FreeToDo Travel Guide
UK & Ireland

Published by: FreeToDo Travel Guides

First Published: 2006

ISBN 10 - 0-9553600-0-5
ISBN 13 - 978-0-9553600-0-8

Copyright © FreeToDo Travel Guides

Printed and bound in India by Gopsons

The information contained within this publication is believed correct at the time of printing. FreeToDo Travel Guides have done their best to ensure the accuracy of the information contained within this publication. However FreeToDo Travel Guides can accept no responsibility for errors, omissions or changes in the details given or the loss, injury or any inconvenience sustained as a result of information contained within this publication. FreeToDo Travel Guides would like readers to be aware that accommodation listings within this publication have not been visited by FreeToDo Travel Guides. The accommodation descriptions are provided by the owners of the individual accommodations. FreeToDo Travel Guides can not accept any liability for any inaccuracy in accommodation descriptions or for any loss, injury or inconvenience sustained as a result of this information. As FreeToDo UK & Ireland is a bi-annual publication changes to opening hours and description of attractions may change over the two year period and readers are advised to confirm details for themselves before visiting any of the attractions or events within this publication.

FreeToDo Travel Guide – UK & Ireland is a unique and comprehensive guide book of **FREE ADMISSION** attractions, activities and events throughout the UK and Ireland.

The information covers a wide range of both indoor and outdoor attractions.

FreeToDo will guide you through the different areas of the UK & Ireland and provide you with information on hundreds of free things to see and do, where ever your interests lie.

Discover the ancient mysteries that surround historic sites and houses from pre historic ruins to the splendour of the country home. Wander with intrepidation around haunted castles and graveyards or marvel at the splendour of majestic cathedrals and churches.

Relax in the surroundings of World famous gardens and beautiful, picturesque walks, watch hand crafted goods being made or visit a wide range of different and unusual exhibitions. For a cultural experience browse the wealth of diverse art galleries and museums, from classical to contemporary, that FreeToDo has to offer.

FreeToDo has compiled this Guide Book of free attractions, activities and events so that it appeals to everyone. Whether you are looking for a full day out, a weekend away or something to pass an hour of two, there's something near you that's **FREE TO DO**.

FreeToDo is more than your average Guide Book. It is a discovery of Free Admission, well known and unusual attractions, indoor and outdoor, close to home or further afield.

Have a fantastic day out for FREE.

INDEX OF COUNTRIES

SCOTLAND

Scotland is a country of myths and mountains, lochs and legends. The lavish history and heritage of the oldest Kingdom in Europe is matched by its majestic landscapes and spectacular scenery. From rolling farmland to imposing mountain ranges, each region of Scotland has its own individual character and appeal.

Scotland also has its busy metropolitan cities, Edinburgh the Capital is known for its yearly festival, the winding, picturesque streets of the Old Town and the contrasting modern shops and cafes. Glasgow has fantastic architecture and culture and the other major Scottish cities of Inverness, Aberdeen, Dundee and Sterling have a lively bustling atmosphere with a wealth of attractions and facilities.

Away from the cities Scotland is well known for its great outdoors and abundance of wildlife. From skiing and golfing to hill walking and fishing there is a wide variety of outdoor sports to enjoy.

Scotland has hundreds of castles and dramatic ruins scattered around the magnificent countryside to explore or enjoy a taste of one of the country's most famous products at the many whisky distilleries that are available.

Whether you are looking for the buzz and nightlife of the city or the relaxing peace and quiet of the country side Scotland has it all.

SCOTLAND

N.E.Highlands-Scotland

ART GALLERIES/ARTS & CRAFTS

Chisholms Highland Dress
47-51 Castle Street, Inverness, Inverness-shire, IV2 3DU
Tel: 01463 234599
Email: info@kilts.co.uk
Website: www.kilts.co.uk
Mon-Sat 09.00-17.30 and 19.00-21.00 in Summer.
Display of kilt making and Scottish Highland dress. From 1745 to the present day, tartans, swords and other weapons on display.

Inverness Museum & Art Gallery
Castle Wynd, Inverness, Inverness-shire, IV2 3EB
Tel: 01463 237 114
Email: contact@invernessmuseum.com
Website: www.invernessmuseum.com
Mon-Sat 09.00-17.00
History of Inverness and the Highlands depicted in displays of natural and human history. Exhibitions include, Inverness and Highlands Silver, Weapons, and Musical Instruments.

Tore Art Gallery
Red Castle Crossroad, Muir-of-Ord Road, Tore, Inverness-shire, IV6 7RT
Tel: 01463 871 444
Email: clare@tore-art-gallery.co.uk
Website: www.tore-art-gallery.co.uk
Daily 10.30-16.30 (Closed Tuesdays) Sunday 12.00-16.30
Showing a large variety of original works from all over Scotland and beyond, exhibitions of contemporary artists and also the base for leading Scottish silversmith Alan Baillie

The Tain Pottery

Aldie, Tain, Ross & Cromarty, IV19 1LZ
Tel: 01862 894 112
Email: sales@tainpottery.co.uk
Website: www.tainpottery.co.uk
April-Oct Mon-Fri 09.00-18.00 Sat & Sun 10.00-17.00 Nov-March Mon-Sat 09.00-17.30
Sundays by appointment only
Their ware has been developed by a team of artisans and the products cover a
diverse method of manufacturing techniques

John O Groats Pottery And Gallery

3 The Crafts Centre, John O' Groats, Wick, Caithness, KW1 4YR
Tel: 01955 611 284
Email: info@jogpot.co.uk
Website: www.jogpot.co.uk
April-Sept Mon-Sat 09.30-17.30 Sun 12.30-17.00 Oct-March Tues-Sat 09.30-17.00
Producing a wide range of hand thrown functional tableware, individual ceramics
and a range of wildlife prints and cards

Hartmount Woodturning

Tigh an Fhraoich, Hartmount, Ross & Cromarty, IV19 1NQ
Tel: 01862 842 511
Please phone for opening times
Custom built wood working shop and display area set in 2 acres of garden.

Knockan Studio and Craft Centre

Knockan, Elphin, Sutherland, IV27 4HH
Tel: 01854 666 261
March-October Mon-Sat 09.00-18.00
Jewellery/Lapidary workshop where Scottish gem stones are cut and set.
Workshop viewing area, Scottish crafts, knitwear, pottery and glass.

Achiltibuie Smokehouse

Achiltibuie, Ullapool, Ross & Cromarty
Tel: 01854 622 353
Email: sifsalmo@globalnet.co.uk
Website: www.summerislesfoods.com
East-Oct Mon-Sat 09.30-17.00
Smokehouse where visitors can view the work areas and see fish being
prepared for smoking and other processes then buy the finished products.

James Pringle Weavers
Holm Mills, Dores Road, Inverness, Inverness-shire, IV2 4RB
Tel: 01463 223 311
Mon-Sat 09.00-17.30 Sun 10.00-17.00
200 year old weaving mill where tartan rugs are still made. Extensive mill shop and Clan tartan centre.

Iceberg Glass Blowing Studio
Victoria Buildings, Drumnadrochit, Inverness, Inverness-shire, IV63 6TX
Tel: 01456 450 601
Summer daily 10.00-20.00 Winter daily 10.00-16.00 Closed Mondays
Glass blowing studio producing solid and hollow glassware. Mostly small delicate pieces, vases, Christmas decorations etc.

Clog and Craft Shop
Invermoriston, Loch Ness, Inverness-shire, IV63 6YA
Tel: 01320 351 318
March-June daily 10.00- 17.00 July-Aug 09.30-18.00 Sept-Oct 10.00-17.00
Leather goods manufacturer and clog maker. Visitors can watch craftsmen at work.

CASTLES

Castle of Old Wick
1 mile south of Wick, Wick, Caithness
Tel: 01667 460 232
Website: www.historic-scotland.gov.uk
Access at any reasonable time
Ruin of a very early Norse Tower House on a spectacular spine of rock projecting into the sea between two narrow gulleys.

Ardvreck Castle
Loch Assynt, 11 miles east of Lochinver, Lochinver, Sutherland
Access at any reasonable time
Built around 1490 this 3 storied ruin stands on the shore of Loch Assynet. After his defeat at Culvain in 1659 the Marquess Of Montrose fled to Assynet but was captured and imprisoned in this castle before being taken to Edinburgh and executed.

Lochindorb

unclassified road off A939, 10 miles NW of Granton On Spey, Granton on Spey, Morayshire
Exterior view only no access to the castle island

The ruins of this 13C castle stand on an island in the Loch. It was occupied in 1303 by Edward I. In 1371 the castle became home to The Wolf Of Badenoch, The Earl Of Buchan who terrorised the area. The castle was dismantled in 1456

CHURCHES & CATHEDRALS

Dornoch Cathedral

On A949, Castle Street, Dornoch, Sutherland
Tel: 01862 810 357
Email: revsbrown@aol.com
May-September during daylight hours

Small cathedral founded in 1224, partly destroyed by fire in 1570 and restored in the 17C, 1835-37 and again in 1924. Fine 13C stonework is still visible.

Hilton of Cadboll Chapel

In the Village Of Hilton, 12 miles NE of Invergordon, Hilton, Inverness-shire
Tel: 01667 460 232
Access at all times

Foundation remains of a small rectangular chapel and modern reconstruction of the famous Pictish Cross Slab found on the site.

Fortrose Cathedral

On the A832, Fortrose, Ross & Cromarty
Tel: 01667 460 232
Grounds open all year round Cathedral Open April-Sept Mon-Sat 09.30-19.00 Sun 14.00-19.00 Oct-March Mon-Sat 09.30-16.00 Sun 14.00-16.00

Surviving fragments of a 13C vaulted undercroft of the chapter house and the south aisle of the 14C nave. Also canopied monument and memorials.

EXHIBITIONS

Ferry Croft Countryside Centre

Ferry Croft, Lairg, Sutherland, IV27 4TP
Tel: 01549 402 160
April, May, September & October 10.00-16.00 June, July & August 10.00-17.00

Tourist information Centre where visitors can learn through audio visual displays the many changes to Sutherland's landscape from the Ice Age to the present day.

John O' Groats
Caithness
Access at all times
Caithness.Famous world wide as the most northerly tip of the UK, the site contains a hotel, souvenir shops and plenty of photo opportunities. However it is actually Dunnet Head along the coast that is truly the most northerly point.

Natural History Display and Ranger Service
Dunnet Pavillion, Dunnet, Castletown, Caithness, KW14 8HY
Tel: 01847 821 531
April-Sept Tues, Wed, Thurs & Fri 14.00-17.00 Sat & Sun 14.00-18.00
Display illustrating the Natural History of Caithness and Sutherland with a nature reserve with guided walks.

Dunnet Head
B8555, 12 miles NE of Thurso, Thurso, Caithness
Access at all times
The most northern point of the Scottish mainland this bold sandstone promontory is 417 feet high and gives spectacular views across the Pentland Fifth to Orkney.

Duncansby Head
18 miles N of Wick, Wick, Caithness
Access at all times
Three huge stone needles stand silently in the sea, surrounded by sandstone cliffs that are severed by huge deep gashes running into the land, one of which is bridged by a natural arch. Spectacular views.

Dornoch Lochans
Davochfin, Dornoch, Sutherland, IV25 3RW
Tel: 01862 810 600
Website: www.dornochlochans.co.uk
Mon-Sat 10.00-22.00 Sun 14.00-18.00
Outdoor recreation in attractive surroundings with fantastic views over the Dornoch Firth.

Falls of Shin Visitors Centre

Falls of Shin, Achany Glen, Lairg, Sutherland, IV27 4EE
Tel: 01549 402 231
Email: info@fallsofshin.co.uk
Website: www.fallsofshin.co.uk
March 21st-October 31st 09.30-18.00 November-March-10.00-17.00
Salmon leap and waterfall always open. Spectacular falls through rocky gorge famous for salmon leaping.

Falls of Rogie

2 miles W of Strathpeffer, Strathpeffer, Ross & Cromarty
Access at all times during daylight hours
Rogie comes from the Norse meaning splashing, foaming river. From the suspension bridge that spans the falls, salmon can be seen leaping.

Cape Wrath

12 miles NW of Durness, Durness, Sutherland
Access at all times
Most northerly NW point of Scotland which has some of mainland Britain's highest sea cliffs at Clo Mor which are 920 feet high.

Eas Coul Aulin Falls

Loch Glencoul, Assynt, Sutherland
Access at all times
The tallest waterfall in Britain, dropping 658ft

Inshriach Nursery

Inshriach, On the B970 4 miles S of Avimore, Aviemore, Inverness-shire, PH22 1QS
Tel: 01540 651 287
Email: drakesalpines@kincraig.com
Website: www.kincraig.com/drakesalpines
Mid Feb-Mid November Sunday-Saturday 09.00-17.00
Show garden and alpine plant nursery growing a variety of alpines, heathers, dwarf shrubs and dwarf rhododendrons.

Glenmore Forest Park Visitors Centre

Ski Road, Glenmore, Aviemore, Inverness-shire, PH22 1QU
Tel: 01479 861 220
Website: www.forestry.gov.uk/recreation
Open all year Visitors Centre daily 09.00-17.00
Glenmore Forest park is situated in the foothills of the Cairngorm National
Nature Reserve.Walks, Cycle routes, picnic sites, lochside activities, bird
watching, visitor centre, etc.

Farigaig Forest

By Inverfarigaig, on S side of Loch Ness, 18 miles SW of Inverness, Inverfarigaig,
Inverness-shire
Tel: 01320 366322
Email: fiona.barnett@forestry.gsi.gov.uk
Open daily all year
Excellent views over Loch Ness and across Inverfarigaig to Dum Boarduit the
site of a vitrified Iron Age fort dating from around 500BC.

Loch Ness

SW of Inverness on A82, Inverness, Inverness-shire
Website: www.lochnessguide.com
Access at all times
This 24 mile long loch in the Great Glen forms part of the Caledonian canal.Up
to 700 feet deep the loch contains the largest volume of freshwater in any lake in
the British isles. Famous world wide for it's mysterious occupant the LOCH
NESS MONSTER !!!!!

Randolph's Leap

off B9007 On the Findhorn River, 7 miles SW of Forres, Forres, Morayshire
Access at all times
Randolph's Leap is the is the most striking point in this valley where River
Findhorn meanders through a deep sandstone gorge.

Smoo Cave

1 miles outside Durness, On the road to Tongue, Durness, Sutherland
Access at all times
Smoo Cave is 200 feet long, 130 feet wide and has a 50 foot high entrance way.

Old Man Of Stoer

Lochinver, Follow road for the Stoer Point Lighthouse, Lochinver, Sutherland
Access at all times
An energetic walk along the cliff top leads to this magnificent red sandstone sea stack.

Sandwood Bay

On A894/A838 N from Scourie, 28 miles N of Lochinver, Blairmore, Sutherland
Access at all times
Beautiful walk that leads to Sandwood Bay which had rock stacks, white beaches and it's own ghosts said to frequent a bothy (cottage) near the shore.

NATURE RESERVE

Forsinard RSPB Nature Reserve

Forsinard Station, Forsinard, on the A897 26 miles inland from Helmsdale, Forsinard, Sutherland, KW13 6YT
Tel: 01641 571 225
Email: forsinard@rspb.org.uk
Reserve open at all times, Visitors Centre Easter-Oct daily 09.00-18.00
46 950 acres of peatland that form a substantial Nature Reserve. The peat bogs contain thousands of bog pools with insect eating plants, dragonflies and rare birds. Guided walks during the summer.

HISTORIC SITES

Dun Dornaigil Broch

10 miles S of Hope, Hope, Sutherland
Access at all times
Well preserved broch standing 22 feet above the entrance passage.

Cnoc Freiceadain Long Cairns

6 miles SW of Thurso, Thurso, Caithness
Tel: 01667 460 232
Access at all times
Two unexcavated Neolithic long horned burial cairns.

Grey Cairns of Camster

off the A9 on the Watten Road, 5 miles N of Lybster, Lybster, Caithness
Tel: 01667 460 232
Access at all times
Two Neolithic chambered burial cairns, one long cairn with projecting horns and two chambers and the other round with a single chamber.

Cairn O'Get

1.5 miles SW of Ulbster, On the A9, Ulbster, Caithness
Tel: 01667 460 232
Access at all times
A horned and chambered burial cairn of Neolithic date.

Hill O' Many Stanes

Mid Clyth, 4 miles NE of Lybster, Lybster, Caithness
Tel: 01667 460 232
Access at all times
Over 22 rows of low slabs arranged in a fan shaped pattern.One theory suggests that the site may had formed a kind of Prehistoric astronomical observatory.

Cain Liath

By the A9, 3 miles ENE of Golspie, Golspie, Sutherland
Access at all times
A typical broch surviving to the first floor level with an associated settlement.

Fyrish Monument

Above the village of Evanton, on Fyrish Hill off A9, Evanton, Ross & Cromarty
Access at all times
This strange monument was built in 1782 by Sir Hector Munroe to provide work for the local people and is a replica of the Indian gateway.

John Cobb Memorial Cairn

Between Invermoriston and Drumnadrochit, By the A82, Drumnadrochit, Inverness-shire
Access at all times
This cairn commemorates the racing driver John Cobb who died near this spot in 1952 whilst attempting to beat the water speed record in his speed boat on Loch Ness.

Corrimony Cairn

Glen Urquhart, 8 miles W of Drumnadrochit, Drumnadrochit, Inverness-shire
Tel: 01667 460 232
Access at all times
Chambered burial cairn surrounded by a kerb of stone slabs outside of which is a ring of standing stones.

Knocknagael Boar Stone

In Highland Council Offices, Glenurquhart Road,, Inverness, Inverness-shire
Tel: 01667 460 232
Mon-Fri 09.30-16.30
A rough stone slab carved with the Pictish symbols of a mirror case and a wild boar. The stone can be viewed at any time through the window.

Clava Cairns

off B9091 6 Miles E of Inverness, Near Culloden, Culloden, Inverness-shire
Tel: 01667 460 232
Access at all times
Two chambered and one ring cairn each surrounded by a circle of standing stones of Neolithic or late Bronze Age origin. This is an extensive historic site situated in beautiful surroundings.

Ardclach Bell Tower

off A939, 8.5 miles SE of Nairn, Nairn, Inverness-shire
Exterior View at all reasonable times
Built in 1655 this two storied, fortified bell tower was used to summon worshipers to Church or to warm them in case of alarm and stands on the hill above the Parish Church of Ardclach.

Ruthven Barracks

on the B907, 0.5 miles S of Kingussie, Kingussie, Inverness-shire
Tel: 01667 460 232
Access at all reasonable times
Ruins of a Infantry barracks built in 1719 and comprising two ranges of quarters and a stable block. The barracks was captured and burnt by Prince Charlie's army in 1746.

MUSEUMS

Clan MacPhersons Museum
Clan House, Main Street, Newtonmore, 1.5 miles S of Avimore on the A86, Newtonmore, Inverness-shire, PH20 1DE
Tel: 01540 673 332
Email: macphersonmuseum@btopenworld.com
May-Oct Mon-Sat 10.00-17.00 Sun 12.00-17.00
Museum depicting the history of the Clan with portraits, photographs and other Macphearson memorabilia.

Queens Own Highlander's Regimental Museum
Fort George, Ardesier, Ardesier, Inverness-shire, IV2 3XD
Tel: 01667 462 800
Email: museum@thehighlanders.com
April -Sept Daily 10.00-18.00 Oct-March Mon-Fri 10.00-16.00
Regimental Museum with collections of medals, uniforms and other items depicting the history of the Queens Own Highlanders, Seaforth Highlanders, The Queens Own Cameron Highlanders and Lovat Scouts.

FARMERS MARKETS

Inverness Farmers Market
Eastgate Shopping Precinct, Inverness City, Inverness, Inverness-shire
Tel: 01309 651 206
Email: debhamish@thescore.fsworld.co.uk
1st Saturday of the month 08.30-15.00
Local produce on sale by local farmers

N.W.Highlands-Scotland

ART GALLERIES/ARTS & CRAFTS

Lime Tree Studio Gallery
The Old Manse, Achintore Road, Fort William, Inverness-shire, PH33 6RQ
Tel: 01397 701 806
Email: info@limetreestudio.co.uk
Website: www.limetreestudio.co.uk
Open daily 10.30-17.00 except Christmas and New Year
Continually changing exhibitions of landscape paintings mainly of North West
Scotland, Workshop Programmes and Stained Glass Exhibition.

Carron Pottery
Carnallt, Strathcarron, Wester Ross, IV54 8YX
Tel: 01520 722 321
Email: robteago@ukonline.co.uk
Website: www.carronpottery.co.uk
March-December Mon-Sat 09.30-17.30 Closed Sundays
Craft shop selling Scottish and local crafts. Visitors can view craftsmen in the
pottery. Art gallery with work by local and National artists, exhibitions, sculptures
and stained glass.

Highland Stoneware Ltd
Lochinver, Sutherland, IV27 4LP
Tel: 01571 844 376
Email: potters@highlandstoneware.co.uk
Website: www.highlandstoneware.com
Mon-Fri 09.00-18.00 Sat (East-Oct) 09.00-17.00
Produce a large range of high-fired, freehand painted ceramics with an
International reputation for quality

Shards Stained Glass
The Old Schoolhouse, Arinacrinachd, By Shieldaig, Strathcarron, Wester Ross, IV54 8XU
Tel: 01520 755 231
Email: schoolhouse@arrina.co.uk
Website: www.shardsstainedglass.co.uk
Easter-October 09.00-18.00 Please phone to confirm open on the day of your visit
A selection of designs from a range of stained glass sun catchers, including wild
life, birds, flowers and sea life

Great Glen Fine Foods

Old Ferry Road, North Ballachulish, Fort William, Inverness-shire, PH33 6RZ
Tel: 01855 821 577
Email: info@greatglenfinefoods.co.uk
Website: www.greatglenfinefoods.co.uk
Shop Open East-Oct Mon-Sat 09.15 -17.15 Sun 10.00-17.30 Factory Open East-Oct
Mon-Sat 09.15-17.15 Sun 10.15-17.15 Factory is not in production at weekends
Confectionery factory and specialty food shop which claims to have the largest
selection of Scottish specialty foods in the world. The factory makes the famous
Islay tablet, and visitors can watch the production process.

Spean Bridge Woolen Mill

Spean Bridge, Inverness-shire, PH34 4EP
Tel: 01397 712 260
Email: info@speanbridgemill.com
March-Oct Mon-Sat 09.00-17.30 Sun 10.00-16.30 Nov-Feb Daily 10.00-17.00
Picturesque weaving mill in former farm steading. Visitors can watch weaving
demonstrations on Hattersley Power Looms.

Glenelg Candles

Art and Craft Centre, Balcraggie, Glenelg, Ross & Cromarty, IV40 8LA
Tel: 01599 522 240
Email: info@glenelgcandles.co.uk
Website: www.glenelgcandles.co.uk
Summer Mon-Fri 09.30-18.00 Sat & Sun 10.00-17.00 Coffee Shop Open April-Oct
Candle workshop where visitors can view the process of hand made candle
production. Wide range of candles, candle holders, oil lamps, Scottish & Celtic
crafts on sale.

Smithy Heritage Centre

Strathcarron, Strathcarron, Wester Ross, IV54 8YS
Tel: 01520 722 722
Email: smithy@balnacra.com
April-October 10.00-17.30 (Closed Sundays)
Restored smithy, set in a plantation of native trees that tells the history of the
building and those who worked in it.

The Studio Jewellery Workshop

Highland Line, Achnasheen, Wester Ross, IV22 2EE

Tel: 01520 720 227

Email: info@studiojewellery.com

Website: www.studiojewellery.com

April-Oct Daily 09.00-17.30

Craft Centre with a craft and jewellery workshop. Visitors can view the craftsmen at work through windows. Silver & Gold jewellery and small silverware items are on sale.

CASTLES

Strome Castle

Stromemore, 4 miles S of Lochcarron, Lochcarron, Wester Ross

Tel: 01599 566 325

Open all year

This ruined castle dates from the 15C and comprises of a ruined square tower, a courtyard entered through a gateway on the north wall and a gateway on the west wall that leads to the headland

Inverlochy Castle

2 miles NE of Fort William, Off the A82, Fort William, Inverness-shire

Exterior View Only

Well preserved 13C castle, in the form of a square with round towers at the corners, the castle belonged to the Comyn family. The largest tower was the Donjon or Keep.

Castle Tioram

Loch Moidart, Moidart, Ardnamurchan, Inverness-shire

Access at all times

Ruined fortress dominating a bracken green islet. Once the home of the Chief Of MacDonalds of Clan Ranald, but the last chief burnt the castle to prevent it falling into the hands of his enemies, the Campbells during the 1715 Jacobite rebellion.

CHURCHES & CATHEDRALS

Croick Church

Croick, 10 miles West of Ardgay, Strathcarron, Wester Ross
Email: enquiries@croickchurch.com
Website: www.croickchurch.com
Open all year
The church and its minister figured prominently in the clearance of Glencalvie in 1845, a tragic event that is recorded in messages scratched on its East window

GARDENS PARKS & WALKS

Victoria Falls

Off A832 12 miles NE of Kinlochewe, Loch Maree, Slattadale, Wester Ross
Access at all times
Waterfall named after Queen Victoria who visited Loch Maree and the surrounding area in 1877.

Falls of Glomach

18 miles E of Kyle of Lochalsh, NE off A87, Kyle of Lochalsh, Ross & Cromarty
Tel: 01599 511 231
Access at all times
One of the tallest waterfalls in Britain at a height of 370 feet. The falls are a 5 mile walk from the car park and set in a narrow cleft in the remote countryside.

West Affric

22 miles E of Kyle of Lochalsh, off A87, Kyle of Lochalsh, Ross & Cromarty
Tel: 01599 511 231
Open all year
Comprising of over 9000 acres of wild and rugged landscape, the area provided magnificent and challenging walks and includes one of the most popular East-West Highland Paths.

Parallel Roads

Glen Roy, on unclassified road off A86, 18 miles NE of Fort William, Fort William, Inverness-shire, PH31 4AG
Access at all times
These parallel roads are hillside terraces marking levels of lakes that were damned by glaciers during the ice age.

Ben Nevis

Loch Linnhe, Near Fort William, Fort William, Inverness-shire

Access at all times

Britain's highest mountain at 4406 feet it is popular with both rock climbers and hill walkers. Best views are from the Northern approach to Fort William or from the Gairlochy Road across the Caledonian canal.

HISTORIC SITES

Glenelg Brochs

8 miles SE of Kyle of Lochalsh, Turn off at Shielbridge on the A87 onto unclassifed road to Glenelg, Kyle of Lochalsh, Ross & Cromarty

Tel: 01667 460 232

Access at all times

Two Iron Age Broch towers standing over 30 feet high, with well preserved structural details.

Well of Seven Heads

off the A82, on the West shore of Loch Oich, Loch Oich, Inverness-shire

Access at all times

A curious well standing above a spring and depicting the grim tale of the execution of seven brothers for the murder of the two sons of a 17C Chief of Keppoch. The well in inscribed in English, Gaelic, French and Latin and is surmounted by the seven heads

Loch Nan Uamh Cairn

off the A830, Lochailort, Arisaig, Inverness-shire

Access at all times

The loch is famous for its association with Bonnie Prince Charlie. A memorial Cairn on the shore marks the spot where Prince Charles Edward Stewart set sail for France in 1746 after having wandered around the Highlands as a fugitive with a price of £30 00

Tayside Scotland

ART GALLERIES/ARTS & CRAFTS

Dundee Contemporary Arts
152 Nethergate, Dundee, Dundee, DD1 4DY
Tel: 01382 909 900
Email: dca@dundeecity.gov.uk
Website: www.dca.org.uk
Galleries Open Tues-Sat 10.30-17.30, Sun 12.00-17.30 Late opening on Thurs till 20.30
Building and Café Bar Open Mon-Sat 10.30-24.00 Sun 12.00-24.00
An arts centre with contemporary art gallery, print studio, shop and café bar

The Meffan Museum & Art Gallery
20 West High Street, Forfar, Angus & Dundee, DD8 1BB
Tel: 01307 464 123
Email: meffan@angus.gov.uk
(Mon-Sat) 10.00-17.00
Stunning display of Pictish stones. Opportunity to walk down the reconstructed
Vennel Of Shoppies. Changing art exhibitions and displays

CASTLES

Broughty Castle Museum
Castle Approach, Broughty Ferry, Angus & Dundee, DD5 2PE
Tel: 01382 436 916
Email: broughty@dundeecity.gov.uk
Website: www.dundeecity.gov.uk/broughtycastle
April-Sep (Mon-Sat) 10.00-16.00 (Sun) 12.30-16.00 Oct-March (Tues-Sat) 10.00-16.00
(Sun) 12.30-16.00 Closed Mondays.
A 15C Estuary Fort, now housing a museum with displays on local history, arms
and armour, sea side life and Dundee's Whaling history.

Dudhope Castle
Dudhope Park,, Barrack Road, Dundee, Angus & Dundee
(exterior view only)
The castle was originally built in the 13C to provide a home for the Hereditary
Constables Of Dundee. By the mid 18C the building contained a woollen mill and
later became a barracks.

Invermark Castle

Glen Esk, Brechin, Angus
Access at all times-Exterior View Only
A ruined fortress which once guarded the vital hill pass to Deeside

Red Castle

Overlooking Lunan Bay, 2 miles NE of Inverkeilor, Montrose, Angus & Dundee
Access at all times
15C red sandstone castle ruins overlooking Lunan Bay. The present remains
replaced an even earlier fort built for William The Lion Heart.

Claypotts Castle

Off the A92 East of Dundee, Broughty Ferry, Angus & Dundee
Tel: 01786 431 324
Exterior View Only
This castle dates from 1569-1588 and has a rectangular central block flanked by
two round towers

CHURCHES & CATHEDRALS

Restenneth Priory

On the B9113 Forfar to Montrose Road, Just over 1 mile outside Forfar, Forfar, Angus &
Dundee
Access at all times
A house of Augustinian Canons probably built by King David on the site of an
earlier church. An interesting feature is the all square tower with a brooch spire.

Cathedral Church of St Paul

Castle Hill, 1 High Street, Dundee, Angus & Dundee, DD1 1TD
Tel: 01382 224 486
Email: email@stpaulscathedraldundee.org
Website: www.stpaulscathedraldundee.org
April-Sept (Tues-Sat) 11.00-15.30 October-March (Tues-Sat) 12.00-15.00
Built in 1853 by Sir George Gilbert Scott the church is designed in beautiful
Neo-Gothic style

St Andrews Kirk and Glasite Hall

King Street, Cowgate, Dundee, Angus & Dundee
Email: petrieduncan@aol.com
(Tue & Thur) 10.00-12.00
Designed by Samuel Bell in 1722 the church has some fabulous stained glass.

St Marys Tower and City Churches
Nethergate, Dundee, Angus & Dundee, DD1 4DG

Tel: 01382 226 271

Email: office@dundeestmarys.co.uk

Website: www.dundeestmarys.co.uk

May-Aug weekdays except Wednesday 10.00-12.00, Sunday 10.00-13.00

This is the most substantial medieval church tower in Scotland dating from 1460 with a hammer beam roof and galleried aisles. There are 232 steps to climb before you can appreciate the view.

EXHIBITIONS

Mills Observatory
Balgay Park, Glamis Road, Dundee, Angus & Dundee, DD2 2UB

Tel: 01382 435 967

Email: mills.observatory@dundeecity.gov.uk

Website: www.dundeecity.gov.uk/mills

Oct-Mar (Mon-Fri) 16.00-22.00 (Sat-Sun) 12.30-16.00 April-Sep (Tue-Fri) 11.00-17.00 (Sat-Sun) 12.30-16.00.

Britain's only full time public observatory with resident astronomer. Displays on astronomy, space exploration and the universe. Viewing instruments include a ten inch refracting telescope for night viewing.

GARDENS PARKS WALKS

Law Hill
Access from Hill Street or Kinghorne Road, Via Law Road, Dundee, Angus & Dundee

Access at all times

The walk to the top of Law Hill gives a superb view over the River Tay and the majestic sweep of the rail bridge which runs along side the ruins of the old bridge which was destroyed during a storm in 1879.

Baxter Park
Dundee, Angus & Dundee, DD1 3RA

Tel: 01382 433 769

Email: baxter.rangers@dundeecity.gov.uk

Daily all year dawn-dusk

Classic Victorian park with boating on Stobmuir Ponds. The park includes a variety of walks, a sandstone pavilion, tennis, bowling and a play park

Monikie Country Park

Panmure Road, Monikie, Broughty Ferry, Dundee, DD5 3QN
Tel: 01382 370 202
Website: www.monikie.org.uk/cntryprk.html
Open all year during daylight hours-opening hours are displayed at the entrance to the park
Countryside park with 140 acres of woodland and open water which is home to a variety of birds and aquatic life

Gannochy Bridge and The Rocks Of Solitude

North of Edzell Village, Edzell, Angus
Access at all times
A riverside walk from Gannochy Bridge to the Rocks Of Solitude

Camperdown Country Park

Coupar Angus Road, Dundee, Dundee, DD2 4TF
Access at all times
735 acre park with something for everybody. Boating pond, pitch and putt and children's play area.

Barnhill Rock Garden

The Esplanade, By Broughty Ferry, Barnhill, Dundee
Website: www.dundeecity.gov.uk/gardens/index.html
Access at all times
Featuring plants and flowers from all over the world, and a woodland walk

Caird Park

Junction of Forfar Road and Kingsway, Dundee, Angus & Dundee
Access at all times
A gift to the city from past industrialists the park now includes Mains Castle. The conservation area of Trottick Ponds with resident swans is just to the North of the park.

HISTORIC SITES

Aberlemno Sculptured Stones

Aberlemno by Forfar, On the B9134, 6 miles NE of Forfar, Aberlemno, Angus & Dundee
Tel: 0131 668 8600
Access at all times. Between October and May the stones are boxed to prevent frost damage-Historic Scotland will confirm when boxes will be removed
The churchyard of Aberlemno contains an upright cross slab with intricate Pictish symbols and three further standing stones beside the road.

The Caterthuns

Near Menmuir, 4 miles North of Brechin, Off the A94, Menmuir, Angus & Dundee

Access at all times

The white and brown Caterthuns are the well preserved remains of iron age hill forts. Features include ramparts and ditches that give a fascinating insight into the skills used by prehistoric man.

Elephant Rock

Lunan Bay between Usan and Boddin, Montrose, Angus

Access at all times

This rock looks like an elephant lumbering out of the sea

Scurdie Ness

Near Montrose, Montrose, Angus

Exterior view only

Marking the headland of the coast line approaching Montrose is this very distinct lighthouse

HISTORIC SITES

Ardestie Earth-House

Off the A92, Between Dundee and Arbroath, Dundee, Dundee

Access at all times

An Iron Age curved underground gallery that has now been exposed. The gallery measures 80 feet in length and was once the cellar of a round house

The Wishart Arch

Cowgate, Dundee, Angus & Dundee

Access at all times

This ancient gateway to the city has both a main carriage arch and a footpath arch.The gate was named after reformer George Wishart who used it as a pulpit to preach from during the plague of 1544.

Museums

Arbroath Museum
Signal Tower, Ladyloan, Arbroath, Angus & Dundee, DD11 1PU
Tel: 01241 875 598
Email: signal.tower@angus.gov.uk
Website: www.angus.gov.uk/history.htm
(Mon-Sat) 10.00-17.00 July & August also open Sundays 14.00-17.00
Houses in the signal tower for the off shore Bellrock Lighthouse the museum depicts the maritime and social history of the area with models, sounds and smells.

Brechin Town House Museum
28 High Street, Brechin, Angus & Dundee, DD9 6ER
Tel: 01356 625 536
Email: brechin.museum@angus.gov.uk
Mon, Tues, Thurs, Fri & Sat 10.00-17.00 Wed 10.00-13.00
The museum houses various exhibitions depicting ancient trades and industries, cathedral, paintings and archaeology, and the rich local history of the city.

Kirriemuir-Gateway To The Glens Museum
32 High Street, Kirriemuir, Angus, DD8 4BB
Tel: 01575 575 479
Mon-Sat (Except Thurs) 10.00-17.00 Thurs 13.00-17.00
A Museum dedicated to the town of Kirriemuir

Montrose Museum
Panmure Place, Montrose, Angus & Dundee, DD10 8HE
Tel: 01674 673 232
Email: montrose.museum@angus.gov.uk
(Mon-Sat) 10.00-17.00
The museum explains the rich history of Montrose with exhibits on prehistory, Jacobites and Maritime Trade. There is also a wild life gallery and a variety of changing exhibitions.

Farmers Markets

Forfar Farmers Market
Forfar Mart, John Street, Forfar, Angus & Dundee
2nd Saturday of the month 09.30-13.00
Farmers Market with local produce for sale

Dundee Farmers Market
Reform Street, Dundee, Angus & Dundee
Jan-November Third Saturday of the month 09.00-16.00
Farmers Market with local produce for sale

NATURE & WILDLIFE

Balgavies Loch
On the A932, 4 miles East of Forfar, Balgavies, Angus
Tel: 01307 818 355
To access the reserve prior permission is required and restricted during the breeding season, but a viewpoint on the A932 has access at all times
A Scottish Wildlife Trust Loch Reserve with a variety of birds and wildlife

Grampian Scotland

ART GALLERIES/ARTS & CRAFTS

Syllavethy Gallery

Montgarrie, Alford, Aberdeenshire, AB33 8AQ

Tel: 01975 562 273

Email: syllavethygallery@hotmail.com.

Website: www.syllavethy.com

Spring-August open 6 days a week September-March please phone to check opening times.
Art Gallery featuring paintings and sculptures by high quality local and
international artists. The gallery specialises in portrait paintings.

Lantern Gallery Of Fine Art

18 South Guildry Street, Elgin, Morayshire

Tel: 01343 546 864

Email: info@lanterngallery.co.uk

Website: www.lantern-gallery.co.uk

(Tue-Sat) 13.00-17.00

Gallery features original paintings, wood sculptures and ceramics. Commissions
painted.

Aberdeen Gallery Heinzel

24 Thistle Street, Aberdeen, Aberdeenshire, AB10 1XD

Tel: 01224 625 629

Email: info@galleryheinzel.com

Website: www.galleryheinzel.com

(Tue-Sat) 10.00-17.30

Featuring permanent and temporary monthly exhibitions of contemporary art,
paintings, sculpture, watercolours and ceramics by Scottish artists both new and
established.

Aberdeen Art Gallery

Schoolhill, Aberdeen City Centre, Off Union Street, Aberdeen, Aberdeenshire, AB10 1FQ

Tel: 01224 523 700

Email: info@aagm.co.uk

Website: www.aagm.co.uk

(Mon-Sat) 10.00-17.00 (Sun) 14.00-17.00

The gallery houses one of the finest small public collections in the UK of 18-20C
works. Including works by British Artists, Spencer, Nash and Bacon. Varied
exhibitions throughout the year.

Fettercairn Distillery

Laurencekirk, Kincardineshire, Laurencekirk, Aberdeenshire, AB30 1YE

Tel: 01561 340 244

Website: www.whyteandmackay.co.uk

May-Sep (Mon-Sat) 10.00-14.30 (Last Tour at 14.00)

One of the oldest licensed distilleries in Scotland. Free guided tours include a "wee dram".

Glendronach Distillery

Forgue, Huntley, Aberdeenshire, AB54 6DA

Tel: 01466 730 202

Email: ljsherriff@hotmail.com

Shop open 09.00-16.00 All year Tours take place Mon-Fri 10.00 and 14.00

Traditional distillery dating from 1825 with floor maltings, peat fire and kiln. The surrounding grounds contain the Gordon Wood, in commemoration of the Gordon Highlanders, where visitors can see Highland cattle.

Glenfiddich Distillery

Dufftown, Banffshire, Dufftown, Aberdeenshire, AB55 4DH

Tel: 01340 820 373

Email: info@glenfiddich.com

(Mon-Fri) 09.30-16.30 Sat 09.30-16.30 Sun 12.00-16.30

Opened in 1887 the distillery produces the only Highland Single Malt Whisky that is distilled, bottled and matured at it's own distillery. Guided tours include Bottling room, gift shop, picnic area and free sample.

Baxter's Highland Village

Fochabers, Speyside, Fochabers, Morayshire, IV32 7LD

Tel: 01343 820 666

Email: highland.village@baxters.co.uk

Website: www.baxters.co.uk

April-Dec 09.00-17.00 Jan-March 10.00-17.00 Daily.

Manufacturers of Quality Scottish Food. The attractions include an old shop museum, George Baxter's Cella , the Baxter's Experience with culinary demonstrations and tastings, specialty shops and audio visual presentations.

Logie Steading

Logie House, Forres, Morayshire, IV36 2QN
Tel: 01309 611 378
Email: panny@logie.co.uk
Website: www.logie.co.uk
End March-Christmas 10.30-17.00
Attractive farm steading that has been converted into workshops for professional craftsmen, including a gunmaker, sealmaker, engraver,potter, textile worker and furniture restorer.

CASTLES

Findlater Castle

By Sandend, Portsoy, Sandend, Aberdeenshire
Access at all times
Cliff Top ruin of a 15C Ogilvie Stronghold.

Mither Tap

Bennachie Hills, Garoich, Aberdeenshire
Access at all times
Iron Age Hill Top Fort.

CHURCHES & CATHEDRALS

Aberdeen Cathedral Church Of St Machar

Chanonry, Old Aberdeen, Aberdeen, Aberdeenshire, AB24 1RQ
Tel: 01224 485 988
Email: office@stmachar.com
Website: www.stmachar.com
Open all year daily 09.00-17.00 Winter 10.00-16.00 except for weddings,funerals and unscheduled events.
The present building dates from 1350-1520, but is built on an ancient site of worship which dates from 580 AD. There had been a Cathedral Church on the site since 1140. The building is a twin towered granite structure.

St Laurence Church

High Street, Forres, Morayshire
Tel: 01309 672 260
Email: barryj.boydstlaurence@btinternet.com
1st Monday in May-Last Friday in Sept 10.00-12.00 & 14.00-16.00
Built in 1904 and opened in 1906 this church stands on a site of an earlier 13C chapel. The main tower and spire reach a height of 120 feet.

Kirk Of St Nicholas

Union Street, Aberdeen, Aberdeenshire
Tel: 01224 643 494
Website: www.kirk-of-st-nicholas.org.uk
May-Sep (Mon-Fri) 12.00-16.00 (Sat) 13.00-15.00
Historic city church and chapel of the oil industry.St Nicholas Kirk contains the best preserved collection of stone effigies surviving from a Scottish medieval church, comprising four male and three female figures.

Kinkell Church

2 miles S of Inverurie, Off the B993, Inverurie, Aberdeenshire
Tel: 01667 460 232
Access at all times
16C ruins of a Parish Church with ornate details.

Deer Abbey

On the A95030, 2 miles W of Mintlaw, Mintlaw, Aberdeenshire
Tel: 01667 460 232
Access at all times
The remains of a Cistercian monastery founded in 1219, a beautiful sight at sunset

St Mary's Kirk

Auchindoir, Off the A994 Between Rhynie and Lumsden on the B9002, Auchindoir, Aberdeenshire
Access at all times
Ruins of a Medieval parish Church including an early 16C Sacrament House.

St Congan's Church

Castle Street, Turriff, Aberdeenshire
Exterior View
13C Church and surrounding church yard containing a variety of sculptured and inscribed stones, in addition to many 16 and 17C memorial stones.

Fyvie Parish Church

East end of Fyvie, Turriff, Fyvie, Aberdeenshire, AB53 8RD
Tel: 01651 891 230
Please phone for opening times
19C Kirk with Tiffany glass windows , a Laird's Pew and a Wine Glass Pulpit

GARDENS PARKS WALKS

Grant Park

Victoria Road, Forres, Morayshire, IV36 3BN
Tel: 01309 673 289
Access at all times
Woodland walks in this sunken garden. Picnic area and children's play area

Cruickshank Botanic Gardens

St Machar Drive, Aberdeen, Aberdeenshire, AB24 3UU
Tel: 01224 272 704
(Mon-Fri) 09.00-17.00 May -Sept (Sat&Sun) 14.00-17.00
11 acres of University gardens featuring herbaceous borders, rock gardens,
terraces and arboretum.

Duthie Park Winter Gardens

Polmuir Road, Aberdeen, Aberdeenshire
Tel: 01224 585 310
Open all year
Europe's largest indoor garden collection. Flora and Fauna from around the
world, fish and birds, "talking" cactus during the summer. Artists in summer,
licensed restaurant.

Aden Country Park

Mintlaw, By Peterhead, Peterhead, Aberdeenshire, AB42 8FQ
Tel: 01771 622 906
Every day during daylight hours
230 acre country park in the grounds of the old Buchan Estate. Attractions
include Nature trails, woodlands, adventure playground, picnic sites, sensory
garden. Ranger events programme from April-October and Wild life Discovery
Centre.

Historic Houses

Provost Skene's House

Guestrow, Off Broad Street, Aberdeen, Aberdeenshire, AB10 1AS
Tel: 01224 641 086
Website: www.aagm.co.uk
Open all year (Mon-Sat) 10.00-17.00 Sun 13.00-16.00
One of Aberdeen's few remaining examples of early burgh architecture. Interior attractions include a suite of Georgian rooms, an Edwardian nursery, 17C wood paneling and ceilings.

James Dun's House

61 School Hill, Off Union Street, Aberdeen, Aberdeenshire, AB10 1JT
Tel: 01224 646 333
Open all year (Mon-Sat) 10.00-17.00
Restored 18C Town House named after the rector of Aberdeen Grammar School when Lord Byron was a pupil. The house contains a museum and a gallery with various exhibitions including photography, arts and crafts, paintings, textiles, science and technology.

Historic Sites

Bridge Of Dee

Holburn Street, Aberdeen, Aberdeenshire
Access at all times
The bridge built in the 1520s by Bishop Gavin Dunbar formerly carried the main road South.Its seven arches span a distance of 400 feet and the medieval structure is adorned by heraldic carvings.

Peel Ring

Off A93, 5 miles NE of Aboyne, Lumphanan, Aberdeenshire
Access at all times
12C mote of Castle mound. 120 feet in diameter and 18 feet high. The site has links with Shakespeare's Macbeth.

Tomnaverie Stone Circle

3 miles NW of Aboyne Off the B9094, Near the Mill Of Westercoull, Aboyne, Aberdeenshire
Tel: 01667 460 232
Access at all times
Bronze Age recumbent stone circle dating back almost 4000 years.

Loanhead Of Daviot Stone Circle

By Inverurie, Daviot, Gordon, Aberdeenshire
Access at all times
Recumbent stone circle dating back 4000 years to the Bronze Age.

Maiden Stone

By Inverurie, 4.5 miles N on the A96 from Inverurie, Garoich, Aberdeenshire
Access at all times
Late Pictish Symbol Stone with relief carvings.

Picardy Stone

By Insch, Off the B922, Insch, Aberdeenshire
Access at all times
Pictish stone circle carved in the 7th Century AD.

Memsie Burial Cairn

Memsie, Near Rathen, Memsie, Aberdeenshire
Access at all times
Large Bronze Age cairn approximately 4000 years old

MUSEUMS

Kings College Visitors Centre

College Bound's, Old Aberdeen, Aberdeen, Aberdeenshire, AB24 5NS
Tel: 01224 273 702
Email: conf.events@abdn.ac.uk
(Mon-Sat)10.00-17.00 (Sun) 12.00-17.00
The history of Aberdeen University told via a multi-media display.

Aberdeen Maritime Museum

Shiprow, Aberdeen, Aberdeenshire, AB11 5BY
Tel: 01224 337 700
(Mon-Sat) 10.00-17.00 (Sun) 12.00-15.00
The story and history of the North East's long association with the sea told via
multi media displays. Including computer visual databases, audio visual theatre
and maritime paintings.

Natural History Centre

University Of Aberdeen, Tillydrone Avenue, Aberdeen, Aberdeenshire, AB24 2TZ
Tel: 01224 274 545
Email: nat.hist@abdn.ac.uk
Open Mon-Fri 09.00-17.00 Please call in advance
Botanic Gardens and Zoology Museum based at Aberdeen University.

Ballater Station Visitors Centre

Station Square, Ballater, Aberdeenshire
Tel: 01339 755 306
Oct-May 10.00-17.00 June-Sept 09.00-18.00
Restored Victorian Railway Station housing displays of the 100 year old history of Royal use. Unique Royal waiting room built for Queen Victoria. The building also houses the Deeside Orientation Centre and a Restaurant.

Tollbooth Museum

Old Pier, The Harbour, Stonehaven, Aberdeenshire, AB39 2JU
Tel: 01771 622 906
12 April-16 October Wednesday-Monday 13.30-16.30 Closed Tuesdays
Museum containing exhibits on local history and fishing.

Brander Museum

The Square, Huntley, Aberdeenshire, AB54 8AE
Tel: 01771 622 906
(Tue-Sat) 14.00-16.30
Local History museum with a collection of Communion tokens and a display of military objects associated with the Huntly born author George Anderson Bey MacDonald.

Carnegie Museum

Town Hall, The Square, Inverurie, Aberdeenshire, AB51 3SN
Tel: 01771 622 906
Monday & Wednesday-Friday 14.00-16.30 Saturday 10.00 -13.00 & 14.00-16.00
Local history museum specialising in archaeology.

Aberdeenshire Farming Museum

Aden Country Park, Near Peterhead, Mintlaw, Aberdeenshire, AB42 5FQ
Tel: 01771 622 906
Email: general@abheritage.demon.co.uk
May 1st-September 30th 11.00-16.30 October 14th-29th 12.00 -16.00
Award winning portrayal of regional farming over the past 200 years including Hareshowe working farm.

Arbuthnot Museum

St Peter's Street, Peterhead, Aberdeenshire, AB42 1QD
Tel: 01779 477 778
Mon-Tue & Thur-Sat 10.00-13.00 & 14.00-16.30 Wed 11.00-13.00
Exhibitions include local history, maritime collections, Inuit artefacts and Arctic
Animals, Arbuthnot coin collection and various temporary displays.

Banff Museum

High Street, Banff, Aberdeenshire, AB45 1AE
Tel: 01771 622 906
June-Sep Mon-Sat 14.00-16.30
Local History including displays of archaeology,arms and armour, astronomy,
Banff silver and Natural History.

Peterhead Maritime Heritage

The Lido, South Road, Peterhead, Aberdeenshire, AB42 2XX
Tel: 01779 473 000
June July & August Mon-Sat 10.30-17.00 Sun 11.30-17.00
The maritime history of Peterhead told via interactive displays and audio visual
presentations. Also art exhibition of Aberdeenshire Heritage paintings.

Falconer Museum

Tollboth Street, Forres, Forres, Morayshire, IV36 1PH
Tel: 01309 673 701
Email: museums@moray.gov.uk
Website: www.falconermuseum.co.uk
Apr-Oct (Mon-Sat) 10.00-17.00 Nov-March (Mon-Thurs) 11.00-12.30 & 13.00-15.30
Local and Natural History displays including a special exhibition of the folk
musicians "The Corries".

Tomintoul Museum and Visitors Centre

The Square, Tomintoul, Tomintoul, Morayshire, AB38 9ET
Tel: 01807 580 285
Email: kris.sangster@moray.gov.uk
March, April, May & October (Mon-Fri) 09.30-12.00 & 14.00-16.00 June-August (Mon-Sat)
09.30-12.00 & 14.00-16.30 September (Mon-Sat) 09.30-12.00 & 14.00-16.00
Depictions of Rural Life, Landscape, Skiing, Wildlife and Local History

Aberdeen University Zoology Museum
Zoology Building, Tilydrone Avenue, Aberdeen, Aberdeenshire, AB24 2TZ
Tel: 01224 272 850
Email: m.gorman@abdn.ac.uk
(Mon-Fri) 09.00-17.00
Collection of zoological specimens ranging from flies to whales, the museum is
part of the Conoco Natural History Centre

FARMERS MARKETS

Elgin Farmers Market
Plain Stones, High Street, Elgin
Third Saturday of the month 09.00-16.00
Farmers Market with local produce for sale

Banchory Farmers Market
Scott Skinners Square, Banchory, Aberdeenshire
Third Saturday of the month 10.00-15.00
Farmers Market with local produce for sale

Fife Scotland

ART GALLERIES/ARTS & CRAFTS

Kin Kraft Centre For Scottish Crafts

Kinross Services Area, Junction 6 on the M90, Kinross, Fife
Tel: 01577 862 041
Email: info@kin-kraft.co.uk
Website: www.kin-kraft.co.uk
10.00-17.00 January 1st week only, Feb Weekends only, March-December Daily (Closed Mondays)
Visitors can observe demonstrations of various crafts with displays and a gift shop.

South Lissens Pottery

22 Church Street, Milnathort, Fife, KY13 9XH
Tel: 01577 865 642
(Mon-Sat) 10.00-18.00 (Sun) 12.00-17.00
A Pottery workshop located in an old church built in 1769. The pottery specialises in traditional and contemporary country pots decorated with unusual lustre effects.

Balbirnie Craft Centre

Balbirnie Park, Near Glenrothes, Markinch, Fife, KY7 6NE
Tel: 01592 753 743
(Mon-Sat) 10.00-17.00, (Sun) 14.00-17.00
Located in the centre of Balbirnie Park in a 18C complex of coach and stable buildings the independently owned craft centre produces leather goods, salt dough products, paintings and prints and gold and silver jewellery.

Shoreline Studio

2 Shore Road, Aberdour, Fife, KY3 0TR
Tel: 01383 860 705
Email: ianmcc@shoreline.demon.co.uk
Website: www.shoreline.sco.fm
Mon-Fri 10.00-17.00 Sat 11.00-17.00
This gallery exhibits works of art of watercolours, prints, ceramics, stained glass, sculpture and jewellery from artists living mainly in Scotland

Crawford Art Gallery

93 North Street, St Andrews, Fife, KY16 9AD
Tel: 01334 74 610
Email: crawfordarts@crawfordarts.free-online.co.uk
Website: www.crawfordarts.free-online.co.uk
(Mon-Sat) 10.00-17.00 (Sun) 14.00-17.00
Founded in 1977, houses all kind of visual art, sculpture, painting, photography, design etc

Church Square Ceramics

4 Church Square, St Andrews, Fife, KY16 9NN
Tel: 01334 477 744
Jul & Aug (Mon-Sat) 09.30-19.00 (Sun) 11.30-16.30, Sep-Jun (Mon-Sat) 09.30-17.30 (Sun) 11.30-16.30.
Working pottery where visitors can watch the potter at work

CASTLES

Burleigh Castle

Near Milnathort, Off the A991, 2 miles NE of Kinross, Kinross, Fife
Tel: 0131 668 8800
(Mon-Sat) 09.00-18.30 (Sun) 14.00-18.30 Keyholder at farm opposite phone 0131 668 8800
A Tower House built around 1500 which was the seat of the Balfours Of Burleigh. The house is now roofless but is otherwise a complete ruin with attractive features such as a defensive Barmkin Wall and a corner tower.

CHURCHES & CATHEDRALS

St Bridget's Kirk

Off the A92 at Dalgetty Bay, 2 miles SW of Aberdour, Aberdour, Fife
Access at all times
The shell of a medieval church altered in the 17C by Protestants. Features include a burial vault with a Laird's loft above for the Earl of Dunfermline

Blackfriar's Chapel

South Street, St Andrews, Fife
Exterior View Only
The vaulted side apse of a church of Dominican Friars rebuilt around 1516.

St Mary's Church

Kirkheugh, St Andrews, Fife
Access at all times
Remains of a small cruciform church situated on the edge of a cliff. The building was the earliest collegiate church in Scotland and was destroyed during the Reformation.

St Fillan's Parish Church

Hawkcraig Road, Aberdour, Fife, KY3 0UP
Exterior View Only-Worship times Sunday 10.30
A small church that dates back to 1123.

GARDENS PARKS WALKS

Lochore Meadows Country Park

Crosshill, Lochgelly, Fife, KY5 8BA
Tel: 01592 414 300
Email: info@lochore-meadows.co.uk
Website: www.lochore-meadows.co.uk
Open all year seven days a week
The area was reclaimed from coal mining waste in the 1960s to form a lake surrounded by beautiful countryside. Displays and a slide show tell the story of the reclamation. Attractions include, wildlife, walks and ancient monuments.

Letham Glen

Scoonie Brae, Leven, Fife, KY8 4SH
Tel: 01592 416 823
Open all year
Picturesque surrounding house a number of activities and attractions. The nature centre had wildlife exhibits, during the summer there are craftsmen in residence, nature trails through the glen, guided tours, pets corner and picnic areas.

Silverburn Estate

Largo Road, Leven, on the A915, Leven, Fife, KY8 5PU
Tel: 01592 416 823
Open all year
Extensive gardens and mature woodlands with a variety of wildlife. Several paddocks are used for the summer grazing of domestic animals such as Shetland ponies, and there is a mini farm with various farm animals and farming equipment.

Balbirnie Park

Near Glenrothes, Markinch, Fife

Tel: 01592 414 100

Access at all times

The park which also houses the Balbirnie Craft Centre includes woodland walks, specimen trees and rhododendrons, bronze age stone circle, golf course, children's play area and a picnic area.

Pittencrieff Park

Dunfermline, Dunfermline, Fife

Tel: 01383 726 313

Access at all times

A 76 acre park, known locally as "The Glen" that was donated to Dunfermline by Andrew Carnegie. Wide open spaces, winter gardens and a children's farm

HISTORIC HOUSES

Pan Ha

Dysart, Fife

Exterior View Only

A group of 17C fisher houses that have been restored by the National Trust For Scotland.

Scotstarvit Tower

Off A916, 2 miles S of Cupar, Ceres, Fife

Summer 13.00-17.00 Keys available from Tarvit Mansion House

A 16C keep owned by the Wymyss family. Ask for the key at the Hill Of Tarvit Mansionhouse, which is in Cupar on the A916. Admission is free but you will need to leave a small deposit for the key

HISTORIC SITES

St Margaret's Cave

Chalmers Street, Dunfermline, Fife, KY12 8DQ

Tel: 01383 314 228

Easter-Sept (Daily) 11.00-16.00

Named after Queen Margaret an 11C queen and saint who came to the cave to seek refuge for meditation and prayer. Later the site of a Catholic pilgrimage.

St Monan's Windmill

St Monan's, 1 mile W of Pitenweem, Pitenweem, Fife
Tel: 01333 739 043
July-Aug 12.00-16.00
A windmill which previously served the nearby salt pans with explanatory
displays.

Alexander III Monument

King's Crag, Pettycur, Kinghorn, Fife
Access at all times
Erected in 1887 to commemorate the death of Scotland's last Celtic King in 1286.

St Fillan's Cave

Cove Wynd, Pitenweem, Fife
Key available from the Gingerbread House Craft Shop And Coffee Shop, 9 High Street,
Pittenweem
The cave dated back to the 7C and was used by the missionary St Fillan.

MUSEUMS

Pittencrieff House Museum

Pitencrieff Park, Dunfermline, Fife, KY12 8QH
Tel: 01383 313 838
April-Sept 11.00-17.00 Oct-March 11.00-16.00
A 17C mansion that was bought by Andrew Carnegie early in the 20C and
converted by Robert Lorimar into three galleries that display a history of the
house and park.

Inverkeithing Museum

The Friary, Queen Street, Inverkeithing, Fife, KY11 1LS
Tel: 01383 313 594
Thurs, Fri, Sat & Sun 11.00-12.30 & 13.00-16.00
Museum displaying the local history of Inverkeithing and Rosyth including one
display on the founder of the Russian Navy, Admiral Greig.

Burntisland Edwardian Fair Museum

102 High Street, Burntisland, Fife, KY3 9AS
Tel: 01592 412 860
Open all year, Mon, Wed, Fri and Sat 10.00-13.00 and 14.00-17.00; Tue and Thu 10.00-13.00 and 14.00-19.00
Museum that tells the story of the Edwardian Fair that came every year to Burntisland, as well as the history of the town itself.

Kirkcaldy Museum & Art Gallery

War Memorial Gardens, Abbotshall Road, Kirkcaldy, Fife, KY1 1YG
Tel: 01592 412 860
Email: kirkcaldy.museum@fife.gov.uk
(Mon-Sat) 10.30-17.00, (Sun) 14.00-17.00
The building houses a collection of fine and decorative arts of local and national importance. These include 18-20C works by Scottish Painters, one of the largest public collections of works by William McTaggart and S.J. Peploe.

Buckhaven Museum

College Street, Buckhaven, 8 miles E of Kirkcaldy, Buckhaven, Fife, KY8 1LD
Tel: 01592 412 860
Tuesday 10.00-13.00 & 14.00-17.00 Thurs 10.00-13.00 & 14.00-17.00 & 17.30-19.00 Friday 14.00-17.00 Sat 10.00-12.30
Museum depicts the history of Buckhaven with emphasis on the fishing industry. Displays include a reconstructed 1920s kitchen and stained glass windows made by local residents.

St Andrew's Museum

Kinburn Park, Doubledykes Road, St Andrews, Fife, KY16 9DP
Tel: 01334 412 690
April-Sep 10.00-17.00, Oct-Mar (Mon-Fri) 10.30-16.00 (Weekends) 12.30-17.00
Opened in Kinburn House in 1991, the museum is housed in a Victorian mansion set in parklands and explores the dramatic heritage of the city from it's beginnings to modern time.

St Andrew's Preservation Trust Museum

12 North Street, St Andrews, Fife, KY16 9PW
Tel: 01334 477 629
Email: trust@standrewspreservationtrust.co.uk
Website: www.standrewspreservationtrust.co.uk
Daily 14.00-17.00
Set in a historic building the museum shows shop reconstruction's, and displays on the fishing and manufacturing industries of St Andrews.

Islands Scotland

ART GALLERIES/ARTS & CRAFTS

Nornova Knitwear
Muness, Uyeasound, Unst, Shetland, ZE2 9DL
Tel: 01957 755 373
Email: admin@nornova.co.uk
Website: www.nornova.co.uk
May-Oct (Daily) 09.00-17.00
Varied exhibitions on wool, Shetland sheep, knitting, hand spinning, lace knitting etc.

Ortak Visitors Centre
Hatston Industrial Estate, Kirkwall, Orkney, KW15 1RH
Tel: 01856 872 224
Email: ortak@ortak.co.uk
(Mon-Sat) 09.00-17.00 (Winter) 09.00-13.00 & 14.00-17.00
The exhibition tells the story of Ortak jewellery and describes how modern jewellery is made. In July and August visitors can watch the resident silversmith at work.

Edinbane Pottery
Edinbane, On the A850 14 Miles from Portree, Edinbane, Isle of Skye, IV51 9PW
Tel: 01470 582 234
Email: stuart@edinbane-pottery.co.uk
Website: www.edinbane-pottery.co.uk
East-Oct (Daily) 09.00-18.00 (Monday-Fri) 09.00-18.00 Rest of Year
Working pottery where visitors can observe the potters at work making a wide range of pots most of which are wood fired.

Skyeskyns
17 Loch Bay, 4.5 miles from the A850, 19 miles N of Portree, Waternish, Isle of Skye, IV55 8GD
Tel: 01470 592 237
Email: clive@skyeskyns.co.uk
Website: www.skyeskyns.co.uk
April-Oct (Daily) 10.00-18.00
Guided tours of the only tanning workshop of its kind in Scotland.On display are traditional tools in use such as the beam, paddles, drum, buffing wheel and combs. Demonstrations of old skills and wide selection of products to buy.

Dandelion Design And Images Gallery

The Captain's House, Stein, Waternish, Isle of Skye, IV55 8GA

Tel: 01470 592 218

Email: cathy@dandelion-designs.co.uk

Website: www.dandelion-designs.co.uk

East-Sep (Daily) 11.00-17.00. Winter months hours vary so please phone 01470-592218 for recorded message.

Craft gallery and workshop producing hand decorated woodcrafts such as clocks, boxes and plaques as well as paintings, jewellery, clothes,books, and cards. Demonstrations by local artist in this listed building on the shore of Loch Bay.

Uig Pottery

The Pier, Uig, Isle of Skye, IV51 9XY

Tel: 01470 542 421

Email: greatpots@uigpottery.co.uk

Website: www.uigpottery.co.uk

Mon-Fri 08.30-18.00 Sun 11.00-16.00

Pottery producing unique functional items.

Aurora Crafts

2 Ose, Struan, Isle of Skye, IV56 8FJ

Tel: 01470 572 208

Apr-Oct (Daily) 09.00-19.00

Craftshop demonstrations of lace and candle making, spinning and weaving and wood turning.

Skye Jewellery

Shore Road, Broadford, Broadford, Isle of Skye, IV49 9AE

Tel: 01471 820 027

Email: info@skyejewellery.co.uk

Website: www.skyejewellery.co.uk

Mon-Sat 09.00-17.30 (Open later in high season) Sundays 11.00-16.30

Workshop that produces its own range of Celtic jewellery. Specialising in cutting and polishing local marble, and hand painted landscapes. Workshop can be viewed from shop.

Castle Keep

Unit 7B1, Portree Industrial Estate, Portree, Isle of Skye, IV51 9BD

Tel: 01478 612 114

Email: rob@castlekeep.co.uk

Website: www.castlekeep.co.uk

(Mon-Fri) 10.00-16.30 All year

Bladesmith making hand forged swords, knives, dirks and traditional Scottish weaponry. Explanatory displays.

Skye Woollen Mill
Dunvegan Road, Portree, Isle of Skye, IV51 9HG
Tel: 01478 612 889
Jun-Sep 09.00-17.30 (Oct-May) 10.00-17.00
Character weaving mill originally producing yarn for Glasgow carpet factories.

Scotia Ceramics Ltd
Coll Pottery, Back, Isle of Lewis, HS2 0JP
Tel: 01851 820 219
Email: admin@scotia-ceramics.com
Apr-Sep (Mon-Sat) 09.00-18.00 Oct-Mar (Mon-Sat) 09.00-17.00
Working pottery making marbled ware and traditional figurines.

Oiseval Gallery
James Smith Photography, Brue, Isle of Lewis, HS2 0QW
Tel: 01851 840 240
Website: www.oiseval.co.uk
(Mon-Sat) 10.30-17.30
Collection of creative Hebridean landscapes by local photographer. Includes the St Kilda Archipelago.

CASTLES

Muness Castle
4 miles NE from pier at Belmont, Off the A968, Unst, Shetland
Tel: 01856 841 815
Access at all times Exterior View Only
A late 16C Tower House with circular towers. It is the most Northerly Castle in the British Isles.

Fort Charlotte
Town Centre, Lerwick, Shetland
Tel: 01856 841 815
1st April-30th Sept (Mon-Sun) 09.30-18.30 1st Oct-31st March (Mon-Sun) 09.30-16.30 Key available locally
Built in 1665 the fort was captured by the Dutch and burned in 1673, the present building was rebuilt in 1781 and comprises a pentagonal fort with corner bastions and huge walls.

Scalloway Castle

In Scalloway, 6 miles W of Lerwick on the A970, Lerwick, Shetland
Tel: 01856 841 815
Open during Shetland Woollen Company Shop hours Mon-Sat 09.30-17.00 Sundays key available from Royal Hotel
A mansion built in medieval style in 1600 by the Earl of Orkney which fell into disuse in 1615

Noltland Castle

On the Island of Westray, 1 mile W of Pierowall Village, Westray, Orkney
Tel: 01856 841 815
11th June-30th Sept Mon-Sun 09.30-18.30
Ruined Z plan tower built between 1560 -1573, but never completed. Impressive winding staircase and large number of gun loops.

Cubbie Row's Castle

On the Island of Wyre, 0.5 miles from pier, Wyre, Orkney
Tel: 01856 841 815
Ferry from Tingwall.(Access at all times)
Probably Scotland's earliest stone castle built around 1145 consisting of a small rectangular tower enclosed in a circular ditch. The ruins of the late 12C Romanesque style St Mary's Chapel are close by

CHURCHES & CATHEDRALS

Pierowall Church

On the S coast of the Island of Westray, In the village of Pierowall, Westray, Orkney
Tel: 01856 841 815
Access at all times
Medieval ruined church with intricately carved tombstones.

Westside Church

Bay of Tuquoy, 3 miles S of Pierowall Village, Westray, Orkney
Tel: 01856 841 815
Access at all times
Roofless 12C Romanesque church.

Eynhallow Church

On the Island of Eynhallow, Eynhallow, Orkney
Access at all times
Ruined 12C church and remains of a group of domestic buildings.

Church of St Magnus

On the Island of Egilsay, Egilsay, Orkney
Access at all times
A complete but roofless ruin of a 12C church, with Irish style round tower,
situated in a dramatic location

St Magnus Cathedral

Broad Street, Kirkwall, Orkney, KW15 1NX
Tel: 01856 874 894
Apr-Sep (Mon-Fri) 09.00-18.00 (Sun) 14.00-18.00, Oct-Mar (Mon-Fri) 09.00-13.00 &
14.00-17.00
The building which is still in regular use as a church was originally built between
1137 and 12.00 with remains of a group of domestic buildings.

Italian Chapel

Lambholm, 7 miles S of Kirkwall off the A961, Lambholm, Orkney
Tel: 01856 781 268
Open all year, daylight hours.
Two Nissen huts that were transformed into a small chapel by Italian Prisoners
Of War.

St Clement's Church

Rodel, At the S end of the Isle of Harris, On the A859, Rodel, Isle of Harris
Access at all times
16C Church built by Alexander MacLeod of Dunvegan and Harris. The interior of
the church contains his elaborately carved tomb

EXHIBITIONS

Unst Boat Haven

Unst Heritage, Haroldswick, Unst, Shetland, ZE2 9EF
May-Sep (Daily) 14.00-17.00
Collection of wooden oar and sail boats built in the last 100 years from Shetland,
Norway and the Faroe Islands. Exhibitions, photographs and documents relating
to aspects of Shetland's maritime history.

The Old Haa

Burravoe, Yell, Shetland
Tel: 01957 722 339
Late April-End of Sept Tues, Thurs & Sat 10.00-16.00 Sun 14.00-17.00
The oldest building in Yell, now a heritage centre and coffee shop with exhibitions and displays on local history

An Tuireann Arts Centre

Struan Road, Portree, Isle of Skye, IV51 9EG
Tel: 01478 613 306
Email: exhibition@antuireann.org.uk
Website: www.antuireann.org.uk
(Mon-sat) 10.00-17.00 Winter Tues-Sat 10.00-17.00
Exhibition gallery for visual arts and crafts and related education events and performances

GARDENS PARKS WALKS

Keen Of Hamar National Nature Reserve

Keen of Hamar, Baltasound, Unst, Shetland
Tel: 01595 693 345
Open daily all year
Important Botanical site with unique habitat and landscape. Specialist plants grow in the Serpentine soil.

Kylerhea Otter Haven

Kylerhea, Isle of Skye
Access at all times
Visitors can walk along specially constructed paths and view otters from the hide. The area also contains eagles, falcons, waders, seabirds and seals.

HISTORIC HOUSES

Knap Of Howar

West Side of Island of Papa Westray, Approx 2.5 miles W of Holland Farm, Papa Westray, Orkney
Tel: 01856 872 044
Access at all times
Two Neolithic rectangular dwellings with stone cupboards and stairs, probably the oldest standing stone houses in NW Europe.

Earl's Palace

In Birsay, 11 miles N of Stromness, At the N end of Mainland Orkney, Stromness, Orkney

Access at all times

Remains of a courtyard palace built in the 16C by the Earl Of Orkney.

Grain Earth House

Hatson, 1 mile NW of Kirkwall, Kirkwall, Orkney

Tel: 01856 841 815

(Access at all times, key available from the Ortak shop in Kirkwall.)

Well built Iron Age Earth House with an underground chamber supported by stone pillars.

Rennibister Earth House

On the A965, 4.5 miles WNW of Kirkwall, Kirkwall, Orkney

Access at all times

Example of an Orkney Earth House with a passage and underground chambers supporting roof pillars.

HISTORIC SITES

Clickhimin Broch

1 mile SW of Lerwick, Beside the A970, Lerwick, Shetland

Access at all times

Good example of a broch tower with other Iron Age buildings.

Mousa Broch

On Isle of Mousa, Accessible from Sandwick 14 miles S of Lerwick on the A970, Mousa, Shetland

Tel: 01856 841 815

Open April-Sept

Finest surviving Iron Age Broch tower over 40 feet high. Visitors can climb to the parapet.

Ness Of Burgi

SE point of Scatness, 1 mile SW of Jarlshof, Jarlshof, Shetland

Access at all times

Defensive stone Blockhouse, with features similar to a broch probably Iron Age.

Taversoe Tuick Chambered Cairn

On the Isle of Rousay, Half a mile west of Trumland Pier, Rousay, Orkney

Access at all times

Neolithic chambered mound with two burial chambers, one above the other.

Quoyness Chambered Tomb

2.5 miles from Kettlehoff Village, Island of Sanday, Sanday, Orkney

Access at all times

A Megalithic tomb with triple walls and a passage with a main chamber and six secondary cells from the Neolithic period.

Holm Of Papa Westray Chambered Cairn

On the Isle of Holm Of Papa Westray, Papa Westray, Orkney

Tel: 01856 841 815

Access at all times

Massive tomb with a long narrow chamber divided into three and containing 14 beehive cells within the walls. Also wall engravings.

Knowe Of Yarso Chambered Cairn

On the Isle of Rousay, On the B9064 3 miles from the pier, Rousay, Orkney

Tel: 01856 751 360

Access at all times

Oval cairn with concentric walls. Enclosing a Neolithic chambered tomb divided into three.

Blackhammer Cairn

N of B9064, On the S coast of Isle of Rousay, Rousay, Orkney

Tel: 01856 751 360

Access at all times

Long Neolithic cairn surrounded by a retaining wall with a megalithic burial chamber divided into seven compartments.

Cuween Hill Cairn

On the A965, 0.5 miles S of Finstown, Finstown, Orkney

Access at all times

Neolithic four chambered burial tomb covered by a low mound. Inside the cairn were found the bones of men,dogs and oxen.

Wideford Hill Cairn

On the W slope of Wideford Hill, 2 miles W of Kirkwall, on the B9056, Kirkwall, Orkney
Tel: 01856 841 815
Access to the chamber is a 0.5 mile hill walk which can be muddy
Three celled Neolithic burial cairn with three concentric walls.

Unstan Chambered Cairn

3.5 miles NNE of Stromness, On the A965, Stromness, Orkney
Tel: 01856 841 815
Access at all times
Neolithic burial chamber divided into five compartments by slabs and covered by
a mound.

Dwarfie Stane

North end of Island of Hoy, Between Quoys and Rackwick, Hoy, Orkney
Tel: 01856 811 397
Access at all times
Unique to the British Isles this huge block of sandstone contains a Neolithic
burial cairn.

Orphir Church and Earls Bu

By the A964, 8 miles WSW of Kirkwall, Kirkwall, Orkney
Access at all times
Earl's Bu are the foundation remains of a possible Viking Palace which stand
near to the ruins of Scotland's only circular medieval church.

Dun Beag Broch

Follow A863 south out of Dunvegan for about 8 miles, Just before village of Struanmore,
Struanmore, Isle of Skye
Tel: 01667 460 232
Access at all times
Fine example of a Hebridean Broch that was apparently occupied up until the
18C.

Quirang

Off unclassified Staffin to Uig road, 19 miles N of Portree, Portree, Isle of Skye
Access at all times
Extraordinary mass of pinnacles and towers into which cattle were driven during
forays. A rough track leads up to the needle, a 120 ft high obelisk, and a large
amphitheatre containing "The Table" a large grass covered rock.

Steinacleit Cairn
S end of Loch An Duin, Shader, 12 miles N of Stornoway, Stornoway, Isle of Lewis
Access at all times
Remains of a building dating from early prehistoric times.

Dun Carloway
On A858, 1.5 miles S of Carloway, 16 miles WNW of Stornoway, Stornoway, Isle of Lewis
Access at all times
One of Scotland's best preserved Iron Age Brochs

Calanais Standing Stones
Calanais, Off the A858, 12 miles W of Stornoway, Stornoway, Isle of Lewis
Site open all year Visitor Centre Open in Summer 10.00-19.00, Winter 10.00-16.00. Closed Sundays.
Unique cruciform arrangement of megaliths, second in importance only to Stonehenge.An avenue of 19 monoliths leads N from a circle of 13 stones fanning out to the S, E & W. There is a small chambered tomb inside the circle. The site dates to around 3000BC

MUSEUMS

Croft House Museum
South Mainland at Voe, Dunrossness, Shetland
May-Sept 10.00-13.00 & 14.00-17.00
This 19C Croft Steading and Watermill have been restored to give a taste of family life as it was over 100 years ago

Tangwick Haa Museum
Eshaness, 40 miles N of Lerwick via the A970 and B9078, Lerwick, Shetland, ZE2 9RS
Tel: 01806 503 389
May-Sep (Mon-Fri) 13.00-17.00, (Weekends) 11.00-19.00
Restored 17C house houses a museum with various exhibitions on aspects of local life, including; agriculture, fishing, spinning and weaving in Northmavine through the ages.

Bonhoga Gallery

Weisdale, 12 miles W of Lerwick, Lerwick, Shetland, ZE2 9LW
Tel: 01595 830 400
(Tues-Sat) 10.30-16.30, (Sun) 12.00-16.30
The gallery includes the Shetland Textile Museum as well as local and national arts and craft exhibitions. There is also a café in the conservatory overlooking the Weisdale Burn.

Shetland Museum

Lower Hillhead, Lerwick, Shetland, ZE1 0EL
Tel: 01595 695 057
Email: museum@sic.shetland.gov.uk
Website: www.shetland-museum.org.uk
(Mon-Wed-Fri) 10.00-19.00, (Tue-Thur-Sat) 10.00-17.00
The museum covers all aspects of the history of Shetland including archaeology from Neolithic to Medieval times, Early Christian Sculpture, Viking grave artefacts, Medieval domestic and fishing items and Maritime and Agricultural history

Scalloway Museum

Main Street, Scalloway, 9 miles W of Lerwick, Scalloway, Shetland, ZE1 0TR
Tel: 01595 880 256
May-Sept Mon-Sat 10.00-12.00 & 14.30-16.00
Local and Norwegian Wartime history including how Norwegians were smuggled out of Norway during World War II.

Borders Scotland

Lindean Mill Glass

Lindean Mill, Galashiels, Scottish Borders, TD1 3PE
Tel: 01750 201 73
Email: info@lindeanmillglass.co.uk
Website: www.lindeanmillglass.co.uk
Mon-Fri 09.00-12.00 & 13.00-16.30
Scotland's premier lead crystal studio where visitors can observe glass wear being made by hand.

Kinsman Blake Ceramics

Barnhouse, Smailholm, Near Kelso, Smailholm, Scottish Borders, TD5 7PH
Tel: 01573 460 666
Open all year, daily 10.00-17.00
Small family pottery specialising in decorative techniques. Visitors are welcome to observe in the workshop. Well stocked show room and gift shop.

Kelso Pottery

The Knowes, Kelso, Scottish Borders, TD5 7BH
Tel: 01573 224 027
Tues -Sat) 10.00-13.00 and 14.00-17.00
Workshop creating a range of simple practical stoneware pottery and pit fire ware.

Tom Davidson Gallery

High Street, Earlston, Scottish Borders, TD4 6BU
Tel: 01896 848 898
Email: info@tomdavidson.co.uk
Website: www.tomdavidson.co.uk
Mon-Sat 10.00-17.00 Closed Tues Afternoons
The Gallery of Tom Davidson one of Scotland's leading exponents of the Linocut. Visitors can observe him at work. The gallery contains his paintings, etchings and lino cuts

Hawick Cashmere Visitors Centre

Trinity Mills, Duke Street, Hawick, Scottish Borders, TD9 9QA
Tel: 01450 372 510
Email: sales@hawickcashmere.com
Website: www.hawickcashmere.com
Mon-Sat 09.30-17.00 Sun 11.00-16.00 (Seasonal please call for details)
Visitors can watch cashmere products being produced and learn more about knitwear manufacturing

Selkirk Glass Visitors Centre

Dunsdalehaugh, Selkirk, Scottish Borders, TD7 5EF
Tel: 01750 209 54
Email: ronhutchinson@selkirkglass.co.uk
Mon-Sat 09.00-17.00 Sun 11.00-17.00 Glassmaking Mon-Fri 09.00-16.30 Sat 11.00-15.00
Watch craftsmen produce glassware, including the well known Selkirk paperweights

Johnnie Armstrong Gallery

Hernderson's Knowe, Teviot Head, Hawick, Scottish Borders, TD9 0LF
Tel: 01450 850 237
Daily 09.00-18.00 Closed Tuesdays
Displays of artefacts and arms from the times of the Border Reivers. Gold and silver jewellery designed and made on site

Scottish Borders Art Glass

Galalaw, Hawick, Scottish Borders, TD9 8PZ
Tel: 01450 371 425
Email: sales@scottishborderartglass.com
Mon-Fri 09.00-17.00 Sat 10.00-15.00
Visitors can watch the skills of the craftsmen of glassmaking, as they produce paperweights and hand blown vases and bowls

Peebles Craft Centre

Newby Court, High Street, Peebles, Scottish Borders, EH45 8AL
Tel: 01721 722 875
Email: woodworkspeebles@aol.com
Daily 10.00-17.00 Not all workshops are open at all times
This craft centre houses a wide variety of different craftspeople including woodworking, ceramics, metal and jewellery. Visitors can watch the craftspeople at work and purchase their finished products

Flat Cat Gallery
2 Market Place, Lauder, Scottish Borders, TD2 6DR
Tel: 01578 722 808
Email: angelamercer@btopenworld.com
Website: www.flatcatgallery.co.uk
Daily 09.30-17.00
Changing exhibitions of paintings, photography, glass and sculpture from a variety of artists

100 Aker Wood Visitors Centre
Annay Road, Melrose, Scottish Borders, TD6 9LW
Tel: 01896 823 717
Email: mark@1stforfencing.com
Website: www.100akerwoodgardencentre.com
Daily 09.00-17.00
This visitors centre combines a gift shop with crafts and paintings from local artists, woodland walks and a garden centre

CASTLES

Roxburgh Castle
Off the A699, 1 mile SW of Kelso, Kelso, Scottish Borders
Access at all times
Remaining earthworks of a once magnificent castle that was destroyed by the Scots in the 15C and the walled Royal Burgh that gave it's name to the County.

Hume Castle
Hume, 3 miles S of Greenlaw, Kelso, Scottish Borders
Access at all times daylight hours
Ruined remains of castle destroyed by Cromwell and partially rebuilt by the Earl of Marchmont. Spectacular views of the Tweed Valley and beyond. Explanatory displays.

CHURCHES & CATHEDRALS

Edrom Church
Edrom Churchyard, Edrom, Off the A6015 3.5 miles NE of Dunns, Edrom, Scottish Borders
Access at any reasonable time
Norman chancel arch from the church dating from around 1105 and built by Thor Longus.

Ladykirk

Off B6470, 5.5 miles NE of Coldstream, Ladykirk, Scottish Borders

Access at any reasonable time

Built in 1500 by James IV in memory of Our Lady who saved him from drowning. The church was built under the order that it should be able to withstand fire and flood, hence it's all stone construction including no wooden rafters and stone pews

Kelso Abbey

Bridge Street, Kelso, Roxburghshire, Kelso, Scottish Borders

Open at all times

The west end of the Great Abbey Church of the Tironensians who were brought to Kelso by David I in 1128. Even in it's present state it remains one of the Great Border Abbeys.

Jedburgh Friary

Jedburgh, Scottish Borders

Access at all times

An ongoing archaeology project has uncovered the remains of this 16C Franciscan building.

Bowden Kirk

Bowden Village, 5 miles E of Selkirk, Bowden, Scottish Borders

Open during daylight hours

Founded in 1128 by the monks of Kelso Abbey. Only fragments of the original building have survived, the exterior still bears the feeling of antiquity but the interior has been remodeled

Cross Kirk

Cross Road, On A703, Peebles, Scottish Borders

Access at all times

The nave and tower of a Trinitarian Friary founded in the late 13C

GARDENS PARKS WALKS

Harestanes Countryside Visitors Centre
Ancrum, Off the A68, 3 miles N of Jedburgh, Ancrum, Scottish Borders, TD8 6UQ
Tel: 01835 830 306
Email: harestanes@scotborders.gov.uk
April-Oct (Daily) 10.00-17.00
Converted farm buildings now house a variety of indoor and outdoor attractions, exhibitions, countryside and guided walks, activities and events. Wildlife gardens and wooden games room.

Wilton Lodge Walled Garden
Wilton Park Road, 0.5 miles from the town centre, Hawick, Scottish Borders, TD9 7JL
Tel: 01450 378 023
Open all year
107 acres of garden with wide variety of shrubberies and mature trees.

Teviot Water Gardens
Kirkbank House, Mid way between Kelso & Jedburgh on the A698, Kelso, Scottish Borders, TD5 8LE
Tel: 01835 850 734
(Daily) 10.00-17.00
Four levels of water gardens in the midst of the beautiful Border's countryside.The lower levelled garden flows down to the River Teviot. Other attractions include explanatory displays and a smokery.

HISTORIC HOUSES

Old Gala House
Scott Crescent, Galashiels, Scottish Borders, TD1 3JS
Tel: 01750 720 096
April-Sept Tues -Sat 10.00-16.00 July-Aug Mon-Sat 10.00-16.00 Also Sun 14.00-16.00 Oct Tues- Fri 13.00-16.00 Sat 10.00-16.00
Dating from 1583 and set in its own grounds. Former home of the Lairds of Gala it is now an interpretative centre. Displays tell the story of the house, it's residents and the growth of the surrounding town.

Sir Walter Scott's Courtroom

Market Place, Selkirk, Scottish Borders, TD7 4BT
Tel: 01750 720 761
Email: museums@scotborders.gov.uk
April-Sept Mon-Fri 10.00-16.00 Sat 10.00-14.00 May-August also open Sundays
10.00-14.00 Oct Mon-Sat 13.00-16.00
This is the building that Sir Walter Scott used between 1804 to 1832 when he
was a Sheriff of Selkirk, and a now a museum dedicated to him

HISTORIC SITES

Edin's Hall Broch

On the NE slope of Cockburns Law, Off the A6112, 4.5 miles from Granthouse,
Berwickshire, Granthouse, Scottish Borders
Access at all times
One of the few Iron Age Brochs in the Lowlands. Sitting in a fort surrounded by
ditches and ramparts. Also remnants of a later settlement that was occupied in
Roman times.

St Ronans Well Interpretive Centre

Wells Brae, on the A72 Gallashiels to Peebles Road, Innerleithen, Scottish Borders, EH44
6JE
Tel: 01721 724 820
Email: rhannay@scotborders.gov.uk
June-Oct Mon-Fri 10.00-13.00 & 14.00-17.00 Sat & Sun 14.00-17.00
Built in 1827 this historic spa with mineral waters was a magnet for the Victorians

Foulden Tithe Barn

Off the A6105, 4 miles SE of Chirnside, Berwickshire, Foulden, Scottish Borders
Access at all times-exterior view only.
Two storey tithe barn with outside stair and crow stepped gables

MUSEUMS

Berwick Main Guard

Palace Green, Berwick Upon Tweed, Berwick, Scottish Borders
Tel: 01289 308 005
June-Sept Daily except Wednesdays 13.00-17.00
Exhibitions and displays on the history of the town, housed with a Georgian
Military Guardhouse.

Coldstream Museum

12 Market Square, Off the A698 Kelso to Cornhill Road, Coldstream, Scottish Borders, TD12 4BD
Tel: 01890 882 630
Email: museums@scotborders.gov.uk
April-Sept Mon-Sat 10.00-16.00 Sun 14.00-16.00 October Mon-Sat 13.00-16.00
A museum with temporary exhibitions and a special display for the Coldstream Guards

Hawick Museum and Scott Art Gallery

Wilton Lodge Park, Hawick, Scottish Borders, TD9 7JL
Tel: 01450 373 457
Email: museums@scotborders.gov.uk
April-Sept Mon-Fri 10.00-12.00 & 13.00-17.00 Sat & Sun 14.00-17.00 Oct-March Mon-Fri
13.00-16.00 Sun 14.00-16.00 Closed Saturdays
Hawick Museum covers displays of manufacturing and local history of the area,
while the Scott Art gallery exhibits art from the 19th and 20C

Tweeddale Museum And Gallery

Chambers Institute, High Street, Peebles, Scottish Borders, EH45 8AG
Tel: 01721 724 820
Email: museums@scotborders.gov.uk
Mon-Fri 10.00-12.00 & 14.00-17.00 Also Easter-Oct Saturdays 10.00-13.00 & 14.00-16.00
Telling the story of Peebles from pre historic times to the present day, the Gallery
offers exhibitions of contemporary arts and crafts

Halliwell's House Museum And Robson Gallery

Halliwell's Close, Market Place, Selkirk, Scottish Borders, TD7 4BL
Tel: 01750 200 96
Email: museums@scotborders.gov.uk
April-Sept Mon-Sat 10.00-17.00 Sun 10.00-12.00 July & August Mon-Sat 10.00-17.30
October Mon-Sat 10.00-16.00
Exploring the life and times of Selkirk through the ages

FARMERS MARKETS

Peebles Farmers Market

East Station Carpark, Peebles
2nd Saturday of the month 09.30-13.30
Farmers market with local produce for sale

Kelso Farmers Market

Town Square, Kelso
The 4th Saturday of the month 09.30-13.30
Farmers market with local produce for sale

NATURE AND WILDLIFE

Bemersyde Moss

4 miles East of Melrose, On a minor road between Melrose and Smailholm, Scottish Borders
Open during daylight hours
This 25 hectare reserve is the breeding colony for some 14 000 pairs of black headed gulls

Dumfries & Galloway Scotland

ART GALLERIES/ARTS & CRAFTS

Border Fine Arts Gallery
Market Place, Langholm, Dumfries & Galloway, DG13 0JQ
Tel: 01387 383 033
(Mon-Fri) 09.00-17.00, (Sat & Sun) 11.00-16.00
Extensive display of current works in addition to previous work housed in museum section.

Castle Douglas Arts Gallery
Market Street, Castle Douglas, Dumfries & Galloway, DG7 1BE
Tel: 01557 331 643
Daily 11.00-14.00
Varied collection of temporary exhibitions focusing mainly on the works of local art and craft groups but also featuring touring exhibitions.

Rockcliffe Gallery
Barons Craig, Rockcliffe, Kirkcudbrightshire, Rockcliffe, Dumfries & Galloway, DG5 4QF
Tel: 01556 630 475
Email: info@rockcliffegallery.co.uk
Website: www.rockcliffegallery.co.uk
Seven days a week from 09.00-21.00
A varied programme of regular changing exhibitions of work by professional artists, the gallery has panoramic views over the open sea to the hills beyond.

Gracefield Arts Centre
28 Edinburgh Road, Dumfries, Dumfries & Galloway, DG1 1NW
Tel: 01387 262 084
Email: arts@dumgal.gov.uk
(Tue-Fri) 09.00-17.00 Sat 10.00-12.00 & 14.00-17.00 Closed Mondays
Changing programme of contemporary visual arts and craft exhibitions and activities. Also exhibitions from the permanent collection of Scottish paintings from 18C to present.

The Waterloo Gallery

Wellington House, Princes Street, Stranraer, Stranraer, Dumfries & Galloway, DG9 7RQ
Tel: 01776 702 888
Email: ann_waterlooartgallery@btopenworld.com
Website: www.thewaterlooartgallery.co.uk
(Tue-Sun) 12.00-17.00
Exhibits paintings by mainly professional Scottish Artists, regular exhibitions.
Unframed original works available to buy

Designs Gallery

179 King Street, On A75 18 miles W of Dumfries, Castle Douglas, Castle Douglas, Dumfries
& Galloway, DG7 1DZ
Tel: 01556 504 552
Email: enquiries@designsgallery.co.uk
Website: www.designsgallery.co.uk
09.30-17.30 (Mon-Sat) Closed Sundays
Focal point for Southwest Scotland Arts and Crafts. Exhibitions and shop selling
products.

Cat's Moustache Gallery

54 St John's Street, Creetown, Dumfries & Galloway, DG8 7JF
Tel: 01671 820 577
Email: rtrevanion@hotmail.com
Website: www.thecatsmoustachegallery.co.uk
Sat & Sun 11.00-17.00
A range of original hand made arts and crafts from Scottish, National and
International artisans

Barnbarroch Pottery

Kippford, Dalbeattie, Dumfries & Galloway, DG5 4LE
Tel: 01556 620 695
Email: barnbarroch-pottery@lineone.net
Website: www.barnbarroch-pottery.com
Showroom open Mon-Sat 09.30-17.00
From large contemporary sculptural ceramics to functional decorative tableware
pottery

Moffat Woolen Mill

Ladyknowe, Moffat, Dumfries & Galloway, DG10 9EP
Tel: 01683 220 134
Email: info@moffatwoollenmill.com
Mar-Oct (Mon-Sun) 09.00-17.30 Nov-Feb (Mon-Sun) 09.00-17.00.
Resident Weaver brings the Scottish Border's weaving tradition alive for visitors,
exclusive range of woollens and tartans and clan tartan centre.

Dalton Pottery

Meikle Dyke, Dalton, Near Lockerbie, Dalton, Dumfries & Galloway, DG11 1DU
Tel: 01387 840 236
Email: info@daltonpottery.co.uk
Website: www.daltonpottery.co.uk
(Mon-Sun) 09.00-17.00 Nov-March Closed Mondays
Working pottery and art experience where visitors can create or paint a pot themselves.

Tolbooth Arts Centre

High Street, Kirkcudbright, Dumfries & Galloway
Tel: 01557 331 556
Mon-Sat 11.00-16.00 June-Sept Sundays also 14.00-17.00
Telling the story of the Kirkcudbright artists colony via an audio visual show, as well as a gallery showing the works of artists and craftmakers who visitors can watch at work

Cornerways Studio

7 Selkirk Road, Kirkcudbright, Dumfries & Galloway
Tel: 01557 331 640
Email: enquiry@cornerwaysart.co.uk
Website: www.cornerwayart.co.uk
Fridays 10.30-17.00 Open till 16.00 in Winter
This small studio situated in the home of the artist Jane B Gibson welcomes visitors on a Friday to view her paintings, miniatures, paperweights and other works of art

Galloway Country Style

59-61 High Street, Gatehouse-Of-Fleet, Dumfries & Galloway, DG7 2HS
Tel: 01557 814 001
Email: toots@gcsltd.freeserve.co.uk
July-Aug (Mon-Sat) 10.00-17.00 (Sun) 11.00-17.30 Sep-Jan (Mon-Sat) 10.00-17.00 (Sun) 11.00-17.00. Closed Sundays in January.
Country Style featuring exhibitions, kilt making and gifts.

CASTLES

Morton Castle

On the A702, near Carronbridge, 17 miles NW of Dumfries, Dumfries, Dumfries & Galloway
Tel: 0131 668 8800
Access at all times
Well preserved 13C ruins of a Hall House the stronghold of the Douglas's

Carsluith Castle

A75 3.5 miles S of Creetown, Carsluith, Dumfries & Galloway
Tel: 0131 668 8800
Open 1st April-30 Sept Mon-Sun 09.30-18.30 1st Oct-31st March Mon-Sat 09.30-16.30 Sun 14.00-16.30
Charming well preserved ruins of a 16C four storied tower house, one of the last owners being the last Abbot of the Sweetheart Abbey.The ruins include a range of 18C outbuildings.

Dunskey Castle

Portpatrick, Portpatrick, Dumfries & Galloway
Access at all times
Early 16C castle ruins perched dramatically on the cliff top. The ruins themselves can be reached by a cliff top footpath that climbs from the old Quarry at the South end of Portpatrick Waterfront.

Lochmaben Castle

1 mile S of Lochmaben, by Castle Loch, Lochmaben, Dumfries & Galloway
Tel: 0131 668 8800
Email: hs.explore@scotland.gsi.gov.uk
Exterior View Only
The ruins of a 14-16C castle which were once the seat of Robert The Bruce's family, the castle itself is set on a promontory in Castle Loch.

Castle Of St John

Town Centre, Stranraer, Dumfries & Galloway
Tel: 01776 705 544
Website: www.dumgal.gov.uk/museums
Open East-Mid Sept Mon-Sat 10.00-13.00 & 14.00-17.00
At this late Medieval Tower House built around 1500, and later used as a Victorian Prison there are displays on prison life and the Covenanters

CHURCHES & CATHEDRALS

St Ninian's Chapel

Isle of Whithorn, On the A747, 4 miles from Whithorn, Isle of Whithorn, Dumfries & Galloway
Tel: 0131 688 8830
Access at all times
13th century chapel thought to be where St Ninian landed

Kagyu Samye Ling Tibetan Buddhist Monastery

Sign posted from Lockerbie and Langholm, Eskdalemuir, Dumfries & Galloway, DG13 0QL

Tel: 01387 373 232

Email: reception@samyeling.org

Website: www.samyeling.org

Visitors are welcome to visit the temple and grounds-Temple open 6.00-22.00 daily

In a quiet rural setting this Tibetan Buddhist Temple and Monastic Community has tranquil walks around the grounds

Chapel Finian

On the A747 5 miles NW of Port William, Port William, Dumfries & Galloway

Tel: 0131 668 8800

Access at all times

The chapel which dates from the 10C was probably named after St Finian who studied at Whithorn. The low walls of the building remain on part of a long raised beach.

Durisdeer Church

On the A702 6 miles NE of Thornhill, Durisdeer, Dumfries & Galloway

Open all year

The church houses the Queensberry Marbles and in the vault below are 29 lead coffins containing ancient remains of the Clan Douglas. The well path was once part of a medieval pilgrimage route to Whithorn.

Lincluden Collegiate Church

Of the A76 1 mile N of Dumfries, Dumfries, Dumfries & Galloway

Tel: 0131 668 8800

Open April-Sept Mon-Sun 09.30-18.30 Oct-March Mon-Sat 09.30-16.30 & Sun 14.00-16.30

Remains of a 15C Collegiate Church which was built by the Duke of Tourane and provided accommodation for its cannons.

Sanquhar Church

Sanquhar, Dumfries & Galloway

Tel: 01659 50596

Key available from Tollbooth.

19C Church which houses an varied display of historic items. Including a medieval stone effigy of a monk, an early medieval cross slab and an effigy of St Nicholas that was discovered to the South of the town.

GARDENS PARKS WALKS

Dalbeattie Forest

Dalbeattie, South of the town on the A710, Dalbeattie, Dumfries & Galloway

Access at all times

The forest is run by the Forest Enterprise Trust and has picnic places and miles of marked wooded and hilly walks, as well as mountain bike trails.

Gray Mare's Tail

Off the A708, 10 miles NE of Moffat, Moffat, Dumfries & Galloway

Tel: 01721 722 502

Access at all times

Spectacular 60 meter waterfall is just one feature on this 2 mile round trip with plenty of wild goats on the way.

Barwinnock Herbs

Off the B7027, N of Newton Stewart, Barrhill, Dumfries & Galloway

Tel: 01465 821 338

Email: visit@barwinnock.com

Website: www.barwinnock.com

Apr-Oct (daily)10.00-17.00

The opportunity to learn about the ancient and modern uses of herbs in this organic herb garden with a great assortment of plants.

Sanquhar-The Historic Walk

Sanquhar, Dumfries & Galloway

Tel: 01659 505 96

Access at all times

Follow the historic plaques throughout the town taking in the 18C Tollbooth, the world's oldest working post office, Cameron Monument and Sanquhar Castle

Glentrool Visitors Centre and Galloway Forest Park

12 miles North of Newton Stewart, Off the A714 at Bargrennan, Newton Stewart, Dumfries & Galloway

Tel: 01671 402 420

March-Sept Mon-Sun 10.30-17.00 Sept-Oct Mon-Sun 10.30-16.30

The Galloway Forest Park offers trails and cycle routes and is famous for Bruce's Stone

The Crichton Estate

1 miles South of Dumfries, Dumfries, Dumfries & Galloway
Tel: 01387 247 544
Email: admin@crichton.org.uk
Website: www.crichton.org.uk
Access at all times
34 hectares of landscaped grounds with rhododendrons, azaleas, a large rock garden, waterfall and ornamental pond

Wood Of Cree

4 miles N of Newton Stewart, via Minnigaff, Newton Stewart, Dumfries & Galloway
Tel: 01671 402 861
Access at all times
RSPB Nature Reserve with spectacular waterfalls.

HISTORIC HOUSES

Robert Burns House

Burns Street, Dumfries, Dumfries & Galloway, DG1 2PS
Tel: 01387 255 297
Website: www.dumgal.gov.uk/museums
April-Sep (Mon-Sat) 10.00-17.00 (Sun) 14.00-17.00 Oct-March (Tue-Sat) 10.00-13.00 & 14.00-17.00
In this house Robert Burns Scotland's National poet spent the last years of his life, and it is now a place of pilgrimage for Burns fans across the globe. The house retains its 18C appearance and contains many relics and artefacts of the famous poet.

Drumcoltran Tower

Dalbeattie, off the A711, 7 miles NE of Dalbeattie, Dalbeattie, Dumfries & Galloway
Tel: 0131 668 8800
April-Sept Mon-Sun 09.30-18.30 Oct-March Mon-Sat 09.30-16.30 Sun 14.00-16.00
16C fortified L Plan Tower House next to 18C Farmhouse.

Orchardton Tower

Off the A711, 1.5 miles S of Palnackie, Palnackie, Dumfries & Galloway
Tel: 0131 668 8800
April-Sept Mon-Sun 09.30-18.30 Oct-March Mon-Sat 09.30-16.30 Sun 14.00-16.00
Common in Ireland this is the only cylindrical style Tower House to be built in Scotland. It dates from the 15C and is set in picturesque surroundings.

HISTORIC SITES

Bruce's Stone

On the A712, 6 miles W of New Galloway, New Galloway, Dumfries & Galloway
Access at all times
The granite boulder situated on Moss Rapploch marks the site where Robert
The Bruce defeated the English in 1307. Legend says that Bruce rested against
the bolder after the battle.

Burnswark

3 miles N of Ecclefechan, Ecclefechan, Dumfries & Galloway
Access at all times
Hilltop Earthwork dating from around 6C B.C. Flanked by two Roman siege
camps dating from the 2C A.D.

Cairnholy

6 miles SE of Creetown, Carsluith, Dumfries & Galloway
Tel: 0131 668 8800
Access at all times
Impressive remains of two chambered cairns dating back to around 2000 B.C.

Kirkmadrine Early Christian Stones

Sandhead, Off the A716 2 miles SW of Sandhead, Sandhead, Dumfries & Galloway
Tel: 0131 668 8800
Access at all times
After the stones at Whithorn the Kirkmadrine stones are the oldest examples in
Scotland dating from the 5th Century and displayed in the porch of a former
church.

Ruthwell Cross

Off the B724, In 7C Ruthwell Church, Ruthwell, Dumfries & Galloway
Tel: 01387 870 249
April-Sept 09.30-18.30 Oct-March Mon-Sat 09.30-16.30 Sun 14.00-16.30
Magnificent stone cross bears runic and Latin inscriptions and dates to around
680 A.D.

Rockcliffe

Off the A710, 7 miles S of Dalbeattie, Dalbeattie, Dumfries & Galloway

Access at all times

The National Trust owns several free sites around the village of Rockcliffe. These include the Motte Of Mark which is an ancient hill fort, Rough Island which is a bird sanctuary with access on foot at low tide and Muckle Land and Jubilee Path.

St Ninian's Cave

3 miles S of Whithorn, Whithorn, Dumfries & Galloway

Tel: 0131 668 8800

Access at all times

The cave is reputed to have been used as a retreat by St Ninian and contains 8C carving. It is reached by an attractive walk from the nearby farmhouse.

Scot's Dyke

2 miles S of Canonbie, Canonbie, Dumfries & Galloway

Restricted Access

This trench and dyke were to mark the border between Scotland and England

Wigtown's Martyrs' Monument

Wigtown, Dumfries & Galloway

Access at all times

A monument to the local 17C Covenanters who were executed for their beliefs during the years of Religious intolerance

The Twelve Apostles

Near Dumfries, 400m off the B729 towards Dunscore, Dumfries, Dumfries & Galloway

Access at all times

Park beside first road on the left and walk 100 meters to the way marker and style. The stone circle is the largest example anywhere on the Scottish mainland.

MUSEUMS

Stranraer Musuem

The Old Town Hall, George Street, Stranraer, Dumfries & Galloway, DG9 7JP

Tel: 01776 705 088

All year Mon-Fri 10.00-17.00 Sat 10.00-13.00 & 14.00-17.00

Displays on local history archaeology and farming including one of Scotland's oldest ploughs

Sanquhar Tollbooth Museum

High Street, Sanquhar, Dumfries & Galloway
Tel: 01659 501 86
April-Sept (Tues-Sat) 10.00-13.00 & 14.00-17.00 (Sun) 14.00-17.00
Located in the 18C Tollbooth the museum tells the story of the area including the world famous Sanquhar knitting, mines and miners of Sanquhar, History and customs of the area, three centuries of local literature and life in Sanquhar jail.

Carsphairn Heritage Centre

Carsphairn, On the A713, NW of Castle Douglas, Carsphairn, Dumfries & Galloway
Tel: 01644 460 220
Open April-Oct Mon-Sat 10.30-17.00 Closed Wednesdays (Sun) 13.00-17.00
Displays of the history of the Parish with permanent displays and themed annual exhibitions.

Dumfries Museum

The Observatory, Rotchell Road, Dumfries, Dumfries & Galloway
Tel: 01387 253 374
Email: davidl@dumgal.gov.uk
Apr-Sep (Mon-Sat)10.00-17.00 (Sun) 14.00-17.00, Oct-March (Tue-Sat) 10.00-13.00 & 14.00-17.00
18C Windmill tower which houses an extensive museum of the history of Southwest Scotland. Large collections include, fossil footprints of prehistoric reptiles, local wildlife and tools and weapons of the earliest people.

The Old Bridge House

Mill Road, Dumfries, Dumfries & Galloway, DG2 7BE
Tel: 01387 256 904
April-Sep(Mon-Sat)10.00-17.00(Sun)14.00-17.00
Dumfries' Oldest house built into the sandstone of Devorgilla Bridge the house is now a museum of everyday life in the town

Savings Banks Museum

7 miles West of Annan, By Dumfries, Ruthwell, Dumfries & Galloway, DG1 4NN
Tel: 01387 870 640
Email: info@savingsbanksmuseum.co.uk
Website: www.savingsbanksmuseum.co.uk
Daily 10.00-16.00 Except Sundays and Mondays from Oct-Easter
This is where the Reverend Henry Duncan opened the first commercial Savings Bank in 1810, the 18C building now houses a collection of early home saving boxes, coins and bank notes from all over the world

Robert Burns Centre

Mill Road, Dumfries, Dumfries & Galloway, DG2 7BE
Tel: 01387 264 808
Website: www.dumgal.gov.uk/museums
April-Sept Mon-Sat 10.00-20.00 Sun 14.00-17.00 Oct-March Tues-Sat 10.00-13.00 & 14.00-17.00
This award winning visitors centre tells the story of the connection between Robert Burns and the town of Dumfries. There is a charge for the Audio-Visual Theatre

Moffat Museum

The Neuk, Church Gate, Moffat, Dumfries & Galloway
Tel: 01683 220 868
East-Sept Mon-Tues Thurs-Sat 10.45-16.15 Sun 13.45-16.15
This museum offers exhibitions on the history of Moffat including local trades, famous people, the railway and farming

NATURE AND WILDLIFE

Mossburn Animal Centre

Off the B7020 from Lochmaben, Hightae, Dumfries & Galloway, DG11 1LE
Tel: 01387 811 288
Email: mail@mossburn.org
Website: www.mossburn.org
Mon-Sun 10.00-16.00
This animal welfare centre gives refuge to a variety of domestic, farm and exotic animals

Ken-Dee Marshes Nature Reserve

Along the Loch Ken-River Dee, Castle Douglas, Dumfries & Galloway
Tel: 01671 402 861
Daily dawn-dusk
This RSPB Nature Reserve offers trails through woodland and marshes. In Winter the area becomes home to many wildfowl

Mull Of Galloway Visitors Centre

Mull Of Galloway, Near Drummore, Drummore, Dumfries & Galloway, DG9 9HP

Tel: 01776 830 682

Email: southrhins@talk21.com

Website: www.mull-of-galloway.co.uk

April-Mid October Mon-Sun 10.00-16.00

This visitors centre offers information on the birds and marine life that are housed in the centre or on the RSPB reserve around the centre

Central Scotland (Perthshire & Stirlingshire)

ART GALLERIES/ARTS & CRAFTS

Fergusson Gallery
Marshall Place, Perth, Perthshire, PH2 8NU
Tel: 01738 441 944
Email: museum@pkc.gov.uk
Website: www.pkc.gov.uk/ah/fergussongallery.htm
(Mon-Sat) 10.00-17.00
Gallery showing work of the Scottish colourist painter John Duncan Fergusson (1874-1961)

Inverbeg Galleries
On the A82, 3 miles N of Luss, Inverbeg, Central, G83 8PD
Tel: 01436 860 277
Email: inverbeg.galleries@visit-lochlomond.com
(Daily) 09.30-17.30 Thursdays 09.30-12.00
Internationally renowned art gallery with one of the largest collections of oil and watercolour paintings and prints in the UK.

Glen Lyon Gallery
Boltachan, Aberfeldy, Perthshire, PH15 2LB
Tel: 01887 820 202
Email: glenlyon.gallery@virgin.net
Website: www.glenlyongallery.com
March-Oct (Daily) Closed Wednesdays. Nov, Dec & Feb 10.00-17.00 Closed Tues Wed Thurs. Closed Jan.
Artist's gallery exhibiting and selling the resident artist's paintings in beautiful surroundings

Village Glass
14 Henderson Street, Bridge of Allan, 4 miles N of Stirling on the A9, Bridge Of Allan, Stirlingshire, FK9 4HT
Tel: 01786 832 137
Email: sales@villageglass.co.uk
Website: www.villageglass.co.uk
Mon-Sat 09.00-17.00 Open Sundays in December
Various craftsman create decorative glassware from fruit and flowers to perfume bottles.

Barbara Davidson Pottery

Muirhall Farm, Muirhall Road, Larbert, Stirlingshire, FK4 4EW
Tel: 01324 554 430
Email: mailroom@barbara-davidson.com
Website: www.barbaradavidson.com
(Mon-Sat) 10.00-17.00
Working pottery in converted 17C farm steading. Handthrown stoneware, mostly functional.

Caithness Glass

Inveralmond Industrial Estate, Perth, Perthshire, PH1 3TZ
Tel: 01738 492 320
Email: visitor@caithnessglass.co.uk
Website: www.caithnessglass.co.uk
Mon-Sat 09.00-17.00 Sundays 10.00-17.00
Visitors can watch the process of glassmaking. Also paperweight museum and gallery.

Edradour Distillery

Moulin, North of Pitlochry, Pitlochry, Perthshire, PH16 5JP
Tel: 01796 472 095
Website: www.edradour.co.uk
Jan & Feb Mon-Sat 10.00-16.00 Sun 12.00-16.00 March-Oct Mon-Sat 09.30-18.00 Sun 12.00-17.00
Smallest distillery in Scotland established in 1825.

Heather Gems

22 Atholl Road, Pitlochry, Perthshire
Tel: 01796 474 391
Mar-Oct 09.00-17.30 Winter (Mon-Sat) 09.00-17.00
Gem factory and visitors centre

Trossachs Woolen Mill

Kilmahog, By Callander, Callander, Perthshire, FK17 8HD
Tel: 01877 330 178
Email: info@trossachswoollenmill.com
Mon-Sun 09.00-17.00
Working weaving mill with goods for sale and Jacob sheep in the field outside.

Buchlyvie Pottery Shop

Main Street, Buchlyvie, Stirlingshire, FK8 3LP
Tel: 01360 850 405
Email: alison_borthwick@hotmail.com
Website: www.buchlyviepotteryshop.com
(Mon-Sat) 09.30-17.30 (Sun) 12.00-17.00.
Working pottery making fine hand cast porcelain. Shop has wide range of pottery,glass and jewellery from all over UK. Potters at work can be seen from the shop.

Crieff Visitors Centre

Muthill Road, Crieff, Perthshire, PH7 4HQ
Tel: 01764 654 014
Email: info@crieff.co.uk
Website: www.crieff.co.uk
Open Seven days 09.00-17.00 Charge for the Highland Drover's Exhibition
Hand made whiskey flagons, tableware and glass paperweights. Visitors can view the production process and see the craftsmen at work. Factory showroom, plant centre.

Strathearn Gallery

32 West High Street, Crieff, Perthshire, PH7 4DL
Tel: 01764 656 100
Email: info@strathearn-gallery.com
Website: www.strathearn-gallery.com
Mon-Sat 10.00-17.00 Sun 13.00-17.00
This gallery exhibits high quality ceramics, glass, jewellery and silversmithing together with paintings, prints and sculpture

Loch Tay Pottery

Fearnan, Aberfeldy, off the A827, Aberfeldy, Perthshire
Tel: 01887 830 251
Open all year round, seven days a week, 10.00-17.00
Former croft housing showroom and workshop. Producing wide variety of stoneware pots

CASTLES

Finlarig Castle

Killin, Across the river Dochart near the golf course, Killin, Perthshire
Access at all times
Ruins of the castle built by Black Duncan of the Cowl a notorious Campbell Laird.

Balvaird Castle

Off the A912, 6 miles Se of Bridge Of Earn, Bridge Of Earn, Perthshire
Tel: 01786 431 324
Exterior View Only. Limited opening-confirm by telephone 01786 431 324
A late 15th-century tower on an L plan, extended in 1581 by the addition of a walled courtyard and gatehouse.

CHURCHES & CATHEDRALS

Church of the Holy Rude

St John's Street, Stirling, Stirlingshire
Tel: 01786 475 275
Easter-Oct 11.00-16.00. Donations Welcomed.
Reputed to be the only church in Scotland still in use that had witnessed a coronation. That of James VI in 1567.

Cambuskenneth Abbey

1 mile E of Stirling, Off the A907, Stirling, Stirlingshire
Summers Only (Exterior view only.)
Abbey ruins founded in 1147 as a house of Augustinian Canons. Robert The Bruce held parliament here in 1326 and James III and his queen were buried on the site. The fine detached tower had survived in good condition.

Innerpeffray Chapel

Off the B8062, Between Crieff and Auchterarder, Crieff, Perthshire
Open Summer Only
A rectangular collegiate church founded in 1508. Still retains its altar, evidence of its furnishings and some painted details.

St Serfs Church

Dunning, Perthshire
(Exterior view only)
Square Romanesque tower and tower arch.

St John's Kirk

St John's Street, Perth, Perthshire
Email: bookings@st-johns-kirk.co.uk
Website: www.st-johns-kirk.co.uk
East-Sep (Mon-Sat) 10.00-12.00 & 14.00-16.00 (Sun) 12.00-14.00 Free Admission but
donation of £1 asked
Consecrated in 1242 the present church dates for the 15C and was restored
between 1923 and 1926 as a war memorial.

Dunkeld Cathedral

Off The A9, High Street, Dunkeld, Perthshire
Tel: 01350 727 792
Email: j.f.moffat@amserve.net
Website: www.dunkeldcathedral.org
April-Sep (Mon-Sat) 09.00-18.30
The Cathedral situated on the banks of the River Tay was originally 12C, The
restored choir is now used as the Parish Church.

Muthill Church & Tower

on th A823, 5 miles S of Crieff, Muthill, Perthshire
Keys to access the grounds available from the Post Office in Muthill
Ruins of an important 15C parish church with tall Romanesque tower at the
West end.

Tullibardine Chapel

Off the A823 Crieff Road, 2 miles NW of Auchterarder, Auchterarder, Perthshire
Open Summers Only
One of the most complete and unaltered medieval churches in Scotland dating
from 1446.

Dunblane Cathedral

The Cross, 7 miles N of Stirling, Dunblane, Perthshire, FK15 0AQ
Tel: 01786 825 388
Email: office@dunblanecathedral.org.uk
Website: www.dunblanecathedral.org.uk
April-Sep (Mon-Sat) 09.30-18.30 (Sun) 14.00-18.00, Oct-March (Mon-Sat) 09.30-16.30
(Sun) 14.00-16.30
The existing structure was built in the 13C by King David on the site of St Blane's
tiny 8C cell, the site now contains partly restored ruins

Royal Burgh of Stirling Visitors Centre

Castle Esplanade, Stirling, Stirlingshire, FK8 1EH
Tel: 01786 479 901
Jan-June 09.30-17.00, July-Aug 09.00-18.30 Sep-Oct 09.30-18.00 Nov-Dec 09.30-17.00
The story of Stirling from the wars of independence and medieval times to the present day.

Mill Trail Visitors Centre

West Stirling Street, Alva, Clackmananshire, KY12 5EN
Tel: 01259 769 696
Email: milltrailvc@aillst.ossian.net
Sept-June 10.00-17.00 Daily July & August 09.00-17.00 Daily
Exhibition telling the story of weaving and spinning in the area. Features the experiences of a 13 yr old working in the mills. Original weaving and knitting looms. Visitors can walk through a modern mill and watch jumpers being made.

Scottish Liqueur Centre

John Murray and Co (Mull) Ltd, On the A9, 5 miles N of Perth, Bankfoot, Perthshire, PH1 4EB
Tel: 01738 787 044
Email: info@scottish-liqueur-centre.co.uk
Website: www.scottish-liqueur-centre.co.uk
Mon-Sat 10.00-17.00 Sun 13.00-17.00
Producing Scottish Liqueurs such as Columba Cream and Scottish Highland Liqueur. There is a visitors centre displaying art works and crafts and of course the opportunity for a free liqueur tasting.

Beatrix Potter Exhibition

Birnam Institute, Station Road, Birnam Near Dunkeld, Dunkeld, Perthshire, PH8 0DS
Tel: 01350 727 674
Email: admin@birnaminstitute.com
10.00-17.00 Daily except Christmas and New Year. Sundays end Nov-mid March
11.30-17.00 Garden open all year
Housed in the Birnam Institute a Victorian building dating from 1883. Beatrix Potter exhibition, garden and woodland walks.

GARDENS PARKS WALKS

Ben Lomond
Main path starts from Rowardennan Car Park, Loch Lomond, Central
Access at all times
Rising from the East shore of Loch Lomond to a height of 3194 feet, the area offers exhilarating walks and spectacular views.

Kings Knot
Below the Castle Rock, Access from Dunbarton Road/Kings Park Road, Stirling, Stirlingshire
Access at all times
The earthworks of a formal garden which were probably constructed in 1628 for Charles I.

The Knock
From James Square in the centre of Crieff, Up Hill Street and turn left up Knock Road,,
Crieff, Perthshire
Access at all times
Small paths lead up the hill to the summit which has marvellous views across Strathearn

Queen Elizabeth Forest Park Centre
Off the A821, 1 miles N of Aberfoyle, Aberfoyle, Stirlingshire
Tel: 01877 382 258
Email: cowal.trossachs.fd@forestry.gsi.gov.uk
Mid March-Mid September Daily 10.00-18.00
First designated a forest park in 1953 to mark the coronation of Queen Elizabeth II, the area contains mountains and moorland, forests and woodland, rivers and lochs, displays, shop, tea room, picnic areas, cycle routes, walks and a forest drive.

Macrosty Park
On the West side of the town, Crieff, Perthshire
Access at all times
This park was named after its benefactor James Macrosty and opened in 1902

Lady Mary's Walk
From the carpark at Macrosty Park, Crieff, Perthshire
Access at all times
This walk was a favourite of Lady Mary the daughter of Sir Patrick Murray of Ochtertyre who gifted the walk to the town in 1815

Trossachs Pier Complex

Loch Katrine, by Callander, 8 miles W of Callander on the A821, Callander, Perthshire, FK17 8HZ

Tel: 01877 376 315

Access at all times

Extensive loch side walks and cycle routes throughout the surrounding area.

HISTORIC HOUSES

Mar's Wark

Top of Castle Wynd, Stirling, Stirlingshire

(Outside view)

Renaissance Mansion built by the Regent Mar in 1570, the façade is the main surviving part

Earthquake House

On the outskirts of Comrie on the A85, Comrie, Comrie, Perthshire

Open all year

In 1874 a small building was constructed to house the seismological apparatus that was developed by the Comrie Pioneers to measure seismic activity in the area

HISTORIC SITES

Stirling Old Bridge

Beside the Customs Roundabout, Off the A9,, Stirling, Stirlingshire

Access at all times

The bridge was built in the 15-16C, with the Southern arch rebuilt in 1749 after it was blown up in the rebellion to prevent the Stewart army entering the town.

Abernethy Round Tower

In Abernethy, On the A913 9 miles SE of Perth, Abernethy, Perthshire

(Summer only)

One of the only two Irish style round towers that still survive in Scotland, dating from the 11C and standing alongside a Pictish stone.

Kinnoull Tower

Kinnoull Hill, Near Perth, Perth, Perthshire

Access at all times-Exterior View Only

Kinnoull Tower was built by the 9th Earl of Kinnoull and is situated near the summit of Kinnoull Hill

Muir O'Fauld Signal Station

Accessed by woodland footpath 1m NE of Trinity Gask, Off the B8062 Crieff to Auchterarder road, Auchterarder, Perthshire

Access at all times

The site of a Roman Watch Tower.

Dunkeld Bridge

Dunkeld, Perthshire

Access at all times

Built in 1809 the bridge is one of the finest built by Thomas Telford. A riverside path runs from the bridge to the site of the famous Birnam Oak, the last relic of Macbeth's Birnam Wood, the path then runs around the village of Birnam.

Dunfallandy Stone

1 mile S of Pitlochry, Off the A924, Pitlochry, Perthshire

Access at all times

A fine Pictish sculptured stone.

Rob Roy's Grave

Balquidder Church Yard, Off the A84, 18 miles NNW of Callander, Balquidder, Perthshire

Access at all times

3 flat gravestones surrounded by railings mark the graves of Rob Roy, his wife and two of his sons. Also contains St Angus stone from the 8C, a 17C bell and old Gaelic bibles.

Blackhall Roman Camps

Ardoch, 0.5 miles N of Braco, Braco, Perthshire

Access at all times

Part of the defences of two Roman marching camps dating from the early 3C.

Fortingall Yew

Fortingall, 9 miles W of Aberfeldy, Fortingall, Perthshire

Access at all times

The surviving part of the great yew set in an enclosure in the church yard is reputed to be over 3000 years old, which possibly makes it the oldest tree in Europe. The village of Fortingall was rebuilt in the 1900.

Falls of Dochart

Killin, Killin, Perthshire

Access at all times

Dramatic waterfalls rush through the centre of this picturesque village. The island of Inchbuie on the river is the setting for the burial ground of the Clan McNab. Key to the island and the graveyard is available from the tourist information centre.

Melville Monument

1 mile N of Comrie, 6 miles W of Crieff, Comrie, Perthshire

Access at all times

Obelisk in memory of Lord Melville (1742-1811) stands on the 840ft Dunmore Hill. Access path is linked to a scenic 4 mile Glen Lednock Circular Walk.

MUSEUMS

Black Watch Regimental Museum

Balhousie Castle, Hay Street, Perth, Perthshire, PH1 5HR

Tel: 01738 621 281

Email: rhq@theblackwatch.co.uk

Website: www.theblackwatch.co.uk

May-Sep (Mon-Sat) 10.00-16.30 Oct-April (Mon-Fri) 10.00-15.30

Balhousie Castle houses the Regimental Headquarters and Museum Of the Black Watch regiment. The museum describes the history of the regiment from 1740 to present day and has displays of silver, colours, uniforms and medals.

Perth Museum & Art Gallery

78 George Street, Perth, Perthshire, PH1 5LB

Tel: 01738 632 488

Email: museum@pkc.gov.uk

Mon-Sat 10.00-17.00

Collections of local history, fine and applied art, archaeology and natural history.

Auchterarder Heritage Centre

90 High Street, Auchterarder, Perthshire, PH3 1BJ
Tel: 01764 663 450
April-Oct (Mon-Sat) 9.30-17.00 (Sun) 11.00-16.30, Nov-March (Mon-Fri) 09.30-12.30
History of the town told via photographs and memorabilia, Information of the railway, local history, the territorial army and church history.

Smith Art Gallery & Museum

Dumbarton Road, Stirling, Stirlingshire, FK8 2RQ
Tel: 01786 400 917
Email: museum@smithartgallery.demon.co.uk
Website: www.smithartgallery.demon.co.uk
(Tue-Sat) 10.30-17.00 (Sun) 14.00-17.00
Displays and exhibitions of the history of Stirling, including fine art and natural history.

FARMERS MARKETS

Stirling Farmers Market

The Foot Of Maxwell Place, Stirling, Stirlingshire
2nd Saturday of the month 09.00-14.00
Farmers market with local produce for sale

Perth Farmers Market

King Edward Street, Perth, Perthshire
1st Saturday of the month 09.00-14.00
Farmers market with local produce for sale

FESTIVALS

Comrie Flambeaux

Village Sqaure, Comrie, Perthshire
31st December
A fire ceremony to mark the coming of the new year, though to have its origins in Pagan times. At midnight eight Flambeaux (burning torches) are piped into the village square and then thrown into the River Earn

Argyll Scotland

ART GALLERIES/ARTS & CRAFTS

Argyll Pottery
Barcaldine, Oban, Argyll & Bute, PA37 1SQ
Tel: 01631 720 503
Website: www.argyllpottery.co.uk
(Mon-Fri) 10.00-18.00 (Sat) 14.00-17.00 Closed Sundays
Pottery producing domestic ware including range of oven ware and individual pieces.

John Street Studio
4 John Street, Oban, Argyll & Bute, PA34 5NS
Tel: 01631 570 470
Email: info@obanart.com
Website: www.obanart.com
Mon-Sat 09.00-17.00
A wide variety of art work in various media with a range of distinctive giftware and jewellery

Mull Pottery
On the Isle Of Mull, Tobermory, Argyll & Bute, PA75 6QA
Tel: 01688 302 347
Email: orders@mullpottery.com
Website: www.mullpottery.com
April-Oct Mon-Sat 10.00-17.00 Sun 11.00-17.00 Nov-March Mon-Sat 10.30-17.00 Sun 11.00-17.00
The gallery displays all the pottery which is made in this studio by skilled craftspeople

Oban Antiques
35 Stevenson Street, Oban, Argyll & Bute, PA34 5NA
Tel: 01631 566 203
Email: oban.antiques@lonan.screaming.net
Mon-Sat 10.00-17.00 (Some seasonal variations)
With silver, jewellery, glass, ceramics and furniture on sale

CASTLES

Kilchurn Castle

NE end of Loch Awe, 2.5 miles from Dalmally, Off the A85, Dalmally, Argyll & Bute

Summer only-public access by boat only

Substantial ruin of a square tower built around 1550. Enlarged in 1693 by the earl Of Breadalbane. The tower incorporates the first ever purpose built barracks in Scotland and the site offers fantastic views down the length of the Loch.

Skipness Castle and Chapel

On the coast at Skipness, On the East Coast Of Kintyre, Off the B8001, Skipness, Argyll & Bute

Access at all times

Exterior view only. 13C castle with 16C tower house, nearby there is a 14C chapel with interesting grave slabs

Carnasserie Castle

On the A816, 2 miles N of Kilmartin, Kilmartin, Argyll & Bute

Access at all times

Combined tower house and hall and previous home of John Carswell, first Bishop of the Isles. Features include fine 16C details. The castle was captured and partially blown up during Argyll's rebellion in 1685.

Castle Sween

East Shore of Loch Sween, Knapdale off the B8025, Knapdale, Argyll & Bute

Tel: 0131 668 8830

Open all year

Probably the oldest stone castle on the Scottish Mainland built in 12C and destroyed by Alexander MacDonald in 1647

CHURCHES & CATHEDRALS

St Mary's Chapel

Top of High Street, In the Townhead area of Rothesay, Isle of Bute, Rothesay, Argyll & Bute

Open all year

Late medieval remains of the chancel of the Parish Church of St Mary with fine tombs.

St Blane's Church

Kingarth, S end of Isle of Bute, 8 miles S of Rothesay, Kingarth, Argyll & Bute

Access at all times

Ruins of a 12C Romanesque chapel set in the foundations of a Celtic monastery.

Ardchattan Priory

On the N side of Loch Etive, 6.5 miles NE of Oban, off the A828, Oban, Argyll & Bute

Open all year

Ruins of a priory founded in 1230 and later. Burned by Cromwell's soldiers in 1654. The remains include numerous carved stones.

Keills Chapel

6 miles SW of Tayvallich, Off the B8025, Tayvallich, Argyll & Bute

Access at all times

Small West Highland Chapel housing a collection of early grave slabs and Keills cross.

Kilmory Knap Chapel

on the shore between Loch Sween and Loch Caolisport, In S Knapdale, Off the B8025, Knapdale, Argyll & Bute

Access at all times

Medieval West Highland Church with a collection of typical grave slabs. In the church is Macmillian's Cross a beautiful example of medieval carving.

Saddell Abbey

On the B842, 9 miles NNW of Campbeltown, Campbeltown, Argyll & Bute

Access at all times

Built in 12C by Somerled, Lord Of The Isles or his son Reginald. Only the walls of the building are now standing with fine sculptured and carved tombstones

GARDENS PARKS WALKS

Crarae Garden

Near Inverary, Crarae, Argyll & Bute, PA32 8YA

Tel: 01546 886 614

Open all year

The garden contains one of the best collections of the Genus Rhododendron in Scotland and extends to around 25 hectares

Ardencraig Gardens

Ardencraig Lane, High Craigmore, Rothesay, Argyll & Bute, PA20 9EZ
Tel: 01700 504 644
May-Sept Mon-Fri 10.30-16.30 Sat& Sun 13.00-16.30
Working greenhouse and garden built between 1919-1923. Houses many rare plants, an aviary and ornamental fish ponds.

Kilmory Castle Garden

Kilmory, Lochgilphead, on the A83, Lochgilphead, Argyll & Bute, PA31 8RA
Tel: 01546 602 127
Open daylight hours.
Established in 1770s when it contained over 100 varieties of rhododendron and supplied plants for Kew Gardens. Now restored and includes woodland walks, nature trails etc.

Tighnabruaich View Point

NE of Tighnabruaich, On the A8003, Tignabruaich, Argyll & Bute
Access at all times
High vantage point with indicators to surrounding sites. Spectacular views

Puck's Glen

Starts at Forestry Commission Carpark, 1 mile S of the Benmore Botanic Garden, Dunoon, Argyll & Bute, PA23 8QU
Access at all times
A walk through mature woodland planted over 100 years ago, the path follows a natural gorge, with dramatic overhanging cliffs and a series of roaring waterfalls.

Crinan Canal

Crinan, Ardrishaig, by Lochgilphead, Lochgilphead, Argyll & Bute
Access at all times
Built in 1793-1801 to carry ships from Loch Fyne to the Atlantic. 9 mile stretch of water with 15 locks now used by pleasure craft. Tow path provides easy walks with magnificent views.

Historic Sites

Monument Hill

Off the old road to Inverary, 2 miles SW of Dalmally, Dalmally, Argyll & Bute
Access at all times
Monument to Duncan ban McIntyre (1724-1812). Known as The Burns of the Highlands

Kilmodan Sculptured Stones

Clachan of Glendareul on the A886, 8 miles N of Colintraive, Colintraive, Argyll & Bute
Access at all times
Group of West Highland carved grave slabs in church yard.

Kilmichael Glassary Cup and Ring Marks

Kilmartin Glen, Near the school house in the village of Kilmichael Glassary, 5 miles N of
Lochgilphead, Kilmichael Glassary, Argyll & Bute
Access at all times
Bronze age cup and ring marks on natural rock outcrop.

McCaig's Tower

On the hill overlooking the town of Oban, Oban, Argyll & Bute
Access at all times
Local banker (1897-1900) employed local craftsmen to build this monument as a
memorial to his family. Inside there is a landscaped courtyard, and an
observation platform.

Clachan Bridge

On the B844, off the A816, 8 miles SW of Oban, connecting the mainland with the Isle Seil,
Oban, Argyll & Bute
Access at all times
Picturesque single arched bridge built in 1792.

Dunchraigaig Cairn

Kilmartin Glen, 1.5 miles S of Kilmartin, Kilmartin, Argyll & Bute
Access at all times
Bronze age cairn excavated in the last century.

Dunadd Fort

Kilmartin Glen, 1 mile W of Kilmartin Glassary, Kilmartin, Argyll & Bute
Access at all times
Spectacular site occupied since the Iron Age,The well preserved hill fort is part
Roman dating from when it was occupied as a stronghold.

Kilmartin Sculptured Stones

Kilmartin Church Yard, On the A816, 9 miles N of Lochgilphead, Kilmartin, Argyll & Bute
Access at all times
Carved West Highland Grave slabs housed in a former mausoleum in the
church. One cross dates from the 16C.

Ri Cruin Cairn

Kilmartin Glen, 1 mile SW of Kilmartin, Kilmartin, Argyll & Bute
Access at all times
Bronze age burial Cairn with the covering removed to reveal three massive cists with axe head carvings.

Glebe Cairn

Kilmartin Glen, Kilmartin, Argyll & Bute
Access at all times
Early Bronze Age burial cairn with two burial chambers.

Nether Largie Cairns

Kilmartin Glen, Between Kilmartin and Nether Largie, Kilmartin, Argyll & Bute
Access at all times
One Neolithic and two Bronze age cairns. Access to the chamber in the North Cairn.

Temple Wood Stone Circles

0.25 miles SW of Nether Largie, 1 mile S of Kilmartin Village, Nether Largie, Argyll & Bute
Access at all times
Circle of upright stones around 3000 years old and remains of an even earlier circle.

St Columba's Cave

The W shore of Loch Killisport, 1 mile N of Ellary, Ellary, Argyll & Bute
Access at all times
Associated with St Columba's arrival in Scotland, the cave contains a rock shelf with an altar above which are carved crosses, a large basin, possibly a stone age mortar which might have been used as a font.

Kilberry Sculptured Stones

At Kilberry Castle, Off the B8024, 17 miles SSW of Lochgilphead, Lochgilphead, Argyll & Bute
Access at all times
Fine collection of medieval sculptured stones gathered from the Kilberry Estate

Columba's Footsteps

West Of Southend, at Keil, Keil, Argyll & Bute

Access at all times

Traditionally believed that St Columba first set foot on Scottish soil near Southend. Footsteps are imprinted in a flat topped rock near the ruins of an old chapel.

Dunaverty Rock

Southend, Kintyre Peninisula, 9 miles S of Campbeltown, Southend, Argyll & Bute

Access at all times

Formerly the site of Dunaverty castle, a MacDonald stronghold. In 1647 around 300 people were put to death here by Covenanters, The rock is known locally as Blood Rock.

MUSEUMS

Campbeltown Museum

Hall Street, Campbeltown, Argyll & Bute, PA28 6BS

Tel: 01586 552 366

(Tue & Thur) 10.00-13.00, 14.00-17.00 and 17.30-19.30, (Wed,Fri,Sat) 10.00-13.00 and 14.00-17.00

Listed building designed by renowned Scottish architect J.J. Burnett. Mainly archaeological and natural history collections with some local history and maritime exhibitions.

FARMERS MARKETS

Tarbert Farmers Market

Harbourside, Tarbert, Argyll

3rd Saturday of the month 10.00-14.00

Farmers Market with local produce for sale

Ayrshire, Strathclyde & Lanarkshire-Scotland

ART GALLERIES/ARTS & CRAFTS

Mackinnon Mills
Kirkshaws Road, Coatbridge, Lanarkshire, ML5 4SL
Tel: 01236 440 702
Open Daily 10.00-17.30 Sat/Sunday 10.00-18.00
Variety of factory exhibitions explaining the manufacturing process of knitwear.
Walk through exhibitions and explanatory display boards guide you through the
mill.

The Ceramic Experience
24 Albion Way, East Kilbride, Strathclyde, G75 0YN
Tel: 01355 263 194
Email: batess@ntlworld.com
Website: www.ceramicx.biz
Daily 10.00-17.00
Creative family activities, featuring pottery painting.

Vennel Gallery
10 Glasgow Vennel, Irvine, Ayrshire, KA12 0BD
Tel: 01294 275 059
Email: vennel@north-ayrshire.gov.uk
Fri, Sat & Sun 10.00-13.00 & 14.00-17.00
Housed in an 18C cottage, the Vennel Gallery includes the Burns Connection
and a small crafts shop

McLean Museum & Art Gallery
15 Kelly Street, Greenock, Strathclyde, PA16 8JX
Tel: 01475 715 624
Email: museum@inverclyde.gov.uk
Open (Mon-Sat) 10.00-17.00.
Beautifully restored building housing a varied collection of Scottish paintings.

Harbour Arts Centre
Harbour Street, Irvine, Ayrshire, KA12 8PZ
Tel: 01294 274 059
Email: admin@harbourarts.org.uk
Website: www.harbourarts.org.uk
(Tue,Wed,Thurs) 10.00-16.00 Also most Fri evenings and alternate Sun afternoons.
Monthly exhibitions

CASTLES

Cadzow Castle

In the grounds of Chatelherault Country Park, Hamilton, Lanarkshire
Exterior View Only, Access at all times.
Constructed between 1500 and 1550 the castle was formerly known as " The Castle In The Woods Of Hamilton"

Cathcart Castle

1 mile S of Rutherglen, At the head of Linn Park, Rutherglen, Lanarkshire
Access at all time during daylight hours
15C stone fortress, now only the foundations survive

CHURCHES & CATHEDRALS

Old Parish Church

Strathmore Road, Hamilton, Lanarkshire, ML3 6AQ
Tel: 01698 281 905
Email: office@hopc.fsnet.co.uk
Website: www.hopc.fsnet.co.uk
Mon-Fri) 10.30-15.30 (Sat) 10.30-12.00. (Sun) after 10.45. Evenings by appointment.
Oldest building in Hamilton, the only church designed by William Adam between 1732-1734. The roof timbers are full of lead shot as they came originally from an old Man Of War. Elaborately detailed engraved glass windows depict the history of the church.

EXHIBITIONS

Summerlee Heritage Park

Heritage Way, Coatbridge, Lanarkshire, ML5 1QD
Tel: 01236 431 261
Daily 10.00-17.00 All year
various exhibitions and displays give a detailed interpretation of the social and industrial history of West of Scotland Communities. Attractions include; historic machinery, period shop interiors and an excavation of the 1835 ironworks.

Strathclyde Country Park

366 Hamilton Road, Motherwell, Strathclyde, ML1 3ED
Tel: 01698 266 155
Email: strathclydepark@northlan.gov.uk
Mon-Fri 11.00-18.45 Sat & Sun 09.00-18.45
Country Side park consisting of 1000 acres of the Clyde Valley. Features include an artificial lake, mixed parkland and woodland, and a variety of recreational features such as watersports, woodland trails, countryside walks, sports pitches & sandy beaches.

Calderglen Country Park

Strathaven Road, East Kilbride, Lanarkshire, G75 0QZ
Tel: 01355 236 644
Email: jim.brockie@southlanarkshire.gov.uk
Summer (Mon-Fri) 10.30-17.00 (Weekends & Public Holidays) 11.30-18.30 Winter months daily 11.30-16.00
Over 300 acres of wooded gorge and parklands including several waterfalls. Attractions include a visitor's centre, grand conservatory, children's zoo, toddler's play area, adventure and special needs play area, horticultural staff and animal keepers.

Palacerigg Country Park

Palacerigg Road, Cumbernauld, Lanarkshire
Tel: 01236 720 047
Email: countryside@northlan.gov.uk
(Apr-Sep) 10.00-18.00 (Oct-Mar) 10.00-16.30
700 Acre Country Park with a Scottish and North European Animal Collection. Species include wild populations of Roedeer, owls, bison, wildcat, linx and moufflon. Attractions include guided tours, explanatory displays, gift shop, tea room & picnic areas.

Gardens Parks Walks/Historic Houses

Chatelherault

Carlise Road, Ferniegair, Hamilton, Lanarkshire, ML3 7UE
Tel: 01698 426 213
Email: liz.macgill@southlanarkshire.gov.uk
Website: www.southlanarkshire.gov.uk
Visitors Centre Mon-Sat 10.00-17.00 Sun 12.00-17.00 Hunting Lodge Mon-Thurs, Sat
10.30-16.30 Sun 12.30-16.30 Park open daylight hours all year
Magnificent hunting lodge and kennels built in 1732 for the Duke of Hamilton
which had now been restored. The grounds contain country walks, an exhibition
on the Clyde Valley, geology and the natural history of the park, 18C Gardens &
terraces.

Eglinton Country Park

Kilwinning, Irvine, Ayrshire
Tel: 01294 214 100
Access at all time
400 acres of parkland in the middle of Irvine set aside for leisure and recreation

Historic Sites

Barochan Cross

In Paisley Abbey, Abbey Close, Paisley, Strathclyde
Tel: 0141 889 7654
Website: www.paisleyabbey.org.uk
Abbey open Mon-Sat 10.00-15.30
A fine free-standing early medieval cross that formerly stood in Houston parish

Auchagallon Stone Circle

4 miles N of Blackwaterfoot, On the East Side of Arran off the A841, Arran, Ayrshire
Access at all time
A bronze age cairn surrounded by fifteen standing stones

Bar Hill Fort

0.5 miles E of Twechar, Access from the B8023 Kirkintilloch to Kilsyth Road, Twechar,
Lanarkshire
Access at all time
The highest hill fort on the line of the Antonine Wall, featuring the foundations of
the headquarters building and bath house. Nearby to the East is another Iron
Age Fort.

Croy Hill

Between Croy and Dullatur, Access from the B802, Dullatur, Strathclyde
Access at all time
The site of a Roman fort situated on the Antonine Wall. Part of the Wall Ditch can be seen beside two beacon platforms on the west side of the hill.

Antonine Wall Dullatur

0.5 miles E of Dullatur Centre, Dullatur, Strathclyde
Access at all time
Well preserved section of the ditch part of the Antonine Wall.

Antonine Wall at Tollpark and Garnhail

W of Castlecary, Castlecary, Lanarkshire
Access at all time
Well preserved section of the ditch of the Antonine Wall.

Castlecary Ruined Fort

on the B816, E of Castlecary Village, Castlecary, Lanarkshire
Access at all time
The reduced earthworks of a fort on the Antonine Wall. Access at all reasonable times.

MUSEUMS

Low Parks Museum

129 Muir Street, Motehill, Hamilton, Lanarkshire, ML3 6BJ
Tel: 01698 328 232
(Mon- & Sat) 10.00-17.00 (Sun) 12.00-17.00
This museum combines the former Hamilton museum with that of the Scottish Rifles Regimental Museum. The building houses several collections including displays on the Clyde Valley, The Hamilton Estate and the Cameronians.

North Ayrshire Museum

Manse Street, Saltcoats, Ayrshire, KA21 5AA
Tel: 01294 464 174
Email: namuseum@globalnet.co.uk
Mon, Tues, Thurs, Fri, Sat 10.00-13.00 & 14.00-17.00
Housed in a former church the museum tells the local history of three towns, Saltcoats, Stevenson and Ardrossan.

Paisley Museum & Art Gallery

High Street, Paisley, Strathclyde, PA1 2BA
Tel: 0141 889 3151
Email: museums.els@renfrewshire.gov.uk
(Tues-Sat) 10.00-17.00 (Sun) 14.00-17.00
Various exhibitions and displays including a huge selection of the famous Paisley Pattern material.

Lanark Museum

8 Westport, Lanark, Lanarkshire, ML11 9HD
Tel: 01555 666 680
Website: www.biggar-net.co.uk/lanarkmuseum
April -Sep (Fri-Sat) 10.30-16.30.
Local history museum with changing exhibitions and displays.

Irvine Burns Museum

28 Eglinton Street, Irvine, KA12 8AS
Email: burns@irvineayrshire.org
Easter-Sept Mon, Wed, Fri, Sat 14.30-16.30 Oct-March Sat 14.30-16.30
Audio-visual presentation about the poet's time in Irvine, also original manuscripts and other displays

FARMERS MARKETS

Kilsyth Farmers Market

Kilsyth
1st Saturday of the month 09.00-14.00
Farmers Market with local produce on sale

Irvine Farmers Market

Rivergate Sqaure, Irvine
2nd Saturday of the month 09.00-14.00
Farmers Market with local produce on sale

Hamilton Farmers Market

Townhead Street, Hamilton, Lanarkshire
3rd Saturday of the month 09.00-14.00
Farmers Market with local produce on sale

Ayr Farmers Market
Kyle Centre Carpark, Ayr, Ayrshire
1st Saturday of the month 09.00-14.00
Farmers Market with local produce on sale

Glasgow City-Scotland

ART GALLERIES/ARTS & CRAFTS

Glasgow Gallery Of Modern Art

Royal Exchange Square, Glasgow, Strathclyde, G1 3AH
Tel: 0141 229 1996
Website: www.glasgowmuseums.com
(Mon-Wed & Sat)10.00-17.00 Thurs 10.00-20.00 (Fri & Sun)11.00-17.00
Glasgow's Modern Art gallery opened in 1996. The modern art, craft and design
collections include a strong selection of Scottish figurative art and works by
Scottish artists.

Hunterian Art Gallery

82 Hillhead Street, Glasgow University, Glasgow, Strathclyde, G12 8QQ
Tel: 0141 330 5431
Email: hunter@museum.gla.ac.uk
Website: www.hunterian.gla.ac.uk
(Mon-Sat) 09.30-17.00
The gallery situated within the University houses William Hunter's collection of
paintings. Including works by Reynolds, Rodin, Rembrant, Tintoretto and
Whistler. There is also a replica of Charles Rennie Mackintosh's town house.

Kelvingrove Art Gallery & Museum

Argyle Street, Glasgow, Strathclyde, G3 8AG
Tel: 0141 287 2699
Website: www.glasgowmuseums.com
(Mon-Thurs & Sat) 10.00-17.00 (Fri & Sun) 11.00-17.00
The building looking like a cross between a cathedral and a castle is home to
Glasgow's main museum and boasts collections that include everything from fine
and decorative arts to archaeology and the natural world.

Collins Gallery

University of Strathclyde, 22 Richmond Street, Glasgow, Strathclyde, G1 1XQ
Tel: 0141 548 2558
Email: collinsgallery@strath.ac.uk
Website: www.collinsgallery.strath.ac.uk
Mon-Fri 10.00-17.00 Sat 12.00-16.00
The Collins Gallery houses a programme of changing exhibitions and events

The Gatehouse Gallery
Roukenglen Road, Glasgow, Strathclyde, G46 7UG
Tel: 0141 620 0235
Email: art@gatehousegallery.co.uk
Website: www.gatehousegallery.co.uk
Sun, Mon, Thurs & Fri 13.30-17.30 Saturdays 11.30-17.30
New exhibitions monthly featuring new exhibitors as well as regular artists

CHURCHES & CATHEDRALS

Glasgow Cathedral
Cathedral Square, Glasgow, Strathclyde, G4 0QZ
Tel: 0141 552 6891
Email: cathedral@amserve.com
Website: www.glasgow-cathedral.com
April-Sep (Mon-Sat) 09.30-18.00 Closes at 17.00 on Sundays Oct-March (Mon-Sun)
09.30-16.00
Dedicated to St. Mungo the patron saint of Glasgow the Cathedral is made up of
a double church which was begun in the 12C and completed some 300 years
later. The lower church contains the crypt of St. Mungo and has been revered
since the 6C.

St Mungo Museum Of Religious Life And Art
2 Castle Street, Glasgow, Strathclyde, G4 0RH
Tel: 0141 553 2557
Mon-Thurs & Sat 10.00-17.00 Fri & Sun 11.00-17.00
Large collection of artefacts representing the diverse number of religions that
have settled throughout the centuries in Glasgow. Salvador Dali's ' Christ Of St.
John Of The Cross' forms the centerpiece to the display.

St Aloysius RC Church
25 Rose Street, Glasgow, G3 6RE
Tel: 0141 332 3039
Email: aloychurch@garnet92.freeserve.co.uk
Mon-Fri 07.30-18.30 Sun 08.30-22.00
St Aloysius is one of the most finely decorated churches in the City Of Glasgow.
The church dates from 1910 and the interior decoration from 1927.

EXHIBITIONS/MARKETS

The Barras
0.25 mile E of Glasgow Cross, Glasgow, Strathclyde
Tel: 0141 552 4601
Email: barras1@tiscali.co.uk
Website: www.glasgow-barrowland.com
Sat & Sun 10.00-17.00
Scotland's largest indoor market named from the old pushcarts or "barrows" formerly used by the stall holders. A Scottish "flea market" and a must for those who enjoy searching for bargains

FESTIVALS

Glasgay Festival
Throughout the city of Glasgow, Glasgow, Strathclyde
Tel: 0141 334 7126
Email: info@glasgay.org.uk
Website: www.glasgay.co.uk
Please see website for annual dates each year 2006 dates 16 Oct-12 Nov
Glasgow's Annual Gay and Lesbian Festival host a variety of events and exhibitions throughout the city with many free programmes

Glasgow West End Festival
Byres Road, Glasgow, Strathclyde
Tel: 0141 341 0844
Email: westend.festival@virgin.net
Website: www.westendfestival.co.uk
Please see website for annual dates each year
Street parties, processions, jazz and opera theatre as well as free concerts

GARDENS PARKS WALKS

Glasgow Botanic Gardens
730 Great Western Road, At Queen Margaret's Drive, Glasgow, Strathclyde, G12 0UE
Tel: 0141 334 2422
Email: gbg@land.glasgow.gov.uk
Gardens (Daily) 07.00-Dusk, Glasshouses (Weekdays) 10.00-16.45. (Sat) 13.-16.45 (Sun)
12.000-16.45. All close at 16.15 in Winter. May be charge for Glasshouses
Displays include herb garden, tropical plants and world famous collection of
orchids. The Kibble Palace is a collection of interlinked greenhouses containing
tree ferns,palm trees, and the tropicarium which houses a tropical rain forest.

Glasgow Green
Greendyke Street, Situated by the River Clyde, Glasgow, Strathclyde, G40
Access at all times
The oldest park in Glasgow situated by the River Clyde. Features include the
Nelson's column a predecessor to London's own and The Arch which is now the
finishing line the thousands of participants of the Glasgow Half Marathon.

Kelvin Grove Park
Otago Street, 1.5 miles W of City Centre, Glasgow, Strathclyde, G12
Access at all times
The park takes it's name from the River Kelvin that flows through it and was set
up in 1852. Features include numerous statues, a massive fountain,duck pond,
play area, exotic trees and open air theatre.

Fossil Grove
Victoria Park, Glasgow, Strathclyde, G14 1BN
Tel: 0141 287 2000
Email: museums@cls.glasgow.gov.uk
Apr-Sep Mon-Thurs & Saturday 10.00-17.00 Fri & Sunday 11.00-17.00
Glasgow's oldest tourist attraction, discovered by accident. Fossil stumps and
roots of trees that grew here 350 million years ago.

Rouken Glen
Giffknock, Glasgow, Strathclyde, G46 7UG
Tel: 0141 577 3105
Open dawn-dusk
One of Glasgow's most attractive parks with shaded walks and waterfall.
Children's playground, boating pond, garden centre and butterfly farm

HISTORIC HOUSES

City Chambers
80 George Square, Glasgow, Strathclyde, G2 1DU
Tel: 0141 287 2000
Open 08.30-17.00 Mon-Fri-Free guided tours weekdays 10.30 & 14.30.
Opened by Queen Victoria in 1888. The interior has many attractive features including the entrance hall's vaulted ceilings, marble and alabaster staircases and a banqueting hall.

Templetons Carpet Factory
Glasgow Green, Glasgow, Strathclyde
Exterior View Only
A Victorian factory built to copy the design of Doge's Palace in Venice

Provand's Lordship
3 Castle Street, Glasgow, Strathclyde, G4 0RH
Tel: 0141 552 8819
Mon-Thurs & Sat 10.00-17.00 Fri & Sun 11.00-17.00
Glasgow's oldest house built in 1471 in which Mary Queen Of Scots is reputed to have stayed. In the past it has been a sweet shop, junk shop, soft drinks factory and the home of the city's hangman. Now restored and houses a museum.

University Of Glasgow Visitors Centre
University Avenue, Glasgow, G12 8QQ
Tel: 0141 330 5511
Email: visitorscentre@gla.ac.uk
Website: www.gla.ac.uk/general/visiting
All year Mon-Sat 09.30-17.00 May-Sept also Sundays 14.00-17.00
This is the fourth oldest University in Britain and the Award Winning Visitors Centre displays the history, organisation and activities of the University through interactive computer displays and hands on information systems

The Willow Tea Rooms
217 Sauchiehall Street, Glasgow, G2 3EX
Tel: 0141 332 0521
Email: tea@willowtearooms.co.uk
Website: www.willowtearooms.co.uk
Mon-Sat 09.00-16.30 Sun 11.00-16.30
The original Mackintosh tea rooms feature many original fittings including fire place and leaded windows

Martyrs' School

Parson Street, Glasgow, G4 0PX
Tel: 0141 552 2356
Website: www.glasgowmuseums.com
Open by appointment all year round please telephone St Mungo Museum on: 0141 553 2557
This building was restored by apprentices of Glasgow City Building and has spectacular roof trusses

Pollok House

Pollok Country Park, 2060 Pollokshaws Road, Glasgow, Strathclyde, G43 1AT
Tel: 0141 616 6410
Email: pollokhouse@nts.org.uk
Daily 10.00-17.00 Free Entry Only Nov-March (April-October £8 Adults and £5 Children)
Dating from the mid 1700 the house had fine gardens and over looks the White Cart River and Pollock Park. Inside the house are the Stirling Maxwell Collections of paintings .

Mitchell Library

North Street, Glasgow, Strathclyde, G3 7DN
Tel: 0141 287 2999
Email: lil@cls.glasgow.gov.uk
Mon-Thurs 09.00-20.00 Fri-Sat 09.00-17.00
The largest public reference library in Europe

HISTORIC SITES

George Square Statues

George Square, Glasgow, Strathclyde
Access at all times
Statues of King George, Queen Victoria, Robert Burns and Robert Peel are amongst the many statues situated in this square

Merchant Square

71-73 Albion Street, Glasgow, Strathclyde, G1 1RB
Tel: 0141 552 5908
08.00-01.00 Daily
A Victorian Courtyard with stone flagged centre, now home to exclusive retail outlets

Glasgow Cross

City Centre, Glasgow, Strathclyde

Access at all times

Marks the centre of the medieval city. The Mercat cross topped by a unicorn marks the spot where people met, where the market was held and where criminals were executed.

Necropolis

Castle Street, Cathedral Square, Glasgow, Strathclyde, G1

Tel: 0141 287 3961

Website: www.glasgownecropolis.org

Dawn-Dusk-Free 2 hr Guided Tours run by the Friends Of Glasgow Necropolis please see website for dates and times.

This site had been a burial ground since the beginning of recorded history and contains some extraordinary Victorian graves. It also includes the grave of 19C Glasgow merchant William Miller who wrote the famous nursery rhyme Wee Willie Winkie

MUSEUMS

Peoples Palace

Glasgow Green, Glasgow, Strathclyde, G40 1AT

Tel: 0141 554 0223

(Mon-Thurs & Sat) 10.00-17.00 (Fri & Sun)11.00-17.00

Museum dedicated to the social history of Glasgow set in a handsome Victorian red sandstone building. The exhibition of the People's Story is dedicated to the ordinary people of Glasgow.

Hunterian Museum

Glasgow University, 82 Hillhead Street, Glasgow, Strathclyde, G12 8QQ

Tel: 0141 330 4221

Email: hunter@museum.gla.ac.uk

Website: www.hunterian.gla.ac.uk

(Mon-Sat) 09.30-17.00

Glasgow's oldest museum housing part of the collections of 18C Glasgow doctor William Hunter. Displays of coins, manuscripts, archaeological artefacts and scientific instruments.

Museum Of Transport

Kelvin Hall, 1 Bunhouse Road, Glasgow, Strathclyde, G3 8DP
Tel: 0141 287 2720
(Mon-Thurs & Sat) 10.00-17.00 (Fri & Sun) 11.00-17.00.
Full size exhibits depict the history of the locomotive. World famous collection of
Clyde built ship models and recreated street scene from the 1950s.

Royal Highland Fusiliers Museum

518 Sauchiehall Street, Glasgow, Strathclyde, G2 3LW
Tel: 0141 332 0961
Email: reg.sec@rhf.org.uk
Website: www.rhf.org.uk
(Mon-Fri) 08.30-16.00
Displaying the history of the famous regiment and the men who served in it.
Exhibits include medals, badges and uniforms.

Scotland Street School Museum

225 Scotland Street, Glasgow, G5 8QB
Tel: 0141 287 0500
Email: museums@cls.glasgow.gov.uk
Website: www.glasgowmuseums.com
Mon-Thurs & Sat 10.00-17.00 Fri & Sun 11.00-17.00
Originally opened in 1906 and designed by Charles Rennie Mackintosh, this
former school is now a museum of education

Glasgow Police Museum

68 St Andrews Square, Glasgow, G1 5PR
Tel: 07788 532 691
Email: curator@policemuseum.org.uk
Website: www.policemuseum.org.uk
April-Oct Mon-Sat 10.00-16.30 Sun 12.00-16.30 Nov-March Tues 10.00-16.30 Sun
12.00-16.30
This museum tells the history of the United Kingdom's oldest police force

The Burrell Collections

2060 Pollockshaws Road, Pollock Country Park, Glasgow, Strathclyde, G43 1AT
Tel: 0141 287 2550
(Mon-Thurs & Sat)10.00-17.00 (Fri & Sun) 11.00-17.00
Custom built modern building housing over 8000 exhibits. Including ancient
Egyptian, Greek and roman artefacts and jade to medieval tapestries and French
impressionist paintings. There are also reconstruction's of medieval castle
rooms.

FARMERS MARKETS

Glasgow Farmers Market

Queens Park & Mansfield Park, Glasgow, Strathclyde

Queens Park 1st & 3rd Saturday of the Month 10.00-14.00 Mansfield Park 2nd and 4th Saturday of the month 10.00-14.00

Farmers Market with local produce on sale

Edinburgh City-Scotland

ART GALLERIES/ARTS & CRAFTS

National Gallery Of Scotland
The Mound, Princes Street, Edinburgh, Midlothian, EH2 2EL
Tel: 0131 220 0917
Email: nginfo@nationalgalleries.org
Website: www.natgalscot.ac.uk
Daily 10.00-17.00 Thursday 10.00-19.00
Many of Scotland's or even the world's most treasured works of art. Rembrant, Raphael, Titian and Rubens displayed in a 19C building.

Scottish National Portrait Gallery
1 Queen Street, Edinburgh, Midlothian, EH2 1JD
Tel: 0131 332 2266
Email: pginfo@nationalgalleries.org
Website: www.natgalscot.ac.uk
Daily 10.00-17.00 Thursday 10.00-19.00
An unequalled collection of Scottish life and history depicted via portraits, paintings, sculptures, miniatures, coins, medallions, drawings, watercolours and photography.

Scottish National Gallery Of Modern Art
75 Bellford Road, Edinburgh, Midlothian, EH4 3DR
Tel: 0131 624 6200
Email: gmainfo@nationalgalleries.org
Website: www.natgalscot.ac.uk
Daily 10.00-17.00
20C Art including Matisse, Magritte and Picasso. Sculptures decorate the grounds.

Dean Gallery
73 Belford Road, Edinburgh, Midlothian, EH4 3DS
Tel: 0131 624 6200
Email: deaninfo@nationalgalleries.org
Website: www.natgalscot.ac.uk
Daily 10.00-17.00
The Dean Gallery displays world class holdings of Dada and Surrealist art by Sir Eduardo Paolozzi, and in the grounds there are sculptures by Bourdelle, Rickey, Paolozzi and Turnbull

Edinburgh City Arts Centre
2 Market Street, Edinburgh, Midlothian, EH1 1DE
Tel: 0131 529 3993
Email: enquiries@city-art-centre.demon.uk
Website: www.cac.org.uk
Mon-Sat 10.00-17.00 Sun 12.00-17.00
Six floors of display galleries. Home of the City's collection of Scottish Art, and one the UK's leading temporary exhibition spaces

Edinburgh Fruit Market Gallery
45 Market Street, Edinburgh, Midlothian, EH1 1DF
Tel: 0131 225 2383
Email: elizabeth@fruitmarket.co.uk
Website: www.fruitmarket.co.uk
Tues-Sat 10.30-17.30
Built in 1938 as a fruit and vegetable market the building is now an acclaimed art gallery with an international reputation for diverse and challenging exhibitions.

Edinburgh Printmakers
23 Union Street, Edinburgh, Midlothian, EH1 3LR
Tel: 0131 557 2479
Email: info@edinburgh-printmakers.co.uk
Website: www.edinburgh-printmakers.co.uk
Tues-Sat 10.00-18.00
Edinburgh's main studio for practising artists who make limited edition prints. Visitors can watch the artists at work and purchase finished prints for sale in the gallery.

Talbot Rice Gallery
University Of Edinburgh Old College, South Bridge, Edinburgh, Midlothian, EH8 9YL
Tel: 0131 650 2211
Email: info.talbotrice@ed.ac.uk
Website: www.trg.ed.ac.uk
Tues-Sat 10.00-17.00
The University of Edinburgh's permanent collection and a contemporary gallery showing temporary exhibitions

Brass Rubbing Centre

Trinity Apse, Chalmers Close, Off Royal Mile, Edinburgh, Midlothian, EH1 1SS

Tel: 0131 556 4364

Website: www.cac.org.uk

Open April -Sept Mon-Sat 10.00-17.00 Sundays in August 12.00-17.00 (Admission Free but charge to make a rubbing)

In the reconstructed 15C Apse of the Trinity Church, collection of casts taken from early Pictish stones. Have a go at making your own brass rubbing.

CASTLES

Lauriston Castle Gardens

Crammond Road South, Davidson Mains, 4 miles from Centre Of Edinburgh on A90, Edinburgh, Midlothian, EH4 5GD

Tel: 0131 336 2060

Email: cac.admin@edinburgh.gov.uk

Website: www.cac.org.uk

Gardens open all year 09.00-Dusk

Charge for entrance to the house but 30 acres of beautiful gardens and parkland with stunning views across the Firth of Forth

Edinburgh Castle

Castle Hill, Royal Mile, Edinburgh, Midlothian, EH1 2NG

Tel: 0131 225 9846

FREE ENTRY ON ST ANDREW'S DAY EACH YEAR (£9.50 admission charge at other times)

This is Edinburgh's top tourist attraction. The castle includes the tiny St Margaret's Chapel, The Honours Of The Kingdom, tells the story of Scotland's Crown Jewels, The Prisoners Of War Exhibition and Mons Meg the cannon which fires at 13.00

St Giles Cathedral

High Street, Royal Mile, Edinburgh, Midlothian, EH1 1RE
Tel: 0131 225 9442
Email: info@stgiles.net
Website: www.stgiles.net
March-Sept (Mon-Fri) 09.00-19.00 Sat 09.00-17.00 Sun 13.00-17.00 Oct-April (Mon-Sat)
09.00-17.00 Sun 13.00-17.00
Principal church of Edinburgh. Contains many memorials to great Scots. Fine
Victorian and 20C stained glass and a magnificent modern organ.John Knox is
apparently buried under the car park. (Free Admission but Suggested Donation)

The Tron Church-Old Town Information Centre and Visitor Attraction

122 High Street, Edinburgh, Midlothian, EH1 1RU
Tel: 0131 225 8408
Email: oldtowninfo@excite.com
Jan-Dec April-Oct Mon-Sun 10.00-17.00 Nov-March Mon-Sun 12.00-17.00
People traditionally gathered around the Tron to celebrate Hogmany. Inside is an
excavated section of Marlin's Wynd, rediscovered after 500 years and now part
of the legendary Edinburgh's Underground City

Greyfriar's Kirk

Greyfriar's Place, Junction with Candlemakers Row, Edinburgh, Midlothian, EH1 2QQ
Tel: 0131 225 1900
Email: administrator@greyfriarskirk.com
Website: www.greyfriarskirk.com
April -Oct (Mon-Fri) 10.30-16.30 (Sat)10.30-14.30 Nov - March Thursdays
13.10-15.30-Churchyard open every day 09.00-18.00
Where the National Covenant was signed in 1638. Scotland's finest collection of
16 and 17C funeral monuments. Near Greyfriar's Bobby the monument to the
faithful Skye terrier whose stayed by his master's grave for 14 years after he was
buried.

Canongate Kirk

Canongate, Royal Mile, Edinburgh, Midlothian, EH8 8BN
Tel: 0131 226 5138
Website: www.canongatekirk.com
Jun-Sep (Mon-Sat) 10.30-16.30
Historic 300 yr old church recently renovated and restored. Parish church of
Holyrood Palace and Edinburgh Castle.

St Triduana's Chapel

At Restalrig Church, Off Restalrig Road South, Edinburgh, Midlothian
Tel: 0131 554 7400
Arrange access Mon-Fri 09.00-17.00 contact St Margaret's Parish Church Restalrig 0131 554 7400
Lower part of the chapel houses the shrine of St Triduana, a Pictish Saint. The hexagonal vaulted chamber is unique.

St Mary's Cathedral

Palmerston Place, Edinburgh, Midlothian, EH12 5AW
Tel: 0131 225 6293
Email: office@cathedral.net
Website: www.cathedral.net
Mon-Fri 07.30-18.00 Sat-Sun 07.30-17.00
Episcopal cathedral built in 1879. Central spire is 276 feet high. Impressive interior.

Parish Church Of St Cuthbert

5 Lothian Road, Edinburgh, Midlothian, EH1 2EP
Tel: 0131 229 1142
Email: office@st-cuthberts.net
Website: www.st-cuthberts.net
April -Sep (Mon-Sat) 10.00-16.00
Seventh church on this site, present one built in 1894 retaining 1790 tower. Renaissance style stalls, marble communion table, mural, stained glass by Tiffany. Famous name graves

GARDENS PARKS WALKS

Princes Street Gardens

Princes Street, Edinburgh, Midlothian, EH2 3AA
Access during daylight hours
These extensive gardens were formed by the draining of the Nor Loch which previously formed a defensive moat for the castle. Now the gardens contain bandstands, walkways, fountains and flowers.There is also one of the world's largest working floral clocks

Arthur's Seat, Sailsbury Crag & Holyrood Park

By Holyrood Palace, Royal Mile, Edinburgh, Midlothian

Access at all times

Arthur's Seat rises 823ft from Holyrood Park next to Holyrood Palace. The Park has been a Royal Park since the 12C. A walk to the summit of Arthur's Seat gives spectacular views of the region and takes about 45mins

Royal Botanic Gardens

20a Inverleith Row, Edinburgh, Midlothian, EH3 5LR

Tel: 0131 552 7171

Email: info@rbge.org.uk

Website: www.rbge.org.uk

Jan,Feb,Nov & Dec Mon-Sun 10.00-16.00 March & Oct Mon -Sun 10.00-18.00 April-Sept Mon-Sun 10.00-19.00 (Charge to visit the Glasshouses)

70 acres of gardens established in 1670 containing glasshouse experience, rock garden, herbaceous border, woodland gardens and arboretum, Chinese collection, azalea lawn, alpine collection and winter garden.

Dunbar's Close

Dunbar's Close, Off the Royal Mile, Edinburgh, Midlothian

Open daylight hours

The gate inside the close gives entrance to a reconstructed 17C garden with flowers, herbs and relaxing places to sit.

Water of Leith Walkway

Visitors Centre, 24 Lanark Road, Edinburgh, Midlothian, EH14 1TQ

Tel: 0131 455 7367

Website: www.waterofleith.org.uk

Access at all times for walks

The Water of Leith runs from the Pentland Hills outside Edinburgh to the Firth of Forth at Leith. A good place to join the riverside walk is at the picturesque village of Dean Village in the city Centre then follow the river East to Leith.

Crammond Village

Crammond, Approx 5 miles W of city centre on A9, Edinburgh, Midlothian

Access at all times

This scenic sea side village offers a variety of pleasant walks. Either towards Cramond Brig, across to Cramond Island at low tide or following the shore road past Barnbougle Castle to Dalmeny Estate and on to South Queensferry.

HISTORIC HOUSES

Parliament Hall

2-11 Parliament Square, Royal Mile, Edinburgh, Midlothian, EH1 1RQ
Tel: 0131 225 2595
Mon-Fri 10.00-16.00
Built 1632-39 this was the seat of Scottish government until 1707. Now the Supreme Law Courts Of Scotland. Parliament Hall has hammer beam roof and portraits by Raeburn and other Scottish artists

National Library Of Scotland

George IV Bridge, Edinburgh, Midlothian, EH1 1EW
Tel: 0131 226 4531
Email: events@nls.uk
Website: www.nls.uk
Exhibition Opening Times-Mon-Fri 10.00-17.00 Saturdays 10.00-17.00 Sundays 14.00-17.00
One of Britain's 4 largest libraries with an unrivalled collection of Scottish History and Culture, various exhibitions on Scottish Themes open to the public

HISTORIC SITES

Grassmarket

Grassmarket, Edinburgh, Midlothian
Access at all times
This area of the old town was originally an agricultural market. Within the Grassmarket is a well preserved section of the old Flodden Wall. The cobbled cross marks the site of the town's old gallows.

Mercat Cross

Royal Mile, Edinburgh, Midlothian
Access at all times
This monument marks the central point of the old town where people would meet, sell goods and make announcements. The cross was reconstructed in the 19c but the original 16C shaft remains.

White Horse Close

Off Royal Mile, Edinburgh, Midlothian
Access at all times
Although this courtyard is now residential it retains much of it's original appearance. It was here at the old White Horse Inn that stage coaches arrived and departed for London

Calton Hill

Waterloo Place, Edinburgh, Midlothian

Access at all times

This impressive hill dominates the city centre and affords spectacular vies of the surrounding area. On the summit sits a 19C copy of the Parthaenon known as Edinburgh's Folly or disgrace as funds ran out before it's completion.

MUSEUMS

Writers Museum

Lady Stairs Close, Lawnmarket, Royal Mile, Edinburgh, Midlothian, EH1 2PA

Tel: 0131 529 4901

Email: enquiries@writersmuseum.demon.co.uk

Website: www.cac.org.uk

Mon-Sat 10.00-17.00 Sundays 12.00-17.00 During August

Commemorates Scotland's 3 most famous writers.Sir Walter Scott, Robert Burns and Robert Louis Stevenson. Houses a collection of memorabilia.

Museum of Edinburgh

142 Canongate, Royal Mile, Edinburgh, Midlothian, EH8 8DD

Tel: 0131 529 4143

Email: cac.admin@edinburgh.gov.uk

Website: www.cac.org.uk

(Mon-Sat)10.00-17.00, Sundays in August 12.00-17.00

16C house showing the history of Edinburgh. Deerskins with thousands of signatures showing the signing of the National Covenant dating from 1638. Old fashioned shop front figurines.

Museum Of Childhood

42 High Street, Royal Mile, Edinburgh, Midlothian, EH1 1TG

Tel: 0131 529 4142

Email: admin@museumofchildhood.fsnet.co.uk

Website: www.cac.org.uk

(Mon-Sat)10.00-17.00 Sundays in August 12.00-17.00

Unique museum with fine collection of toys, dolls, dolls' houses, costumes and nursery items.

The People's Story

Canongate Tollbooth, 163 Canongate, Royal Mile, Edinburgh, Midlothian, EH8 8DE
Tel: 0131 529 4057
Website: www.cac.org.uk
(Mon-Sat) 10.00-17.00 . Sundays in August 12.00-17.00
This building was once the prison and courthouse for the Canongate area.
Museum looks at the history of the real people of Edinburgh from 18C to modern
day. Displays include a reconstructed coopers workshop and a 1940s kitchen.

Royal Museum Of Scotland

Chambers Street, Edinburgh, Midlothian, EH1 1JF
Tel: 0131 247 4422
Email: info@nms.ac.uk
Website: www.nms.ac.uk
Daily 10.00-17.00
Scotland's premier museum housed in a spectacular Victorian glass topped
building. An amazing range of permanent galleries and temporary exhibitions.
From Egyptian treasures to stuffed elephants.

Museum Of Fire

Brigade Headquarters, Lauriston Place, Edinburgh, Midlothian, EH3 9DE
Tel: 0131 228 2401
Mon-Fri 09.00-16.30 Closed 1-14 Aug
Oldest municipal fire brigade in the UK. Range of fire engines dating from 1806
& displays.

Newhaven Heritage Museum

24 Pier Place, Newhaven, Edinburgh, Midlothian, EH6 4LP
Tel: 0131 551 4165
Daily 12.00-16.45
Museum telling the story of the historic fishing village of Newhaven and its people

FARMERS MARKETS

Edinburgh Farmers Market

Castle Terrace, Edinburgh, Midlothian
Every Saturday 09.00-14.00
Farmers Market with local produce on sale

Lothians-Scotland

ART GALLERIES/ARTS & CRAFTS

Stenton Gallery

Stenton, On the B6370 3 miles from the A1 at East Linton, Stenton, East Lothian, EH42 1TE

Tel: 01368 850 256

Email: bic@stentongallery.com

Website: www.stentongallery.com

Fri-Wed 11.00-17.00 during exhibitions (phone for details) 01368 850256

Shows the best contemporary art from Scotland and elsewhere.

Kittiwake Gallery and Artists Workshop

Units 1 & 2, The Steading, Northfield Farm, St Abbs, East Lothian, TD14 5QF

Tel: 018907 715 88

Email: derick@kittiwak.demon.co.uk

Website: www.kittiwak.demon.co.uk

March 1st-Easter 12.00-16.00 Easter-October 31st 10.30-17.00 20th Nov-12 Dec 11.30-16.00

Converted 19C farm steading creates a venue for showing Fredrick J Watson's wildlife and local scenery water colours.

Carberry Candle Cottage

Carberry, Musselburgh, East Lothian, EH21 8PZ

Tel: 0131 665 5656

Email: carberry@candles.co.uk

Website: www.candles.co.uk

Mon-Sat 09.00-17.00 Sun 12.00-17.00

Factory shop with large range of candles, candle making demonstrations and coffee shop.

Peter Potter Gallery

10 The Sands, Haddington, East Lothian, EH41 3EY

Tel: 01620 822 080

Email: info@peterpottergallery.org

Website: www.peterpottergallery.org

Mon-Sat 10.00-16.30 Sun 11.00-16.30

A series of exhibitions of paintings, prints, pottery, ceramics, jewellery and wood craft. Coffee shop serving light lunches

CASTLES

Hailes Castle
Off the A1, 1.5 miles SW of East Linton, East Linton, East Lothian
Access at all times
Beautifully situated ruin, incorporating a 13C fortified manor a 16C chapel and 2 vaulted prison pits.

Fast Castle
Off the A1107, 4 miles NW of Coldingham, Coldingham, Berwickshire
Access at all times
Impressive remains of a Home stronghold perched on a cliff above the sea.

Hume Castle
On the B6364, Between Kelso and Greenlaw, Hume, Berwickshire
April-Oct Access at all times Jan-March Key available from the large house opposite the castle
Ruined castle giving good views of the Tweed Valley and beyond.

EXHIBITIONS

National Flag Centre
Main Street, Athelstaneford, North Berwick, East Lothian, EH39 5BE
Tel: 01368 863 239
Open April - Sept Mon - Sun 10.00-17.00
Plaque by church tells the story of the origins of St Andrews cross (the Saltire) which was first adopted as the Scottish Flag at this place. Book of Saltire is exhibited in the 18C church.

CHURCHES & CATHEDRALS

Dunglass Collegiate Church
West off the A1, signposted Bilsdean, 1 mile NW of Cockburnspath, Cockburnspath, Berwickshire
Website: www.historic-scotland.gov.uk
Access at all times
Cross shaped church with vaulted nave,choir and transepts all with stone slab roofs. Founded 1450

Edrom Church

Edrom Churchyard, Off the A6015, 3.5 miles NE of Duns, Edrom, Berwickshire

Access at all times

e Norman chancel arch built by Thor Longus about 1105.

Borthwick Parish Church

Borthwick, 2 miles Se of Gorebridge, Borthwick, Midlothian

Open all year daily

Largely Victorian Church. Aisle and vault dating from 15C, 12C apse and memorials from 18 & 19C. 2 15C effigies thought to be the best preserved in Scotland.

Crichton Collegiate Church

Crichton Village, Off the B6367, 1.5 miles E of Gorebridge, Crichton, Midlothian

Tel: 01875 320 364

Email: johnlglamotte@aol.com

Summer Only Sunday 14.00-16.00 Advisable to phone ahead of visiting

Medieval Church built by William Crighton in 1449, with unique 19C stained glass windows

Saint Martin's Kirk

On the East Outskirts of Haddington, Off the A1, Haddington, Haddington, East Lothian

Website: www.historic-scotland.gov.uk

Access at all times

Ruined nave of a Romanesque Church altered in the 13C

St Mary's Parish Church

Sidegate, Haddington, East Lothian, EH41 4BZ

Tel: 01620 823 109

April-Sep (Mon-Sat) 11.00-16.00 (Sun) 14.00-16.30

14C Medieval cruciform church. East Lothian's "Cathedral". Completely restored 1971-1973. Features Burne Jones and Sax Shaw windows, Lammermuir pipe organ. Situated beside the River Tyne.

Dalmeny Parish Church

Main Street, Dalmeny, 15 miles W of Edinburgh, Dalmeny, West Lothian

Key available from Manse or Post Office Open April-Sept Sundays 14.00-16.30

Best preserved Norman Church in Scotland dating from the 12C.

Kirk of Calder

Main Street, Mid Calder, 12 miles W of Edinburgh, Mid Calder, West Lothian, EH53 0AN
Tel: 01506 882 495
Email: minister@kirkofcalder.com
Website: www.kirkofcalder.com
May-Sep 14.00-16.00
16C Parish Church that won the West Lothian award for conservation in 1992.

St Michael's Parish Church

Crosshouse, Linlithgow, West Lothian, EH49 7AL
Tel: 01506 842 188
Email: info@stmichaels-parish.org.uk
Website: www.stmichaelsparish.org.uk
Summer Daily 10.30-16.00 Winter (Oct-April) 10.30-13.30
Medieval Parish Church consecrated in 1242 on the site of an earlier church. Place of Mary Queen Of Scots baptism. Contemporary aluminium crown on tower which replaced the medieval one in 1820.

GARDENS PARKS WALKS

Dunbar Cliff Top Trail

Starts at Dunbar Harbour, Dunbar, East Lothian
Access at all times
A great walk with views across the Firth of Forth and is less than a mile long. There are some quite steep slopes and a number of steps

Polkemmet Country Park

The Park Centre, Whitburn, West Lothian, EH47 0AD
Tel: 01501 743 905
Email: mail@beecraigs.com
Website: www.beecraigs.com
All year dawn-dusk
Public park with mature woodland, rhododendrons, picnic and barbecue sites & play areas.

Almondell and Calderwood Country Park

Near Broxburn, Broxburn, West Lothian, EH52 5PE
Tel: 01506 882 254
All year dawn-dusk
Extensive riverside and woodland walks in former estate with large picnic and grassy areas. Visitors centre housed in old stable block has large freshwater aquarium, displays on local and natural history

Beecraigs

The Park Centre, Linlithgow, West Lothian, EH49 6PL
Tel: 01506 846 256
Email: mail@beecraigs.com
Website: www.beecraigs.com
Daily dawn-dusk

Wide range of leisure and recreational pursuits within 370 hectares. Archery, orienteering, fly fishing, walks & trails, trim course, play area, bicycle trails, picnic areas, barbecue sites, fish farm, horse route, deer farm, caravan and camping site.

Edinburgh Canal Centre

27 Baird Road, Bridge Inn, Ratho, Midlothian, EH28 8RA
Tel: 0131 333 1320
Email: info@bridgeinn.com
Website: www.bridgeinn.com
Mon-Sat 12.00-23.00 Sun 12.30-23.00

Towpath for walks or cycling along the Union canal. Play area and wild fowl reserve. Inn was built in 1750 and became a canal-side inn with the opening of the canal in 1822.

Muiravonside Country Park

The Law, Whitecross, Linlithgow, West Lothian, EH49 6LW
Tel: 01506 845 311
Apr-Sep (Mon-Fri) 09.00-17.00 (Sun) 10.00-18.00 Oct-March (Weekends only)10.00-16.00

170 acres of woodlands, parklands and gardens of the Muiravonside Estate, home of the Stirling family for 150 years. Attractions include and auditorium, relics of the industrial past, dovecot, burial ground, summer house and children's farm.

John Muir Country Park

To the West of Dunbar, The approach to the main car park is from the A1 along the A1087., Dunbar, East Lothian
Tel: 01620 827 421
Jan-Dec Open all day

Cliffs, dunes, salt marshes, woodlands, scrub and grassland habitats on a beautiful part of the coastline

Roslin Glen Country Park

Roslin Glen, On the B7003 between Roslin Village and Rosewell, Roslin, Midlothian
Tel: 01875 821 990
Jan-Dec Mon-Sun 08.00- Dusk

Woodland walks past Roslin Castle, the gun powder mills and on towards Roslin Chapel.

HISTORIC HOUSES

Greenknowe Tower

On the A6105 Earlston Road, 0.5 miles W of Gordon, Gordon, Berwickshire
Website: www.historic-scotland.gov.uk
Access at any reasonable time
A Handsome Tower House on an L-Plan design. Built in 1581 and still retaining it's iron gate.

HISTORIC HOUSES/MUSEUMS

Kinneil House

On the Western outskirts of Bo'ness, Of the A904, Bo'ness, West Lothian, EH51 0PR
Email: callendar.house@falkirk.gov.uk
Museum Mon-Sat 12.30-16.00 Exterior View Only Of House
15C tower set in public park. Transformed into the stately home for the Duke's of Hamilton in the 1660s (Outside view Only) Museum housed in stable block tells the story of the park from Roman times to modern day

HISTORIC SITES

Doonhill Homestead

Dunbar, Off the A1, 2 miles S of Dunbar, Dunbar, East Lothian
Website: www.historic-scotland.gov.uk
Access at all times
The site of a wooden hall of a 6C British chief and of a later 7C Anglican chief's hall

Wool Stone

on the B6370 at Stenton, 5 miles SW of Dunbar, Stenton, East Lothian
Access at all times
Medieval Wool Stone used formerly for the weighing of wool at Stenton Fair now stands on the green. Also a 14C Rood Well and the old Doocot.

Preston Market Cross

0.5 miles S of Prestonpans, Prestonpans, East Lothian
Access at all times
Only surviving example of a market cross of it's type still on it's original site. 17C design.

Dere Street Roman Road

Soutra, on the B6438 off the A68 beside Soutra Aisle, Soutra, Midlothian

Access at all times

A good stretch of the Roman Road that ran from Corbridge beside Hadrian's Wall to Cramond

MUSEUMS

Dunbar Town House Museum

High Street, Dunbar, East Lothian

Tel: 01368 863 734

Email: info@dunbarmuseum.org

Website: www.dunbarmuseum.org

April-Oct (Daily) 12.30-16.30 Nov-March Sat & Sun 14.00-16.30

A 16C town house now home to a museum of local history and archaeology.

John Muir's Birth Place

126 High Street, Dunbar, East Lothian, EH42 1JJ

Tel: 01368 865 899

Email: info@jmbt.org.uk

Website: www.jmbt.org.uk

April-Oct Mon-Sat 10.00-17.00 Sun 13.00-17.00 Nov-March Wed-Sat 10.00-17.00 Sun 13.00-17.00

The birthplace of John Muir founding figure of the world wide conservation movement born in 1838. The flat is furnished in period style to give an indication of the conditions that the Muir family lived in.

Prestongrange Industrial Heritage Museum

Morrison's Haven, Prestonpans, East Lothian, EH32 9RY

Tel: 0131 653 2904

Email: info@prestongrangemuseum.org

Website: www.prestongrangemuseum.org

April-Oct Mon-Sun 11.00-16.00

Industrial Museum on former colliery site, historic Cornish beam engine. Locomotive steam engine operates on the 1st Sunday of every month

Scottish Agricultural Museum

Ingilston, By Edinburgh Airport, Newbridge, Midlothian, EH28 8NB
Tel: 0131 333 2674
Email: jps@nms.ac.uk
Website: www.nms.ac.uk
March-October Mon-Sun 10.00-17.00 October-March Mon-Fri 10.00-17.00
Scotland's National Museum of Country Life. Interpretative and audio displays.

Queensferry Museum

53 High Street, South Queensferry, West Lothian, EH30 9HP
Tel: 0131 331 5545
Mon, Thurs , Fri & Sat 10.00-13.00 & 14.15-17.00 Sun 12.00-17.00 Closed Tues & Wed
Museum telling the story of the town known as the "Queen's Ferry" in honour of
Queen Margaret who died in 1093 and encouraged pilgrims to use the ferry
crossing to travel to the shrine of St Andrew.

Bennie Museum

9-11 Mansefield Street, Bathgate, West Lothian, EH48 4HU
Tel: 01506 634 944
Email: thornton@benniemuseum.freeserve.co.uk
Website: www.benniemuseum.homestead.com
April-Sep 10.00-16.00, Oct-March 11.00-15.30
Local heritage museum with almost 5000 artefacts. Postcards and photographs
from 1890s onwards, fossils, Roman glass and coins found in Bathgate. Relics
from Prince Charles Edward Stewart and the Napoleonic War.

FARMERS MARKETS

Haddington Farmers Market

Outside the Corn Exchange, Court Street, Haddington, East Lothian
Website: www.haddingtonfarmersmarket.co.uk
Last Saturday of the month 09.00-13.00
Farmers Market with local produce on sale

ENGLAND

England - What ever it is you're looking for you're sure to be able to find it in England.

The Capital City of London is one of the most exciting in the World. Full of history and character and yet modern, vibrant and stylish. London has fantastic museums and galleries, historical buildings and monuments, beautiful parks and a wealth of interesting places to visit. Also the home of the Royal Family and Parliament which makes London a fantastic place to visit.

Outside the Capital the rest of England is very diverse. From quaint old villages full of historical interest, to enormous National Parks such as the Lake District and Dartmoor, large cities overflowing with culture and entertainment and beautiful sandy beaches and coast lines.

Although England is only separated from the European mainland by a short stretch of water, the country has its own unique identity and character that can change dramatically from region to region yet remains quintessentially English throughout.

Where ever you go in England a sense of history is always present from castles, palaces and stately homes, to cathedrals, ancient churches and majestic ruins. Yet the large multi-cultural cities are modern and fashionable with a wide variety of culture, entertainment and retail facilities.

ENGLAND

North West-England

ART GALLERIES/ARTS & CRAFTS

Tate Liverpool
Albert Dock, Liverpool, Merseyside, L3 4BB
Tel: 0151 702 7400
Email: liverpoolinfo@tate.org.uk
Website: www.tate.org.uk/liverpool
Tues-Sun 10.00-17.50
Home of the National collection of modern art, this gallery has four floors of art,
daily talks, shop and café. A definite place to visit . Admission to The Tate
Collection is free, charge for special exhibitions

Haworth Art Gallery
Haworth Park, Manchester Road, Accrington, Lancashire, BB5 2JS
Tel: 01254 233 782
Email: haworth@hyndburnbc.gov.uk
14.00-17.00 Weds, Thurs & Fridays 12.00-16.30 Sat & Sun
This gallery houses the finest collection of Tiffany Art Glass in public hands
outside the USA. The collection has over 140 pieces of mosaics and tiles and
over 70 examples of Favrile glass vases.

Mid Pennine Gallery
Yorke Street, Burnley, Lancashire, BB11 1HD
Tel: 01282 421 986
Email: info@midpenninearts.org.uk
Website: www.midpenninearts.org.uk
Mon-Sat 10.00-17.00 , Tues 10.00-13.00
This gallery offers a wide range of exhibitions, paintings, sculptures, glass and
photography.

Manchester City Art Gallery
Mosley Street, North of St Peter's Square, Manchester, Greater Manchester, M2 3JL
Tel: 0161 235 888
Website: www.manchestergalleries.co.uk
(Tue-Sun) 10.00-17.00
The huge collection of high Victorian art includes the finest collection of works by
Pre-Raphaelite artists in the country.

Walker Art Gallery

William Brown Street, Liverpool City Centre, Liverpool, Merseyside, L3 8EL

Tel: 0151 478 4199

Email: thewalker@liverpoolmuseums.org.uk

Website: www.liverpoolmuseums.org.uk/walker

(Daily) 10.00-17.00

This art gallery has one of the country's finest provincial art collections. The works range from the 14C to the present day and include artists such as Rembrant, Poussin, Rubens and other 17C masters.

Castlegate House

Cockermouth, Lake District, Cockermouth, Cumbria, CA13 9HA

Tel: 01900 822 149

Email: gallery@castlegatehouse.co.uk

Website: www.castlegatehouse.co.uk

Mon, Fri & Sat 10.30-17.00 Sun 14.20-16.30 Closed Tues, Wed & Thurs

Contemporary changing selection of displays specialising in the works of some of the most accomplished artists of the local area.

Salford Museum And Art Gallery

Peel Park, The Crescent, Salford, Greater Manchester, M5 4WN

Tel: 0161 736 2649

Email: salford.museum@salford.gov.uk

Website: www.salford.gov.uk/salfordmuseum

(Mon-Fri) 10.00-16.45, (Sat & Sun) 13.00-17.00

Houses the most extensive Lowry exhibition in the country and an impressive collection of Victorian Art. The museum also houses a reconstructed Victorian Street, where visitors can experience the sights and sounds of Victorian Salford

Whitworth Gallery

University Of Manchester, Whitwork Park, Oxford Road, Manchester, Greater Manchester, M15 6ER

Tel: 0161 275 7450

Email: whitworth@man.ac.uk

Website: www.whitworth.man.ac.uk

(Mon-Sat) 10.00-17.00 (Sun) 14.00-17.00

A selection of works from British artists such as Staples, Moore, Frink and Hepworth are displayed alongside a variety of pieces from lesser known sculptors. A further gallery displays watercolours from such artists as Turner, Constable and Blake

Manchester Craft Centre

17 Oak Street, Off Tib Street, Northern Quarter, Smithfield, Manchester, Greater Manchester
Tel: 0161 832 4274
Email: info@craftanddesign.com
Website: www.craftanddesign.com
(Mon-Sat) 10.30-17.30 (Also Sundays in December)
The building houses a wide display of various skills and crafts and provides a great opportunity to purchase ceramics, fabrics, earthenware, jewellery and decorative art.

Castle Park Arts Centre

Off Fountain Lane, Off Mill Street, Frodsham, Cheshire, WA6 6SE
Tel: 01928 735 832
Email: enquiries@castle-park-arts.co.uk
Website: www.castle-park-arts.co.uk
Open Tues-Sat 10.00-12.30 & 14.00-16.30 Sunday 14.00-16.30
Castle Park is in the market town of Frodsham and is known for its beautiful floral gardens. The arts centre is in a restored clock tower and stable block, and contains galleries and craft work shops ranging from painting to sculptures.

Potters Barn

Roughwood Lane, Hassall Green, Sandbach, Cheshire, CW11 4XX
Tel: 01270 884 080
Website: www.thepottersbarn.f2s.com
Open all year 09.30-17.30
Home made gifts for home and garden this traditional working pottery holds classes group visits and children's parties

Church Farm Crafts

Marton, 3 miles N of Congleton, on the A34 in Marton, Marton, Cheshire, SK11 9HF
Tel: 01260 224 344
April-Sept Mon-Fri 09.30-18.00 Sat,Sun 09.30-17.00 Oct -March Mon-Fri 09.30-17.30 Sat, Sun 09.30-16.30
Crafts farm containing workshops, ranging from glass blowing to oak furniture, there is also a coffee shop

Cedar Farm Galleries

Back Lane, Mawdesley, Near Ormskirk, Mawdesley, Lancashire, L40 3SY
Tel: 01704 822 101
Email: info@cedarfarm.net
Website: www.cedarfarm.net
Open Tues-Sun 10.00-17.00
Contemporary crafts, picture framing, artists materials, world wide exotica, coffee shop and special teas.

Blakemere Craft Centre

Chester Road, Sandiway, Northwich, Cheshire, CW8 2EB
Tel: 01606 883 261
Website: www.blakemere-shoppingexperience.com
Open Tues-Fri 10.00-17.00 Sat & Sun 10.00-17.30
Attractions include over 30 different types of craft shops and work shops, falconry centre, children's play area , coffee shop and restaurant.

Welltrough Dried Flowers

Welltrough Hall Farm, Lower Withington, Near Macclesfield, Macclesfield, Cheshire, SK11 9EF
Tel: 01477 571 616
Mon-Fri 09.00-17.00 Sat & Sun 10.00-17.00
Workshops and demonstrations. Silk and dried flowers, containers and arrangements. 8 showrooms and an all year Christmas Room.

The Grundy Art Gallery

Queen Street, Blackpool, Lancashire, FY1 1PX
Tel: 01253 478 170
Email: grundyartgallery@blackpool.gov.uk
Mon-Sat 10.00-17.00
A display of old Blackpool plus Victorian oils, contemporary prints and changing exhibitions

Oswaldtwistle Mills

Moscow Mill, Collier Street, Oswaldtwistle, Lancashire, BB5 3DF
Tel: 01254 871 025
Email: info@o-mills.co.uk
Website: www.o-mills.co.uk
Mon-Sat 09.30-17.30 Sun 11.00-17.00
Combining retail outlets with craft workshops and events. Visitors can watch the resident artists and craftsmen at work, as well as follow nature trails and visit the weavers cottage

Blackburn Museum & Art Gallery

Museum Street, Blackburn, Lancashire, BB1 7AJ
Tel: 01254 667 130
Email: janet.leeming@blackburn.gov.uk
Website: www.blackburnworld.com
Tues-Sat 10.00-16.45 all year
Opened in 1874 and houses the largest icon collection outside London's Victoria and Albert Museum. This museum has the only permanent gallery of Indian and Pakistani culture in the North West

Thornthwaite Galleries

Near Keswick, Thornthwaite, Cumbria, CA12 5SA
Tel: 01768 778 248
Email: enquiries@thornthwaite.net
Website: www.thornthwaite.net
10.30-17.00 Daily except Tuesdays
Known to exhibit the very best in fine art, craftsmanship and traditional skills

Lady Lever Art Gallery

Port Sunlight Village, Higher Bebington, Merseyside, CH62 5EQ
Tel: 0151 478 4136
Email: ladylever@liverpoolmuseums.org.uk
Website: www.ladyleverartgallery.org.uk
10.00-17.00 Daily
Houses a fine collection of 18 & 19C paintings, ceramics and sculptures. Known for its Pre-Raphaelite pictures

Harris Museum and Art Gallery

Market Square, Preston, Lancashire, PR1 2PP
Tel: 01772 258 248
Email: harris.museum@preston.gov.uk
Mon, Wed-Sat 10.00-17.00 Tues 11.00-17.00 Sun 11.00-16.00
Houses collections of British art, glass and costumes with a programme of over 20 art exhibitions each year

Cheshire Workshops

Near Chester, Burwardsley, Cheshire, CH3 9PF
Tel: 01829 770 401
10.00-17.00 Daily
Visitors can try their hand at candle dipping, clay modelling and badge making, also many craftmakers displaying their skills on site

Cheshire Farm Real Dairy Ice Cream

Drumlan Hall Farm, Newton Lane, Tattenhall, Cheshire, CH3 9NE
Tel: 01829 770995
Email: enquiries@cheshirefarmicecream.co.uk
Website: www.cheshirefarmicecream.co.uk
April-Oct 10.00-17.30 Daily Nov-March 10.30-17.00 Daily
30 different types of ice cream and sorbets made from the milk of the farm's 300 cows, visitors can even watch the cows being milked

CASTLES

Chester Castle

Castle Street, Chester, Cheshire
April -Sep (Daily) 10.00-17.00, Oct-March (Daily) 10.00-16.00
Set into the angle of the city walls, the Agricola Tower is a 12th-century tower
which contains a fine vaulted chapel.

Penrith Castle

Castlegate, Opposite the train station, Penrith, Cumbria, CA11 7HX
Tel: 0191 269 1214
The park is open 07.30-21.00 during summer and 07.30-16.30 During winter
The ruins that remain of this castle were originally built in the 14C as a bastion
against raids from the North.

Brough Castle

Brough, 8 miles SE of Appleby, Brough, Cumbria
Website: www.english-heritage.org.uk
Access at all reasonable times
A 12C Keep, which replaces an earlier stronghold which was destroyed by the
Scots in 1174

CHURCHES & CATHEDRALS

Carlisle Cathedral

Castle Street, Carlisle, Cumbria, CA3 8TZ
Tel: 01228 548 151
Email: office@carlislecathedral.org.uk
Website: www.carlislecathedral.org.uk
(Mon-Sat) 07.30-18.15, (Sun) 07.30-17.00
Inside the Cathedral the East window that dates from the 14C features some of
the finest examples of 14C stained glass in the country. In the NW corner a flight
of steps lead down to the treasury which is packed with glittering chalices and
communion sets

Lancaster Priory

Castle Hill, At the side of Lancaster Castle, Lancaster, Lancashire, LA1 1YZ
Tel: 01524 65338
Email: lancasterpriory@yahoo.co.uk
Website: www.priory.lancs.ac.uk
Mon-Sat 10.00-16.30 Sunday 10.00-16.30
This church dates from the 11C and there has been a church on this site since 630AD. The present building is mainly 15C and still retains some 14C features including a Saxon doorway at the West end and finely carved choir stalls.

Manchester Cathedral

Cathedral Yard, Manchester, Greater Manchester, M3 1SX
Tel: 0161 835 4030
Email: office@manchestercathedral.com
Website: www.manchestercathedral.org.uk
Mon-Fri 08.00-19.00 Sat 08.00-17.00 Sun 08.30-19.30 Visitors Centre Mon-Fri 10.00-16.30
Sun 11.30-14.00
This cathedral offers worship, concerts, recitals, guided tours and a gift shop and possesses a fine example of 15C woodcarvings. New visitor's centre and restaurant and exhibition areas

Liverpool Cathedral

Saint James Mount, Liverpool, Merseyside, L1 7AZ
Tel: 0151 702 7217
Email: lew.eccleshall@liverpoolcathedral.org.uk
Website: www.liverpoolcathedral.org.uk
Daily 08.00-18.00 Admission is free but a donation is suggested
The largest Anglican Cathedral in Britain with superb views from the tower

Metropolitan Cathedral Of Christ The King

Mount Pleasant, Liverpool, Merseyside, L3 5TQ
Tel: 0151 709 9222
Email: met.cathedral@boltblue.com
Website: www.liverpoolmetrocathedral.org.uk
Daily 08.00-18.00, Closes at 17.00 on Sundays in Winter. Visitors Centre open Mon-Fri 10.00-17.00 Sat 10.00-17.00 Sun 11.00-16.00
This very modern Roman Catholic Cathedral was designed by Sir Frederick Gibberd and consecrated in 1967. Most noted for its stained glass. Guides available to show you round as well as historical information, refreshments and gifts on hand

Birkenhead Priory

Priory Street, Birkenhead, Cheshire, CH41 5JH

Tel: 0151 666 1249

Summer Wed-Fri 13.00-17.00 Sat/Sun 10.00-17.00. Winter Wed-Fri 12.00 -17.00 Sat/Sun 10.00-16.00

Founded in 1150, this Norman Priory has stunning views from the vantage point of St Mary's Tower.

Goodshaw Chapel

Goodshaw Avenue, 2 niles N of Rawtenstall, Crawshawbooth, Lancashire

Tel: 0161 242 1400

Website: www.english-heritage.org.uk

Telephone the keyholder for details of access

An 18C Baptist Church which retains all of its original furnishings

St Mary & St Michael's Church

Great Urswick, Ulverston, Cumbria, LA12 0TD

Tel: 01229 582 053

Website: www.urswick.freeuk.com

Daily 10.00-15.00

A 10C Church, the oldest in Furness, with Georgian gallery, Pre-Viking Tunwinni Cross and triple decker pulpit

Sawley Abbey

3.5 miles N of Clitheroe, Off the A59, Sawley, Lancashire

Tel: 01282 661 702

Website: www.english-heritage.org.uk

April-Sept 10.00-18.00 Oct-March 10.00-16.00 Daily

The remains of a Cistercian Abbey which was founded in 1148

GARDENS PARKS & WALKS

Fletcher Moss Botanical Gardens and Parsonage Gardens

Wimslow Road, Didsbury, Rusholm, Manchester, Greater Manchester

Dawn-Dusk

Situated in a large park the gardens contain a landscaped area that includes ponds, shrubs, rare pines and firs and an imaginative selection of cacti and flowers.

The Pennine Way

Edale to Kirk Yetholm, Peak District
Email: enquiries@thepennineway.co.uk
Website: www.thepennineway.co.uk
Access at all times

Start of the Pennine way is sign posted from outside the "Old Nags Head" pub in Edale.The walk covers 250 miles across the backbone of England to Kirk Yetholm on the Scottish Border. The Pennine Way is one of the most popular walks in the country

Stadt Moers Country Park

Pottery Lane, Whiston, Knowsley, Merseyside
Tel: 0151 489 1239
Open dusk-dawn. Visitors Centre 13.00-16.30 on Sat & Sun

Nature reserve with various programmes of events and activities.

Wirral Country Park

Station Road, Thurstaston, Wirral, Thurstaston, Merseyside, CH61 0HN
Tel: 0151 648 4371
Email: wirralcountrypark@wirral.gov.uk
Dawn-Dusk

There are guided walks , boat trips, children's activities and a twelve mile footpath through this Country Park which has cracking views across the Dee Estuary.

Haigh Hall Country Park

Junction 6 of the M61, Take the B5239 to Aspull then onto Haigh, Wigan, Wigan, Greater Manchester, WN2 1PE
Tel: 01942 832 895
Email: hhgen@wlct.org
Daily 10.00-16.00 Weekends 10.00-17.00

Set in 250 acres, this Country Park has woodland walks, nature trails and a playground.

Clifton Country Park

Clifton House Road, Clifton, Salford, Greater Manchester, M27 6NG
Tel: 0161 793 4219
Email: clifton.countrypark@salford.gov.uk
Website: www.salford.gov.uk/cliftoncountry.htm
Open dawn-dusk

Within this 80 acre park there is a lake, ponds, woodlands, grasslands, wet land areas and also a Visitor Centre with details of walks

Halewood Country Park

Off Okell Drive, Halewood, Halewood, Merseyside, L26 7XB
Tel: 0151 488 6151
Park Open dawn-dusk Visitor Centre open 1.00-16.30 on Saturday, Sunday
Set in a former railway junction, this park has extensive footpaths and bridal way networks as well as a programme of events and activities.

Blackleach Country Park

John Street, Walkden, Salford, Greater Manchester, M28 3PQ
Tel: 0161 790 7746
Email: blackleach.countrypark@salford.gov.uk
Website: www.salford.gov.uk/blackleach.htm
Open dawn-dusk
What used to be a chemical works has been transformed into a 100 acre park, there is also a bird sanctuary and nature trails

Hollingworth Lake Country Park

Rakewood Road, Littleborough, Lancashire
Tel: 01706 373 421
Open all year Visitors Centre Open March Mon-Fri 11.00-16.00 Sat & Sun 10.30-17.00
April-Sept Daily 10.30-18.00 Oct Mon-Fri 11.00-16.00 Sat & Sun 10.30-17.00
This country park has a 2.25 mile walk around a watersports lake and wonderful views of the Pennines

Wycoller Country Park

Off A6068, 2.5 miles E of Colne, Colne, Lancashire
Tel: 01282 870 253
Email: countrysideservices@env.lancscc.gov.uk
Website: www.lancshire.gov.uk/environment
Open all year dawn-dusk
A Country Park and conservation area with Bronte associations. Within the park are the ruins of Wycoller Hall, reputed to be Ferndean Manor in Charlotte Bronte's Jane Eyre

Heaton Park

Middleton Road, Preswitch, Manchester
Tel: 0161 773 1085
Open all year
600 acre park with lake, golf course and working tram.

HISTORIC HOUSES

Heaton Hall

Heaton Park, Prestwich, Manchester, Greater Manchester, M25 5SW
Tel: 0161 773 1231
Website: www.manchestergalleries.org.uk
April - October Wed - Sun 10.00-17.30
This late Georgian gentry house has many original features, including furniture and paintings.

Chetham's Library

Long Millgate, Manchester, Greater Manchester, M3 1SB
Tel: 0161 834 7961
Email: librarian@chethams.org.uk
Website: www.chethams.org.uk
Monday to Friday 9.00-12.30 and 13.30-16.30
The first free Public Library in the world with over 100 000 books, many rare.

Weavers Triangle Visitors Centre

85 Manchester Road, Burnley, Lancashire, BB11 1JZ
Tel: 01282 452 403
East-End Sept Sat-Tues 14.00-16.00 October Sun 14.00-16.00
Giving visitors the chance to discover what it was like to live in a 19C mill town
.With walks along the Liverpool canal towpath and looking at buildings used for spinning mills, foundries, weaving sheds and even a school.

Lytham Windmill

Lytham Green, East Beach, Lytham St Anne's, Lancashire, FY8 5LD
Tel: 01253 794 879
Easter & Late May-Early September Mon-Fri 10.30-16.30 Closed between 13.00-14.00
This windmill houses an exhibition on the history and workings of the windmill and overlooks the Ribble Estuary

Walton Hall Park & Heritage Centre

Walton Hall Gardens,, Walton Lea Road, Higher Walton, Warrington, Cheshire
Tel: 01925 602 336
Email: waltonhall@warrington.gov.uk
Website: www.warrington.gov.uk/waltongardens
Park Open Daily 08.00-dusk Heritage Centre Open Summer 10.30-17.00 Winter
10.30-16.15
The grounds of Walton Hall are open daily and there is an exhibition in the Heritage Centre focusing on the Greenall family life and history and Walton Hall estate. There is also an exhibition on Lewis Carroll

Wythenshawe Hall

Wythenshawe Park, Wythenshawe Road, Northenden, Northenden, Greater Manchester, M23 0AB

Tel: 0161 998 2331

Website: www.manchestergalleries.org.uk

June until September, Saturdays only, 10.00-17.00

Home of the Tatton family for 400 years, this house dates back to 1540 and is feet in 250 acres of parkland

HISTORIC SITES

Minerva Shrine

Edgars Field, Handbridge, Chester, Cheshire

Access at all times

A roman shire to the Goddess Minerva which is 4 feet 9 inches tall and 2 feet 6 inches wide. This is the only rock cut Roman Shrine in its original location in the UK.

Barrow Bridge Village

Barrow Bridge Road, Off Moss Bank Way, Bolton, Lancashire

Access at all times

Small village created during the Industrial Revolution built by the owners of the local mill to house their workers. Picturesque cottages with history trails and information centre

Sandbach Crosses

Market Square, Sandbach, Cheshire

Tel: 01260 271 095

Website: www.english-heritage.org.uk

Access at all reasonable times

Believed to date from the 9C these two massive crosses are carved with Biblical scenes including the Nativity Of Christ and the Crucifixion

Ambleside Roman Fort

200 yards West of Waterhead carpark, Waterhead, Ambleside, Cumbria

Website: www.english-heritage.org.uk

Access at all reasonable times

The remains of a 1st and 2nd century fort built to guard the Brougham to Ravenglass Roman Road

Peel Tower

Holcombe Hill, Holcombe Village, Ramsbottom, Lancashire, BL8 4NR
Tel: 0161 253 5353
Email: afrost@bury.gov.uk
Exterior View at all times. Access to the interior may be restricted
Built as a memorial to Sir Robert Peel, the former Prime Minister. There are 160 steps to the top of this 120 foot stone tower where views of the surrounding countryside can be seen for miles

King Arthur's Round Table

Eamont Bridge, 1 Mile S of Penrith, Penrith, Cumbria
Website: www.english-heritage.org.uk
Access at all reasonable times
A Prehistoric earthwork encompassed by a ditch and outer bank, 162 feet in diameter

Shore Road Pumping Station

Woodside, Birkenhead, Cheshire, CH41 6DN
Tel: 0151 650 1182
East-Oct Sat & Sun 13.00-17.00 Nov-Easter Sat & Sun 12.00-16.00
This restored working pump was used to clear water from the railway tunnel beneath the Mersey

Chester Town Crier

At the Ancient Cross, Junction of Bridge Street, Watergate Street and Eastgate Street, Chester, Cheshire
Tel: 01244 311 736
Email: david@creativecommunications.biz
Website: www.creativecommunications.biz
At Noon every Tuesday-Saturday from May-August
Witness an old traditional town crier in the heart of Chester. The shout lasts about 15mins

Long Meg and Her Daughters

Little Salkeld, Penrith, Cumbria
Access at all times
The third largest stone circle in England suggested to date from 2500-2000 BC

Roman Amphitheatre

Vicars Lane, Chester, Cheshire
Tel: 0161 242 1400
Unrestricted Access

This Roman Amphitheatre was estimated to have held over 7000 spectators, making it the largest of its kind in Britain.

Ravenglass Roman Bath House

Off minor road leading to the A595, 0.25 miles E of Ravenglass, Ravenglass, Cumbria
Website: www.english-heritage.org.uk
Access at all reasonable times

Remains of the Bath House for the Roman Fort of Ravenglass, the walls which stand 4 meters high are amongst the most complete remains in Britain

MUSEUMS

Imperial War Museum

Trafford Wharf Road, Trafford Park, Manchester, Greater Manchester, M17 1TZ
Tel: 0161 836 4000
Email: info@iwmnorth.org.uk
Website: www.iwm.org.uk
Mar-Oct Mon-Sun 10.00-16.00 Nov-Feb 10.00-17.00

Displays and collections showing the impact of War on the 20C and 21C

Towneley Hall Art Gallery and Museum

Off Todmorden Road, 1 mile from Burnley city Centre, Burnley, Lancashire, BB11 3RQ
Tel: 01282 424 213
Email: towneleyhall@burnley.gov.uk
Website: www.towneleyhall.org.uk
Free for Burnley residents, children and student only. Charge for non-residents.

This 14C house contains a Museum and features oil paintings, English watercolours, 18C glass wear, furniture and natural history exhibits. Also the museum of local crafts & industries which had displays on Burnley's recent social and industrial history

Rossendale Museum

Whittaker Park, Haslingden Road, Rawtenstall, Rossendale, Lancashire, BB4 6RE
Tel: 01706 244 682
Email: rossendalemuseum@btconnect.com
Sat, Sun, Tues, Wed, Thurs Apr-Oct 13.00-14.30 Nov-Mar 13.00-16.00
This museum displays an impressive collection of fine art and furniture, natural history, local industrial and domestic artefacts and stuffed animals. Former 19C mill owners mansion recently restored to its original glory

Bolton Museum

Le Mans Crescent, Bolton, Bolton, Lancashire
Tel: 01204 332 211
Email: museum.customerservices@bolton.gov.uk
Website: www.boltonmuseums.org.uk
Mon- Sat 09.00-17.00 Closed Sun
Renown for its collection of Egyptian antiquities this museum also has a wild life gallery, activity centre and collections of natural and social history, archaeology and local history

Manchester Museum

Oxford Road, Manchester, Greater Manchester
Tel: 0161 275 2634
Website: www.museum.man.ac.uk
Sun, Mon 11.00-16.00 Tues-Sat 10.00-17.00
A variety of exhibitions and attractions that include a fabulous Egyptian collection, and a three tiered mammal gallery that has a multitude of stuffed exhibits and an aquarium containing a ten foot long boa-constrictor.

Gallery Of Costumes

Platt Hall, Platt Field Park, Wilmslow Road, Rusholm, Manchester, Greater Manchester, M14 5LL
Tel: 0161 224 5217
Website: www.manchestergalleries.org
Open last Saturday of every month 10.00-17.00
This unusual museum depicts the various fashions and styles throughout the ages and places a degree of emphasis on Manchester's past history as a textile centre, and the clothes of the working class people

Grosvenor Museum

27 Grosvenor Street, Chester, Cheshire, CH1 2DD
Tel: 01244 402 008
Email: srogers@chestercc.gov.uk
(Mon-Sat) 10.30-17.00 (Sun) 14.00-17.00
This museum gives an insight into the Roman history of Chester. Displays cover
a wide range of subjects including, The City Buildings, Legionary Systems,
Grave Sites, Defences, Daily Life and Culture. There is also a collection of
Roman tombstones

Nantwich Museum

Pillory Street, Nantwitch, Cheshire, CW5 5BQ
Tel: 01270 627 104
Email: nantwitch.museum@virgin.net
Website: www.nantwitchmuseum.org.uk
Apr-Sep (Mon,-Sat) 10.30-16.30, Oct-March (Tues-Sat) 10.30-16.30
The museum comprises a variety of cottage industry artefacts that give an insight
into the town's past, including cheese making, salt making and shoe making.

The Dock Museum

North Road, Barrow-in-Furnace, Cumbria, LA14 2PW
Tel: 01229 894 444
Email: dockmuseum@barrowbc.gov.uk
Website: www.dockmuseum.org.uk
East-Oct (Tues-Fri) 10.00-17.00 (Sat-Sun) 11.00-17.00 Nov-Easter (Wed- Fri) 10.30-16.00
(Sat & Sun) 11.00-16.30
The museum is situated in a dried out graving dock where shipped used to be
repaired and now contains a history of the town's ship building past told through
a variety of media.

Manchester Museum

University Of Manchester, Oxford Road, Manchester, Manchester, M13 9PL
Tel: 0161 275 2634
Website: www.museum.man.ac.uk
(Tues-Sat) 10.00-17.00 Mon & Sun 11.00-16.00
A variety of exhibitions and attractions that include a fabulous Egyptian
collection, and a three tiered mammal gallery that has a multitude of stuffed
exhibits and an aquarium containing a ten foot long boa-constrictor.

National Football Museum

Sir Tom Finney Way, Deepdale, Preston, Lancashire, PR1 6RU

Tel: 01772 908 442

Email: enquiries@nationalfootballmuseum.com

Website: www.nationalfootballmuseum.com

Tues-Sat 10.00-17.00 Saturday Matchdays 10.00-15.00 & 16.45-18.00 Midweek Matchdays 10.00-19.30 Sun 11.00-17.00

This museum shows how the game came to be invented, individuals and teams who helped shape the game as well as an art gallery dedicated to the world of football

Portland Basin Museum

Portland Place, Aston-Under-Lyne, Lancashire, OL7 0QA

Tel: 0161 343 2878

Email: portland.basin@tameside.gov.uk

Tues-Sun 10.00-17.00

Local exhibits of the working canal and rail systems

Prescot Museum

34 Church Street, Prescott, Knowsley, Merseyside, L34 3LA

Tel: 0151 430 7787

Email: prescot.museum.dlcs@knowsley.gov.uk

Website: www.knowsley.gov.uk/leisure/museum

All year Tues-Sat 10.00-13.00 & 14.00-17.00 Sun 14.00-17.00

An 18C town house with exhibits and displays showing the traditional watch makers workshop and hand tools

Lancaster City Museum

Market Square, Lancaster, Lancashire, LA1 1HT

Tel: 01524 646 37

Email: lancaster.citymuseum@mus.lancscc.gov.uk

Website: www.lancsmuseums.gov.uk

Mon-Sat 10.00-17.00

Housing displays of local archaeology, Royal Lancashire Militia and the Kings Own Royal Lancaster Regiment

World Museum Liverpool

William Brown Street, Liverpool, Merseyside, L3 8EN

Tel: 0151 478 4399

Email: themuseum@liverpoolmuseums.org.uk

Website: www.liverpoolmuseum.org.uk

Daily 10.00-17.00

Collections from the Amazonian Rain Forests to the riches of an Egyptian Tomb, this is one of Britain's finest Museums

The Queens Lancashire Regiment Museum

Fulwood Barracks, Watling Street Road, Fulwood, Lancashire, PR2 8AA
Tel: 01772 260 362
Email: rhq.qlr@talk21.com
Tues-Thurs 09.30-16.30
An extensive collection of books, documents and artefacts. This is one of the largest Military Heritage Collections in the North West

Park Bridge Heritage Centre

The Stables, Park Bridge, Aston-Under-Lyne, Lancashire, OL6 6DL
Tel: 0161 330 9613
All year Wed-Thurs 12.00-16.00 Summer Sat & Sun 11.00-17.00 Winter Sat & Sun 10.00-16.00
Trace the history of this iron rolling mill through the remains of the building and other artefacts

Greater Manchester Police Museum

Newton Street, Manchester, Manchester, ME1 1ES
Tel: 0161 856 3287
Email: police.museum@gmp.police.uk
Website: www.gmp.police.uk
Tues 10.30-15.30 or by appointment
This museum is housed in a Victorian Police Station, and is complete with original prison cells

NATURE AND WILDLIFE

Marshside

Near Southport, Southport, Merseyside
Tel: 01704 536 378
Roads alongside the fields are open at all time. Two hides open daily 8.30-17.00
Some of the best lowland wet grassland in the North West of England and an important refuge for pink footed geese

Hodbarrow

Millom, Cumbria
Tel: 01697 351 330
Access at all times
Wading birds and water fowl can be seen on the fresh water lagoons

Campfield Marsh

Bowness-On-Solway, Bowness-On-Solway, Cumbria

Tel: 01697 351 330

Access at all times

See Oyster Catchers, Grey Plovers and Bartailed Godwits

Haweswater

Near Bampton, Brampton, Cumbria

Tel: 01931 713 376

Access at all times

The only place in England where golden eagles nest. Farms and houses were pulled down, coffins removed from the graveyard and the church demolished to create this lake, at low tide visitors can see the remains of the villages emerging.

Morecambe Bay

Near Morecambe, Morecambe, Lancashire

Tel: 01524 701 601

Access at all times

This reserve's sand flats and salt marshes are vital feeding ground for thousands of wading birds and wild fowl.

Animal World and Butterfly House

Moss Bank Park, Moss Bank Way, Bolton, Lancashire, BL1 6NQ

Tel: 01204 334 050

April-Sept 10.00-16.30 Oct-March 10.00-15.30 Fridays 10.00-14.30

Animal World offers a living environment for animals and birds from chipmunks to wildfowl, the Butterfly House offers a tropical environment for butterflies, reptiles and tropical plants

FARMERS MARKETS

Carlisle Farmers Market

City Centre, Carlisle, Cumbria

1st Friday of the month 10.00-15.30

Farmers market with local produce on sale

Penrith Farmers Market

Market Square, Town Centre, Penrith, Cumbria

3rd Tuesday of the month 09.30-14.30

Farmers market with local produce on sale

Colne Farmers Market

Market Street Carpark, Outside and In Market Hall, Colne, Lancashire
3rd Saturday of the month
Farmers market with local produce on sale

Manchester Farmers Market

Old Smithfield Market, Northern Quarter, Manchester
2nd Saturday of the month 08.00-16.00
Farmers market with local produce on sale

EVENTS

Blackpool Illuminations

Blackpool Promenade, Blackpool, Lancashire
Website: www.visitblackpool.com/illuminate.asp
2006 1st September-5th November. Please call or see website for other annual dates.
The famous Blackpool Illuminations burst into life every night along the six miles
of Promenade for 66 nights

The West Country-England

ART GALLERIES/ARTS & CRAFTS

Marine House at Beer Arts & Pottery

Fore Street, Beer, Seaton, Devon, EX12 3EF
Tel: 01297 625 257
Email: info@marinehouse-at-beer.co.uk
Website: www.marinehouse-at-beer.co.uk
Summer Tues-Sun 10.00-17.30 Winter Tues-Sun 10.00-17.00 Closed Mondays except in High Season
This gallery features some of Britain's best craftspeople and artists, with constantly changing exhibitions of paintings, pottery, glass wear, jewellery etc.

Cheddar Sweet Kitchen

Daghole Cottages, Water Lane, Cheddar, Somerset, BS27 3QJ
Tel: 01934 743810
March-October Mon-Sun 11.00-17.00 Jun-Sept Open until 18.00 1 Nov-End Feb Weekends Only
A small scale sweet factory that has been run by the Mizzen family for generations. Visitors can see the high quality work put in by the family as they make their sweets the old fashioned way, then sample the end products in the shop.

Cornwall Pearl

Southway, Quintrell Downs, Newquay, Cornwall, TR8 4LE
Tel: 01637 872 991
Email: pearl.2004@virgin.net
1 Jan-31 Dec Mon-Sun 09.30-17.30 Closed Christmas Day only
Known to house one of the largest selections of pearl jewellery in England. Staff work on the premises with pearls and precious stones.

Burton Art Gallery

Kingsley Road, Bideford, Devon, EX39 2QQ
Tel: 01237 471 455
Email: friends@burtonartgallery.co.uk
Website: www.burtonartgallery.co.uk
Tues-Sat 10.00-17.00 Sun 14.00-17.00
This gallery has various exhibitions on arts and crafts including examples of North Devon pottery.

Falmouth Art Gallery

Municipal Buildings, The Moor, Falmouth, Cornwall, TR11 4SN

Tel: 01326 313 863

Website: www.falmouthartgallery.com

Mon-Sat 10.00-17.00

Temporary exhibitions of contemporary art as well as a permanent collection of 20C paintings.

The Devon Guild Of Craftsmen

Riverside Mill, Bovey Tracey, Devon, TQ13 9AF

Tel: 01626 832 223

Email: devonguild@crafts.org.uk

Website: www.crafts.org.uk

All year round 09.00-17.30 Closed 24-25 Dec & 1 Jan

This grade 2 listed building has a wide variety of displays including furniture, wood work, textiles, ceramics and jewellery. There is also a shop and café.

Somerset Guild Of Craftsmen Gallery

Hurst Works, Martock, Somerset, TA12 6JU

Tel: 01935 825 891

Email: homegallery@somersetguild.co.uk

Website: www.somersetguild.co.uk

Open Mon-Sat 10.00 -17.00 (April-Christmas Sundays) 10.00-16.00

Featuring hand made crafts of furniture, fabrics, wood carving, jewellery and print making.

Spacex Gallery

45 Preston Street, Exeter, Devon, EX1 1DF

Tel: 01392 431 786

Email: mail@spacex.co.uk

Website: www.spacex.co.uk

Tues-Sat 10.00-17.00

Collection of art by regional, national and international artists.

Newlyn Art Gallery

4 Causewayhead, Penzance, Cornwall, TR18 2SN

Tel: 01736 363 715

Email: mail@newlynartgallery.co.uk

Website: www.newlynartgallery.co.uk

Mon-Sat 09.30-17.00 Please check exhibition programme before visiting

Changing exhibitions featuring a wide range of artists from local to international.

Cornish Goldsmiths

Tolgus Mill, Near Portreath, Cornwall, TR16 4HN
Tel: 01209 218 198
Email: info@cornishgoldsmiths.com
Website: www.cornishgoldsmiths.com
Mon-Sat 09.30-17.30 Sun 10.30-16.30
Come see the Cornish Crown Jewels, or watch our goldsmiths at work, or even
pan for gold yourself

English Hurdle

Curload, Stoke St Gregory, Taunton, Somerset, TA3 6JD
Tel: 01823 698 418
Email: hurdle@enterprise.net
Website: www.hurdle.co.uk
Mon-Fri 08.00-17.00 Sat 09.00-13.00
Working willow farm with craftsmen on site, making baskets and producing
hurdle. Finished products can be seen displayed in the garden.

CASTLES

Saint Catherine's Castle

Saint Catherine's Point, Fowey, Cornwall, PL23 1JH
Access at all times
This ruined castle was built by Thomas Teffry on the orders of Henry VIII. The
ruins give fantastic views across the estuary.

Castle An Dinas

Goss Moor, 1 mile N of A30, Cornwall, Cornwall
Access at all times
Dating from 200-300BC this amazing hill fort dating from the Iron Age has circles
of ditches and ramparts 850 feet in diameter

Nunney Castle

Nunney, $3\frac{1}{2}$ miles SW of Frome, off A361, Frome, Somerset, BA11
Access at all times
This complete 14C castle was built by Sir John Delamare (who later became the
Sheriff Of Somerset) using the style of French architects, with a distinct compact
tower, and surrounded by a deep moat.

Bayards Cove Fort

Located in Dartmouth, On the river front, Dartmouth, Devon

Access at all times

Built in 1509-1510 this small artillery fort was to protect the entrance of the inner haven.

CHURCHES & CATHEDRALS

Saint Andrew's Church

Winterbourne Tomson, Blandford, Forum, Blandford, Dorset

Open all year daily

An 11C village church built of stone and flint which is a delight both from the outside and within.

Oare Church-Saint Mary's Church

Oare, Lynton, Lynton, Somerset

Open all year

Features of this church include, a 19C tower, 15C chancel, and a 12C font. This church was also the scene of Lorna Doone's wedding in the novel written by R.D. Blackmore.

Loughwood Meeting House

Dalwood, Axminster, Devon, EX13 7DU

Tel: 01392 881 691

Open all year

Remaining unaltered since the 18C this meeting house was built by the Baptist congregation in 1653 at that time anyone attending a service in such a church faced trial and imprisonment.

Saint Lawrence Chapel

Saint Lawrence Lane, Ashburton, Devon, TQ13 7DD

Tel: 01364 653 414

Website: www.stlawrencechapel.ik.com

May-Sep, Tues, Thur-Sat 14.00-16.30 (Closed on Wednesdays)

Housing one of the finest examples of plasterwork in a public building, this chapel also covers an exhibition on the history of the chapel and grammar school.

Culbone Church

St Beuno, Culbone, Porlock, Minehead, Somerset
Open all year
Known as the smallest complete Parish Church in England, at only 35 feet in length, (the chancel is 10 feet wide, and the nave is 12 feet 3 inches wide, and there is only 30 seats.) Features include: the 15C pews, Norman font and Saxon windows.

GARDENS PARKS & WALKS

Royal Victoria Park

Entrance to park from Queen Street or Marlborough Lane, Bath, Wiltshire, BA1 2NR
Tel: 01225 425 066
Open all year daily 09.00-Dusk
These are the city's largest open spaces containing an aviary and beautiful botanical gardens.

Sydney Gardens

Behind Holburne House, Bathwick, Bath, Wiltshire, BA2 1EE
Tel: 01225 477 101
Open dawn-dusk
This was formerly a venue for concerts and firework displays as witnessed and written about by Jane Austen in her novels.

Dunkery Beacon

Exford, Exmoor, Exford, Somerset
Access at all times
A four mile walk stretches from Exford to Dunkery Beacon which is Exmoor's highest point rising 1700 feet.

Weston Mouth

On the East Devon Coast, Between Sidmouth and Seaton, Sidmouth, Devon
Access at all times
This is one of the areas most attractive and isolated beaches.

Meadfoot Beach

Meadfoot Sea Road, Torquay, Devon, TQ1 2LQ
Tel: 01803 294 339
Access at all times
A 12 mile long coastal walk through Daddyhole plain.

Tregenna Castle Gardens

St Ives, Cornwall
Tel: 01736 795 254
10.00-Dusk
72 acres with stunning views overlooking St Ives Bay. Main attractions include a sub-tropical walled garden and a recently created water garden.

Barricane Beach

Ilfracombe, Just North of Woolacombe Sands, Woolacombe, Devon
Access at all times
This beach is famous for the numerous tropical shells that was h up on its shores from the Caribbean..

Lands End

Penzance, Approx nine miles West of Penzance, Penzance, Cornwall
Access at all times (Parking Fee for cars)
The actual location is a public right of way and there is a platform to view the sights of the Irish Lady, the Armed Knight and Dr Syntax Head.Stand on the edge of England and gaze out across the sea.

Exe Estuary

Near Exeter, Exeter, Devon
Tel: 01392 824 614
Access at all times
This reserve offers coastal grazing marsh on opposite sides of the estuary. Visitors can see thousands of ducks, geese, lapwing and redshank

Marazion Marsh

Marazion, 4 miles from Penzance, Marazion, Cornwall
Tel: 01736 711 682
Access at all times
This reserve has Cornwall's largest reed bed and is home to two special rare birds which visit on migration-The Spotted Crane and Aquatic Warbler

HISTORIC HOUSES

Kirkham House
Kirkham Street, Paignton, Devon, TQ3 3AX
Tel: 0117975 0700
Every Sunday in July & Aug 14.00-17.00 Please check with Englsih Heritage for futher opening times.
Permanent collection of furniture , fabrics and pottery designed to imitate the interior of a 14C house.

Ashton Windmill
Chapel Allerton, Axbridge, Somerset
Tel: 01278 435399
Easter through to September, Sunday 14.30-16.30 July and August, Wednesday 14.30-16.30
Unique 18th century flour mill with fantastic view of Cheddar Gorge, Somerset Levels and Brent Knoll.

Church House
Widecombe-In-The-Moor, Newton Abbot, Devon, TQ13 7TA
Tel: 01364 621 321
Open daily to visitors when not in use as the village hall
This 1537 brew house is leased to the Village for use as the Village Hall.

Meare Fish House
Meare, Glastonbury, Somerset
Access at any reasonable time. The key for the house is available from Manor House farm
A 14C Hill house with fish ponds that would have been built for the Abbey, who were at the time in charge of fisheries. The fish ponds have since dried up.

Oldway Mansion
Torquay Road, Paignton, Devon, TQ3 2TD
Tel: 01803 207 933
April-Oct Daily 09.00-17.00 Nov-March Mon-Fri 09.00-17.00 Guided tours of the house have a small charge of approx £1 but there is free admission without a guided tour
Known for its marble staircase, main hall and glass work, this 1873 mansion was bought by The Paignton Council in 1946 to be used as a Civic Centre. The mansion was built in 1874 by Isaac Merritt Singer, founder of the sewing-machine empire.

HISTORIC SITES

Glastonbury Tor
Glastonbury, Somerset
Access at all times
Dramatic and spectacular views over Somerset, Dorset & Wiltshire. At the summit the remaining tower of the Church of St Michael dating from the 15C is being extensively repaired. The remains of the church stand on an earlier church site.

Mayflower Steps
Sutton Harbour, Plymouth, Devon
Access at all times
These steps commemorate the sailing of the Pilgrim Fathers

Grimspound
2 miles NE of Postbridge, Dartmoor, Dartmoor, Devon
Access at any reasonable time
Bronze Age Village consisting of 24 circular huts.

Halliggye Fogou
E of Garras on Trelowarren Estate, 5 miles SE of Helston off B3293, Garras, Cornwall
Reasonable Daylight Hours Access April-Oct Completely blocked between Nov-March Free Entry to the monument but there is a charge for the Estate
A mysterious underground chamber, associated with Iron Age villages and normally used for refuse or storage.

Men-An-Tol
Madron, Penzance, Cornwall
Access at all times
Neolithic free standing stones with the hole which could have been an entrance to a burial chamber

Blackbury Camp
South Leigh, Colyton, Devon
Access at all times
Dating from 200 BC-AD 100 this Iron Age Hill Fort is surrounded by a bank and ditch.

Ballowall Barrow

1 miles W of St Just, Near Carn Gloose, St Just, Cornwall
Website: www.english-heritage.org.uk
Access at all reasonable times
A Bronze Age chambered tomb which includes an entrance grave and a series of burial chambers

Carn Euny Ancient Village

1.25 miles SW of Sancreed, Off the A30, Sancreed, Cornwall
Website: www.english-heritage.org.uk
Access at all reasonable times
Foundations of stone huts and curved underground passages survive from this Iron Age settlement

Dupath Well

1 mile E of Callington, Off the A388, Callington, Cornwall
Website: www.english-heritage.org.uk
Access at all reasonable times
An almost complete Well house constructed from Granite block stands over a holy well which dates from the 15C

Hurlers Stone Circles

On Bodmin Moor, off the B3254, 0.5 miles NW of Minions, Liskeard, Cornwall
Website: www.english-heritage.org.uk
Access at all reasonable times
Dating from 1500 BC these three Bronze Age stone circles are one of the best examples of ceremonial standing stones in the South West of England

King Doniert's Stone

On Bodmin Moor, off the B3254, 1 mile NW of St Cleer, St Cleer, Cornwall
Website: www.english-heritage.org.uk
Access at all reasonable times
This 9C cross is believed to commemorate the King Of Cornwall who drowned in AD 875

St Breock Downs Monolith

3.75 miles SW of Wadebridge, Off an unclassified road to Rosenannon, St Breock, Wadebridge
Website: www.english-heritage.org.uk
Access at all reasonable times
Cornwall's heaviest Prehistoric standing stone, weighing 16.75 tonnes and was originally 16 feet high

Lydford Castle and Saxon Town

Lydford, off the A386, 8 miles S of Okehampton, Devon

Website: www.lydford.co.uk

Access at all reasonable times

A 12C Tower stands above the Gorge of the River Lyd and the earthworks of the Norman Fort lie to the South

MUSEUMS

City Museum And Art Gallery

Queens Road, Bristol, BS8 1RL

Tel: 01779 223 571

Email: general_museum@bristol-city.gov.uk

(Daily) 10.00-17.00

The museum has various exhibits on archaeology,geology and natural history.Including a large collection of eastern art and Egyptology

Plymouth City Museum

Drake Circus, Plymouth, Devon, PL4 8AJ

Tel: 01752 304 774

Email: enquiry@plymouthmuseum.gov.uk

Website: www.plymouthmuseum.gov.uk

Tues-Fri 10,00-17,30 Sat 10.00-17.00 Closed Sundays and Mondays

This free attraction offers collections and exhibitions of works by Caufmann, Reynolds, Watteau and many more.

Industrial Museum

Princes Wharf, Wapping Road, Bristol, BS1 4RN

Tel: 01179 251 470

All year Sat-Wed 10.00-17.00

A collection of vehicles and maritime models.With over 400 exhibits

Royal Albert Memorial Museum

Queen Street, Exeter, Devon, EX4 3RX

Tel: 01392 265 858

Email: ramm@exeter.gov.uk

(Mon-Sat) 10.00-17.00

A wide range of curious exhibits from stuffed animals to different building styles throughout the different cities.

Museum Of North Devon

The Square, Barnstaple, Devon, EX32 8LN
Tel: 01271 346 747
Email: museum@northdevon.gov.uk
Website: www.devonmuseums.net
Tues- Sat 10.30-16.30
The museum displays exhibitions on wildlife and 18C pottery.

Daphne du Maurier Literary Centre

5 South Street, Fowey, Cornwall, PL23 1AR
Tel: 01726 833 616
Email: literarycentre@fowey.co.uk
(Daily) Mid May-Sep 10.00-17.00
The building contains a small exhibit on the life and works of Daphne DuMaurier.

Penlee House Gallery And Museum

Morrab Road, Penzance, Cornwall, TR18 4HE
Tel: 01736 363 625
Email: info@penleehouse.org.uk
Website: www.penleehouse.org.uk
Free On Saturdays Only 10.00-17.00
The house contains various maritime scenes and artefacts

FARMERS MARKETS

Buckfastleigh Farmers Market

Buckfastleigh, town centre across from the Globe Inn, Dartmoor, Devon
Tel: 01803 762 674
Every Thursday 10.00-13.00
Fresh food from local farmers, also local crafts and refreshments.

NATURE AND WILDLIFE

Mousehole Wild Bird Hospital

Raginnis Hill, Mousehole, Near Penzance, Penzance, Cornwall, TR19 6SR
Tel: 01736 731 386
Email: mouseholebirdhospital@hotmail.com
Open daily
This hospital accepts any bird in need of care. Visitors are welcome.

Ham Wall

Near Ashcott, Ashcott, Somerset
Tel: 01458 860 494
Access at all times
An internationally important wetland covering 469 acres, marsh harriers, otters and dragonflies can be seen on the open water

Chapel Wood

Near Braunton, Braunton, Devon
Tel: 01392 432 691
Access at all times
A small reserve with the remains of an old hill fort and a historic chapel

Hayle Estuary

Hayle, Hayle, Cornwall
Tel: 01736 711 682
Access at all times
Important location for over-wintering ducks and geese

The Donkey Sanctuary

Sidmouth, Off the A3052 between Sidmouth and Branscombe, Sidmouth, Devon, EX10 0NU
Tel: 01395 578 222
Email: enquiries@thedonkeysanctuary.com
Website: www.thedonkeysanctuary.org.uk
Open all year
Founded in 1969 on a farm near Sidmouth, over 9000 donkeys have been rescued by this sanctuary.

FARMERS MARKETS

Tavistock Farmers Market

Bedford Square, Tavistock, Devon
Tel: 01822 820 360
Email: info@tavistockfarmersmarket.com
Website: www.tavistockfarmersmarket.com
2nd and 4th Saturday of the month 09.00-13.00
Farmers Market with local produce for sale

Exeter Farmers Market

Princesshay, Exeter, Devon
Every Thursday 09.00-14.00
Farmers Market with local produce for sale

Callington Farmers Market

Town Hall, Callington, Cornwall
2nd and 4th Friday of the month 09.00-12.00
Farmers Market with local produce for sale

Wellington Farmers Market

Wellington Scout Hall, Wellington, Somerset
Tel: 01458 830 801
3rd Saturday of the month 09.00-13.00
Farmers Market with local produce for sale

Weston Super Mare Farmers Market

Town Square, Weston Super Mare, Somerset
Tel: 01934 634 850
2nd Saturday of the month 09.30-14.00
Farmers Market with local produce for sale

Glastonbury Farmers Market

St Johns Carpark, Glastonbury, Somerset
4th Saturday of the month 09.00-13.00
Farmers Market with local produce for sale

London To The Severn-England

ART GALLERIES/ARTS & CRAFTS

Cheltenham Art Gallery and Museum

Clarence Street, Cheltenham, Gloucestershire, GL50 3JT
Tel: 01242 237 431
Email: artgallery@cheltenham.gov.uk
Website: www.cheltenhammuseum.org.uk
(Mon-Sat) 10.00-17.20 First Thursday of each month open at 11.00
The museum offers great displays on social history and there is a room
dedicated to the Arts & Crafts movement.

Cecil Higgins Art Gallery

Castle Lane, Bedford, Bedfordshire, MK40 3RP
Tel: 01234 211 222
Email: chag@bedford.gov.uk
Website: www.cecilhigginsartgallery.org
Tues-Sat 11.00-17.00 Sun 14.00-17.00
This is the original home of Cecil Higgins, the rooms of this Victorian Mansion
have been re-created to their original period style. The Gallery includes
exhibitions of water colours, drawings, ceramics and glass.

Bohun Gallery

15 Reading Road, Henley-on-Thames, Oxfordshire, RG9 1AB
Tel: 01491 576 228
Website: www.bohungallery.co.uk
Mon,Tues, Thurs-Sat 09.30-13.15, 14.15-17.00
Displaying artists include Mary Fedden, John Piper and Elizabeth Frink

Hook Norton Pottery

East End Farm House, Hook Norton, Bambury, Oxon, OX15 5LG
Tel: 01608 737 414
Email: info@hooknorton-pottery.co.uk
Website: www.hooknortonpottery.co.uk
Mon-Fri 09.30-17.00
This studio takes the visitor through the different stages of pottery production
from glazing to decorating

Yellow Hat Tribe

Brookfield Ostrich Farm, Church Westcote, Chipping Norton, Oxfordshire, OX7 6SJ
Tel: 01993 832 042
Email: irene@yellowhat-tribe.com
Website: www.theyellowhat-tribe.com
Daily 10.00-18.00
Set on an Ostrich Farm and offers paintings, prints and cards created on site for sale

Taurus Crafts

The Old Park, Off the A48, 0.5 mile SW of Lydney, Lydney, Gloucestershire, GL15 6BU
Tel: 01594 844 841
Email: enquire@tauruscrafts.co.uk
Website: www.tauruscrafts.co.uk
Daily 10.00-17.30
A craft centre with craft units, gift shop, working pottery and restaurant

Ruskin Mill

Old Bristol Road, 4 miles South of Stroud, Nailsworth, Gloucestershire, GL6 0LA
Tel: 01453 837 537
Email: maria.fischer@ruskin-mill.org.uk
Website: www.ruskin-mill.org.uk
Daily 10.00-17.00
Craft centre located within an 1820's woollen ill, with local artists, regular exhibitions and evening classes and events

Winchcombe Pottery

Becketts Lane, 1 miles North of Winchcombe on Broadway Road, Winchcombe, Gloucestershire, GL54 5NU
Tel: 01242 602 462
Email: mike@winchcombepottery.co.uk
Website: www.winchcombepottery.co.uk
Mon-Fri 08.00-17.00 Sat 10.00-16.00 Sun May-Sept 12.00-16.00
This pottery was established in 1926 on the site of an older 1800's pottery, today the pottery produces a range of hand thrown domestic stonewear pots

Ruardean Garden Pottery

At the west end of Ruardean, Just past Malt Shovel, Ruardean, Gloucestershire, GL17 9TP
Tel: 01594 543 577
Website: www.ruardeanpottery.com
Mon-Sat 09.00-17.30 and March-Sept Sunday 13.00-17.00
Visitors can browse displays of pots and also see the frost proof garden terracotta pots being made

Rooksmoor Mills

Bath Road, 1 mile South of Stroud on the A46, Stroud, Gloucestershire, GL5 5ND
Tel: 01453 872 577
Mon-Sat 09.00-17.00 Sun 10.30-16.30
Situated in a 19C Cotswold stone woollen mill, visitors can view several retail outlets including makers of natural floor coverings and cane furniture

Harts Barn Flower And Craft Centre

Monmouth Road, Longhope, Gloucestershire, GL17 0QD
Tel: 01452 830 954
Website: www.fweb.org.uk/hartsbarn
April-Sept Tues-Sun 10.00-17.30 Oct-March Tues-Sun 10.00-16.00
This building which dates from 1068 was originally the Norman Hunting Lodge for the Forest Of Dean. The building is now home a wide variety of different crafts

Hart Gold and Silversmiths

The Old Silk Mill, Sheep Street, Chipping Campden, Gloucestershire, GL55 6DS
Tel: 01386 841 100
Email: gofh@hartsilversmiths.co.uk
Website: www.hartsilversmiths.co.uk
Mon-Fri and Saturday Mornings
Specialising in hand made silver visitors are welcome to watch the craftsmen at work

Cotswold Woollen Weavers

Filkins, 3 miles NE of Lechlade, Gloucestershire, GL7 3JJ
Tel: 01367 860 491
Email: wool.weavers@dial.pipex.com
Mon-Sat 10.00-18.00 and Sun 14.00-18.00
A large mill shop offering the woven garments and a museum all housed in 18C buildings

Cotswold Pottery

Clapton Row, Bourton-on-the-Water, Gloucestershire, GL54 2DN
Tel: 01451 820 173
Email: potts@cotswoldpottery.co.uk
Website: www.cotswoldpottery.co.uk
Mon-Sat 09.30-17.00 Sun 10.30-17.00
Offering a wide range of hand made pottery from this small family run business

Painswick Woodcrafts

3 New Street, Painswick, Gloucestershire, GL6 6XH
Tel: 01452 814 195
Website: www.painswick.co.uk
Mon-Sat 09.30-17.00 Jan & Feb 09.30-16.00
Offering a wide range of woodware by Dennis French with occasional
demonstrations

CASTLES

Wallingford Castle Gardens

Castle Street, Wallingford, Wallingford, Oxfordshire
Tel: 01491 835 373
Open April-Oct 10.00-18.00 Nov-March 10.00-15.00
Wallingford castle was demolished by Oliver Cromwell, but the earthworks
,gardens and limited ruins remain.

Deddington Castle

East End of Deddington, 17 miles from Oxford, Deddington, Oxfordshire
Access at all times
This 12C castle which was in ruin by the 14C is now completely demolished and
only the earthworks remain visible.

CHURCHES & CATHEDRALS

Champs Chapel

Chapel Square, East Hendred, Wantage, East Hendred, Oxfordshire, OX12 8J
Tel: 01235 833 466
Apr-Sept Suns 14.30-16.30 Oct-Mar, 1st Sun in Month 14.30-15.30
Restored in 1974 this Grade I listed 15C Chapel was built by The Carthusian
Monks. It now houses a museum dedicated to local history

Prinknash Abbey

2.5 miles NE of Painswick, Cranham, Gloucestershire, GL4 8EX
Tel: 01452 812 455
Email: prinknash@waitrose.com
Website: www.prinknashabbey.org.uk
Open all year daily Summer 09.00-17.30 Winter 09.30-16.30 (Charge for pottery tour)
Set in 250 acres this world famous Benedictine monastery is home to the world
reputed pottery

St Giles Church

Church Lane, Stoke Poges, Slough, Buckinghamshire, SL2 4PE
Tel: 01753 644 177
Email: smnevard@aol.com
Website: www.stokepogeschurch.org
Daily 09.30-16.30
The church dates mostly from the 13th and 14th centuries and is the burial place of poet Thomas Grey

Saxon Tower Of St Michael

Cornmarket Street, Oxford, Oxfordshire
Tel: 01865 240 940
April-Oct Mon-Sat 10.00-17.00 Sun 12.00-17.00 Nov-March Mon-Sat 10.00-16.00 Sun 12.00-16.00 (Admission to church Free, charge to climb the tower)
This 11C tower at St Michael's Church claims to be Oxford's oldest building. Previous visitors to this church include King Charles I , William Shakespeare and William Morris who was actually married in this church

GARDENS PARKS & WALKS

The Oxfordshire Way

Bourton-on-the-Water to Henley-on-Thames, Bourton-on-the-Water, Oxfordshire
Access at all times
A 65 mile walk through stunning landscapes and scenery passing through two areas Outstanding Natural Beauty

Sundon Hills Country Park

5 miles N of Luton, Sundon, Bedfordshire
Tel: 01582 608 489
Open at any reasonable time
This Country Park includes Nature Walks, outstanding landscapes, picnic area and other interesting nature features.

The Herb Farm

Peppard Road, Sonning Common, Reading, RG7 9NJ
Tel: 01189 724 220
Email: herbfarm@herbfarm.co.uk
Website: www.herbfarm.co.uk
Farm open daily 10.00-17.00
Over 200 varieties of herbs are grown at this farm, together with wild flowers and old style roses. There is also a large gift shop on site.

Priory Country Park

Barkers Lane, Bedford, Bedfordshire, MK41 9SH
Tel: 01234 364 213
Open at any reasonable times
At Over 300 acres, this Country Park includes two lakes and riverside. There are guided walks, fishing for all and bird watching hides.

California Country Park

Nine Mile Ride, Finchampstead, Finchampstead, Wokingham
Tel: 01189 342 016
Open daily 09.00-17.00 £1 car parking charge at weekends and easter and summer holidays
Covering 150 acres and including a six acre lake, there is also public coarse fishing, paddling pool, adventure play area and café.

Emberton Country Park

Emberton, On the A509 1 mile S of Olney, Olney, Buckinghamshire, MK46 5DB
Tel: 01234 711 575
Email: embertonpark@milton-keynes.gov.uk
Park open all year
The River Ouse, five lakes and 200 acres of park land make up this Country Park. Attractions include boating, orienteering, camping and nature trails.

Cyril Hart Arboretum

200 yards South of Speech House, on the B4226, Cinderford, Gloucestershire
Tel: 01594 833 057
Open all year daily
A woodland site with small arboretum with trails, sculptures and a picnic site

Annual Cheese Rolling

Coopers Hill, Birdlip, Gloucestershire
Spring Bank Holiday Mondays
This custom originally ensured the villagers right to graze sheep on this hill. The "cheese" is rolled down the hill and who ever reaches the bottom first claims it

Cirencester Park

Park Street/Cecily Hill, Cirencester, Gloucestershire
Tel: 01285 640 410
Open 08.00-17.00
Cirencester Park is home to Lord Bathgate and although his house is not open to the public, the park is one of the finest examples of geometric landscaping in Britain

Ernest Wilson Memorial Garden

Leysbourne High Street, Chipping Campden, Gloucestershire
Tel: 01386 841 206
Email: visitchippingcampden@lineone.net
Daily 08.00-Dusk
Chipping Campden born Earnest Wilson the famous plant collector who introduced over 1200 new species of trees and shrubs to Britain is commemorated with this garden

HISTORIC HOUSES

Merton College

South Side of Merton Street, South of Oxford High Street, Oxford, Oxfordshire, OX1 4JD
Tel: 01865 276 310
Website: www.merton.ox.ac.uk
(Mon-Fri) 14.00-16.00 (Sat,Sun) 10.00-16.00
Historically this is the most important college in the University town of Oxford and was founded in 1264

All Souls College

The Broad Street Area, Oxford, Oxfordshire, OX1 4AL
Tel: 01865 279 379
Email: enquiries@all-souls.ox.ac.uk
Website: www.all-souls.ox.ac.uk
Weekdays 14.00-16.00
The college boasts twin mock Gothic towers and a coloured sundial designed by Sir Christopher Wren.

Exeter College

Enter from Turrel Street, Oxford, Oxfordshire, OX1 3DP
Tel: 01865 279 600
Email: academic.administrator@exeter.ox.ac.uk
Website: www.exeter.ox.ac.uk
(Daily) 14.00-17.00
This college has one of Oxford's most elaborate chapel's

Houghton House

1 mile NE of Ampthill, Off A421, Bedford, Bedfordshire
Tel: 01223 455 532
Access at any reasonable time
17C country house ruins which are believed to be "House Beautiful" in Bunyan's "The Pilgrims Progress ".

Antiques At Wendover

The Old Post Office, 25 High Street, Wendover, Buckinghamshire, HP22 6DU
Tel: 01296 625 335
Email: antiques@antiquesatwendover.co.uk
Website: www.antiquesatwendover.co.uk
Mon-Sat 10.00-17.30 Sun 11.00-17.00
This Tudor building is now used as an antiques centre, housing approx. 30 dealers. The barn has been restored and now houses a gallery for Aviation Art.

The Great Witcombe Roman Villa

5 miles SE of Gloucester, Between Stroud and Cheltenham, off the A417/A46, Gloucester, Gloucestershire
Tel: 01451 862 000
Email: aonb@cotswold.gov.uk
Exterior view only daily at any reasonable time
This large Roman Villa was built around three sides of a courtyard and had a luxurious bath house

Minster Lovell Hall and Dovecote

Minster Lovell, 3 miles W of Witney, Minster Lovell, Oxfordshire, OX8 5RN
Dovecote exterior view only, Hall access at any reasonable time
Situated on the bank of the River Windrush is the ruins of a large 15C manor. In the 18C a skeleton was found said to be that of Lord Lovell

Swalcliffe Barn

Shipston Road, Swalcliffe, Banbury, Oxfordshire, OX15 5DR
Tel: 01295 788 278
April-Oct Sundays 14.00-17.00
A fine example of a half cruck barn and now houses a collection of local agricultural and trade vehicles. Restored in 1992 by English Heritage and recognised as one of the major barns of England

HISTORIC SITES

White Horse Hill

6 miles West of Wantage, Uffington, Oxfordshire
Access at all times
This 373 foot long horse is carved into the North facing slope of the Downs.

Belas Knap Long Barrow

Near Charlton Abbots, Charlton Abbots, Gloucestershire

Access at all times

This is a Neolithic long barrow that dates from around 3000 BC and is the best preserved burial chamber in England. The chamber tombs that housed the remains of 31 Stoneage people have been opened up so that visitors can see inside

Uley Bury

Uley, 6 miles from Stroud, Uley, Gloucestershire

Access at all times

This is amongst the largest hill forts in Britain. A walk to the fort is approximately 2 miles but motorists can park in the car park near the fort itself.

Banbury Cross

Horsefair, Banbury, Oxfordshire

Access at all times

This Neo Gothic monument erected in 1859 was to celebrate the marriage of Queen Victoria's Eldest daughter and is immortalised in the famous Nursery Rhyme

North Leigh Roman Villa

East End, 2 miles N of North Leigh, North Leigh, Oxfordshire

Access at all times There is a viewing window for the mosaic tile floor

The most stunning feature of this large Roman built courtyard villa is an almost complete mosaic tiled floor

Maharajahs Well

Stoke Row, Henley-On-Thames, Oxfordshire

Access at all times

Built in 1863 this Indian style well stands an impressive 20 foot high with iron and guilt decoration.

Woodchester Roman Mosaic Plinth

Adjacent to Woodchester Church Yard, 2 miles S of Stroud, Woodchester, Gloucestershire

Tel: 01453 872 340

Access at all times

Describing the Woodchester Roman pavement and Woodchester Roman Villa this plinth is opposite the church yard, the original site of the villa

De Grey Mausoleum

1.5 miles W of the A6 at Silsoe, Attached to the church, Flitton, Bedfordshire
Website: www.english-heritage.org.uk
Weekends only. Contact the key keeper in advance-Mrs Stimson, 3 Highfield Road, Flitton
Sculptured tombs and monuments from the 16th-19thC, Dedicated to the De Grey family of Wrestpark

Wayland's Smithy

On the Ridgeway, 0.75 miles NE of B4000 Ashbury-Lambourn Road, Uffington, Oxfordshire
Website: www.english-heritage.org.uk
Access at all reasonable times
A Neolithic burial site, surrounded by a small circle of trees. Associated with Wayland the Saxon God of metalworking

Cirencester Amphitheatre

Chesterton Lane, Next to the bypass, Cirencester, Gloucestershire
Tel: 0117 975 0700
Access at all times
One of the largest and best preserved Roman Amphitheatres from the 2C in Britain

MUSEUMS

Bate Collection

Faculty Of Music, Saint Aldate's, Oxford, Oxfordshire, OX1 1DB
Tel: 01865 276 139
Email: bate.collection@music.ox.ac.uk
Website: www.bate.ox.ac.uk
Mon-Fri 14.00-17.00 Sat (Full Term Only) 10.00-12.00
This museum contains England's most comprehensive collection of woodwind instruments.

Museum Of Modern Art

30 Pembroke Street, Oxford, Oxfordshire, OX1 1BP
Tel: 01865 722 733
Email: info@modernartoxford.org.uk
Website: www.modernartoxford.org.uk
Tues-Sat 10.00-17.00 Sun 12.00-17.00
The gallery displays a variety of modern art and has 2 exhibits on show at the same time.

Museum Of The History Of Science

In the Old Ashmolean Building, Broad Street, Oxford, Oxfordshire, OX1 3AZ
Tel: 01865 277 280
Website: www.mhs.ox.ac.uk
(Tue-Sat) 12.00-16.00 (Sun) 14.00-17.00
The museums displays microscopes and early calculators.

Ashmolean Museum

Beaumont Street, Oxford, Oxfordshire, OX1 2PH
Tel: 01865 278 000
Website: www.ashmol.ox.ac.uk
(Tue-Sat) 10.00-17.00 (Sun) 12.00-17.00
This is the oldest public museum in the country and has a variety of displays
including Egyptian artefacts, eastern and Italian art.

University Museum Of Natural History

Parks Road, Oxford, Oxfordshire, OX1 3PW
Tel: 01865 270 949
Email: info@oum.ox.ac.uk
Website: www.oum.ox.ac.uk
(Daily) 12.00-17.00
The museum includes a working bee hive and impressive fossil dinosaurs

Luton Museum

Wardown Park, Luton, Bedfordshire, LU2 7HA
Tel: 01582 546 722
Email: museum.gallery@luton.gov.uk
Tues-Sat 10.00-17.00, Sun 13.00-17.00
Collections of lace, Victorian displays, archaeology and natural history are on
show in this Museum.

Benson Veteran Cycle Museum

The Bungalow, 61 Brook Street, Benson, Wallingford, Oxfordshire, OX10 6LH
Tel: 01491 838 414
April-Aug 09.00-13.00 by prior arrangement with owner
Veteran and vintage cycles dating from 1818-1925

John Bunyan Museum

Mill Street, Bedford, Bedfordshire, MK40 3EU
Tel: 01234 213 722
Tues-Sat 11.00-16.00
Museum dedicated to the famous writer and author of "The Pilgrims Progress"
Collections include his personal effects and 60 of his published works.

Abingdon Museum

County Hall, Market Place, Abingdon, Oxfordshire, OX14 3HG
Tel: 01235 523 703
Website: www.abingdon.gov.uk
Daily 10.30-16.00
Contains local historical and archaeological displays housed within this 1678
County Hall.

Tetbury Police Museum

The Old Courthouse, 63 Long Street, Tetbury, Gloucestershire, GL8 8AA
Tel: 01666 504 670
Email: tetburypolicemuseum@btinternet.com
Website: www.tetbury.com/policemuseum
Mon-Fri 09.30-15.00
Offers visitors the chance to view the police office, former magistrates court and
the police cells with displays of uniforms and equipment

Swinford Museum

Fox House, 3 miles NE of Lechlade, Filkins, Gloucestershire, GL7 3JQ
Tel: 01367 860 209
May-Sept 1st Sunday of the month 14.00-17.00
One of Oxford's oldest and smallest museums housed in a 17C cottage.
Displaying a collection of domestic and agricultural tools.

Gloucester City Museum And Art Gallery

Brunswick Road, Gloucester, Gloucestershire, GL1 1HP
Tel: 01452 396 131
Email: city.museum@gloucester.gov.uk
Website: www.gloucester.gov.uk
Tues-Sat 10.00-17.00
This museum houses displays of natural science and archaeology, and a fine art
art gallery

Pitt Rivers Museum

South Parks Road, Oxford, Oxfordshire
Tel: 01865 270 927
Email: prm@prm.ox.ac.uk
Website: www.prm.ox.ac.uk
Daily 12.00-16.30
This collection is of artefacts collected from around the world by
Lieutenant-General Pitt Rivers and others

Wotton-Under-Edge Heritage Centre

The Chipping, Wotton-Under-Edge, Gloucestershire, GL12 7AD
Tel: 01453 521 541
Website: www.wottonheritage.com
Summer Tues-Fri 10.00-13.00 & 14.00-17.00 Sat 10.00-13.00 Winter Tues-Fri 10.00-13.00 &
14.00-16.00 Sat 10.00-13.00
This museum offers photos and pictures relating to Wotton and the surrounding
district

NATURE & WILDLIFE

Donnington Fish Farm

Condicote Lane, Off the A424, 1 mile NW of Upper Swell, Upper Swell, Gloucestershire,
GL54 1EP
Tel: 01451 830 873
Email: donnifish@chalkh.force9.co.uk
Summer-Oct Daily 10.00-17.30 Nov-March Tues-Sun 10.00-17.00
Set in the beautiful Cotswolds and housed in an 18C stone barn this trout farm
allows visitors to feed the fish and also buy their produce at the shop

A Home Of Rest For Horses

West Croft Stables, Slad Lane, Near Lacey Green, Princes Risborough, Buckinghamshire,
HP27 0PP
Tel: 01494 488 464
Email: info@homeofrestforhorses.co.uk
Website: www.homeofrestforhorses.co.uk
All year daily 14.00-16.00
Visitors can feed the animals at this stable which can house up to 120 horses

St James City Farm

23 Albany Street, Tredworth, Gloucester, Gloucestershire, GL1 4NG
Tel: 01452 305 728
Summer 09.30-17.00 daily Winter Tues-Sun 10.00-16.00
This farm provides hands on contact with farm animals there is also an outdoor picnic site

Edward Richardson and Phyllis Amey Reserve

0.5 miles North of Lechlade, Lechlade, Gloucestershire
Tel: 01452 383 333
Email: info@gloucestershirewildlifetrust.co.uk
Open all year daily
Two areas of wetland and grassland with water birds being the main attraction.

FARMERS MARKETS

Chipping Norton Farmers Market

Market Square, Chipping Norton, Oxfordshire
4th Friday of the month 08.30-13.00
Farmers Market with local produce for sale

St Albans Farmers Market

Town Hall Square, Market Place, St Albans, Hertfordshire
2nd Sunday of the month 10.00-15.00
Farmers Market with local produce for sale

Tewkesbury Farmers Market

Tewkesbury Abbey Carpark, Tewkesbury, Gloucestershire
Tel: 01684 272249
Email: tewkesbury@gafm.org
2nd Saturday of the month 09.00-14.00
Farmers Market with local produce for sale

Cirencester Farmers Market

Cirencester Cattle Market-Leisure Centre, Cirencester, Gloucestershire
Tel: 01453 834777
Email: simonsmith@pdcarter.co.uk
2nd and 4th Saturday of the month 09.00-13.00
Farmers Market with local produce for sale

Central England-England

ART GALLERIES/ARTS & CRAFTS

Herbert Art Gallery

Jordan Well, Coventry, East Midlands, CV1 5QP
Tel: 024 7655 2386
Email: info@theherbert.org
Website: www.theherbert.org
(Mon-Sat) 10.00-17.30, (Sun) 12.00-17.00
Most outstanding exhibits are Luca's "Bacchus And Ariadne" which fills an entire wall and the famous portrait of King George III by Sir Thomas Lawrence.

Barber Institute Of Fine Art

University Of Birmingham, Edgbaston Park Road, Edgbaston, Birmingham, West Midlands, B15 2TS
Tel: 0121 414 7333
Email: info@barber.org.uk
Website: www.barber.org.uk
(Mon-Sat) 10.00-17.00, (Sun) 12.00-17.00
World class collection of European masters from the 13C onwards. Rembrants, Ruben, Degas and Matisse.

Walsall New Art Gallery

Gallery Square, Walsall, West Midlands, WS2 8LG
Tel: 01922 654 400
Email: info@artatwalsall.org.uk
Website: www.artatwalsall.org.uk
Tues-Sat 10.00-17.00 Sun 12.00-17.00 Closed Mondays
A wide ranging number of impressive collections which include The Garman Ryan Collection, Permanent Art Collection, The Garman Ryan Epstein Collection and the Epstein Collection Archive and Library

Derby Museum And Art Gallery

The Strand, Derby, Derbyshire, DE1 1BS
Tel: 01332 716 659
(Mon) 11.00-17.00, (Tue-Sat) 10.00-17.00, (Sun) 14.00-17.00.
Work by local 18C artist Joseph Wright and a wide range of important collections including porcelain, paintings, archaeology, history, geology and wildlife.

Stop House

Oxford Canal Tow Path, Braunston, Northamptonshire, NN11 7JQ
Tel: 01788 890 666
Email: braunston@britishwaterways.co.uk
Please call for opening times
Small exhibition explaining about the canal, the boats, the marina and the locks.
The house is where tolls used to be collected from passing boats

Wolverhampton Art Gallery

Lichfield Street, Wolverhampton, West Midlands, WV1 1DU
Tel: 01902 552 055
Email: info@wolverhamptonart.org.uk
Website: www.wolverhamptonart.org.uk
Mon-Sat 10.00-17.00
Award winning gallery with permanent exhibits of 18, 19 & 20C paintings and
sculptures. The gallery also houses the largest collection of contemporary art in
the region.

Ikon Gallery

1 Oozells Square, Brindleyplace, Birmingham, West Midlands, B1 2HS
Tel: 0121 248 0708
Email: art@ikon-gallery.co.uk
Website: www.ikon-gallery.co.uk
Open Tues-Sun 11.00-18.00
Ikon is one of Europe's premier venues for new art. Ikon organises gallery tours,
special events, educational workshops and public talks.

Beckford Silk

The Silk Printing Centre, Ashton Road, Beckford, Gloucestershire, GL20 7AU
Tel: 01386 881 507
Email: sales@beckfordsilk.co.uk
Website: www.beckfordsilk.co.uk
Open Mon-Sat 09.00-17.30
The silk printing centre is a design studio where textile designs are created and
developed. Visitors have a printers eye view of the process of hand printing silk.

Harts Barn Flower and Craft Centre

Harts Barn Farm, Monmouth Road, Longhope, Gloucestershire, GL17 0QD
Tel: 01452 830 954
Apr 1 - Sep 30 (Tues-Sun) 10.00-17.30 October 1st - March 31st (Tues-Sun) 10.00-16.00
An extensive range of local crafts and exhibitions and a flower barn with all the
flowers grown on site.

Ye Olde Pork Pie Shoppe and Sausage Shop

Dickinson and Morris, 10 Nottingham Street, Melton Mowbray, Leicestershire, LE13 1NW

Tel: 01664 482 068

Email: dickinsonandmorris@porkpie.co.uk

Website: www.porkpie.co.uk

Open daily except Sundays 08.00-17.00

Producers of authentic Melton Mowbray pork pies. Visitors can watch demonstrations of hand raising pork pies.

Old Dairy Farm Centre

Upper Stowe, Weedon, Northamptonshire, NN7 4SH

Tel: 01327 340 525

Email: helen.brodie@old-dairy-farm-centre.co.uk

Website: www.old-dairy-farm-centre.co.uk

Open all year daily 10.00-17.30 Jan & Feb closes at 16.30

The workshops include an iron worker, furniture maker, antiques, clothes and needlecrafts with demonstrations

Derwent Crystal Limited

Shaw Croft, Ashbourne, Derbyshire, DE6 1GH

Tel: 01335 345 219

Email: sales@derwentcrystal.co.uk

Website: www.derwentcrystal.co.uk

Gift Shop Open Mon-Sat 09.00-17.00 Displays Mon-Fri 09.00-13.30

Displays of blowing, manufacturing and decorating of full lead English crystal glass wear.

Brewery Art

Brewery Court, Cirencester, Gloucestershire, GL7 1JH

Tel: 01285 657 181

Email: admin@breweryarts.org.uk

Website: www.breweryarts.org.uk

Open all year Mon-Fri 10.00-17.00 Sat 09.30-17.30

Converted brewery housing 17 workshops including a jeweller, glass blower, upholsterer and ceramicist.

Alford Pottery

Commercial Road, Alford, Lincolnshire, LN13 9EY

Tel: 01507 463 342

May-Sept Mon-Sat 09.00-17.00 Oct-April Mon-Fri 09.00-17.00 (Closed 12.30-13.30 for lunch)

Stone wear pottery is hand made on the premises. There is a small showroom where pots can be purchased and the working area viewed.

Conderton Pottery

The Old Forge, Conderton, Tewkesbury, Gloucestershire, GL20 7PP
Tel: 01386 725 387
Email: toffmilway@telco4u.net
Website: www.toffmilway.co.uk
Open All year 09.30-17.00
Hand made salt glazed stonewear are made by crafts men on the premises. All parts of the workshop are open to view

Manor Stables Craft Centre

Manor Stables, Lincoln Road, Fulbeck, Lincolnshire, NG32 3JN
Tel: 01400 272 779
Website: www.cuttinglane.com
Open Tue-Sun 10.30-16.30
Houses individual craft workshops including spinning weaving, clock maker, saddlery, and home made produce.

Sharpe's Pottery Visitors Centre

23 West Street, Swadlincote, Derbyshire, DE11 9DJ
Tel: 01283 222 600
Email: sdcollections@btconnect.com
Website: www.sharpes.org.uk
Mon-Sat 10.00-15.30
Exhibits and displays tell the story of the South Derbyshire pottery industry from the 16-20C

Stockwith Mill

Harrington Road, Hagworthingham, Spilsby, Lincolnshire, PE23 4NE
Tel: 01507 588 221
Email: info@stockwithmill.co.uk
March-Oct Tues-Sun 10.30-18.00 Nov & Dec Thurs-Sun 10.30-17.00
A 17C watermill with a permanent exhibition on the poet Tennyson. There is also an art gallery, craft shop and country walks

Newark Town Treasures and Art Gallery

Newark Town Hall, Market Place, Newark, Nottinghamshire, NG24 1DU
Tel: 01636 680 333
Email: post@newark.gov.uk
Website: www.newarktowntreasures.co.uk
Mon-Fri 11.00-16.00 Sat 12.00-16.00
The Town Treasures consist of Civic Regalia, Civic Plate and Civic Gifts. The Gallery has a permanent exhibition on work by Sir William Nicholson and Sir Stanley Spencer and runs temporary exhibitions throughout the year

Wroxeter Roman Vineyard

Glebe Farm, Near Shrewsbury, Wroxeter, Shropshire, SY5 6PQ
Tel: 01743 761 888
Email: wine@wroxetervineyard.co.uk
Website: www.wroxetervineyard.co.uk
Mon-Sat 10.00-17.00 Sun 11.00-17.00
Producers of red wine and quality sparkling wine with free winetasting at the shop.The vineyard is situated on the site of Uriconium Roman City

The Lace Centre

Severn's Building, Castle Road, Nottingham, Nottinghamshire, NG1 6AA
Tel: 0115 941 3539
Open all year
An exhibition of Northern Lace housed within a 14C building. Bobbin Lace demonstrations on Thursdays 14.00-16.00

CASTLES

Clun Castle

Offa's Dyke, Off the A488, Clun, Shropshire
Access at any reasonable time
The castle was built after the Norman Conquest to defend the Welsh Borders but was abandoned in the 16C. It's most striking feature is the huge grey stone tower on a mound.

Oakham Castle

The Market Place, Oakham, Rutland, LE15 6HW
Tel: 01572 758 440
Email: museum@rutland.gov.uk
Mon-Sat 10.30-17.00 Sun 14.00-16.00
Built 1191 all that remains is the banqueting hall and fragment of wall. The banqueting hall has whitewashed walls covered with horse shoes dating back to an ancient custom where dignitaries had to present an ornamental horseshoe when visiting Oakham

Saint Briavels Castle

Youth Hostel Association, St Briavels, Lydney, Gloucestershire, GL15 6RG
Tel: 01594 530 272
Email: stbriavels@yha.org.uk
Open at any reasonable time now a youth hostel
This 12C castle is now used as a youth hostel and is set in the marvellous walking countryside.

Clifford Castle

Clifford, Near Hay-on-Wye, Clifford, Herefordshire
Tel: 01497 831 798
Open all year at all times
Traditional birth place of fair Rosamund, The remaining ruins of this 11C castle comprise of a gatehouse hall and round tower

Moreton Corbet Castle

Moreton Corbet, off B5063 7 miles NE of Shrewsbury, Moreton Corbet, Shropshire
Open all year at all times
At this site you will find the remains of the castle with a small 13C keep, an substantial remains of an Elizabethan Mansion.

Caer Caradoc

Church Stretton, Church Stretton, Shropshire
Access at all times
This hill fort is reputed to be the site of Caractacus' last stand. Also linked to King Arthur. The legendary cauldron of Di-Wrnach which contains the treasures of Britain and the magical sword is hidden in a cave below the summit of Caer Caradoc

Bolingbroke Castle

In Old Bolingbroke, 16 miles N of Boston, Old Bolingbroke, Lincolnshire
Tel: 01529 461 499
Website: www.english-heritage.org.uk
April-Sept 09.00-21.00 Oct-March 09.00-19.00
The remains of a 13C hexagonal castle, the birthplace of Henry I in 1367

Acton Burnell Castle

In Acton Burnell, 8 miles S of Shrewsbury, Acton Burnell, Shropshire
Website: www.english-heritage.org.uk
Access at any resonable time
A shell of a fortified 13C manor house and one of England's most romantic ruins. The site of the first Parliament where the Commons were represented

CHURCHES & CATHEDRALS

Holy Trinity Church

Old Town, Stratford, Warwickshire, CV37 6BG
Tel: 01789 266 316
Email: office@stratford-upon-avon.org
Website: www.stratford-upon-avon.org
March - October Mon-Sat 09.00-17.00 Sun 12.30-17.00 April-Sept Mon-Sat 08.30-18.00
Sun 12.30-17.00 Nov - Feb Mon-Sat 09.00-16.00 Sun 12.30-17.00
This fine gothic building that was built between the 13 & 15C, is the final resting
place of William Shakespeare. The original wooden spire of the church was
replaced in the 18C. £1 donation asked to visit Shakespeare's Grave

Saint Chad's

St Chad's Terrace, Quarry Park, Shrewsbury, Shropshire
Tel: 01743 365 478
Email: saint.chads@ukonline.co.uk
Website: www.stchadsshrewsbury.org.uk
Mon-Fri 10.00-13.00
England's largest round church with it's celebrated wedding cake tower. The
church was consecrated in 1792 .The graveyard was used in the film " A
Christmas Carol" as the location of Scrooge's grave

Shrewsbury Abbey

Abbey Foregate, Shrewsbury, Shropshire, SY2 6BS
Tel: 01743 232 723
Email: jane@shrewsburyabbey.com
Website: www.shrewsburyabbey.com
Daily 10.00-15.00
This abbey was a Benedictine Monastery founded in 1080. The most impressive
feature is the large window of Heraldic glass from the 14C. Original Norman
door, and four original nave pillars with connecting arches from the original
church building

Church Of The Holy Sepulchre

Sheep Street, Peacock Place, Northampton, Northamptonshire
Tel: 01604 754782
Email: john@crusader-round.fsnet.co.uk
May-Sep Wed 12.00-14.00, Sat 14.00-16.00
The church was built at the same time as the castle in 1100 and is probably
Northampton's oldest building. It is one of only four examples of a round church
in the country, and is still used as a Parish Church

Pershore Abbey

Church Street, Pershore, Worchestershire, WR10 1DT
Tel: 01386 552 071
Email: vicar@pershoreabbey.fsnet.co.uk
Website: www.pershoreabbey.fsnet.co.uk
Abbey Open Daily 09.00-17.00 Visitors Centre Open East - Sept Sat 10.00-17.00 Sun 14.30-18.00
This ancient abbey church which was founded in the 7C, is now a flourishing Parish Church. Major features include a fine lantern tower with ringing platform, decorative vaulting and a newly restored tower.

Kingswood Abbey Gatehouse

Kingswood, 1 mile SW of Wotton-Under-Edge, Kingswood, Gloucestershire, GL12
Exterior view at any reasonable time. Key for interior available from 3 Wotton Rd, Abbey St, 10.00-15.30 weekdays
This 16C gatehouse is the only surviving remnant of a Cistercian Abbey dating from the middle ages.

Croyland Abbey

East Stree, Croyland, Lincolnshire, PE6 0EN
Tel: 01733 210 763
Email: mail@croyland.co.uk
Website: www.croylandabbey.co.uk
Open all year 08.00-dusk Daily
A Benedictine Abbey founded in AD 716. Surviving original features include a 15C aisle (now used as Parish Church) 12C Norman arch, and 13C West front.

Croxden Abbey

Croxden, 5 miles NW of Uttoxeter off A522, Croxden, Staffordshire
Access at any reasonable time
This Cistercian abbey was founded in 1176 and today visitors can wander around the ruined remains.

The Tupholme Abbey Ruins

On the B1190 2 miles E of Bardney, Bardney, Lincolnshire
Email: info@lincsheritage.org
Website: www.lincsheritage.org
Open dawn-dusk
The ruins of this 12C permonstratensian abbey are set in twenty acres of grassland which include a picnic site. Features include the refectory wall standing to eaves height and a unique readers pulpit.

Birmingham Cathedral

Colmore Row, Birmingham, West Midlands, B3 2QB
Tel: 0121 262 1840
Email: enquiries@birminghamcathedral.com
Website: www.birminghamcathedral.org.uk
Winter Weekdays 07.30-18.00 Summer Weekdays 07.30-16.00 Weekends 09.00-16.00
English Baroque style church built in the early 18C with beautifully restored city
centre church yard. Famous for its four large stained glass windows designed by
Sir Edward Burne - Jones

Derby Cathedral

18-19 Iron Gate, Derby, Derbyshire, DE1 3GP
Tel: 01332 341 201
Email: office@derbycathedral.org
Website: www.derbycathedral.org
Daily 08.30-18.00
The Cathedral's medieval tower is the second highest in England at 212 feet,
features of interest include the World famous wrought iron screen by Robert
Bakewell. Visitor's Centre across the road

Gloucester Cathedral

2 College Green, Gloucester, Gloucestershire, GL1 2LR
Tel: 01452 528 095
Email: office@gloucestercathedral.org.uk
Website: www.gloucestercathedral.org.uk
Open daily 08.30-17.00 Guided tours available Mon-Sat 10.30-16.00 Sun 12.00-14.30
The Cathedral interesting features include an exhibition, treasury, crypt, chapter
house and precincts.

Hereford Cathedral

5 The Cloisters, Hereford, Herefordshire, HR1 2NG
Tel: 01432 374 0200
Email: office@herefordcathedral.co.uk
Website: www.herefordcathedral.org
Open daily 07.30-17.30 Sun open till 15.30
This cathedral was built on the site of a 7C church and has a mixture of styles
from Norman to early English

Leicester Cathedral

21 St Martin's, Leicester, Leicestershire, LE1 5DE
Tel: 0116 262 5294
Email: cathedral@leicester.anglican.org
Website: www.cathedral.leicester.anglican.org
Open daily 07.30-17.00
The only medieval cathedral with three spires, dating from 1195. A major Christian centre for 1300 years. The cathedral's treasures include an 8C illuminated manuscript, medieval tiled floor , the Lichfield Gospels and 16C and 19C glass windows

Worcester Cathedral

College Green, Worcester, Worchestershire, WR1 2LH
Tel: 01905 611 002
Email: info@worcestercathedral.org.uk
Website: www.cofe-worcester.org.uk
Open daily 07.30-18.00
Interesting features include, King John's tomb, Prince Arthur's chantry, Norman Crypt and chapter house.

Church Of St Mary

Church Street, Edwinstowe, Mansfield, Nottinghamshire, NG21 9QA
Tel: 01623 822 430
East-Oct 12.00-16.00
This 12-15C Church is supposed to be where Robin Hood married Maid Marrion, and is also the original burial place of King Edwin of Northumbria

Langley Chapel and Gatehouse

Acton Burnell, Near Shrewsbury, Acton Burnell, Shropshire, SY5
Access at any resonable time
A small 17C chapel with 17C wooden fittings and furniture

St Mary Magdalene Church

Market Place, Hucknall, Nottinghamshire, NG15
Tel: 0115 963 2033
Email: richard@hucknall-parish-church.org.uk
Website: www.hucknall-parish-church.org.uk
Mon-Thurs 10.00-12.00 & 14.00-16.00 Fri 10.00-16.00 Sat 10.00-12.00
Lord Byron and his ancestors are buried in a family vault within this church. The church also contains a collection of stained glass by eminent Victorian stained glass artists

Thornton Abbey and Gatehouse

18 miles NE of Scunthorpe, Ulceby, Lincolnshire, DN39 6TU

Abbey open Daily 10.00-18.00 Gatehouse (April-Sep) 1st and 3rd Sunday in the month 12.00-18.00 (Oct-March) 3rd Sunday in month 12.00-16.00

The abbey was founded in 1139 and its remains can still be seen. The 11C Gatehouse is recognised as one of the grandest in Europe

Lilleshall Abbey

On unclassified road off the A518, 4 miles N of Oakengates, Between Telford and Newport, Oakengates, Shropshire

Tel: 0121 625 6820

Website: www.english-heritage.org.uk

Access at any resonable time

Ruins of an Abbey of Augustinian Cannons dissolved in 1538, as well as the remains of a 12th and 13thC Church

GARDENS PARKS & WALKS

Forest Of Dean Sculpture Trail

Beechenhurst Lodge, Near Coleford, Forest Of Dean, Gloucestershire

Tel: 01594 833 057

Website: www.forestofdean-sculpture.org.uk

The trail is open Dawn-Dusk daily it starts and ends at Beechenhurst Lodge Open April -Oct 10.00-18.00 Nov-March 10.00-17.00

An easy walk through the forest that is littered with art work and sculptures including a giant chair sitting at the top of a hill.

Sarehole Mill

Cole Bank Road, Hall Green, Birmingham, West Midlands, B13 0BD

Tel: 0121 777 6612

Website: www.birmingham.gov.uk/sarehole

Mill open to visitors April-Oct Tues-Sun 11.30-16.00

This restored water mill dates from 1765 and the mill and surrounding area have close connections with J R R Tolkein. Across the road is a house where he spent 4 years of his childhood . Many of his ideas were inspired by the building and the gloomy lake

Sherwood Forest Country Park

Edwinstowe, Mansfield, Nottinghamshire, NG21 9HN
Daily dawn-dusk to visit the outdoor areas of the park
450 acres of oak and silver birch trees that are crammed with footpaths and
trails. In the forest is the Major Oak, where Maid Marion and Robin Hood
plighted their troth.

David Austin Roses-Rose Garden

Bowling Green Lane, Albrighton, 8 miles W of Wolverhampton, Albrighton, Shropshire
Tel: 01902 376 300
Email: plant_centre@davidaustinroses.co.uk
Website: www.davidaustinroses.com
Daily 09.00- 17.00
This 2 acre rose garden is considered to be one of the best in the world. There
are five main areas covering over 700 varieties of roses, but concentrating
mainly on David Austin's English Rose.

Kenchester Water Gardens

Church Road, Lyde, Hereford, Herefordshire, HR1 3AB
Tel: 01432 270 981
Mon-Sat 09.00-17.30 Sun 10.30-16.30
This water garden centre has a national collection of water lilies. Displays
include plants, fountains, landscapes, fish and tropical and marine aquariums.

University Of Leicester Botanic Garden

Glebe Road, Oadby, Leicester, Leicestershire, LE2 2NE
Tel: 0116 271 2933
Email: hortltr@ukonline.co.uk
Website: www.le.ac.uk/biology/botanicgarden/
Open all year Mon-Fri 10.00-16.00 Sat & Sun 3rd week in March-2nd week in November
10.00-16.00
This 16 acre Botanic Garden consists of several individual gardens including
rock garden, roses, trees and heather gardens

Belper River Gardens

Matlock Road, Belper, Derbyshire, DE56
Tel: 01773 841 482
Open dawn-dusk
Popular river garden often used for film and tv locations. There is a Summer
programme of concerts and theatre as well as rowing boats and motor boats for
hire.

Haddonstone Showgarden

Haddonstone Ltd, The Forge House, East Haddon, Northamptonshire, NN6 8DB
Tel: 01604 770 711
Email: info@haddonstone.co.uk
Website: www.haddonstone.co.uk
Open all year, Mon-Fri 09.30-17.00
Beautiful walled Manor garden that displays classic garden ornaments including
fountains, sundials, bird baths and urns.

Sandwell Valley Country Park

Salters Lane, Sandwell, West Bromwich, West Midlands, B71 4BG
Tel: 0121 553 0220
All year dawn-dusk. Free in the week but there is a small charge at weekend and bank
holidays,
1700 Acres of woodlands, nature trails, lakes and picnic sites

Sutton Park & Visitors Centre

Park Road, Towngate, Sutton Park, Sutton Coldfield, West Midlands, B74 2YT
Tel: 0121 355 6370
Email: sutton.park.visitor.centre@birmingham.gov.uk
Winter 10.00-16.30 Summer 10.00-19.00 Daily
This is Birmingham's largest park with 2400 Acres of woodlands, lakes, walks,
picnic areas and play areas. The whole site is a Natural Nature Reserve

HISTORIC HOUSES

Aston Hall

Trinity Road, Aston, Birmingham, West Midlands, B6 6JB
Tel: 0121 327 0062
Open Easter to the end of October Tuesday to Sunday 11.30 -16.00. Closed Mondays
Spectacular turreted Jacobean mansion with roughly 20 rooms open to the
public. Including the panelled long gallery which runs the entire width of the
house

Billinghay Old Vicarage Cottage and Parish Office

Church Street, Billinghay, Lincolnshire, LN4 4HN
Tel: 01526 861 845
Email: tic_sleaford@n-kesteven.gov.uk
Please contact for exact opening times
This thatched cottage dates from 1650 and has a display of old village
photographs

Oak House

Oak Road, West Bromwich, West Midlands, B70 8HJ

Tel: 0121 553 0759

April-Sept Mon, Tues, Wed & Fri 10.00-17.00 Sat & Sun 14.00-17.00 Oct-March Mon, Tues, Wed, Fri 10.00-16.00 Sat 13.30-16.00

Elizabethan period house with unique lantern tower and many panelled rooms houses a collection of English Oak furniture dating from the 16 & 17C.

Haden Hill House

Halesowen Road, Cradley Heath, West Midlands, B64 7JU

Tel: 01384 569 444

Website: www.lea.sandwell.gov.uk/museums/hadenhill.htm

Tues -Fri 10.00-17.00, Sat & Sun 13.00-17.00

Grade 2 listed Victorian building of three storeys. Features many architectural styles including Gothic, Dutch, Tudor and Classical.

Sutton Scarsdale Hall

Sutton Scarsdale, Between Chesterfield and Bolsover, Chesterfield, Derbyshire, S44

Tel: 01604 735 400

Summer Daily 10.00-18.00 Winter Daily 10.00-16.00

The shell of a great 18C Baroque Mansion which was designed in 1721. English Heritage have restored the building to make it safe and visitors can now see fragments of its former rich plaster decoration

Moseley Hall Ice House

Moseley Private Park, Alcester Road, Moseley, West Midlands, B13 8DD

Tel: 0121 449 2133

Exterior view at all times. Occasional weekend openings to the interior please telephone for details 0121 449 2133

This 18C ice house was recently excavated and restored by the Moseley Society and is in a remarkably good state of preservation.

The Old House

High Town, Hereford, Herefordshire, HR1 2AA

Tel: 01432 260 694

Email: llatcham@herefordshire.gov.uk

Website: www.herefordshire.gov.uk

Open all year Tues-Sat 10.00-17.00 April-Sep Sun 10.00-14.00

Built in 1621 and furnished in 17C style throughout its three floors, the house includes kitchen and bedrooms originally part of Butchers Row. There is also an interpretative display on Hereford during the Civil War

Bishop Asbury Cottage

Newton Road, Great Barr, West Midlands, B42

Tel: 0121 553 0759

Email: oakhouse@sandwell.gov.uk

Open to public on selected days in the year please contact for dates

The boyhood home of Francis Asbury who was sent to America in 1771 and became the first American Methodist Bishop.

Revolution House

61 High Street, Old Whittington, Chesterfield, Derbyshire, S41 9LA

Tel: 01246 345 727

Email: museum@chesterfieldbc.gov.uk

Website: www.chesterfieldbc.gov.uk

April-Sept 11.00-16.00 Daily except Tues

300 years ago this cottage was an alehouse and it was here that three noblemen met to plan to overthrow King James II in favour of William and Mary of Orange. Today period 17C furniture, exhibitions and a video tell the story of the Revolution

The Manor House

Manor Road, Donington le Heath, Coalville, Leicestershire, LE67 2FW

Tel: 01530 831 259

Email: museums@leics.gov.uk

Website: www.leics.gov.uk/museums

April -Sept Mon-Sun 11.30-17.00 Oct, Nov & March Mon-Sun 11.30-15.00 Dec-Feb Sat & Sun 11.30-15.00

The Manor House allows visitors to see how people lived in the Medieval, Tudor and Stewart times and has many fine oak furnishings and a period herb garden

Belgrave Hall

Church Road, Belgrave, Leicestershire, LE4 5PE

Tel: 0116 266 6590

Email: gordon001@leicester.gov.uk

Feb-Nov Sat-Wed 11.00-16.30 Sun 13.00-16.30

This Queen Anne Country House was built between 1709 and 1713 has reconstructed period rooms and is famous for its ghostly sightings and unexplained paranormal activity

Greens Mill and Science Centre

Windmill Lane, Sneinton, Nottinghamshire, NG2 4QB
Tel: 0115 915 6878
Email: access@ncmg.demon.co.uk
Website: www.greensmill.org.uk
Wed-Sun 10.00-16.00 all year
A Grade II listed building and one of a few working inner city windmills in Britain
where visitors can discover the process of turning grain into flour

HISTORIC SITES

Arthur's Stone

Dorstone, On the A465 to Hereford take the B4347 to Dorstone, 7 miles E of Hay-on-Wye off
B4348, Dorstone, Herefordshire
Access at any reasonable time
A prehistoric burial chamber formed of large blocks of stone.

Fotheringhay Castle Site

Castle Farm Cottage, Off the A605, 4 miles from Oundle, Fotheringhay, Northamptonshire,
PE8 5HZ
Tel: 01832 226 326
Email: oundletic@east-northamptonshire.gov.uk
Open dusk-dawn Closed 7-14 Jan
There are no buildings standing at this site, but the grassy mound of
Fotheringhay Castle in where Richard III was born in 1452 and Mary Queen Of
Scots was executed in 1587, thistles still grow on the site.

Great Witcombe Roman Villa

Witcombe, 5 miles SE of Gloucester off the A417, Whitcombe, Gloucestershire
Tel: 01451 862 000
Email: aonb@cotswold.gov.uk
Access at any reasonable time-Exterior View Only
Built around three sides of a courtyard the remains of a large villa overlook an
enchanting valley

Nesscliffe Hill and Kynaston's Cave

Nesscliffe, On the A5, Nesscliffe, Shropshire
Access at all times
Nesscliffe Hill stands in a Country Park surrounded by woods and footpaths,
popular with rock climbers.Kynaston Cave is where the highwayman Humphrey
Kynaston lived and died after he was outlawed for his debts.

Notgrove Long Barrow

1.5 miles NW of Notgrove, On the A436, Notgrove, Gloucestershire
Tel: 0117 975 0700
Email: customers@english-heritage.org.uk
Access at any resonable time
A Neolithic Burial Mound which opens from a stone built general passage and
has chambers for human remains.

Cirencester Roman Amphitheatre

Next to bypass on the W of Cirencester, Cirencester, Gloucestershire
Tel: 0117 975 0700
Email: customers@english-heritage.org.uk
Access at any resonable time
Large well preserved Roman amphitheatre still rises 25 feet above the ground
and once held stone terraces and wooden seating for 8 000 spectators

Bolsover Cundy House

Craggs Road, Bolsover, Derbyshire
Tel: 01246 822 844
Website: www.english-heritage.org.uk
Access at any resonable time
This 17C Conduit House used to supply water to Bolsover Castle and has been
recently restored

Mitchell's Fold Stone Circle

Stapeley Hill, Chirbury, Shropshire
Tel: 0121 625 6820
Access at any resonable time
A Prehistoric Bronze Age stone circle with only 15 of the original 30 stones still
visible

Julian's Bower

Back Street, Alkborough, Scunthorpe, Lincolnshire, DN15 9JN
Tel: 01724 720 484
Access at any resonable time
A turf cut maze dating from Roman times with an explanatory plaque

Eleanor Cross

Village of Geddington, Off the A43 between Kettering and Corby, Geddington,
Northamptonshire
Website: www.english-heritage.org.uk
Access at any resonable time
This stone cross is only one of three remaining that mark the places where the
funeral cortege of Eleanor Of Castile (Wife of Henry I) rested on the journey from
Harby in Nottinghamshire, where she died, to Westminster Abbey her final
resting place

EXHIBITIONS

Ellesmere Mere Visitors Centre

Mereside, Ellesmere, Shropshire, SY12 0PA
Tel: 01691 622 981
Email: ellesmere.tourism@shropshire-cc.gov.uk
March-Oct Daily Nov & Dec Weekends only
Tourist information and visitors centre with beautiful gardens and woodlands.

Barton Clay Pits Visitors Centre

The Old Boat House, Waterside Road, Barton-upon-Humber, Lincolnshire, DN18 5BA
Tel: 01724 297 388
Nature Reserve open all year daily Visitors Centre open East-Sept Weekends
The clay pits form a Nature Reserve that stretch for five miles along the Humber
Bank. The information centre has details on the area

FESTIVALS

Artsfest

Birmingham, West Midlands
Website: www.artsfest.org.uk
Please see website for exact dates each year
UK's largest free arts festival with events across the city centre.

MUSEUMS

Warwickshire Museum

The Market Place, Swan Street, Warwick, Warwickshire, CV34 4SA
Tel: 01926 412 500
Email: museum@warwickshire.gov.uk
Website: www.warwickshire.gov.uk/museum
Tues - Sat 10.00-17.30, May - Sept only Sun 11.30-17.00
Various displays including geological and wildlife exhibits, a huge tapestry dating from 1647 depicting a map of the country, and a video exhibit about the 1694 Great Fire.

Saint John's House

Saint John's, Cotton End, Warwick, Warwickshire, CV34 4NF
Tel: 01926 412 021
Email: museum@warwickshire.gov.uk
Website: www.warwickshire.gov.uk/museum
Tue-Sat 10.00-17.00 (Sun May-Sept Only) 14.30-17.00
Small museum housing displays of period costume and social history exhibits.

Broadfield House Glass Museum

Compton Drive, Kingswinford, West Midlands, DY6 9NS
Tel: 01384 812 745
Email: glass.museum@dudley.gov.uk
Website: www.glassmuseum.org.uk
Tues-Sun 12.00-16.00
This glass museum has a collection of approx 10 000 glass items, there is also a glassmaking studio where visitors can watch the craftsmen at work

Walsall Leather Museum

Littleton Street West, Wisemore, Walsall, West Midlands, WS2 8EQ
Tel: 01922 721 153
Email: leathermuseum@walsall.gov.uk
Website: www.walsall.gov.uk/leathermuseum/
Tues-Sat 10.00-17.00 Sun 12.00-17.00 (Nov-March closes at 16.00)
Displays the history of the development of the leather industry and its effect on the town.

Birmingham Museum and Gallery

Chamberlain Square, Birmingham, West Midlands, B3 3DH
Tel: 0121 303 2834
Email: bmag_enquiries@birmingham.gov.uk
Website: www.bmag.org.uk
Mon-Thurs 10.00-17.00 Fri 10.30-17.00 Sat 10.00-17.00 Sun 12.30-17.00
This museum and gallery offers temporary exhibitions and permanent collections covering archaeology, industrial history and fine art

Museum Of The Jewellery Quarter

75-79 Vyse Street, Hockley, Birmingham, West Midlands, B18 6HA
Tel: 0121 554 3598
Website: www.bmag.org.uk
East-Oct Tues-Sun 11.30-16.00
This museum is in the Old Smith and Pepper Jewellery workshop and gives demonstrations and tours of the working life at the turn of the century

Soho House

Soho Avenue, Off Soho Road, Hansworth, Birmingham, West Midlands, B18 5LB
Tel: 0121 554 9122
Website: www.bmag.org.uk
East- Oct Tues-Sun 11.30-16.00
The former home of Industrialist Matthew Boulton with original items of his work on display.

Jewry Wall and Archeology Museum

St Nicholas Circle, Leicester, Leicestershire, LE1 4LB
Tel: 01162 254 971
Email: museums@leicester.gov.uk
Feb-Nov Sat & Sun 11.00-16.30
The history of Leicester from Pre-Historic to Present day. Roman relics, Fosse Way milestones, mosaic pavement and beautiful medieval glass.

Central Museum And Art Gallery

Guildhall Road, Northampton, Northamptonshire, NN1 1DP
Tel: 01604 838 111
Email: museums@northampton.gov.uk
(Mon-Sat) 10.00-17.00 Sun 14.00-17.00
Exceptional displays of shoes including silk slippers, clogs and high heeled 19C court shoes as well as displays on local history from Roman times to the present.

Buxton Museum And Art Gallery

Terrace Road, Buxton, Derbyshire, SK17 6DA

Tel: 01298 246 58

Email: buxton.museum@derbyshire.gov.uk

East-Sept Tue-Fri 09.30-17.30 Sat 09.30-17.00 Sun 10.30-17.00 Sept-East Tues-Fri
09.30-17.30 Sat 09.30-17.00

This museum includes Georgian Rooms, a Roman Temple and displays of local
rocks, minerals and archaeological finds.

The Old Rectory Museum

Rectory Place, Loughborough, Leicestershire, LE11 1UW

Tel: 01509 843 297

April-Oct Sat 10.00-16.00

This museum displays archaeological finds from in and around Loughborough,
and is housed in a 13C stone rectory

Ludlow Museum

11-13 Castle Street, Ludlow, Shropshire, SY8 1AS

Tel: 01584 873 857

Email: ludlow.museum@shropshire-cc.gov.uk

April-Oct Mon-Sat 10.30-13.00 & 14.00-17.00 June-Aug Sun 10.30-13.00 & 14.00-17.00

Details the early history of the area through an interactive gallery

Shrewsbury Museum And Art Gallery

Barker Street, Shrewsbury, Shropshire, SY1 1QH

Tel: 01743 361 196

Email: museums@shrewsbury.gov.uk

Website: www.shrewsburymuseums.com

Jan-Mid Sept Mon-Sat 10.00-17.00 Sun 10.00-16.00 Mid Sept-Dec Tues-Sat 10.00-16.00

Collections and displays of costume, geology. local and natural history and
archaeology. Plus special exhibitions including major contemporary art

Derby Industrial Museum

Silk Mill Lane, Off Full Street, Derby, Derbyshire, DE1 3AF

Tel: 01332 255 308

All year Mon 11.00-17.00 Tues-Sat 10.00-17.00 Sun 14.00-17.00

Details the history of Derby's industries including a collection of Rolls Royce aero
engines and a railway engineering gallery

North Lincolnshire Museum
Oswald Road, Scunthorpe, Lincolnshire, DN15 7BD
Tel: 01724 843 533
Tues -Sat 10.00-16.00 Sun 13.00-16.00
A regional museum for North Lincolnshire with a changing programme of temporary exhibitions plus a display of local history

NATURE & WILDLIFE

Ulverscroft Nature Reserve
6 miles SW of Loughborough, Loughborough, Leicestershire
Access at all times
This Nature Reserve is part of the ancient forest of Charnwood, during the spring time Ulverscroft is covered with bluebells

FARMERS MARKETS

Mansfield Farmers Market
Buttercross Market, Westgate, Mansefield, Nottinghamshire
3rd Tuesday of the month 09.00-15.00
Farmers Market with local produce on sale

Worcester Farmers Market
Royal Worcester, Severn Street, Worcester, Worcester, Worcestershire
1st Sunday of the month 10.00-14.00
Farmers Market with local produce on sale

Stafford Farmers Market
Market Square, Stafford, Staffordshire
2nd Saturday of the month 09.00-16.00
Farmers Market with local produce on sale

Market Rasen Farmers Market
Market Place, Market Rasen, Lincolnshire
1st Tuesday of the month 09.00-15.30
Farmers Market with local produce on sale

Leicester Farmers Market
Market Place, Leicester, Leicestershire
Last Wednesday of the month 09.00-14.00
Farmers Market with local produce on sale

Oswestry Farmers Market
The Bailey Head, Ostwestry, Shropshire
Tel: 01691 68022
Last Friday of the month 09.00-14.00
Farmers Market with local produce on sale

East Anglia-England

ART GALLERIES/ARTS & CRAFTS

Babylon Gallery

Babylon Bridge, Waterside, Ely, Cambridgeshire, CB7 4AU
Tel: 01353 669 022
Email: info@babylongallery.co.uk
Website: www.adec.org.uk/babylon
Tues-Sat 10.00-16.00 Sun 11.00-17.00
This gallery has a programme of contemporary visual arts and mixes touring exhibitions with curated exhibitions by local and regional artists

Kettles Yard

University Of Cambridge, Castle Street, Cambridge, Cambridgeshire, CB3 0AQ
Tel: 01223 352 124
Email: mail@kettlesyard.com.ac.uk
Website: www.kettlesyard.co.uk
Summer Tues-Sun 13.30-16.30 Winter Tues-Sun 14.00-16.00
A collection of 20C paintings and sculptures also temporary exhibitions, talks and discussions.

The John Russell Gallery

4-6 Wherry Lane, Ipswich, Suffolk, IP4 1LG
Tel: 01473 212 051
Email: a.coe@artone.co.uk
Website: www.artone.co.uk/gallery.html
Mon-Sat 09.30-17.00
Represents over 160 of East Anglia's painters and sculptors

Cambridge Contemporary Art

6 Trinity Street, Cambridge, Cambridgeshire, CB2 1SU
Tel: 01223 324 222
Email: info@cambridgegallery.co.uk
Website: www.cambridgegallery.co.uk
Mon-Sat 09.00-17.30 Sundays 11.00-16.00
Changing exhibitions of painting, sculptures, crafts and furniture, by acknowledged masters, established artists and new talent.

Steeple Bumpstead Pottery and Gallery

Church Street, Steeple Bumpstead, Haverhill, Essex, CB9 7DB
Tel: 01440 730 260
Mon-Sat 10.00-18.00 Sunday 14.00-18.00
Working pottery with gallery set within a Victorian Village School.

Wroxham Barns

Tunstead Road, Hoveton, Norfolk, NR12 8QU
Tel: 01603 783 762
Email: info@wroxham-barns.co.uk
Website: www.wroxham-barns.co.uk
Open Daily 10.00-17.00
Rural craft centre which houses a selection of different crafts men's workshops
set in 18C barns, also on site is a gift shop and tea room

Norwich Puppet Theatre

St James, Whitefriars, Norwich, Norfolk, NR3 1TN
Tel: 01603 629 921
Email: info@puppettheatre.co.uk
Website: www.puppettheatre.co.uk
All year Mon-Fri 09.30-17.00 Building and foyer free to view-charge for puppet shows
Housed within a pre-formation Church. The building contains many original
architectural features including a 14C doorstep, 17C memorial stones and an
octagonal tower. The foyer was once the Lady Chapel and now displays puppets
from the past 20 years

The Pottery

Next to the Ship Inn, Narborough, Near King's Lynn, Narborough, Norfolk, PE32 1TE
Tel: 01760 337 208
All year daily 09.00-18.00
Visitors can watch hand made pottery, sculptures and garden pots being made,
the products can be viewed and purchased in the shop

Norwich Gallery

Norwich School Of Art And Design, 3-7 Redwell Street, Norwich, Norfolk, NR2 4SN
Tel: 01603 756 247
Email: nor.gal@nsad.ac.uk
Website: www.norwichgallery.co.uk
All year Mon-Sat 10.00-17.00
Exhibits work by contemporary living artists, provides exhibitions of new works
by artists of International reputation and provided a programme of talks,
seminars and events

CASTLES

Weeting Castle

Weeting, 2 miles N of Brandon off B1106, Weeting, Norfolk

Tel: 01604 730 320

Access at any reasonable time

Ruins of a Medieval Manor House with a rectangular moat

Baconsthorpe Castle

Baconsthorpe, $\frac{3}{4}$ mile N of village of Baconsthorpe off unclassified, Baconsthorpe, Norfolk

Access at any reasonable time

Remains of a 15C fortified house and moat.

Berkhamsted Castle

Berkhamsted, Berkhamsted, Hertfordshire

Tel: 01536 402 840

1st April-30 Sept Daily 10.00-18.00 1st Oct-31March Daily 10.00-16.00

Remains of an 11C motte and bailey castle. William the Conqueror finally accepted the surrender of the Saxons at Berkhamsted, after his defeat of King Harold at Hastings. Contact the keyholder on 01442 871737

Castle Acre Castle

At the end of Castle Acre, 5 miles N of Swaffham, Castle Acre, Norfolk

Access at any reasonable time

Set by the side of a village are the remains of a Norman Manor House which was built into a castle

CHURCHES & CATHEDRALS

Norwich Cathedral

The Close, Norwich, Norfolk, NR1 4DH

Tel: 01603 218 303

Email: linnie@cathedral.org.uk

Website: www.cathedral.org.uk

Open Daily 07.30-18.00 (Closes at 19.00 Mid may-Mid Sept) Free Guided tours Mon-Sat 10.45, 12.00 & 14.15

Norwich cathedral is definitely one attraction to visit if you're in the area. Guided tours can be arranged or you can wander around the building and soak up the interior architecture yourself for free.

St Edmundsbury Cathedral

Angel Hill, Bury St Edmunds, Suffolk, IP33 1LS

Tel: 01284 754 933

Email: cathedral@burycathedral.fsnet.co.uk

Website: www.stedscathedral.co.uk

Daily 08.00-18.00

This has been a site for worship for nearly 1000 years. The nave of the present church dates from 1503 and the church has been expanded over the decades including the building of a gothic style lantern tower which was completed in 2004

Whipsnade Tree Cathedral

Whipsnade, Near Dunstable, Whipsnade, Bedfordshire

Tel: 01582 872 406

Email: henryblyth@yahoo.co.uk

Website: www.nationaltrust.org.uk/whipsnadetreecathedral

Open at all times

This cathedral was created by Edmund Kell Blyth, a local landowner. After the first world war Edmund planted a variety of trees that have now matured to give the effect of the knave, transepts, cloisters and chapels of a large outdoor cathedral.

St Benets Abbey

Ludham, take the turning near Ludham Hall Farm, Ludham, Norfolk, NR29

Open all year at all times Access to this abbey is from the River Bure or a farm track from the minor road off the A1062

Ruins of a monastery founded on land granted by King Canute in 1020 AD.The most unusual feature is that there is an 18C brick windmill inside the church ruins. There is a legend that a monk can be seen hanging from the belltower on each night of 25th May

Ramsey Abbey Gatehouse

Abbey School, Off B1096, Ramsey, Cambridgeshire, PE17 1DH

Tel: 01480 301 494

Exterior view only. Interior can be visited on certain days throughout the year please telephone 01480 301494 for details

This gatehouse dates from the 15C and is decorated with ornate carvings and Oriel windows. Ruins of the monastery are situated on an island in the Fens

Duxford Chapel

Opposite Whittlesford Station, Off the A505, Cambridge, Cambridgeshire

Tel: 01223 443 000

Website: www.english-heritage.org.uk

Access at any reasonable time

A Medieval Chapel which was once part of the St. John Hospital

Roman Catholic Cathedral Of St John The Baptist

Unthank Road, Norwich, Norfolk, NR2 2PA
Tel: 01603 624 615
Email: enq@stjohncathedral.co.uk
Website: www.stjohncathedral.co.uk
All year daily 07.00-20.00

Gifted to the city of Norwich by the 15th Duke of Norfolk, the building of this Cathedral commenced in 1894 and was finished in 1910. With some of the finest 19C stained glass in Europe this building is a magnificent example of 19C Gothic Revival

Isleham Priory Church

Isleham, On the B1104, Mildenhall, Cambridgeshire
Tel: 01223 582 700
Website: www.english-heritage.org.uk
Access at any reasonable time-Contact the key keeper-Mrs R Burton, 18 Festival Road, Isleham

This early Norman Church has survived and is remarkably well preserved, despite being converted into a barn for use by a local farmer

GARDENS PARKS & WALKS

Sewell Cutting

Just West Of Dunstable, Entrances via Sewell Lane or Frenchs Avenue, Dunstable, Bedfordshire
Access at all times

This nature reserve is most noted for its orchids and chalklands flora. It runs through an old railway just South of Dunstable.

Barton Hills Natural Nature Reserve

Just South of Barton, 5.5 miles North of Luton, South Bedfordshire, Barton, Bedfordshire
Access at all times

This nature reserve protects precious chalkland flowers, insects and butterflies on the Barton Hills. Also in the area is Barton Springs a popular tourist attraction in the early 1900s and can be found by following the field paths to the Icknield Way.

Dunstable Downs

On the B4541 Dunstable to Whipsnade road, Dunstable, Bedfordshire
Tel: 01582 608 489
Email: dunstabledowns@nationaltrust.org.uk
Access at all times

The Dunstable Downs are 130 acres of public access in The Chilterns Area of Outstanding Natural Beauty. With many walks , spectacular views, visitors centre and a picnic area.

Greensand Ridge Walk

From Leighton Buzzard to Chicksands, Leighton Buzzard, Bedfordshire
Access at all times

This 40 mile footpath runs North East across the entire country from Leighton Buzzard to Chicksands.

Abbey Botanical Gardens

Angel Hill, Bury St Edmunds, Suffolk
Tel: 01284 757 490
Mon-Sat 07.30 to half an hour before dusk Sun 09.00-half an hour before dusk

This Botanical Garden includes a Chinese tree of heaven planted in the 1830s. Other features include a riverside walk, aviaries and a tea shop and the recent addition of the World's First Internet Bench !

The Norfolk Broads-Weavers Way

From Cromer to Great Yarmouth, Cromer, Norfolk
Access at all times

Walkers should head for the 56 mile long Weaver's Way, a picturesque long distance footpath that winds through the best and most beautiful parts of The Broads.

Norfolk Coast Path

From Hunstanton to Cromer, Hunstanton, Norfolk
Access at all times

This scenic walk runs from Hunstanton to Cromer and features sand dunes and salt marshes

Wandlebury Country Park

Wandlebury Ring, Gog Magog Hills, Babraham, Cambridgeshire, CB2 4EA
Tel: 01223 243 830
Email: admin@cpswandlebury.org.uk
Website: www.cpswandlebury.org.uk
All year dawn-dusk
A countryside park with Nature Reserve, Roman Road public footpath and other
circular walks

HISTORIC HOUSES

Ipswich Ancient House

30 Buttermarket, Ipswich, Suffolk
Exterior View-Visitors can see the interior when the Lakeland shop is open
This 17C house is now used as a shop so visitors can feel free to browse the
shop's interior and look at the original features inside.The exterior of the house
has some extraordinary plaster work.

Christchurch Mansion

Christchurch Park, Ipswich, Suffolk
Tel: 01473 433 554
April-October (Tue-Sat) 10.00-17.00, (Sun) 14.30-16.30 Nov-March (Tues-Sat) 10.00-16.10
Sun 14.30-16.10
This Tudor building supports 17C Dutch gables and is set in 65 acres of Park
land.The building also contains the Wolsey Art Gallery

Toad Hole Cottage

Howhill, Ludham, Norfolk, NR29 5PG
Tel: 01692 678 763
Email: toadholeinfo@broads-authority.gov.uk
Website: www.broads-authority.gov.uk
East, April, May & Oct Mon-Fri 10.30-13.00 & 13.30-17.00 Sat & Sun 10.30-17.00 June-Sept
Daily 09.30-18.00
This is an old eel catcher's cottage dating from the 18C that shows the home and
working life on the marshes about a hundred years ago

Thetford Warren Lodge

Thetford, 2 miles West of Thetford off the B1107, Thetford, Norfolk
Tel: 01233 582 700
Access at any reasonable times
This ruin can only be viewed from the outside and is of a two storey medieval
game keepers lodge set in woods.

Blakeney Guild Hall

In Blakeney off A149, Blakeney, Norfolk
Tel: 08453 006 116
Access at any reasonable times
The remains of a large 14C building probably a merchants house.

The Ipswich Unitarian Meeting House

Friars Street, Ipswich, Suffolk, IP1 1TD
Tel: 01473 218 217
Open May 1 - Sep 30 Tues & Thurs 12.00-16.00 Sat 10.00-16.00 Services Sunday 10.45
Built in 1699 and opened in 1700 this Grade I listed building is one of the finest
surviving meeting houses in the country. It is an example of a purpose built
timber framed meeting house

Foster's Windmill

Swaffham Prior, Cambridge, Cambridgeshire, CB5 0JZ
Tel: 01638 741 009
Email: info@fostersmill.co.uk
Website: www.fostersmill.co.uk
Second Sunday of each month 13.00-17.00
Visitors are able to climb this four sailed working windmill and see each stage of
the milling process, a range of stone ground flours from organic grain are
available to purchase in the shop.

HISTORIC SITES

Scotts Grotto

24-38 Scotts Road, Ware, Hertfordshire
Tel: 01920 464 131
Website: www.scotts-grotto.org
April-Sept Saturdays 14.00-16.30
This grotto extends 67 feet into the hillside, there are passages and six
chambers decorated with pebbles, shells, fossils and flints. As this grotto is unlit
you would benefit from bringing a torch.

Clare Castle Country Park

Malting Lane, Clare, Sudbury, Suffolk
Tel: 01787 277 491
Open dawn - dusk Charge for car park
This 30 acre country park contains history and nature trails, visitors centre, a
Victorian railway station and the remains of a Norman Motte & Bailey Castle

Moulton Packhorse Bridge

In Moulton off B1085, 4 miles E of Newmarket, Moulton, Suffolk
Access at all times
A magnificent medieval four arched bridge over the River Kennett.

Caister Roman Site

Near Caister-on-Sea, 3 miles N of Great Yarmouth, Great Yarmouth, Norfolk
Access at any reasonable times
Here you will find the remains of a Roman site, which was possibly a fort

Cambridge American Cemetery

Madingley, 3 miles W of Cambridge on the A1303, Madingley, Cambridgeshire, CB3 7PH
Tel: 01954 210 350
Summer Daily 09.00-18.00 Winter Daily 09.00-17.00
This cemetery with visitor reception and memorial chapel is operated and
maintained by the American Battle Monuments Commission

MUSEUMS

Sailor's Reading Room

East Cliff and East Street, Southwold, Suffolk, IP18 6EL
Tel: 01502 723 782
Good Fri-31st October Daily 09.00-17.00 1st Nov-Good Fri 09.00-15.30
Built in the mid 1800s in an attempt to keep fishermen out of the local public
houses. The interior of this building is decorated with model ships and various
examples of nautical text.

Sedgwick Museum Of Earth Sciences

University Of Cambridge, Downing Street, Cambridge, Cambridgeshire, CB2 3EQ
Tel: 01223 333 456
Email: sedgwickmuseum@esc.cam.ac.uk
Website: www.sedgwickmuseum.org
(Mon-Fri) 09.00-13.00, 14.00-17.00 (Sat) 10.00-16.00
The museum contains various collections including fossils and skeletons of
dinosaurs and mammals.

Whipple Museum Of Science

University Of Cambridge, Free School Lane, Off Pembroke Street, Cambridge,
Cambridgeshire, CB2 3RH
Tel: 01223 330 906
Email: hps-whipple-museum@lists.cam.ac.uk
Website: www.hps.cam.ac.uk/whipple
(Mon-Fri) 12.30-16.30
The museum contains a wide array of scientific instruments.

Museum Of Archaeology and Anthropology

University Of Cambridge, Downing Street, Cambridge, Cambridgeshire, CB2 3DZ
Tel: 01223 333 516
Email: cumaa@hermes.cam.ac.uk
Website: www.museum-server.archanth.cam.ac.uk
Summer June-September Tues -Sat 10.00-16.30
This fascinating museum has a wide variety of extensive collections that focus on
anthropology and archaeology from around the world. An also features an
exhibition that shows the development of the city from pre-historic times to the
present day.

Scott Polar Research Institute

University Of Cambridge, Lensfield Road, Cambridge, Cambridgeshire, CB2 1ER
Tel: 01223 336 540
Email: enquiries@spri.cam.ac.uk
Website: www.spri.cam.ac.uk
Tues-Sat 14.30-16.00
This museum was founded in 1920 and dedicated to the memory of Captain
Scott, inside the museum are various exhibitions of articles from his expeditions.

Bridge Cottage

Flatford, East Bergholt, Suffolk, CO7 6UL
Tel: 01206 298 260
Email: flatfordbridgecottage@nationaltrust.org.uk
1 March-30 April Wed -Sun 11.00-17.00 1 May-30 Sept Daily 10.30-17.30 1 Oct-29 Oct
Daily 11.00-16.00 1 Nov-17 Dec Wed-Sun 11.00-15.30 6 Jan-25 Feb Sat & Sun 11.00-15.30
The cottage has been painstakingly restored and now houses a collection of
memorabilia to the artist John Constable.

Fitzwilliam Museum
Trumpington Street, Cambridge, Cambridgeshire, CB2 1RB
Tel: 01223 332 900
Email: fitzmuseum-enquiries@lists.cam.ac.uk
Website: www.fitzmuseum.cam.ac.uk
Tues-Sat 10.00-17.00 Sun 12.00-17.00
Contains an Internationally renowned collection of European paintings and sculpture, as well as Egyptian, Greek and Roman antiquities

FARMERS MARKETS

Cambridge Farmers Market
Market Square, Cambridge, Cambridgeshire
Every Sunday 10.30-16.30
Farmers Market with local produce for sale

Sudbury Farmers Market
St Peters Church, Market Hill, Sudbury, Suffolk
Last Friday of the month 09.00-13.00
Farmers Market with local produce for sale

Beccles Farmers Market
Beccles Heliport, Beccles, Suffolk
1st and 3rd Saturdays of the month 09.00-13.00
Farmers Market with local produce for sale

Norwich Farmers Market
Norfolk Showground, Norwich, Norfolk
Tel: 01953 681 715
Email: rholland@norfolkevents.co.uk
Website: www.norwichfarmersmarket.co.uk
2nd Saturday of the month at Norfolk Showground and at the Forum, Norwich City centre on the 1st and 3rd Sundays of the month 10.00-15.00
Farmers Market with local produce for sale

Fakenham Farmers Market
Town Square, Fakenham, Norfolk
4th Saturday of the month 09.00-13.00
Farmers Market with local produce for sale

Animal Health Trust Visitors Centre

Lanwades Park, Kentford, Newmarket, Suffolk, CB8 7UU

Tel: 01638 751 000

Email: info@aht.org

Website: www.aht.org.uk

All year Mon-Fri 10.00-16.00

Exhibitions and information give an insight into the veterinary work of this charity

Hampshire/Dorset/Wiltshire-England

ART GALLERIES/ARTS & CRAFTS

Southampton Art Gallery

Civic Centre, Commercial Road, Southampton, Hampshire, SO14 7LP
Tel: 023 8083 2277
Email: art.gallery@southampton.gov.uk
(Tue-Sat) 10.00-17.00, (Sun) 13.00-16.00
The museum has a good collection of 20C British artists including Sutherland, Piper and Spenser.

Russell-Cotes Museum

East Cliff Promenade, Bournemouth, Dorset, BH1 3AA
Tel: 01202 451 858
Email: diane.edge@bournemouth.gov.uk
Website: www.russell-cotes.bournemouth.gov.uk
(Tue-Sun) 10.00-17.00
The building displays the collections gathered by the Russell-Cotes family, especially oriental souvenirs, 17C-20C paintings and sculptures

The John Hansard Gallery

University Of Southampton, Highfield, Southampton, Hampshire, SO17 1BJ
Tel: 023 8059 2158
Email: info@hansardgallery.org.uk
Website: www.hansardgallery.org.uk
Open during exhibitions Tues-Fri 11.00-17.00 Sat 11.00-16.00
This gallery draws national and international audiences with its programme of exhibitions and events

Millais Gallery

Southampton Institute, East Park Terrace, Southampton, Hampshire, SO14 0YN
Tel: 023 8031 9916
Email: millais.gallery@solent.ac.uk
Website: www.millais.solent.ac.uk
Monday 13.00-17.00 Tues,Wed & Fri 10.00-17.00 Thurs 10.00-19.00 Sat 12.00-16.00
Exhibitions of local interest and a variety of work by young artists or student work

Guildhall Gallery
The Broadway, Winchester, Hampshire, SO23 9LJ
Tel: 01962 848 289
Email: museums@winchester.gov.uk
Website: www.winchester.gov.uk
April-Oct Mon-Sat 10.00-17.00 Sun 12.00-17.00 Nov-March Tue -Sat 10.00-16.00 Sun
12.00-16.00
This Gallery has a collection of fine arts, drawings and sculptures.

Walford Mill Crafts Centre
Stone Lane, Wimborne, Dorset, BH21 1NL
Tel: 01202 841 400
Email: info@walfordmillcrafts.co.uk
Website: www.walfordmillcrafts.co.uk
Mon-Sat 10.00-17.00 Sun 12.00-17.00 Closed Mondays Jan-Mar
Three workshops offering silk weaving, stained glass and jewellery where you
can watch the craftspeople at work and buy their products

Edwin Young Collection
Salisbury Library and Gallery, Market Place, Salisbury, Wiltshire, SP1 1BL
Tel: 01722 410 614
Mon 10.00-19.00 Tues, Wed & Fri 09.00-19.00 Thur & Sat 09.00-17.00
A collection of watercolours and drawings of the 19C by Edwin Young .Other
exhibitions held during the year by local artists

The Biscuit Bakery
Morcombelake, Bridport, Dorset, DT6 6ES
Tel: 01297 489 253
Email: enquiries@moores-biscuits.co.uk
Website: www.moores-biscuits.co.uk
Mon-Fri 09.00-17.00 Sat 09.00-13.00
Established in 1880 this bakery continues to make ten varieties of traditional
biscuits. Visitors can watch the biscuits being made and there is also a small
gallery with original West Country paintings and bakery history

Lacock Pottery
1 The Tanyard, Church Street, Lacock, Wiltshire, SN15 2LB
Tel: 01249 730 266
Email: simone@lacockbedandbreakfast.com
Website: www.lacockbedandbreakfast.com
Daily 10.00-17.00
Visitors can purchase hand made pottery, porcelain and stonewear all made on
the premises, and see the potters at work at certain times

Marlborough Crafts Centre

St Peter's Church, High Street, Marlborough, Wiltshire, SN8 1HQ
Tel: 01672 511 453
Mon-Sat 10.00-16.30
Selling home made arts and crafts

Selborne Pottery

The Plestor, Selborne, Alton, Hampshire, GU34 3JQ
Tel: 01420 511 413
Email: sales@selbornepottery.co.uk
Website: www.selbornepottery.co.uk
Mon-Fri 09.30-18.00 Showroom only Sat & Sun 12.00-17.00
Situated behind Selborne gallery this pottery offers a large range of hand thrown
and decorated stoneware including teapots, vases and mugs

Viables Craft Centre

Harrow Way, Basingstoke, Hampshire, RG22 4BJ
Email: info@viables.demon.co.uk
Tues-Fri 10.00-16.00, Saturdays 10.00-15.30
Craft workshops of woodturning, weaving, glass working, gold smith and many
more are offered in this Victorian farm building. Different workshops may have
different opening times.

Bartley Heath Pottery

North Warnborough, Hook, Hampshire, RG29 1HD
Tel: 01256 702 163
Email: mick@bartleyheathpottery.co.uk
Website: www.bartleyheathpottery.co.uk
Mon-Sat 10.00-16.30
Hand made pottery and stoneware by Lesley and Michael Dixon, When the
potters are working visitors are welcome to watch

The Allen Gallery

Church Street, Alton, Hampshire, GU34 2BW
Tel: 01420 82802
Tues-Sat 10.00-17.00
Housing an outstanding ceramics collection believed to be one of the best in
Southern England

Swindon Art Gallery

Bath Road, Old Town, Swindon, Wiltshire, SN1 4BA
Tel: 01793 466 556
Mon-Sat 10.00-17.00 Sun 14.00-17.00
One of the most significant collections of 20C British Art outside the Tate Gallery

Flora Twort Gallery

Church Path Studio, 21 The Square, Petersfield, Hampshire, GU32 3HJ
Tel: 01730 260 756
Tues-Sat 09.30-17.00
Paintings of local interest by local artists

CASTLES

Maiden Castle

2 miles south of Dorchester Town Centre, Access off A354, Dorchester, Dorset
Access at any reasonable time
This is the most impressive of Dorchester's many Pre Roman sites and features a massive ruined hill fort roughly the size of 50 football pitches which would have been home to approx 200 families

Sandsfoot Castle

Old Castle Road, Weymouth, Dorset
Access at all times
The ruins of this castle which was built by Henry VIII looks out majestically across Portland harbour

Christchurch Castle and the Norman House

Near The Priory, Christchurch, Dorset
Access at any reasonable time
Built in the late 11C this castle was used in the Anarchy about 1147 and in the 1645 Civil War. The Norman Constables House was built in 1160 to house the towns bailiff and has the oldest Norman chimney in Britain.

Ludgershall Castle and Cross

On the North side of Lundgershall, Off A342, Ludgershall, Wiltshire
Access at any reasonable time
Only the ruins of this 12C royal hunting palace and late medieval cross remain.

Titchfield Abbey

Located $\frac{1}{2}$ mile N of Titchfield, Off A27, Titchfield, Hampshire
Tel: 01329 842 133
1 April-30 Sept Daily 10.00-18.00 1-31Oct Daily 10.00-17.00 1 Nov-31 March Daily
10.00-16.00
The remains of this 13C abbey are just beyond the grand Tudor gatehouse

Netley Abbey

Netley Abbey Village, 4 miles SE of Southampton on the A3025, Netley Abbey, Hampshire
Tel: 02392 581 059
Website: www.netleyabbey.info
Access at any reasonable time
A 13C Abbey which now lays in ruins and is reported to be haunted.

St Mary's Church

The Plestor, Selborne, Alton, Hampshire, GU34 3JQ
09.00-18.00 (or dusk if earlier)
This church has many medieval features and a late Norman Nave. There are two
stained glass windows to commemorate Gilbert White who was the curate of
Selborne

Chisbury Chapel

0.25 miles E of Chisbury off the A4, 6 miles E of Marlborough, Chisbury, Wiltshire
Tel: 01672 513 989
Access at any reasonable time
A thatched 13C chapel now used as a farm building

St Peter's Church

Churchpath, The Square, Petersfield, Hampshire, GU32 3HS
Tel: 01730 260 213
Email: petersfield@stpeters.fsbusiness.co.uk
Open all year daily
St Peters was once described as one of the most interesting Norman Churches
in Hampshire. Inside there is superb craftsmen made English Oak screens
providing a Lady Chapel and meeting room

Malmesbury Abbey

Abbey Row, Malmesbury, Wiltshire, SN16 0AA
Tel: 01666 824 339
Email: office@malmesburyabbey.com
Website: www.malmesburyabbey.com
Summer Daily 10.00-18.00 Winter Daily 10.00-16.00
Founded by Saint Aldhelm in Saxon times this Norman Abbey is now the Parish Church. Famous for being the burial place of King Athelstane (895-940)

GARDENS PARKS & WALKS

Shell Bay

Swanage, Swanage, Dorset
Access at all times
This magnificent long beach is composed of icing sugar like sand.

Chesil Beach

Ferrybridge, Weymouth, Dorset
Tel: 01305 760 579
Access at all times
A 200 yard wide, 50 foot high bank of pebbles that stretches for 18 miles

Gold Hill

Shaftesbury, 10 miles North of Blandford, Shaftesbury, Dorset, SP7
Access at all times
This is the best point for terrific views over the town of Shaftsbury. The most famous street in Shaftsbury, this ancient cobbled street features on countless boxes and calendars.

Braxton Herb and Rose Garden

Braxton Courtyard, Lymore Lane, Milford On Sea, Hampshire, SO41 0TX
Tel: 01590 642 008
Email: info@braxtongardens.co.uk
Website: www.braxtongardens.co.uk
Mon-Sat 09.30-17.00 Sunday 10.00-16.00
Two magnificent gardens set out around the original brick barns of a Victorian farmyard. The walled garden was originally a herb garden and has now been extended to include perennials and the Rose Garden contains almost 350 roses of 100 varieties.

Barton Farm Country Park

Pound Lane, Bradford Upon Avom, Wiltshire, BA15 1LF
Open daily
Combining several short and longer country walks along the Kennet and Avon Canal. A haven for wildlife. Within the park is a magnificent 14C Tithe Barn which was built to store the Abbey's tithes.

Yateley Common Country Park

Between Yateley and the A30, Yateley, Hampshire, GU46 6BB
Tel: 01252 870 425
Email: vicky.booth@hants.gov.uk
Access at all times
One of Hampshires largest commons known for its unspoilt heathlands and natural history and infamous for its highwaymen and smugglers

HISTORIC HOUSES

The Great Hall

The Castle, Winchester, Hampshire
Tel: 01962 846 476
Email: the.great.hall@hants.gov.uk
March-Oct Daily 10.00-17.00 Nov-Feb Daily 10.00-16.00
Features King Arthur's round table. This is the only surviving part of Winchester Castle and there is also a 13C Herb Garden named after Queen Eleanor.

Northington Grange

4 miles N of New Alresford, Northington, Near Winchester, Northington, Hampshire
Tel: 02392 581 059
Exterior View Only 1 April-30 Sept Daily 10.00-18.00 1-31 Oct Daily 10.00-17.00 1 Nov-31 March Daily 10.00-16.00 (Closes at 15.00 June & July)
Built at the beginning of the 18C this is a magnificent example of a Neo Classical Country House. Onegin, starring Liv Tyler and Ralph Fiennes was filmed here

HISTORIC SITES

Maumbury Rings

SE of Dorchester, A short walk from the town centre, Dorchester, Dorset
Access at all times
This is the ancient site where the Romans held vast Gladiatorial combats.

Cerne Abbas Giant

16 miles W of Blandford, Cerne Abbas, Dorset
Website: www.cerneabbas.org.uk
Access at all times
Here you can view the enormous chalk giant that has been carved into the hillside and stands 180 feet high and is 2000 years old.

Avebury Stone Circle

Avebury, Near Malborough, Avebury, Wiltshire, SN8 1RF
Tel: 01672 539 250
Email: avebury@nationaltrust.org.uk
Access at all times
The village of Avebury stands in the middle of an ancient stone circle that rivals Stonehenge, and access is free.

Silbury Hill

Just off the A4 between Devizes and Marlborough, Just S of Avebury, Avebury, Wiltshire
Access at all times .
This is the largest Neolithic artificial Prehistoric mound in Europe There are explanatory plaques at the site

Woodhenge

1.5 miles N of Amesbury, off A345 just S of Durrington, Durrington, Wiltshire
Access at any reasonable time
Consists of six concentric rings of timber posts, this Neolithic ceremonial monument of c2300 BC points to the rising sun on Midsummer's Day. Discovered in 1925

Kingston Russell Stone Circle

2 Miles N of Abbotsbury, Follow footpath for 1 miles off the minor road to the Hardy Monument, Abbotsbury, Dorset
Access at all times
This stone circle is thought to date from the Bronze Age and have been constructed about 4000 years ago. It consists of 18 stones.

Pewsey Horse

Off the A345 towards Amesbury, Pewsey, Wiltshire
Tel: 01380 729 408
Access at all times
The Pewsey Horse is 20 meters long and 14 meters high and is best seen between Marlborough and Salisbury. Designed by George Maples to commemorate the coronation of King George VI

Alton Barnes White Horse

Milkhill, Alton Barnes, Devizes, Wiltshire, SN10
Access at all times
Considered the Arabian Stud of Whitshire's Eight White Horses and was cut in
1812 by the landowner Mr Robert Pile

Crop Circles

Pewsey Vale, Pewsey, Wiltshire
Tel: 01380 725 380
Access at all times
Crop circles have been appearing in this area for years. With the finest
formations located around the Marlborough Downs and Pewsey Vale

Bratton Camp and White Horse

Westbury, Wiltshire, BA13
Tel: 01373 827 158
Access at all times
The White Horse is the oldest in Wiltshire and is the main landmark in the area

Hackpen Hill White Horse

Hackpenhill, Marlborough, Wiltshire, SN8
Access at all times
Cut in 1837 to commemorate the coronation of Queen Victoria and best viewed
on the minor road to Fiddlers Hill

Marborough White Horse

Marlborough College, Marlborough, Wiltshire, SN8
Access at all times
This horse was cut in 1804 by the boys of Marlborough School. Not easily visible
from roads but best on foot by the footpath along the river from Manton to
Marlborough

The Sanctuary-Avebury

Overton Hill, Avebury, Wiltshire, SN8
Tel: 01985 843 600
Access at all times
A series of concentric circles of concrete blocks and pillars marking the positions
of stone and post holes thought to span several centuries of the Late Neolithic
Period

Devizes White Horse

Roundway Hill, Devizes, Wiltshire, SN10

Access at all times

The Devizes White Horse was cut in 1999 to mark the millennium and is a major landmark for the town of Devizes

MUSEUMS

Southampton Maritime Museum

Wool House, Town Quay Road, Southampton, Hampshire, SO14 2AR

Tel: 023 8063 5904

Email: historic.sites@southampton.gov.uk

(Tue-Fri) 10.00-16.00 (Sat) 10.00-13.00 & 14.00-16.00 (Sun) 13.00-16.00

At this museum visitors can listen to recorded voices of various survivors of the Titanic disaster

Winchester City Museum

The Square, Winchester, Hampshire

Tel: 01962 848 269

Email: museums@winchester.gov.uk

Website: www.winchester.gov.uk

Apr-Oct Mon-Sat 10.00-17.00 Sun 12.00-17.00 Nov - March Tues-Sat 10.00-16.00 Sun 12.00-16.00

Rest of the year closed on Mondays. The museum displays various collections and exhibits detailing local history.

Wiltshire Heritage Museum

41 Long Street, Devizes, 7 miles from Avebury, Devizes, Wiltshire, SN10 1NS

Tel: 01380 727 369

Email: wanhs@wiltshireheritage.org.uk

Website: www.wiltshireheritage.org.uk

Free Admission Mondays 10.00-17.00 and Sundays 12.00-16.00 Charge at all other times.

The museum houses various collections of prehistoric finds, including the "Marlborough Bucket" that dates from the 1st Century BC and is decorated with bronze relief's

Bedwyn Stone Museum

91 Church Street, In Great Bedwyn, between Hungerford and Marlborough, Great Bedwyn, Wiltshire, SN8 3PF
Tel: 01672 870 234
Please call for opening times
The art of the stone mason and his craft has been shown here by the Lloyd family for more than 200 years.

Bear Museum

38 Dragon Street, Petersfield, Hampshire, GU31 4JJ
Tel: 01730 265 108
Website: www.bearmuseum.co.uk
Open Tues-Sat 10.00-16.30
This museum was the worlds first Teddy Bear Museum. Activities include singing to rhymes and playing with the bears. Housed in a 17C building

The Willis Museum

Market Square, Basingstoke, Hampshire, RG21 7QD
Tel: 01256 465 902
Mon-Fri 10.00-17.00 Sat 10.00-16.00
Local working museum with collections of archaeology and natural science. Specialist collection of watches and clocks

Trowbridge Museum

The Shires, Court Street, Trowbridge, Wiltshire, BA14 8AT
Tel: 01225 751 339
Email: info@trowbridgemuseum.co.uk
Website: www.trowbridgemuseum.co.uk
Tues-Fri 10.00-16.00 Sat 10.00-17.00
This was the towns last working woollen mill and the museum tells the story of its people and its past

Museum Of Computing

University Of Bath, Marlowe Avenue, Walcot, Swindon, Wiltshire, SN3 3JR
Tel: 01793 872 146
Website: www.museum-of-computing.org.uk
Mon-Thurs 08.30-18.00 Fri 08.30-17.00 Sat 09.00-13.00
Displaying many collections of software, home computers and hand held electronic games

Richard Jefferies Museum

Marlborough Road, Coate, Swindon, Wiltshire
Tel: 01793 466 556
May-Sept 1st and 3rd Sunday 14.00-17.00
This museum is situated in the old Victorian cottage which was the birthplace of Victorian writer Richard Jefferies

Curtis Museum

High Street, Alton, Hampshire, GU34 1BA
Tel: 01420 82802
Email: musmtc@hants.gov.uk
Website: www.hants.gov.uk/museum/curtis
Tues-Sat 10.00-17.00
This museum displays local crafts such as Victorian toys, dolls and houses, as well as local and natural history

Portsmouth City Museum

Museum Road, Portsmouth, Hampshire, PO1 2LJ
Tel: 023 9282 7261
Email: info@portsmouthrecordsoffice.co.uk
Website: www.portsmouthcitymuseums.co.uk
April - Sept Daily 10.00-17.30 Oct-March 10.00-17.00
This museum documents the history of Portsmouth and includes audio visual displays.

FARMERS MARKETS

Winchester Farmers Market

Middle Brook Street and Middle Brook Street Carpark, Winchester, Hampshire
Last Sunday of the month 10.00-14.-00
Farmers Market with local produce for sale

Christchurch Farmers Market

Saxon Square, Christchurch, Dorset
1st Friday of the month 09.00-13.00
Farmers Market with local produce for sale

Shaftsbury Farmers Market

Town Hall, Shaftsbury, Dorset
1st Saturday of the month 09.00-13.00
Farmers Market with local produce for sale

Devizes Farmers Market
Market Place, Devizes, Wiltshire
1st Saturday of the month 09.00-13.30
Farmers Market with local produce for sale

Bradford Upon Avon Farmers Market
Westbury Gardens, Bradford-Upon-Avon, Wiltshire
Tel: 01225 712 334
3rd Thursday of the month 09.00-13.30
Farmers Market with local produce for sale

Yorkshire-England

ART GALLERIES/ARTS & CRAFTS

Graves Art Gallery
Top Floor of the City Library, Surrey Street, Sheffield, Yorkshire, S1 1XZ
Tel: 0114 278 2600
Mon-Sat 10.00-17.00
The gallery houses various collections, the majority of which are by 19 & 20C British Artists, including Turner, Nash, Gwen John and various Pre-Raphaelite artists.

Ruskin Gallery
Millennium Galleries, Arundel Gate, Sheffield, Yorkshire, S1 2PP
Tel: 0114 278 2600
Mon-Sat 08.00-17.00 Sun 11.00-17.00
The building houses the Collection Of Saint George, which was set up to improve the cultural lives of working people of Sheffield. The collection includes, watercolours, paintings, medieval illustrated manuscripts and minerals

Leeds City Art Gallery
The Headrow, Leeds, West Yorkshire, LS1 3AA
Tel: 0113 247 8248
Email: city.art.gallery@leeds.gov.uk
Website: www.leeds.gov.uk/artgallery
Mon, Tues & Thurs-Sat 10.00-17.00 Wed 10.00-20.00 Sun 13.00-17.00
This gallery contains one of the best and most varied collections of art outside London. There are changing selections from the permanent exhibitions of 19 & 20C art and sculpture.

York Art Gallery
Exhibition Square, York, Yorkshire, YO1 7EW
Tel: 01904 687 687
Email: art.gallery@ymt.org.uk
Website: www.yorkartgallery.org.uk
Open Daily 10.00-17.00
Extensive collections of British and Early Northern European paintings. The gallery also hosts year round special exhibitions.

1853 Gallery

Salts Mill, Shipley, Saltaire, West Yorkshire, BD18 3LB
Tel: 01247 531 163
Email: post@saltsmill.demon.co.uk
Website: www.saltsmill.org.uk
Open Daily 10.00-17.30
Permanent exhibition of Bradford born David Hockney's works

Gissing Centre

2-4 Thompsons Yard, Westgate, Wakefield, West Yorkshire, WF1 2TP
Tel: 01924 255 047
May-Sept Sat 14.00-16.00
This centre houses displays and memorabilia connected to Gissing and
Wakefield's literary life

Dean Clough Galleries

Dean Clough, Halifax, Yorkshire, HX3 5AX
Tel: 01422 250 250
Email: dean.clough.ltd@deanclough.com
Website: www.deanclough.com
Open Daily 10.00-17.00
This gallery houses contemporary art and design by Northern artists. Also home
to the Henry Moore studio

Gallery II

Chesham Building, The University Of Bradford, Richmond Road, Bradford, Yorkshire, BD7
1DP
Tel: 01274 235 495
Email: gallery@bradford.ac.uk
Weekdays 11.00-15.00
Changing exhibitions and lunchtime contemporary music showcases

The Cat Pottery

West Burton, Wensleydale, North Yorkshire, DL8 4JW
Tel: 01969 663 273
Email: info@catpottery.co.uk
Website: www.catpottery.co.uk
Open Mon-Fri 09.30-16.00 Sat & Sun 10.00-14.00
Visitors to this pottery can view the unusual ceramic and stone cats being made
first hand by the crafts men on site

White Rose Candles

Wensley Mill, Wensley, Leyburn, North Yorkshire, DL8 4HR
Tel: 01969 623 544
Email: whiterosecandles@freenet.co.uk
Website: www.whiterosecandles.co.uk
Feb 10.00-Dusk April-Oct 10.00-17.00 Nov & Dec 10.00-Dusk Closed Jan & March (Please check open on day of your visit)
Visitors can watch various decorative processes from hand dipping to casting of the home made candles produced on site

The Teapottery Ltd

Leyburn Business Park, Leyburn, North Yorkshire, DL8 5QA
Tel: 01969 623 839
Email: info@teapottery.com
Website: www.teapottery.co.uk
Open daily 09.00-17.00
Visitors can browse in the Teapottery shop, take tea in the refreshment area or watch the collectable teapots being made

Littlethorpe Potteries

Pottery Lane, Littlethorpe, Ripon, Yorkshire, HG4 3LS
Tel: 01765 603 786
Email: mail@littlethorpepotteries.co.uk
Website: www.littlethorpepotteries.co.uk
Mon-Fri 09.00-17.00 Sat 09.00-12.00
Charge for guided tours but visitors to the shop can look around free without a guide and browse the wide collection of on site products including terracotta pots made using Littlethorpe clay deposits.

CASTLES

Sandal Castle

Manygates Lane, Sandal, Wakefield, West Yorkshire, WF2 7DG
Tel: 01924 305 352
Castle grounds open dawn-dusk Visitors Centre Summer (Mon-Sun) 11.00-16.30 Winter Weekends 11.00-16.00
This excavated medieval castle sits on a vantage point overlooking the site 15C Battle Of Wakefield. On site visitors centre contains a centre with displays and models and has fabulous views over the nearby Calder Valley

Skipsea Castle

Skipsea Village, 8 miles West of Bridlington, Skipsea, Yorkshire

Access at any reasonable time

This is a motte and bailey castle that dates from the Norman period. The outer bailey is under the care of English Heritage.

Castle Hill

Off Lumb Lane, Near Almondbury, Hudersfield, Yorkshire

Tel: 01484 223 830

Access to Castle Hill at all times for details of the opening hours of Victoria Tower please contact the Tolson Museum on 01484 223830

This Iron Age Fort has outstanding and stunning views of the surrounding areas. On the top of this hill is the impressive Victoria Tower.

CHURCHES & CATHEDRALS

Easby Abbey

Below Richmond Castle, 1 mile SE of Richmond off B6271, Richmond, Yorkshire

Apr-Sep (Daily) 10.00-18.00, Oct (Daily) 10.00-17.00, Nov-March (Daily) 10.00-16.00

The ruined Abbey was founded in 1152 by Premonstratensian Canons, also known as the White Monks. The ruins that remain are extensive and there is a 13C refectory which is still in remarkable condition.

Holy Trinity

Just off Goodramgate, By Lady Row, York, Yorkshire, YO1 2LF

Tel: 01904 613 451

Apr 1-Sep 30 Mon-Sat 10.00-17.00, Sun 12.00-17.00 Oct 1-Mar 31 Tue-Sat 10.00-16.00

This 15C church is renowned for it's East window, jumbled box pews and a saddle back tower, which is an unusual feature in English Churches.

Kirkstall Abbey

Abbey Road, Leeds, West Yorkshire

Access during daylight hours

The ruined building, which is one of the city's most important medieval relics was built by Cistercian Monks from Fountains Abbey between 1152 and 1182.

Haworth Parish Church

Top of Main Street, Haworth, Yorkshire
Open daily 09.00-17.00
This church and the village in which is resides has gained its fame from the Bronte sisters who lived in the village. The church contains the Bronte family vault and was also the setting for Charlotte Bronte's wedding in 1864.

Bolton Priory

Bolton Abbey Town, 5 miles East of Skipton, Bolton Abbey, Yorkshire
Email: office@boltonpriory.org.uk
Website: www.boltonpriory.org.uk
Daily 08.00-dusk (or 19.00 if earlier) Closes at 16.00 on Fridays
The ruins of this former monastic building were once part of an Augustinian community that was founded by Cecily De Romille in 1120. The nave of the building which was incorporated into the village church in 1170 has survived remarkably well

St Olave's Church

Marygate, York, Yorkshire
Tel: 01904 625 186
Website: www.stolave.org.uk
Mon-Fri 09.00-17.00
This 14C Church with 18C restoration, sits on Pre-Norman foundations

St Martin-le-Grand

Coney Street, York, Yorkshire
Tel: 01904 625 186
Mon-Fri 09.00-17.00
Small chapel and garden of rest are now situated on the site of the 15C Church of St Martin-le-Grand

Howden Minster

Howden, Goole, Howden, Yorkshire, DN14 7BL
Tel: 01430 430 332
Website: www.english-heritage.org.uk
Daily 08.30-17.15 Winter 08.30-16.15
A large Cathedral-like 14C Church, the chancel and chapterhouse can be viewed from the outside only

St Michael-le-Belfrey

High Petergate, York, Yorkshire
Tel: 01904 624 190
Email: admin@st-michael-le-belfrey.org
Mon-Sat 11.00-16.00 Winter opening times vary please contact to confirm
This church is known for containing an enlarged page from its Registers, which began in 1565 and which records the Baptism of Guy Fawkes

Monk Bretton Priory

17 Abbey Lane, Barnsley, Yorkshire, S71 5QD
Tel: 01226 204 089
Email: admin@monkbrettonpriory.org.uk
Website: www.monkbrettonpriory.org.uk
29th March-30th Sept 10.00-18.00 1st Oct-31st Oct 10.00-17.00 Nov & Dec 10.00-16.00
This Priory was founded in 1153 and now only the ruins of the abbey and the 14C gatehouse remain.

GARDENS PARKS & WALKS

Sheffield Botanical Gardens

Clarkhouse Road, Sheffield, Yorkshire, S10 2LN
Tel: 0114 276 6496
Website: www.sbg.org.uk
Gardens Summer Weekdays 08.00-19.45 Weekends 10.00-19.45 Winter Weekdays 08.00-16.00 Weekends 10.00-16.00 Glass Pavilions Winter Daily 11.00-15.30 Summer Daily 11.00-17.00
The 19 acres of landscaped gardens and glass Paxton pavilions with the Botanical Gardens provide the perfect place to relax and walk.

Graves Park Animal Farm

Hemsworth Road, Norton, Sheffield, Yorkshire
Tel: 0114 258 2452
Email: friends@gravespark.org
Website: www.gravespark.fsnet.co.uk
Open - Mon-Sun 08.00-16.00
Located within Sheffield's largest park, which also includes picnic areas and a café. Feel free to wander round and pet the various species of animals.

Heeley City Farm

Richards Road, Heeley, Sheffield, Yorkshire, S2 3DT
Tel: 0114 258 0482
Email: farm@heeleyfarm.org.uk
Website: www.heeleyfarm.org.uk
Open Mon-Sun 09.30-17.00 (Closes at 16.30 in Winter)
Set in four acres this farm includes rare breeds of animals, demonstrations and environmental information, peat free plant garden, café and children's play area

Cow and Calf Rocks

Hangingstone Road, Ilkley, Yorkshire
Access at all times
Easily reached from the town centre of Ilkley, The Cow is a spectacular rock face that rises 50 feet, whilst the nearby calf is obviously smaller in size

HISTORIC HOUSES

Bolling Hall

Bolling Hall Road, Bradford, West Yorkshire, BD4 7LP
Tel: 01274 723 057
Website: www.bolling.net
Open Wed, Thurs & Fri 11.00-16.00, Sat 10.00-17.00, Sun 12.00-17.00
This house contains architecture from several different historical periods,including a medieval tower and an 18C wing. The rooms are decorated with period furnishings and there is also a stunning Central Hall with a gallery and early stained glass windows

Ilkley Manor House

Castle Yard, Church Street, Ilkley, Yorkshire, L529 9DT
Tel: 01943 600 066
Tues 14.00-16.00 Wed-Sat 11.00-17.00 Sun 13.00-16.00
This house which dates from the 16 & 17C was probably the vicarage or a farmers house and was built on the site of an original Roman Fort. Notable features include a 17C king post roof and privy. There is also a museum and art gallery within the building

Oakwell Hall and Country Park

Nutter Lane, Birstall, Batley, West Yorkshire, WF17 9LG

Tel: 01924 326 240

Email: oakwell.hall@kirklees.gov.uk

Website: www.oakwellhall.f9.co.uk

ONLY FREE 1 NOV - 28 FEBRUARY outwith special events. Admission charge at other times Open Mon-Fri 11.00-17.00, Sat & Sun 12.00-17.00,

An Elizabethan Manor House dating from 1583, but decorated in 17C style with period furniture. The house stands in its original 11 acre estate which includes period gardens.

Top Withens

Near Haworth, Haworth, West Yorkshire

Access at all times

A ruined farmhouse situated on the desolate moor is reputed to have been the inspiration for the house in Emily Bronte's Wuthering Heights, The walk to the ruin takes in the beautiful scenery and passed the Bronte Falls and the Bronte Chair

The Guildhall

Behind Mansions House, St Helen's Square, York, Yorkshire, YO1 9QN

Tel: 01904 551 049

May-Oct Mon-Fri 09.00-17.00 Sat 10.00-17.00 Sun 14.00-17.00 Nov-April Mon-Fri 09.00-17.00

A rebuilt version of the original 15C building which was damaged in 1942 by fire. The interior has a Victorian Council Chamber, Stained Glass depicting the history of York and a number of roof bosses depicting animals and faces

Burton Agnes Manor House

Burton Agnes Village, On the A166 5 miles SW of Bridlington, Bridlington, Yorkshire, YO25 4NB

Tel: 01904 601 901

Website: www.english-heritage.org.uk

April-Oct 11.00-17.00 Daily

A well preserved Norman House encased in brick during the 17 & 18C

Wilberforce House

High Street, Hull, Yorkshire, HU1 1NQ

Mon-Sat 10.00-17.00 Sun 13.30-16.30

The birthplace of William Wilberforce, who is famous for his fight against slavery

HISTORIC SITES

Gainsthorpe Deserted Medieval Village
Hibaldstow, Brigg, Yorkshire
Tel: 01904 601 974
Email: janet.burrows@english-heritage.org.uk
Access at any reasonable time
Within this excavated medieval village there are the earthworks of peasant houses, gardens and streets.

Julian's Bower
Back Street, Alkborough, Scunthorpe, Yorkshire, DN15 9JN
Tel: 01724 720 484
Access at any reasonable time
A turf cut maze wit panoramic views over the site from the rivers Ouse & Trent. Information details on site.

Stanwick Iron Age Fortifications
Forcett, Located on a minor road off A6274, Richmond, North Yorkshire
Access at any reasonable time
An immense 850 acre earthwork site, part of which has been excavated to show ramparts and rock cut ditches

Cup and Ring Marked Rocks
Ilkley Moor, Ilkley, Yorkshire
Access at all times
Examples of these carved rocks can be found all around Britain and are associated with Bronze Age burials

Bar Walls
York, Yorkshire
Tel: 01904 621 756
Daily 08.00-dusk
One of the best view of the City Of York, is from the city's Medieval Walls. A walk round the complete circumference of the walls takes a couple of hours.

MUSEUMS

Craven Museum
Town Hall, High Street, Skipton, North Yorkshire, BD23 1AH
Tel: 01756 706 407
Email: museum@cravendc.gov.uk
April-Sept Mon-Sat 10.00-17.00 Sun 13.00-16.00 Oct-March Mon-Fri 12.30-16.00 Sat 10.00-16.00
The museum illustrated the geology, flora & fauna, folk history and archaeology of Craven. A variety of displays include bicycles, policemen's helmets, flints, fossils, snuff boxes, grandfather clocks and a hippopotamus skull!

Whitby Lifeboat Museum
Pier Road, Harbour Front, Whitby, North Yorkshire, YO21 3PU
Tel: 01947 602 001
Website: www.whitby-uk.com/lifeboat
East-Oct Daily 10.00-16.00 (Subject to weather)
This museum is the best of its kind in the country. The life boat crew at Whitby have won more gold medals for Gallantry than any other crew in Britain. The museum contains the last ever hand rowed life boat that was used well into the 20C

Bagshaw Museum
Wilton Park, Batley, West Yorkshire, WF17 0AS
Tel: 01924 326 155
Email: bagshaw.museum@kirklees.gov.uk
Open - Mon-Fri 11.00-17.00 Sat & Sun 12.00-17.00
This museum covers displays and exhibitions from across the continents, including the rain forests and Egyptian tombs, as well as a range of local history

Hull and East Riding Museum
36 High Street, Old Town, Hull, Yorkshire, HU1 1PS
Tel: 01482 613 902
Website: www.hullcc.gov.uk/museums
Mon-Sat 10.00-17.00 Sun 13.30-16.30
This museum covers 235 million years of history from pre historic times to the Dark Ages.

Doncaster Museum and Art Gallery

Chequer Road, Doncaster, South Yorkshire, DN1 2AE
Tel: 01302 734 293
Email: museum@doncaster.gov.uk
Website: www.doncaster.gov.uk/museums
Mon-Sat 10.00-17.00 Sun 14.00-17.00
Displays of archaeology, geology and the regimental museum of the Kings Own Yorkshire Light Infantry.

Bradford Industrial and Horses at Work Museum

Moorside Road, Eccles Hill, Bradford, West Yorkshire, BD2 3HP
Tel: 01274 435 900
Email: industrial.museum@bradford.gov.uk
Open Tues-Sat 10.00-17.00 Sun 12.00-17.00 Steam Days usually held on Wednesdays 10.00-16.30
This Victorian working mill includes textile machinery, engines, mill owner's house and workers cottages. There is a shire horse demonstration twice daily

Museum Of South Yorkshire Life

Cusworth Hall, Cusworth Lane, Doncaster, Yorkshire, DN5 7TU
Tel: 01302 782 342
Email: museum@doncaster.gov.uk
Mon-Fri 10.00-17.00 Sat 11.00-17.00 Sun 13.00-17.00
The Museum is housed within Cusworth Hall, an 18C Country House

Bedale Museum

Bedale Hall, Bedale, Yorkshire, DL8 1AA
Tel: 01677 423 797
East-Sept Mon, Tues, Wed & Fri 14.00-16.00 Sat 10.00-12.00
A museum of local artefacts related to local trades, including a 1748 fire engine.

National Railway Museum

Leeman Road, York, Yorkshire, YO26 4XJ
Tel: 01904 621 261
Email: nrm@nmsi.ac.uk
Website: www.nrm.org.uk
Daily 10.00-18.00
An impressive collection of locomotives and railway artefacts.

Hull Maritime Museum

Queen Victoria Square, Hull, Yorkshire, HU1 3DX
Mon-Sat 10.00-17.00 Sun 13.30-16.30
This Museum aims "to preserve and make available the Maritime History of Hull
and East Yorkshire through artefacts and documents."

Streetlife Museum Of Transport

High Street, Hull, Yorkshire, HU1 1PS
Tel: 01482 613 902
Mon-Sat 10.00-17.00 Sun 13.30-16.30
A motorcar and carriage gallery, a street scene including shops and exhibition
area are all housed within this museum

NATURE AND WILDLIFE

Fairburn Ings

Fairburn, Just off the A1, Fairburn, West Yorkshire
Tel: 01977 603 796
Main Car Park 09.00-dusk. 2 public paths open at all times. Visitors Centre Weekdays
09.30-16.30 Weekends 09.30-17.00
An ideal place to see wetland birds up close throughout the year

FARMERS MARKETS

Doncaster Farmers Market

Goose Hill, Doncaster Market, Doncaster, Yorkshire
Email: doncaster.markets@doncaster.gov.uk
1st and 3rd Wednesday of the month 10.00-16.00
Farmers Market with local produce for sale

York Farmers Market

Parliament Street, York, Yorkshire
Tel: 01904 551 355
Email: york.market@york.gov.uk
Normally held on the 29th of the Month 09.00- 16.30
Farmers Market with local produce for sale

North East-England

BALTIC The Centre For Contemporary Art

South Shore Road, Gateshead, Tyne and Wear, NE8 3BA

Tel: 0191 478 1810

Email: info@balticmill.com

Website: www.balticmill.com

Mon-Sun 10.00-18.00 Thurs 10.00-20.00

One of Europe's largest venues with 5 galleries of contemporary art housed in a converted flour mill

Shipley Art Gallery

Prince Consort Road, Gateshead, Tyne and Wear, NE8 4JB

Tel: 0191 477 1495

Email: info@twmuseum.org.uk

Website: www.twmuseum.org.uk

Mon-Sat 10.00-17.00 Sun 14.00-17.00

This gallery offers a display of jewellery, ceramics and glass along with historic art work and temporary exhibitions

Sunderland Museum and Art Gallery

Mowbray Park, Borough Road, Sunderland, Tyne and Wear, SR1 1PP

Tel: 0191 553 2323

Email: info@twmuseum.org.uk

Website: www.twmuseum.org.uk

Mon-Sat 10.00-17.00 Sun 14.00-17.00

The museum tells the history of the city focusing on how ships were built here and sent all over the world. In the art gallery are several L S Lowry drawings that date from 1936 when he visited the North East to recuperate.

The Laing Gallery

Higham Place, Newbridge Street, Newcastle, Tyne and Wear, NE1 8AG

Tel: 0191 232 7734

Email: info@twmuseum.org.uk

Website: www.twmuseum.org.uk

Mon-Sat 10.00-17.00 Sun 14.00-17.00

A permanent display of British art from Reynolds to John Hoyland with a few Pre-Raphaelite artists featured. Look out for the works of John Martin 1789-1854, a self taught local artist who specialised in mythical and biblical scenes.

Phoenix Hot Glass Studio and Gallery

Riverside Studios, 1-2 Fowlers Yard, Back Silver Street, Durham, County Durham, DH1 3RA
Tel: 0191 384 7773
Email: phgs@netcomuk.co.uk
Website: www.phoenixhotglass.com
Glass Studio-Wed-Sat 11.00-16.00 Glass Gallery-Tues-Sat 11.00-16.00
Visitors are welcome to watch the process of producing hand made glass.

St Aidans Winery

Holy Island, Lindisfarne, Northumberland, TD15 2RX
Tel: 01289 389 230
Email: info@lindisfarne-mead.co.uk
Website: www.lindisfarne-mead.co.uk
Jan-April Mon-Fri, April-December Daily
Northumberland's traditional local drink, once made by the monks of Lindisfarne
Priory is now made and sold at this winery

Chain Bridge Honey Farm

Horncliffe, Of the A698, 5 miles SW of Berwick Upon Tweed, Berwick Upon Tweed,
Northumberland, TD15 2XT
Tel: 01289 386 362
Email: info@chainbridgehoney.co.uk
Website: www.chainbridgehoney.co.uk
April-Oct Mon-Sat 10.30-17.00 Sun 14.00-17.00 Nov-March Mon-Fri 09.00-17.00
History and displays of bee-keeping practices, the history of bees and wasps
and observation hides. A wide variety of products made with the help of bees
including cosmetics, candles and polish

Northumberland Cheese Farm

Make Me Rich Farm, Greenlane, Blagdon, 5 miles S of Morpeth, Blagdon, Northumberland,
NE13 6BZ
Tel: 01670 789 798
Email: enquiries@northumberland-cheese.co.uk
Website: www.northumberland-cheese.co.uk
Daily 10.00-17.00
Visitors can watch cheeses being made and taste free samples of the finished
product.

The Biscuit Factory

16 Stoddart Street, Newcastle, Tyne and Wear, NE2 1AN
Tel: 0191 261 1103
Email: art@thebiscuitfactory.com
Website: www.thebiscuitfactory.com
Tues-Sat 10.00-20.00 Sun & Mon 11.00-17.00
Two floors of exhibition space and two floors of artist's studios with paintings, prints, sculpture and furniture from over 100 Local, National and International artists

Hatton Gallery

University Of Newcastle Upon Tyne, The Quadrangle, Newcastle, Tyne and Wear, NE1 7RU
Tel: 0191 222 6059
Email: hatton-gallery@ncl.ac.uk
Website: www.ncl.ac.uk/hatton
All year 10.00-17.00 daily except Sundays
A collection of 15-20C paintings, drawings and sculptures

CASTLES

Kielder Castle

Border Forest Park, Kielder Water, Northumberland National Park, Northumberland, Northumberland
Tel: 01434 250 209
Email: p.kirkham@forestry.gsi.gov.uk
Website: www.kielder.org
East-Sep (Daily) 10.00-17.00 and till 18.00 in Aug, Oct-East (Sat & Sun) 11.00-16.00
The castle was built in 1775 as a hunting lodge for the Duke Of Northumberland and now houses a information and exhibition area dedicated to the work of the forestry commission.

Bowes Castle

Bowes, Off A66, 4 miles W of Barnard Castle, Bowes, County Durham
Tel: 0191 269 1200
Website: www.english-heritage.org.uk
Access at any reasonable time
A huge 12C stone keep overlooking the River Gretna Valley

Harbottle Castle

Harbottle, 5 miles west of Rothbury, Harbottle, Northumberland

Access at all times

This 12C castle has been in ruins since the 17C. Built for Henry II by the Umfraville family it is best known as being taken by Robert the Bruce in 1318.

Berwick Castle

Located in town centre off Castlegate, Berwick Upon Tweed, Northumberland

Access at all times

The 16C gun tower and the west wall are all that remain of this 12C castle

Edlingham Castle

Edlingham, On minor road off B6341 6 miles SW of Alnwick, Edlingham, Northumberland

Access at any reasonable time

A 13C hall, house and courtyard of the 14C and a tower of the 15C are some of the features to see if you visit the ruins of this castle.

Hylton Castle

Craigavon Road, Hylton Castle Estate, Sunderland, Tyne and Wear

Website: www.english-heritage.org.uk

Access at all reasonable times

Built between 1374 and 1420 the gatehouse still stands whilst only the remains of the castle can be seen

CHURCHES & CATHEDRALS

Hulne Priory

Bailiffgate, Ratten Row, Alnwick, Northumberland

Park open dawn-dusk

The remains of a 13C Carmelite monastery. Amidst the crumbling ruins are several carved stone monks.This priory was featured in the film Robin Hood-Prince Of Thieves

Durham Cathedral

Palace Green, Durham, County Durham, DH1 3EH

Tel: 0191 386 4266

Email: enquiries@durhamcathedral.co.uk

Website: www.durhamcathedral.co.uk

Mon-Sat 09.30-18.15 Sun 12.30 -17.00 (17th June-8th September open until 20.00)

This magnificent Norman Cathedral is a shrine to St Cuthbert

Cathedral Church Of St Nicholas

St Nicholas Street, Newcastle, Tyne and Wear
Email: office@stnicnewcastle.co.uk
Website: www.newcastle-ang-cathedral-stnicholas.org.uk
(Mon-Fri) 07.00-18.00, (Sat) 08.30-16.00 (Sun) 07.00-12.00 & 16.00-19.00
The Cathedral dates from the 14 & 15C and has a remarkable tower that was
erected in 1470. Inside the church and behind the High altar is one of the largest
funerary brasses in England, that is etched with nearly life sized figures.

Egglestone Abbey

1.5 miles South East of Barnard Castle, Egglestone, Northumberland
Tel: 0191 269 1200
Access at any reasonable time
Only the ruins remain of this Abbey with stands between Yorkshire and County
Durham. This site is definitely worth a visit.

Hexham Abbey

Hexham, Northumberland, NE46 3NB
Tel: 01434 602 031
Email: admin@hexhamabbey.org.uk
Website: www.hexhamabbey.org.uk
09.30-17.00 Oct-April, 09.30-19.00 May-Sept
Features of this 12C Abbey include the stone "Saint Winfrid's Chair", the
coronation seat for the Kings of Northumberland. There is also an excellent
visitors centre and guided tour.

St Paul's Church and Monastic Site

Church Bank, Jarrow, Tyne and Wear, NE32 3DZ
Tel: 0191 489 7052
Church open Mon-Sat 10.00-16.00 Sun 14.30-16.00 Monastic Site open April-Oct
10.00-17.30 Mon-Sat Sun 14.00-17.30 Nov-March Mon-Sat 10.00-16.30 Sun 12.00-16.30
This church has been in continuous use for over 1,300 years and contains The
Dedication Stone 23 Apr AD685. The Monastic Site has been excavated and
now shows the remains of the late Medieval Monastery.

GARDENS PARKS & WALKS

Hulne Park

Ratten Row, Alnwick, Northumberland, NE66 1NQ
Tel: 01665 510 777
Daily 09.00-17.00 (Dogs not allowed)
A large expanse of wooded hills that has a three mile hike hidden inside starting from the picturesque remains of Hulne Priory. Entrance to park at Ratten Row

Borough Woods/Scotch Gill Wood

Off the B6343, Morpeth to Mitford Road, Morpeth, Northumberland
Access at all times
Covering 30 acres of the Wansbeck Valley this is an excellent example of an ancient native broadleaf woodland. The Scotch Gill Wood with nature reserve and walks is nearby

Queen Elizabeth II Country Park

Woodhorn, Ashington, Off the A189, Ashington, Northumberland
Tel: 01670 856 968
Open all year 10.00-17.00
This park includes a 40 acre lake and the parkland is ideal for walks and nature trails

Project 2000 Botanic Gardens

Lannercost Park, East Cramlington, Off the B1326 towards Seaton Delaval, East Cramlington, Northumberland
Tel: 01670 714 353
Gardens always open Visitors Centre open dawn-dusk
This seven hectare site includes a nature reserve, botanic garden and circular walk

Bede's Way

From St Peter's in Wearmouth to St Paul's in Jarrow, Wearmouth, Tyne and Wear
Tel: 0191 460 2600
Website: www.greatnorthforest.co.uk
Access at all times
This 10 mile walk would have been a pilgrimage between St Peter's and St Paul's monasteries in the 7th and 8th Century

Kielder Water and Forest

Northumberland National Park, Kielder, Northumberland
Website: www.kielder.org
Access at all times

This is the largest forest in Britain and one of the largest man made forests in Europe. Covering an area of over 230 square miles. Kilder Water is the largest man made lake in Western Europe with a 27 mile shoreline.

The Garden Station

Langley, Hexham, Northumberland
Tel: 01434 684 391
Email: nilston@easynet.co.uk
Website: www.thegardenstation.co.uk
May 4th-Sept 2nd Sat & Sun 10.00-17.00

This Victorian railway station has been restored and now houses art exhibitions and a shop. The outside of the station includes a beautiful secret summer garden and a woodland walk that leads from the garden under railway bridges and into the woods

HISTORIC HOUSES

Bessie Surtees House

41-44 Sandhill, Newcastle, Tyne and Wear, NE1 3JF
Tel: 0191 269 1200
Open all year Mon-Fri 10.00-16.00

Principal rooms can be viewed of these two 16th & 17thC Merchant's houses the ground floor of one of the houses has an exhibition detailing the history of the buildings

HISTORIC SITES

Hadrians Wall

Stretches from Newcastle to Carlisle, Newcastle
Website: www.hadrians-wall.org
Access at all times

Built by the Roman Emperor in 122AD, it stretched from Newcastle to Carlisle. Today only portions of the wall are standing. The most visible remains can be seen between Chollerford and Gilsland within the Northumberland National Park

Berwick Town Walls

Surrounding Berwick Upon Tweed, On the North Bank of the River Tweed, Berwick Upon Tweed, Northumberland

Tel: 01289 330 733

Access at all times

The walls and ramparts completely encircle the old town and were built by Queen Elisabeth I to protect Berwick from Scottish raids

Arbeia Roman Fort and Museum

Baring Street, South Shields, Tyne and Wear, NE33 2BB

Tel: 0191 456 1369

Email: info@twmuseum.org.uk

Website: www.twmuseums.org.uk

East & April-Oct Mon-Sat 10.00-17.30 Sun 13.00-17.00 Free Admission to fort and museum, charge for Time Quest

Excavated Ruins and reconstructions of buildings to show what life was like in Roman Britain. This was the military supply base for 17 forts along the wall.

Auckland Castle Deer House

Auckland Park, On the A68, Bishop Auckland, County Durham

Website: www.auckland-castle.co.uk

April-Sept Daily 10.00-18.00 Oct-March Daily 10.00-16.00

This Deer House was built in 1760 to provide deer with shelter and food

Derwentcote Steel Furnace

Forge Lane, Hamsterley, Tyne and Wear

Tel: 0191 269 1200

Website: www.english-heritage.org.uk

April-Sept 13.00-17.00 Sundays

This is the earliest and most complete 18C steel making furnace to have survived in Britain

Gateshead Angel Of The North

Durham Road, Low Eighton, Gateshead, Tyne and Wear, NE9 6AA

Tel: 0191 478 4222

Access at all times

Britain's largest sculpture weighing 200 tonnes, 20 meters high and a wing span of 54 meters

Gateshead Millennium Bridge

South Shore Road, Gateshead, Tyne and Wear, NE8 3AE
Tel: 0191 478 4222
Email: steverichards@gateshead.gov.uk
Website: www.gateshead.gov.uk/bridge
Access at all times
A stunning pedestrian and cycle bridge which operates like a giant eyelid slowly opening, forming an arc under which ships can pass

MUSEUMS

Dorman Museum

Linthorpe Road, Middlesbrough, Cleveland, TS5 6LA
Tel: 01642 813 781
Email: dormanmuseum@middlesbrough.gov.uk
Website: www.dormanmuseum.co.uk
28th Feb-31 Oct (Tue-Sun) 10.00-17.30 Winter (Tues-Sun) 09.00-16.30 Closed Mondays
A selection of exhibitions and displays dedicated to local history.

Wylam Railway Museum

Falcon Terrace, Wylam, Northumberland, NE41 8EE
Tel: 01661 852 174
Email: wylampc@btinternet.com
Open all year Tues & Thurs 14.00-19.30 Sat 09.00-12.00
This museum shows the history and importance of Wylam and the railways.
Remembering local railway pioneers such as George Stephenson

Museum Of Hartlepool

Maritime Avenue, Hartlepool, County Durham, TS24 0XZ
Tel: 01429 860 006
Email: info@hartlepoolsmaritimeexperience
(Daily) 10.00-17.00
The museum gives visitors the opportunity to trace the history of the town and climb the Port's original lighthouse. Moored outside is the museum's largest exhibit the paddle steamer PSS Wigfield Castle.

Newcastle Discovery

Blandford Square, Newcastle, Tyne and Wear, NE1 1JA

Tel: 0191 232 6789

Email: info@twmuseum.org.uk

Website: www.twmuseums.org.uk

(Mon-Sat) 10.00-17.00 (Sun) 14.00-17.00

The museum tells the history of the town through various displays and exhibits covering maritime history, pioneering inventors, armed forces, local costumes and fashion.This is the regions biggest free museum.

Woodhorn Colliery Museum

Queen Elisabeth II Country Park, Off the A189, Woodhorn, Ashington, Northumberland, NE63 9YF

Tel: 01670 856 968

Email: d.tate@wansbeck.gov.uk

Website: www.woodhorn.org.uk

New Building open from Autumn 2006 please see website for opening times.

This stunning new attraction is open from Autumn 2006 and is housed in a fantastic new landmark building. There are interactive displays about the culture and mining heritage of the area, galleries, records and archives room an education centre and a cafe.

House of Hardy Museum

Willowburn, Alnwick, Northumberland, NE66 2PF

Tel: 01665 510 027

Email: sales@houseofhardy.co.uk

Website: www.houseofhardy.co.uk

Open Mon-Fri 9.00- 17.00. Sat 10.00-17.00.

A history of rods and fishing tackle from the worlds finest manufacture of these products.

Kirkharle Courtyard

Off the B6342 Between the A68 and the A696, Near Kirkharle, Near Wallington, Kirkhale, Northumberland, NE19 2PE

Tel: 01830 540 426

Email: enquiries@kirkharlecourtyard.net

Website: www.kirkharlecourtyard.net

Open all year Daily 10.00-17.00

Changing exhibitions, fine art and English furniture making as well as a collection of vintage bicycles. Birthplace of Capability Brown

Chantry Bagpipe Museum

Bridge Street, Morpeth, Northumberland, NE61 1PJ
Tel: 01670 500 717
Email: info@bagpipemuseum.org.uk
Website: www.bagpipemuseum.org.uk
All year Mon-Sat 10.00-17.00 Sundays in Summer 11.00-16.00
The chantry bagpipes are unique to Northumbria and this museum follows the development and history of the bagpipes

Otterburn Mill

Otterburn Mills Ltd, Otterburn, Northumberland, NE19 1JT
Tel: 01830 520 225
Email: enquiries@otterburnmill.co.uk
Website: www.otterburnmill.co.uk
Open all year Daily 9.00- 17.30. Sum 11.00-17.00
This working woollen mill houses a display on old woollen mill machinery and a museum as well as a mill shop where you can buy their products on site.There is also a 25 acre field for picnics and walks.

Museum Of Antiquities

University Of Newcastle Upon Tyne, Kings Walk, Newcastle, Tyne and Wear, NE1 7RU
Tel: 0191 222 7846
Email: m.o.antiquities@ncl.ac.uk
Website: www.museums.ncl.ac.uk
Mon-Sat 10.00-17.00
The principal museum of archaeology in North East England, detailing the history of the region especially the Roman frontier and Hadrian's Wall

Shefton Museum

University Of Newcastle Upon Tyne, Armstrong Building, Newcastle, Tyne and Wear, NE1 7RU
Tel: 0191 222 8996
Email: a.r.parkin@ncl.ac.uk
Website: www.ncl.ac.uk/antiquities
Mon-Fri 10.00-16.00
A collection of archaeological material from the Greek world, with examples of Greek painted pottery, a range of armour and sculptures

Stephenson Railway Museum

Middle Engine Lane, North Shields, Tyne and Wear, NE29 8DX
Tel: 0191 200 7146
Website: www.twmuseums.org.uk
May-Sept Tues-Thurs 11.00-15.00 Weekends 11.00-16.00
Visitors can relive the days of the steam engine with this museum dedicated to railway engines

Sunderland Museum and Winter Gardens

Burdon Road, Sunderland, Tyne and Wear, SR1 1PP
Tel: 0191 553 2323
Website: www.twmuseums.org.uk
Mon-Sat 10.00-17.00 Sun 14.00-17.00
This museum tells the story of Sunderland from pre-historic times to the present day. The Winter Garden is a display of some of the world's most exotic flowers and plants

Tynemouth Volunteer Life Brigade Museum

Spanish Battery, Tynemouth, Tyne and Wear, NE30 4DD
Tel: 0191 296 0434
Tues-Sat 10.00-15.00 Sun 10.00-12.00
This museum contains artefacts and rescue equipment dating from the wreck of " The Stanley" in 1864 to modern day and a selection of nautical memorabilia

FARMERS MARKETS

Amble Farmers Market

Amble Town Square, Amble, Northumberland
Tel: 01665 712929
Last Friday of the month 10.00-14.00
Farmers Market with local produce for sale

Hexham Farmers Market

Market Place, Hexham, Northumberland
Tel: 01434 673 326
Email: hallshill@tinyonline.co.uk
2nd Saturday and 4th Saturday of the month 09.00-13.30
Farmers Market with local produce for sale

Barnard Castle Farmers Market

Market Place, Barnards Castle, County Durham
Tel: 0771 967 3739
1st Saturday of the month 10.00-15.00
Farmers Market with local produce for sale

Darlington Farmers Market

Market Square, Darlington, County Durham
3rd Friday of the month 09.00-16.00
Farmers Market with local produce for sale

FESTIVALS

Newcastle Community Green Festival

Leazes Park, Newcastle, Tyne and Wear
Tel: 0191 232 1750
Email: newcastle_greenfest@hotmail.com
During May please contact tourist board for exact dates
This festival offers positive solutions to environmental problems, through artists, musicians and children's activities

Surry Kent And Sussex-England

ART GALLERIES/ARTS & CRAFTS

Star Gallery
Castle Ditch Lane, Lewes, East Sussex, BN7 1YJ
Tel: 01273 480 218
Email: info@stargallery.co.uk
Website: www.stargallery.co.uk
Mon-Sat 11.00-17.30 During Exhibitions
The gallery presents an ever changing selection of exhibitions by various artists

Firstsite @ The Minories Art Gallery
74 High Street, Colchester, Essex, CO1 1UE
Tel: 01206 577 067
Email: info@firstsite.uk.net
Website: www.firstsite.uk.net
Mon-Sat 10.00-17.00
The region's premier contemporary visual arts organisation. Exciting year round exhibitions and events

Pooh Corner
High Street, Hartfield, East Sussex, TN7 4AE
Tel: 01892 770 456
Email: shop@pooh-country.co.uk
Website: www.pooh-country.co.uk
Mon-Sat 09.00-17.00 Sun 11.00-17.00
This 300 year old shop is where Christopher Robin went shopping with his nanny, and now houses the largest selection of poohphernalia in the world

Wilkin's Of Tiptree-Jam Museum
Tiptree, 8 miles from Colchester, Tiptree, Essex
Tel: 01621 815 407
Email: tiptree@tiptree.com
Website: www.tiptree.com
Mon-Sat 10.00-17.00 June-August also Sunday 12.00-17.00
Home of the world famous Tiptree jams. There is a museum, Jam Factory Visitors Centre, Shop and Tea Room on site.

Biddenden Vineyards

Little Whatmans, Gribble Bridge Lane, Biddenden, Ashford, Kent, TN27 8DF

Tel: 01580 291 726

Email: info@biddendenvineyards.com

Website: www.biddendenvineyards.com

Open Mon-Sat 10.00-17.00 Sun 11.00-17.00 (Closed Sun Jan & Feb)

Kent's oldest commercial vineyard with 22 acres of vines. See the winery and sample the apple juice, cider and wines produced at this vineyard.

Evegate Craft Centre

Evegate, Smeeth, Kent, TN25 6SX

Tel: 01303 812 334

Email: evegate-central@msn.com

Website: www.denaploy.co.uk/evegate

Mon -Sun 10.00-17.00 (Some shops closed on Mon)

Home to antique restorers, silversmiths, picture framers, potters and other fascinating crafts

Elham Valley Vineyards

Elham Valley Road, Breach, Barham, Kent, CT4 6LN

Tel: 01227 831 266

Mon-Fri 09.00-17.00, Sat 12.00-18.00

Set in the most beautiful valley in Kent, visitors can wander through the rows upon rows of vines and sample the produce made on site. There is also a pottery and small animal sanctuary on site.

Wooden Spoon Preserving Company

The New Oast, Coldharbour Farm, Wye, Kent, TN25 5DB

Tel: 01233 813 326

Email: info@thewoodenspoon.co.uk

Website: www.thewoodenspoon.co.uk

Factory Shop Mon-Fri 09.30-16.30

View the delicious range of home preserves being made through a viewing window in the factory shop. These preserves are produced entirely by hand using only the finest ingredients.

Bosham Walk Art and Crafts Centre

Bosham Lane, Bosham, Sussex, PO18 8HX

Tel: 01243 572 475

Email: dscottsb@aol.com

Website: www.bosham-walk.co.uk

Daily 10.00-17.30 Nov-March Mon-Fri 10.00-17.00 Sat & Sun 10.00-17.30

Bosham Walk is an arcade of 17 individual craft shops, where visitors can watch the crafts people at work

Ballard's Brewery

Unit C, The Old Sawmill, Nyewood, Rogate, Sussex, GU31 5HA
Tel: 01730 821 301
Email: info@ballardsbrewery.org.uk
Website: www.ballardsbrewery.org.uk
Mon-Fri 08.00-16.00
Visitors are shown the workings of this brewery and given a chance to sample the beer

Cinque Ports Pottery

The Monastery, Conduit Hill, Rye, Sussex, TN31 7LE
Tel: 01797 222 033
Email: info@cinqueportspottery.co.uk
Website: www.cinqueportspottery.co.uk
Mon-Fri 09.00-17.00 Sat 10.00-17.00
The pottery was established in 1957 in an Augustinian Friary. Visitors can experience the process of a working pottery from the public viewing gallery on weekdays

Tenterden Vineyard

Smallhythe, Tenterden, Kent, TN30 7NG
Tel: 01580 763 033
Email: tourism@chapeldownwines.co.uk
Website: www.chapeldownwines.co.uk
Mon-Sun 10.00-17.00
Visitors can view our gift shop, herb garden and plant centre along with a free tasting of our award winning wines. Charge for guided tours

Lamberhurst Vineyard

Ridge Farm, Lamberhurst, Kent, TN3 8ER
Tel: 01892 890 170
Open 10.00-17.00 Daily
Visitors can purchase wines, liqueurs and gifts there are also free tastings,a garden centre, bistro and on site pub. Charge for guided tours.

Romney Marsh Craft Gallery

Lydd Library, Old School, Skinner Road, Lydd, Kent, TN29 9HN
Tel: 01797 320 131
Email: melanie.powell@kent.gov.uk
Mon, Tues & Thurs 10.00-13.00 & 14.00-16.30 Fri 10.00-13.00 & 14.00-18.00 Sat 10.00-13.00
Changing exhibitions of contemporary crafts including jewellery, silverwear, textiles and ceramics

Mill Yard Craft Centre
Swan Street, West Malling, Kent, ME19 6LP
Tel: 01732 845 888
09.30-17.00 Daily
Visitors can watch craftsmen at work at this crafts centre, housed within a 16C
barn and carriage house

CASTLES

Bramber Castle
West of the village of Bramber, 12 miles NW of Brighton, Bramber, West Sussex
Access at any reasonable time
The castle stands on a wood covered hill overlooking Bramber village

Eynsford Castle
In Eynsford, Off the A225, Junction 3 off the M25, Eynsford, Kent, DA4 0JF
Tel: 01793 414 910
Website: www.english-heritage.org.uk
April-Sept 10.00-18.00 daily Oct-Nov & Feb-March 10.00-16.00 daily Dec-Jan 10.00-16.00
Wed-Sun
One of the first stone castles to be built by the Normans, the moat and remains
of the curtain wall and hall can be seen

Sutton Valence Castle
In Sutton Valence Village on A274, 5 miles SE of Maidstone, Sutton Valence, Kent
Email: admin@suttonvalence.org.uk
Website: www.suttonvalence.org.uk
Access at all reasonable times
The ruins of a 12C stone keep.

Churches & Cathedrals

Rochester Cathedral

The Precincts, Rochester, Kent, ME1 1SX
Tel: 01634 843 366
Email: cathedral@rochester.anglican.org
Website: www.rochestercathedral.org
(Daily) 07.30-18.00
This cathedral was once home to the remains of St William Of Perth a Scottish baker who started out on a pilgrimage to the holy land in 120, unfortunately his pilgrimage was cut short in Rochester where he was robbed and murdered.

Chichester Cathedral

West Street, Chichester, Sussex, PO19 1PX
Tel: 01243 782 595
Website: www.chichestercathedral.co.uk
Summer (Daily) 07.00-19.00, Winter 07.00-18.00
The spire of this cathedral can be see from out at sea and the interior is famous for it's contemporary art.

St John's Abbey Gate

St John's Lane, Clerkenwell, Colchester, Essex, EC1M 4DA
Tel: 01206 282 931
Access at any reasonable time-Exterior View Only
All that survives from this Benedictine abbey is this quaint gatehouse in East Anglian flintwork.

Guildford Cathedral

Stagg Hill, Guildford, Surrey, GU2 7UP
Tel: 01483 565 287
Website: www.guildford-cathedral.org
Open all year daily 8.30-17.30
Consecrated as recently as 1961 and designed by Edward Maufe. Features include marble floors and soaring arches.

Boxgrove Priory

Church Lane, Boxgrove, 4 miles E of Chichester on minor road off A27, Boxgrove, West Sussex, PO18 0ED
Tel: 01243 774 045
Access at any reasonable time
Founded in 1177, this is a wonderful example of Early English architecture. Sites worth noting are the 16C painted ceiling and the Chantry Chapel dating 1534.

All Saints Parish Church

Tudeley, Near Tonbridge, Tudeley, Kent
Tel: 01732 357 648
Email: patricia@tudeley.org
Website: www.tudeley.org
Summer Mon-Sat 09.00-18.00 Winter Mon-Sat 09.00-Dusk
This ancient church is renowned for its stained glass windows by Marc Chagall

Waverley Abbey

2 Miles SE of Farnham, Off the B3001, Near Elstead Village, Farnham, Surrey
Website: www.waverley.gov.uk/abbey
Access at all reasonable times
Established in 1128 by William Gifford, Bishop of Winchester, Waverley was the
first Cistercian Abbey in England

Knights Templar Church

On the Western Heights above Dover, Dover, Kent
Website: www.english-heritage.org.uk
Access at all reasonable times
The foundations of a small Medieval Church where King John may have made
subjection to the Papal Legate

GARDENS PARKS & WALKS

The White Cliffs of Dover Visitors Centre

Upper Road, Langdon Cliffs, Dover, Kent, CT16 1HJ
Tel: 01304 202 756
Email: whitecliffs@nationaltrust.org.uk
Visitors Centre Open March - Oct Mon-Sun 10.00-17.00, Nov - Feb Mon-Sun 11.00-16.00
These spectacular cliffs dominate the town of Dover and have provided literary,
and romantic inspiration over the years, particularly with loved ones sailing off to
fight in the war.

Winchelsea Beach

Winchelsea, 2 miles SW of Rye, Winchelsea, East Sussex
Website: www.winchelseabeach.org.uk
Access at all times
This beautiful expanse of shore line is composed of pebbles and offers some
fantastic views.

Beachy Head

From Eastbourne take Dukes Drive from the sea front, Eastbourne, East Sussex
Access at all times
This is the most dramatic stretch of the Sussex coastline with 575 ft high cliffs
and a lighthouse below.

Buchan Country Park

Horsham Road, Crawley, West Sussex, RH11 9HQ
Tel: 01293 542 088
Park Open all year Summer 08.00-20.00 Winter 08.00-18.00 (or dusk if earlier) Countryside
Centre Sundays 13.00-17.00
This 170 acres of county park contains woodland walks and trails. There is also
a visitors centre which arranges activities and events.

GARDENS PARKS & WALKS/HISTORIC HOUSES

Saint Hill Manor

Saint Hill Road, East Grinstead, West Sussex, RH19 4JY
Tel: 01324 326 711
Website: www.sainthillmanor.org.uk
Open all year-daily tours.14.00-17.00 on the hour.
This Victorian mansion was the home of L. Ron Hubbard the founder of
Scientology and there are guided tours of the house. The house has stunning
grounds which include a lake, a rose garden, and woods to wander around within
this Victorian garden.

GARDENS PARKS & WALKS

Cudmore Grove Country Park

Bromans Lane, East Mersea, Essex, CO5 8UE
Tel: 01206 383 868
Open daily 8.00-dusk
Designated nature reserve for birdwatching and nature, this park also boasts of
long sandy beaches, grasslands and picnic areas.

High Woods Country Park

Turner Road, Colchester, Essex, CO4 5JR
Tel: 01206 853 588
Open at all times.
300 acres of grassland, woodland, farmland and wetland all within 2 miles from the Town centre.

Highdown Chalk Gardens

Littlehampton Road, Worthing, West Sussex, BN12 6PE
Tel: 01903 239 999
April-Sept Mon-Sat 10.00-18.00 Oct-Nov Mon-Fri 10.00-16.30 Dec-Jan Mon-Fri 10.00-16.00
Feb-March Mon-Fri 10.00-16.30
This garden offers a collection of rare plant and trees.

HISTORIC HOUSES

Watt's Charity

Six Poor Travellers House, Maidstone Road, Rochester, Kent, ME1 1SE
Tel: 01634 842 194
Tues-Sat 14.00-17.00
These 16C Alms Houses were featured in Charles Dickens short story " The Seven Poor Travellers". The inside features galleried Elizabethan bedrooms.

Southover Grange

Southover Road, Lewes, Sussex, BN7 1TP
Tel: 01273 484 999
Exterior view of house. Gardens Open all year dawn-dusk
The grange that was built in 1575 still retains it's priory and beautiful gardens, the building now houses the local registry office and is popular for weddings. The gardens surrounding the Grange are open to the public and stunning

Medieval Undercroft

72 High Street, Guildford, Surrey
East-Sep (Tue, Thur) 14.00-16.00 (Sat) 12.00-16.00
Well preserved 13C basement of vaulted arches.

Old Soar Manor

Plaxtol, Borough Green, Kent, TN15 0QX
Tel: 01732 810 378
3rd April-30th Sept Mon, Tues, Wed, Thurs, Sat & Sun 10.00-18.00
A 13C Knight's dwelling. There is a ghost of a servant said to haunt the Chapel.

The Guildhall

High Street, Guildford, Surrey, GU1 3AA
Tel: 01483 444 035
Open Tues & Thurs for guided tours at 14.00 & 15.00
This former 16 & 17C Courtroom and Council Chamber houses the civic plate. A wonderful bracket clock dating 1683 dominates the building.

St Augustine's Cross

2 miles East of Minster, Off the B29048, Ebbsfleet, Kent
Tel: 0800 696 996
Access at any reasonable time
This cross marks the site of arrival of St. Augustine in AD 597.

St Leonard's Tower

On unclassified road W of A228, 1 mile from West Malling, West Malling
Tel: 01732 870 872
Exterior View at any reasonable time. Interior view by appointment please contact West Malling Parish Council on 01732 870872
Viewing is restricted to the outside only of this Norman Tower.

The Packhouse

Hewett's Kilns, Tongham Road, Runfold, Surrey, GU10 1PJ
Tel: 01252 781 010
Website: www.packhouse.com
Mon-Fri 10.30-17.30 Sat & Sun 10.00-17.30
One of the largest antiques centres in Surrey with over 100 stall holders housed within a large Grade II listed building

Hogs Back Brewery Ltd

Manor Farm, The Street, Tongham, Surrey, GU10 1DE
Tel: 01252 783 000
Email: enquiries@hogsback.co.uk
Website: www.hogsback.co.uk
Mon & Tues 10.00-18.00 Wed-Fri 10.00-20.30 Sat 09.00-18.00 Sun 10.00-16.00
24 Real Ales are brewed at this independent brewery. A viewing gallery in the brewery shop allows visitors to watch the brewery in action. Charge for tours.

Ifield Watermill

Hyde Drive, Ifield West, Crawley, Sussex, RH11 0PL
Tel: 01293 539 088
Open last Sunday of the month May-Sept 14.30-17.00
Currently being restored by volunteers from the Crawley Museum Society, this watermill features a working waterwheel and displays of local history and milling machinery

Nutley Windmill

Crowborough Road, Nutley, Sussex
Tel: 01435 873 367
Email: nutley_mill@talk21.com
Open last Sunday of the month March -Sept 14.30-17.30
Nutley Windmill was built in 1670 but moved to its preset site in 1830 and is the oldest working mill in Sussex.

Temple Manor

Knight Road, Strood, Kent, ME2 2AH
Tel: 01634 338 110
Website: www.english-heritage.org.uk
April-Sept 10.00-18.00 Sundays Oct 10.00-16.00 Sundays
Constructed in the 13C, Temple Manor was the house of the Knight's Templar

Union Windmill

Mill Hill, Cranbrook, Kent
Tel: 01580 712 256
Sat April-Sept 14.30-17.00 2nd Weekend in May & Mid July-End Aug Sun 14.30-17.00
This is the tallest working smock mill in England and was built in 1814

HISTORIC SITES

Kit's Coty House and Little Kit's Coty House

Kits Coty, Bluebell Hill, West of the A229, 2 miles North of Maidstone, Maidstone, Kent
Website: www.english-heritage.org.uk
Access at all reasonable times
Remains of two prehistoric burial chambers

Reculver Towers and Roman Fort

Reculver, 3 miles East of Hernebay, Reculver, Kent, CT6 6SS
Tel: 01227 740676
Website: www.english-heritage.org.uk
Exterior view at all times
A 12C landmark with twin towers and the walls of a Roman Fort

EXHIBITIONS

Beachy Head Countryside Centre

Beachy Head Road, Beachy Head, Eastbourne, East Sussex, BN20 7YA
Tel: 01323 737 273
Summer Daily 10.00-16.00 Winter Weekends only 10.00-15.30
Exhibitions of the history and ecology of Beachy Head

NATURE & WILDLIFE

Aldborough Hall Farm

Aldborough Road North, Aldborough Hatch, Ilford, Sussex, IG2 7TD
Tel: 020 8597 6540
Tues-Sat 09.00-17.00 Sun 10.00-16.00
This farm has rescued animals, as well as pick your own produce and picnic area

MUSEUMS

Bognor Regis Wireless Museum

69 High Street, Bognor Regis, Sussex, PO21 1RY
Tel: 01243 865 636
April-Oct Tues-Sun 10.30-16.30
A museum of domestic radio, television equipment, military and associated radio

Chichester District Museum

29 Little London, Chichester, West Sussex, PO19 1PB
Tel: 01243 784 683
Email: Districtmuseum@chichester.gov.uk
Website: www.chichester.gov.uk/museums/
(Tue-Sat) 10.00-17.30
The museum is situated in a former corn store and has various displays and exhibitions concentrating on local life. The exhibits date from pre-history to the reign of our current monarch, Elizabeth II.

Chichester Guildhall Museum

The Priory, Priory Road, Chichester, West Sussex
Tel: 01243 784 683
7June-13 Sept Sat Only 12.00-16.00
The guildhall museum is situated in a 13C Franciscan church in the centre of Priory Park

Guildford Museum

Castle Arch, Quarry Street, Guildford, Surrey, GU1 3SX
Tel: 01483 444 750
Email: museum@guildford.gov.uk
(Mon-Sat) 11.00-17.00
The museum was founded in 1898 and now houses the largest collection of archaeology, local history and needlework in Surrey

The Guildhall Museum

High Street, Rochester, Kent, ME1 1PY
Tel: 01634 333 111
Email: guildhall.museum@medway.gov.uk
(Daily) 10.00-16.30
The museum contains a model of King John's siege of the castle and an exhibition on the prison ships there are also two rooms dedicated to Charles Dickens.

Whitstable Museum And Gallery

Oxford Street, Whitstable, Kent, CT5 1DB
Tel: 01227 276 998
Website: www.whitstable-museum.co.uk
Mon-Sat 10.00-16.00 July & August also Sundays 13.00-16.00
The museum features a photographic display of the town of Whitstable in its hey day with special exhibitions on oysters, diving and shipping.

Tunbridge Wells Museum And Art Gallery

Civic Centre, Mount Pleasant, Tunbridge Wells, Kent, TN1 1JN
Tel: 01892 554 171
Website: www.tunbridgewellsmuseum.org
(Mon-Sat) 09.30-17.00 Sundays 10.00-16.00
The museum displays varied collections including dolls, toys and games,
Tunbridge Wear, National & Social History, Costumes and Textiles and Fine Art.

Brighton Museum And Art Gallery

Royal Pavillion Gardens, Brighton, East Sussex, BN1 1EE
Tel: 01273 290 900
Email: visitor.services@brighton-hove.gov.uk
Tues 10.00-19.00 Wed-Sat 10.00-17.00 Sun 14.00-17.00
The museum has a varied number of exhibits including nouveau furniture,
paintings, pottery and porcelain

Booth Museum Of Natural History

194 Dyke Road, Brighton, East Sussex, BN1 5AA
Tel: 01273 292 777
Email: booth.museum@brighton-hove.gov.uk
(Mon-Sat) 10.00-17.00 (Sun) 14.00-17.00
The museum houses collections of stuffed birds, animals and skeletons and the
building was purpose built to house Mr E. T. Booth's Collections.

FARMERS MARKETS

Guildford Farmers Market

Guildford High Street, Guildford, Surrey
1st Tuesday of the month 11.30-15.30
Farmers Market with local produce for sale

Woking Farmers Market

Town Square, Woking, Surrey
3rd Thursday of the month 11.00-15.00
Farmers Market with local produce for sale

Hailsham Farmers Market

Hailsham Cattle Market Site, Hailsham, East Sussex
Tel: 01323 833 359
2nd Saturday of the month 09.00-13.00
Farmers Market with local produce for sale

Haywards Heath Farmers Market

Carpark next to Iceland Food Store, Hayward Road, Haywards Heath, West Sussex

3rd Thursday of the month 09.00-14.00

Farmers Market with local produce for sale

Arundel Farmers Market

Market Square, Jubilee Gardens, Arundel, West Sussex, BN18 9DF

Tel: 01798 865804

1st Thursday and 3rd Saturday of the month 09.00-13.00

Farmers Market with local produce for sale

London City-Inner London-England

Tate Modern
Bankside, London, Inner London, SE1 9TG
Tel: 020 7887 8000
Website: www.tate.org.uk
Sunday-Thurs 10.00-18.00 Fri & Sat 10.00-22.00
The Tate Modern collection comprises the national collection of British art from the year 1500 to the present day, and of international modern art.

Tate Britain
Millbank, London, Inner London, SW1P 4RG
Tel: 020 7887 8000
Website: www.tate.org.uk
(Daily) 10.00-17.50
One of London's most famous galleries,housing the collection of National British Paintings including British Art 1500-1900, British Art 1900-2004, Dunveen Galleries, Turner Collection and a wide range of exhibitions and events under one neo-classical roof

National Gallery
Trafalgar Square, London, Inner London, WC2N 5DN
Tel: 020 7747 2885
Email: information@ng-london.org.uk
Website: www.nationalgallery.org.uk
Daily 10.00-18.00, (Wed) 10.00-21.00,
Founded in 1824 with just 38 pictures, now houses over 2000 western European paintings from 13C-1900. Comfortable interior with Chesterfield sofas, marble and wooden floors add to the atmosphere and there are guided tours for those who feel daunted.

National Portrait Gallery
2 Saint Martin's Place, just North of Trafalgar Square, London, Inner London, WC2H 0HE
Tel: 020 7306 0055
Website: www.npg.org.uk
Daily 10.00-18.00 Late night opening Thurs & Fri until 21.00
The gallery was founded in 1856, its aim being to collect paintings of Royal and political figures through the ages, an aim which has been definitely achieved. One of the most prized exhibits is the only known portrait of the writer William Shakespeare.

Wallace Collection

Hertford House, Manchester Square, London, Inner London, W1U 3BN
Tel: 020 7563 9500
Website: www.wallacecollection.org
Daily 10.00-17.00 Free Guided Tours on weekdays at 13.00 also Wed & Sat 11.30 and Sundays 15.00
The hallway and state drawing room of this 18C house have been restored to their original splendour and now house an extraordinary selection of furniture, paintings and porcelain. Home of the Laughing Cavalier by Franz Hals

Camden Arts Centre

Arkwright Road, Corner of Finchley Road, London, Inner London, NW3 6DG
Tel: 020 7472 5500
Email: info@camdenartscentre.org
Website: www.camdenartscentre.org
Tues, Thurs, Fri, Sat, Sun 10.00-18.00 Wed 10.00-21.00
This is the Borough of Camden's Community Arts Centre which houses three galleries that host contemporary exhibitions.

Chisenhale Gallery

64 Chisenhale Road, London, Inner London, E3 5QZ
Tel: 020 8981 4518
Email: mail@chisenhale.org.uk
Website: www.chisenhale.org.uk
(Wed-Sun)13.00-18.00
This late Victorian warehouse that backs onto a canal provides an unusual location for a selection of various innovative art forms

The Royal Institute Of British Archetects

66 Portland Place, London, Inner London, W1B 1AD
Tel: 020 7580 5533
Email: info@riba.org
Website: www.riba.org
Exhibition Floors Mon-Fri 10.00-18.00 Sat 10.00-17.00
The gallery which was built in 1934 is a celebration to the great and good within the architects profession.

Serpentine Gallery

Kensington Gardens, Near Albert Memorial, London, Inner London, W2 3XA
Tel: 020 7402 6075
Email: information@serpentinegallery.org
Website: www.serpentinegallery.org
(Daily) 10.00-18.00
The gallery in housed in a former tea pavilion with French windows that look out across Hyde Park. There are a variety of exhibitions which are enhanced by the quality of natural light that floods the building.

Association Gallery

Association Of Photographers Gallery, 81 Leonard Street, London, Inner London, EC2A 4QS
Tel: 020 7739 6669
Email: gallery@aophoto.co.uk
Website: www.the-aop.org
(Mon-Fri) 10.00-18.00, (Sat) 12.00-16.00
Opened in 1986 the gallery stages around 20 exhibitions of contemporary photography every year and has an exhibition of association photographers award winners work each march.

Photographers' Gallery

5 & 8 Great Newport Street, London, Inner London, WC2H 7HY
Tel: 020 7831 1772
Email: info@photonet.org.uk
Website: www.photonet.org.uk
(Mon-Sat) 11.00-18.00 Thurs Late nights 11.00-20.00 Sunday 12.00-18.00
Opened in 1971 the gallery was the first of its kind in England and has continued to promote contemporary photography over the last 30 years.

Flowers East Gallery

82 Kingsland Road, London, E2 8DP
Tel: 020 7920 7777
Email: gallery@flowerseast.com
Website: www.flowerseast.com
Tues-Sat 10.00-18.00 Sun 11.00-17.00
An internationally recognised showcase for new British art

20th Century Gallery

821 Fulham Road, Fulham, London, SW6 5HG
Tel: 020 7384 1334
Email: chapmanprints@aol.com
Website: www.hilarychapmanfineprints.co.uk
Mon-Fri 10.00-18.00 Sat 10.00-13.00
Established artists offering affordable prints in addition to changing exhibitions

London International Gallery Of Children's Art

255 Finchley Road, London, NW3 6LU
Tel: 020 7435 0903
Email: info@ligca.org
Website: www.ligca.org
Tues-Thurs 16.00-18.00 Fri-Sun 12.00-18.00
Devoted to art produced by children both locally and from around the world

White Cube

48 Hoxton Square, Hoxton, London, N1 6PB
Tel: 020 7930 5373
Email: enquiries@whitecube.com
Website: www.whitecube.com
Tues-Sat 10.00-18.00 During exhibitions
Housed in a 1920s industrial building this gallery shows a variety of contemporary art. The gallery was established in April 2000 and maintains a programme of major solo exhibitions

CHURCHES & CATHEDRALS

Southwark Cathedral

London Bridge, London, Inner London, SE1 9DA
Tel: 020 7367 6700
Email: cathedral@dswark.org.uk
Website: www.dswark.org/cathedral
Mon-Fri 07.30-18.00 Sat & Sun 08.30-18.00
The oldest parts of the building date from the 12C, but after the reformation it fell into disrepair and was used as both a pig sty and a bakery. In 1905 the building was restored as an Anglican Cathedral .Admission Free but Donation Suggested.

St Bartholomew The Great

West Smithfield, London, Inner London, EC1A 7JQ
Tel: 020 7606 5171
Email: admin@greatstbarts.com
Website: www.greatstbarts.com
(Tues-Fri) 08.30-17.00 (Closes at 16.00 Mid Nov-Mid Feb), (Sat) 10.30-13.30, (Sun) 08.30-13.00 & 14.30-20.00
The only surviving part of a Norman priory founded in 1123. This is London's oldest and most atmospheric church.

St Botolph's Church

Aldgate, London, Inner London, EC3N 1AB

Tel: 020 7283 1670

Email: ajktherapies@hotmail.com

Website: www.stbotolphs.org.uk

Mon-Fri & Sun 10.00-15.00 (Not open on Saturdays)

This church which was built in 1744 is noted for it's highly original ceilings which are lined with angels and adorn the galleried interior.

St Bride's Church

Fleet Street, Blackfriars, London, Inner London, EC4Y 8AU

Tel: 020 7427 0133

Email: info@stbrides.com

Website: www.stbrides.com

(Mon-Fri) 08.00-18.00, (Sat) 11.00-15.00, (Sun) 10.00-13.00 & 17.30-19.30

This is the Fleet Street Church of the press, printing and journalism. When the church was gutted during the blitz the devastation revealed many Roman and Saxon remains which are now displayed in the crypt.

St Helen's Church

Great St Helen's, Bishopsgate, London, Inner London, EC3A 6AT

Tel: 020 7283 2231

Email: st-helens@st-helens.org.uk

Website: www.st-helens.org.uk

(Mon-Fri) 09.00-17.00

The building was founded in the 13C and contains a 14C Nuns Chapel and 15C Gothic arches. The interior also contains many medieval and Tudor monument to London dignitaries, which has lead to the church being known as The Westminster Abbey of The City.

St Magnus The Martyr

Lower Thames Street, London, Inner London, EC3R 6DN

Tel: 020 7626 4481

Email: rector@stmagnus.fsnet.co.uk

Website: www.stmagnusmartyr.org.uk

(Tue-Fri) 10.00-16.00, (Sun) 10.00-13.00 Free recitals on most Tuesdays at 13.00

This medieval building stood on the road that lead to the Old London Bridge and it's interior was described by TS Elliot as an inexplicable splendour of Ionian white and gold.

St Mary-Le-Bow

Cheapside, London, Inner London, EC2V 6AU

Tel: 020 7248 5139

Email: administrator@bowbells.dircon.co.uk

Website: www.stmarylebow.co.uk

Mon-Fri 06.30-18.00

The bells of this church are the origins of the tradition that only those born within hearing distance of the Bow Bells can claim to be true Cockney's.The church was built by Sir Christopher Wren and displays a white tower topped with a dragon weathercock

GARDENS PARKS & WALKS

Regents Park

Park Crescent, London, Inner London, NW1

Tel: 020 7486 7905

Email: klewis@royalparks.gsi.gov.uk

Website: www.royalparks.gov.uk

(Daily) 05.00- 30 mins before dusk.

The park contains a boating lake with resident herons on the island, tennis courts, a café and an impressive open air theatre. A walk in Queen Mary's Gardens is one of the pleasures of London.

Hyde Park

Hyde Park Corner, Knightsbridge, London, Inner London, W2

Tel: 020 7298 2100

Email: hyde@royalparks.gsi.gov.uk

Website: www.royalparks.gov.uk

(Daily) 05.00-Midnight

This is the largest park in Central London and contains a variety of things to do and see. One of the most entertaining is listening to the soap box orators declaring their right to Free Speech on Sundays. The park is however best avoided after dark

Kensington Gardens

Bayswater, High Street, Kensington, London, Inner London

Tel: 020 7298 2100

Website: www.royalparks.gov.uk

Daily 06.00-dusk

There are a variety of things to do in the gardens including the sunken gardens, the round pond, elfin oak, children's puppet shows and playground, and a café "The Orangery"

St James Park

The Mall, London, Inner London, SW1
Tel: 020 7930 1793
Email: stjames@royalparks.gsi.gov.uk
Website: www.royalparks.gov.uk
(Daily) 05.00 - Midnight
The bridge that spans the lake in the park is one of the best places to view Buckingham Palace from. #The lake is a wildfowl sanctuary for pelicans, ducks, geese, and black swans.There is a children's playground and refreshments available in the Cake House

Tibetan Garden

Geraldine Mary Harmsworth Park, St George's Road, London, SE1 6ER
Tel: 020 7242 4988
Email: peacegarden@tibet-foundation.org
Website: www.tibetanpeacegarden.com
Dawn-Dusk
Dedicated to peace this Tibetan Garden was opened by the Dalai Lama himself

Camley Street Natural Park

12 Camley Street, London, NW1 0PW
Tel: 020 7833 2311
Email: info@lwtcamleyst.cix.co.uk
Website: www.wildlondon.org.uk
Mon-Thurs 09.00-17.00 Sat & Sun Summer 11.00-17.00 Sat & Sun Winter 10.00-dusk
An internationally acclaimed reserve on the banks of the Regents Canal includes a meadow and woodlands providing a natural environment for a rich variety of plant life

Gillespie Park Nature Reserve

191 Drayton Park, Islington, London, N5 1PH
Tel: 020 7354 5162
Access at all times
This Nature Reserve offers habitat to a range of wildlife through its woodland, meadows and ponds

Holland Park

The Stable Yard, Holland Park, Ilchester Place, London, W8 6LU
Tel: 020 7471 9813
Email: leisure.services@rbkc.gov.uk
Website: leisure.services@rbkc.gov.uk
Daily 07.30-half an hour before dusk
The largest park in the Royal Borough and boasts formal and informal gardens as well as tennis courts, football pitch and netball court

Haggerston Park

Audrey Street, Hackney, London, E2 8QH
Tel: 020 7739 6288
Summer Mon-Sun 07.00-21.30 Winter Mon-Sun 07.00-16.00
Within this park there is a café, extensive gardens and the Hackney City Farm
with pigs, sheep, ducks and rabbits

Springfield Park

Springfield Mansion, Springfield, Hackney, London, E5 9EF
Tel: 020 7886 9674
Summer Mon-Sun 07.30-21.30 Winter Mon-Sun 07.30-16.30
This parks spans the grounds of what used to be three private houses.
Springfield House survived and is open to the public, the old glasshouses are
now a tropical conservatory with pond

Queens Park

Kingswood Avenue, Brent, London, NW6
Tel: 020 8969 5661
Email: queens.park@corpoflondon.gov.uk
Dawn-Dusk
This Victorian Park includes an 1891 listed bandstand, tennis courts, children's
playground, a children's farm and woodland walks

Keats House Garden

Keats Grove, Hampstead, London, NW3 2RR
Tel: 020 7435 2062
Email: keatshouse@corpoflondon.gov.uk
Website: www.keatshouse.org.uk
Nov 9-March 20 Tues-Sun 13.00-17.00 March 22-Oct 30 Tues-Sun 12.00-17.00
The gardens of two originally semi detached houses, in one of which the poet
John Keats lodged. The houses were converted into one dwelling in 1838 and
the exterior remains much the same. Charge for entry to the house but exterior
view and gardens free.

Historic Houses

Prince Henry's Room

17 Fleet Street, London, Inner London, EC4Y 1AA
Tel: 020 7936 4004
(Mon-Fri) 11.00-14.00
One of the few buildings that survived the Great Fire Of London. It was built in 1611 and named after James I eldest son. The interior has an intact plaster ceiling and oak panelling and is now the home of a collection dedicated to Samuel Pepys

Freemason's Hall

60 Great Queen Street, London, Inner London, WC2 5AZ
Tel: 020 7831 9811
(Mon-Fri) 10.00-17.00 Sat 10.30-13.00 (Admission to the interior by booked guided tours only - book tours at the hall)
This is the central meeting place for the 8660 Masonic lodges throughout the UK. The interior contains acres of white marble and green jade that stretches from floor to ceiling.

Old Bailey

Corner of Newgate Street and Old Bailey, London, Inner London, EC4M 7BH
Tel: 020 7248 3277
(Mon-Fri) 10.00-13.00 & 14.00-16.30 No under 14s and 14-16s only with adult
The Central criminal Court has witnessed some of the most famous trial's in London's history.Including Oscar Wilde, Dr Crippen, Peter Sutcliffe. Built on the site of the famous Newgate Prison. The Public are allowed to watch the trials taking place

Events

Oxford V Cambridge Boat Race

The River Thames, Between Putney Bridge and Chiswick Bridge, London
Website: www.theboatrace.org
March annually-please check website or tourist board for exact date
The annual rowing contest between England's two oldest and most famous Universities Oxford and Cambridge

HISTORIC SITES

Kensal Green Cemetery
Harrow Road, Kensal Green, London, W10 4RA
Tel: 020 8969 0152
Email: hvn@cix.co.uk
Website: www.kensalgreen.co.uk
April-Sept Mon-Sat 09.00-17.30 Sun 10.00-17.30 Oct-March Mon-Sat 09.00-16.30 Sun
10.00-16.30
One of the best examples of Victorian culture with an amazing array of
tombstones and historical figures

MUSEUMS

Museum Of London
150 London Wall, London, EC2Y 5HN
Tel: 020 7600 0807
Email: info@museumoflondon.org.uk
Website: www.museumoflondon.org.uk
Mon-Sat 10.00-17.50 Sun 12.00-17.50
Telling the history of London and the life of Londoners from pre-historic times to
modern

Science Museum
Exhibition Road, Kensington, London, SW7 2DD
Tel: 0870 870 4868
Email: sciencemuseum@nmsi.ac.uk
Website: www.sciencemuseum.org.uk
Daily 10.00-18.00
This museum houses the world's largest and most significant collection of the
history of science, technology, medicine and history. With more than 10 000
exhibits including the Apollo Space 10 Command Module.

Islington Museum
Islington Town Hall, Upper Street, Islington, London, N1 2UD
Tel: 020 7527 2837
Wed-Sat 11.00-17.00 Sun 14.00-16.00
Tells the story of Islington through exhibitions and displays

National Army Museum

Royal Hospital Road, Chelsea, London, Inner London, SW3 4HT
Tel: 020 7730 0717
Email: info@national-army-museum.ac.uk
Website: www.national-army-museum.ac.uk
(Daily) 10.00-17.30
The purpose of this museum is to make the history of the British soldier accessible to all. The museum displays life size figures from a variety of eras, but rather than famous people, it uses real people with real stories

Geffrye Museum

Kingsland Road, Shoreditch, London, Inner London, E2 8EA
Tel: 020 7739 9893
Email: info@geffrye-museum.org.uk
Website: www.geffrye-museum.org.uk
Tues-Sat 10.00-17.00 Sun 12.00-17.00
Originally the building was almshouses that were built in 1715 and converted into a museum of furniture and interior design in 1914. There are a variety of rooms reconstructed in period style that make an atmospheric journey through the ages.

Percival David Foundation Of Chinese Art

53 Gordon Square, London, Inner London, WC1H 0PD
Tel: 020 7387 3909
Email: sp17@soas.ac.uk
Website: www.pdfmuseum.org.uk
(Mon-Fri) 10.30-17.00
This collection is the finest of its kind outside China.There are 1,700 items in the permanent collection that mostly date form the 10-18C although there are some earlier pieces from the Tang Dynasty.

Bethnal Green Museum Of Childhood

Cambridge Heath Road, Bethnal Green, London, Inner London, E2 9PA
Tel: 020 8980 2415
Email: bgmc@vam.ac.uk
Website: www.museumofchildhood.org.uk
Re opens Autumn 2006 please check opening hours are still the same Daily 10.00-17.50
Closed Fridays
Inside the 19C building is a mammoth collection of dolls, trains, cars, children's clothes, books and puppets. Including some exquisite Japanese ceremonial dolls.

Petrie Museum Of Egyptian Archaeology

University College London, Malet Place, London, Inner London, WC1E 6BT
Tel: 020 7679 2884
Email: petrie.museum@ucl.ac.uk
Website: www.petrie.ucl.ac.uk
Tues - Fri 13.00-17.00 Sat 10.00-13.00
A variety of ancient artefacts are displayed including the oldest garment in the world dating from 3000BC and underwear dating from 2400BC, as well as an exhumed pot burial with a skeletal occupant still squatting inside!

British Museum

Great Russell Street, London, Inner London, WC1B 3DG
Tel: 020 7323 8299
Email: information@thebritishmuseum.ac.uk
Website: www.thebritishmuseum.ac.uk
Sat-Wed 10.00-17.30 Thurs & Fri 10.00-20.30
This is London's No1 tourist attraction and is in fact a live encyclopaedia being one of only two museums in the world that fulfils the concept of having all branches of human knowledge under one roof.

Sir John Soane's Museum

13 Lincoln's Inn Fields, London, Inner London, WC2A 3BP
Tel: 020 7405 2107
Website: www.soane.org
(Tue-Sat) 10.00-17.00, First Tue of every month also 18.00-21.00
The museum houses collections of Indian drawings, Christopher Wren's watch, casts of ancient sculpture and Soane's own architectural plans and models.

Bank Of England Museum

Bartholomew Lane, Off Threadneedle Street, London, Inner London, EC2R 8AH
Website: www.bankofengland.co.uk/museum
(Mon-Fri) 10.00-17.00
The museum tells the 300 year old history of the bank, and was designed by Sir John Soane in 1793. Attractions include figures in period costume and the opportunity to come depressingly close to a stack of gold bars!

Clock Makers Company Museum

The Clockroom, Guildhall Library, Aldermanbury, London, Inner London, EC2P 2EJ
Email: keeper@clockmakers.org
Website: www.clockmakers.org
(Mon-Sat) 09.30-16.30.
The oldest collection of time pieces in the world. Including the watch worn by Sir Edmond Hillary when he climbed Everest, and John Harrison's prize winning chronometer

NATURE & WILDLIFE

Kentish Town City Farm
1 Cressfield Close, Camden, London, NW5 4BN
Tel: 020 7916 5421
Tues-Sun 09.30-17.30
This City Farm offers a community garden with a traditional farm stock of cows, pigs, sheep, goats, poultry and horses

FARMERS MARKETS

Islington Farmers Market
Essex Road, Opposite Islington Green, Islington, London, Inner London, N1
Every Sunday 10.00-14.00
Farmers Market with local produce for sale

MARKETS

Portobello Market
Portobello Road and Portobello Green, Notting Hill, London, W11
Tel: 020 7375 0441
Website: www.portobelloroad.co.uk
Saturdays 08.00-17.00
London's most famous market and a great place to browse for cheap and secondhand clothing, jewellery and antiques

Church Street Market
Church Street and Bell Street, London, NW8
Mon-Sat 08.00-17.00 (Church Street) Fri-Sat 08.00-17.00 (Bell Street)
At Church Street you will find household goods and fruit and veg, where as at Bell Street you will find the more unusual items such as cookery ingredients from the Middle East

Spitalfields Market
Commercial Street, Tower Hamlets, London, E1
Mon-Fri 11.00-15.00 Sun 09.30-17.30
Shops and stalls offer books, clothes, bread, cakes, fruit and veg and organic meat and produce

Camden Market

Camden Lock Place, Camden, London, NW1
Tel: 020 7284 2084
Website: www.camdenlockmarket.com
Daily 10.00-18.00
Offering clothes, arts & crafts, jewellery, food produce, antiques and bric a brac

Chapel Market

Chapel Street, Islington, London, N1
Tues- Sun 09.00-18.00
This colourful market sells household items, records, and clothes

Camden Passage

Upper Street, Islington, London, N1
Tel: 020 7359 0190
Weds 07.00-14.00 & Sat 08.00-16.00 (Antiques) Thurs 10.00-16.30 (Books) Sun 10.00-14.00 (Farmers Market)
Antiques, silverwear, jewellery and watches are all on offer in this covered walkway

Ridley Road Market

Ridley Road, Hackney, London, E8 2NP
Tel: 020 8356 3367
Mon-Wed 09.00-15.00 Thurs 09.00-12.00 Fri & Sat 10.00-17.00
This is the place in East London to get African, Asian, Caribbean and Mediterranean produce at cheap prices

Columbia Road Flower Market

Columbia Road, Tower Hamlets, London, E1
Tel: 020 7377 8963
Email: columbia_flower_market@blueyonder.co.uk
Website: www.columbia-flower-market.freewebspace.com
Sunday 08.00-14.00
Flowers, plants, pots and all types of garden items are available from this colourful and lively market

Nags Head Market

22 Seven Sisters Road, Islington, London, N7 6AG
Tel: 020 7607 3527
Mon-Sat 08.00-17.00 Sun 07.00-14.00
This indoor market offers cheap electrical goods, clothes and knick knacks

FESTIVALS

Notting Hill Carnival
Notting Hill, London, W10 5AS
Tel: 020 8964 0544
25th and 26th August
Steel Bands, Floats, Food and Dance are all part of this West Indian Carnival
that has grown into an International Event

Outer London-England

ART GALLERIES/ARTS & CRAFTS

Kenwood House-Iveagh Bequest

Hampstead Lane, London, Outer London, NW3 7JR
Tel: 020 8348 1286
Website: www.english-heritage.org.uk
April - Oct Daily 10.00-17.00 Nov - March Daily 10.00-16.00
This house contains a number of outstanding paintings and pieces of furniture.
Most notable are Rembrant's self portraits, Rare Vermeers and Renold's portrait
of Nelson's mistress, Lady Hamilton dressed up as a nun.

Matt's Gallery

42-44 Copperfield Road, London, Outer London, E3 4RR
Tel: 020 8983 1771
Email: info@mattsgallery.org
Website: www.mattsgallery.org
Wed-Sun 12.00-18.00 During Exhibitions
At this gallery artists are given free reign to do what ever they like with the space
and visitors can puzzle and enthuse over the latest creations.

CHURCHES & CATHEDRALS

Christ Church Spital Fields

Commercial Street, London, Outer London, E1 6LY
Tel: 020 7247 7202
Website: www.christchurchspitalfields.org
Tues 11.00-16.00 Sun 13.00-16.00
The building was built in 1714 to provide a place of worship for the Huguenot Silk
Weavers. The church is best viewed at night when the white floodlit bulk looms
above the dark warehouses of Commercial Street.

St Mary's Rotherhithe

St Marychurch Street, Rotherhithe, London, Outer London, SE16 4JE
Tel: 020 7231 2465
Website: www.stmaryrotherhithe.org
Daily 08.00-18.00
This church was built in 1715 by local sailors and watermen. The communion
table in the Lady Chapel and two of the Bishops Chairs were constructed from
timber salvaged from the warship Fighting Temeraire. The interior can be viewed
through glass.

St Anne's Church

Corner of Commercial Road and the Three Colt Street, Limehouse, London, Outer London, E14 7HP

Tel: 020 7987 1502

Sunday Services 10.30-12.00. Access to the church can be organised by calling 020 7515 0977

The church was built in what was originally open fields between 1712 and 1724 and boasts Britain's second highest Clock Tower. The only one that beats it is Big Ben which was built by the same maker as the Clock tower at St Anne's Limehouse.

St Margaret's Church

The Broadway, Barking, Outer London, IG11 8AS

Tel: 020 8594 2932

Website: www.saintmargarets.org.uk

09.00-15.30

This 12C church was built on the site of Barking Abbey. Explorer Captain Cook was married here in 1762

Barking Abbey

The Broadway, Barking, Outer London, IG11 8AS

Dawn- Dusk

Only a few ruins and foundation stones remain of this Abbey which during the 16C was the second largest in England

GARDENS PARKS & WALKS

Greenwich Park

Charleton Way, Greenwich, London, Outer London, SE10 8QY

Tel: 020 8858 2608

Email: greenwich@royalparks.gsi.gov.uk

Website: www.royalparks.gov.uk

(Daily 06.00-Dusk)

This riverside park is famous for its Tudor and Stewart history, and over 20 Saxon grave mounds have been identified within the park. The view from the park to the river is one of the best in London and in Summer brass bands perform in the afternoons.

Hampstead Heath

Parliament Hill, Hampstead, London, Outer London, NW3

Tel: 020 7482 7073

(Daily) Open 24 hours.

This varied semi landscaped heath with its variety of things to do has become one of London's most popular green spaces. In addition fun fairs are held on the Heath on Easter, May and August Bank Holidays.

Victoria Park

Old Ford Road, London, Outer London, E3

(Daily) 06.00-Dusk

Large ponds and tea rooms within the park give it a peaceful and relaxed atmosphere that invites you to linger a while rather than just pass through. At the main Sewardstone Road entrance stand the Dogs Of Alcibiades that were first placed there in 1912

Alexandra Park

Muswell Hill, London, Outer London, N22

Tel: 020 7272 2825

Daily 24 hours

This steeply sloping park gives great views over the city of London and has many kids attractions and sports facilities. There are also fun fairs at the park on Bank Holidays.

Waterlow Park

Highgate Hill, London, Outer London, N6 5HG

Tel: 020 7272 2825

(Daily) 07.00-Dusk

This beautiful park has steep slopes, ponds, fabulous trees, and an aviary as well as sports facilities and a children's play area for the under 5s. There is also a garden café in the 16C Lauderdale House.

High Elms Country Park

Shire Lane, Farnborough, Bromley, Outer London, BR6 7JH

Tel: 01689 862 815

Daily 07.00- Dusk

250 Acres of beautiful estate offering gardens, meadows and woodland walks

Scadbury Park

Old Perry Street, Chislehurst, Bromley, Outer London, BR7 6LS

Tel: 020 8658 1593

Daily 07.00-Dusk

Scadbury Park offers a network of paths for public access to over 300 acres of countryside

Ravenscourt Park

Paddenswick Road, Hammersmith, Outer London, W6 0UA

Tel: 020 8748 3020

Daily 07.30-Dusk

A great park for children and families with designated play areas and children's' paddling pool

Richmond Park

Robin Hood Gate, Kingston Vale, Kingston, Outer London

Tel: 020 8948 3209

Summer 07.00-dusk Winter 7.30- dusk

This is the largest open space in London covering 2500 acres. An excellent park for cycling, rambling and riding in what was once a Medieval Deer Park

Hampstead Heath Open Air Ponds

Parliament Hill, Hampstead, Outer London, NW3

Tel: 020 7485 3873

Daily 07.00-21.00

Seasonal swimming in open air ponds on Hampstead Heath

Eastbrookend Country Park

The Chase, Dagenham Road, Dagenham, Greater London

Tel: 020 8595 4155

Open daily

This park is home to the Chase Nature Reserve which is a haven for around 170 different birds during Winter migration

Bushy Park

Hampton Court Gate, Off Hampton Court Road, Hampton, Outer London, TW12 2EJ

Tel: 020 8979 1586

Pedestrians 05.00-22.30 Vehicles 06.30-Dusk

This Deer Park also features garden areas and a children's playground

Morden Hall Park

Morden Hall Road, Morden, Outer London, SM4 5JD
Tel: 020 8545 6850
Email: mordenhallpark@nationaltrust.org.uk
Daily 08.00-18.00
This is a 125 acre park with the River Wandle running through it. The park consists of hay meadows, wetlands, old estate buildings and an impressive rose garden with over 2000 roses.

The Brent Reservoir

Cool Oak Lane, Barnet, Outer London, NW9
Access at all times
The Reservoir and surrounding land are home to many protected water birds, and is a countryside oasis for city dwellers

HISTORIC HOUSES

Hogarth's House

Hogarth Lane, Great West Road, London, Outer London, W4 2QN
Tel: 020 8994 6757
Apr-Oct (Tue-Fri) 13.00-17.00, (Sat-Sun) 13.00-18.00, Nov-March (Tue-Fri) 13.00-16.00 (Sat-Sun) 13.00-17.00 Closed throughout January.
The country retreat of this famous painter has been fully restored to it's 18C glory and contains over 200 of his prints. However his most famous work of art The Rakes Progress is a copy.

MUSEUMS

Ragged School Museum

46-48 Copperfield Road, London, Outer London, E3 4RR
Tel: 020 8980 6405
Email: enquiries@raggedschoolmuseum.org.uk
Website: www.raggedschoolmuseum.org.uk
Only FREE First Sunday of every Month) 14.00-17.00
Founded by Dr Barnardo to educate and feed poor children. The museum is now housed in what was one of the largest schools in London and has now been restored to its original state, and includes a reconstructed Victorian Classroom

Horniman Museum

100 London Road, Forest Hill, London, Outer London, SE23
Tel: 020 8699 1872
Website: www.horniman.ac.uk
Daily 10.30-17.30 Gardens Mon-Sat 07.15-Dusk Sundays 08.00-Dusk
Houses a variety of the 19C tea merchant Fredrick Horniman's collections. With
natural history hall with stuffed animals,music room where visitors can listen to
and play instruments from all over the world, sunken gardens and small zoo with
farm animals

William Morris Gallery

Lloyd Park, Forest Road, London, Outer London, E17 4PP
Tel: 020 8527 3782
Website: www1.walthamforest.gov.uk/wmg
(Tue-Sat, First Sun every month) 10.00-13.00 & 14.00 -17.00
Opened in 1950 this was the childhood home of the late Victorian designer
William Morris. Part is dedicated to William Morris and selection of his
memorabilia whilst part is devoted to his associates who made his designs what
they are today

Crystal Palace Museum

Anerley Hill, London, Outer London, SE19 2BA
Tel: 07956 587 257
Website: www.crystalpalacefoundation.org.uk
Sundays 11.00-17.00
Built in 1851 to house the Great exhibition, the museum tells the story of the
exhibition is situated in an old engineering school where John Logie Baird
invented the television.The extensive grounds contain amusement park with life
size dinosaur models

Livesey Museum

682 Old Kent Road, London, Outer London, SE15 1JF
Tel: 020 7639 5604
Email: info@liveseymuseum.org.uk
Website: www.liveseymuseum.org.uk
(Tue-Sat) 10.00-17.00
Since becoming a museum in 1974 the building has hosted a variety of
temporary exhibitions, most of which are aimed at children.

Vestry House Museum

Vestry Road, Walthamstow, London, Outer London, E17 9NH

Tel: 020 8509 1917

Email: vestry.house@al.lbwf.gov.uk

(Mon-Fri) 10.00-13.00 & 14.00-17.30, (Sat) 10.00-13.00 & 14.00-17.00

This museum is dedicated to two of the areas most famous sons. Alfred Hitchcock and Fredrick Bremer who designed Britain's first motor car. Bremer's 1894 vehicle is on display inside the building which also has good exhibitions on costumes and toys.

Wandsworth Museum

The Court House, 11 Garrett Lane, London, Outer London, SW18 4AQ

Tel: 020 8871 7074

Email: wandsworthmuseum@wandsworth.gov.uk

Website: www.wandsworth.gov.uk

Tues-Fri 10.00-17.00 Sat & Sun 14.00-17.00

This local museum displays exhibits dedicated to the development of social history in the Borough of Wandsworth from medieval times to the present day. Attractions include interactive displays and children's quizzes.

Royal London Hospital Archives and Museum

Whitechapel, London, Outer London, E1 1BB

Tel: 020 7377 7608

Email: jonathan.evans@bartsandthelondon.nhs.uk

(Mon-Fri) 10.00-16.30

Part of this museum is dedicated to Joseph Merrick (The Elephant Man) who in the 1880s was first a patient and then an exhibit at the Royal London Hospital. The rest of the museum tells the history of the hospital and medicine in general.

North Woolwich Old Station Museum

Pier Road, North Woolwich, London, Outer London, E16 2JJ

Tel: 020 7474 7244

Jan-Nov Sat&Sun 13.00-17.00

This museum is dedicated to The London And North Eastern Railway. On the first Sunday of the Summer months steam engines chug up and down outside. The museum houses a 1920s ticket office and various steam train memorabilia such as station signs.

Valence House Museum

Becontree Avenue, Dagenham, Outer London, RM8 3HT
Tel: 020 8227 5293
Website: www.barking-dagenham.gov.uk
Tues-Fri 09.30-16.30 Sat 10.00-16.00
This museum houses numerous displays and exhibitions from a Victorian
Servant's Parlour to Stone Age tools

RAF Museum

Grahame Park, Hendon, Barnet, Outer London, NW9 5LL
Tel: 020 8205 2266
Email: hendon@rafmuseum.org.uk
Website: www.rafmuseum.org.uk
Daily 10.00-18.00
Britain's only museum dedicated to all things related to aviation.

The Bromley Museum

The Priory, Church Hill, Orpington, Outer London, BR6 0HH
Tel: 01689 873 826
Email: bromley.museum@bromley.gov.uk
April-Oct Sun-Fri 13.00-17.00 Sat 10.00-17.00 Nov-March Closed on Sundays
A museum with displays of artefacts charting the history of Bromley

Church Farmhouse Museum

Greyhound Hill, Hendon, Barnet, Outer London, NW4 4JR
Tel: 020 8203 0130
Website: www.churchfarmhousemuseum.co.uk
Mon-Thur 10.00-13.00 & 14.00-17.00 Sat 10.00-13.00 & 14.00-17.30 Sun 14.00-17.30
Built around 1660 this is one of the oldest surviving houses in the area and is
now a museum with exhibitions, period furniture and displays of arts and crafts

Hampstead Museum-Burgh House

New End Square, Hampstead, Outer London, NW3 1LT
Tel: 020 7431 0144
Email: hampsteadmuseum@talk21.com
Website: www.burghhouse.org.uk
Wed-Sun 12.00-17.00
Museum detailing the history of Hampstead including the areas famous writers
and artists such as Constable

FARMERS MARKETS

Blackheath Farmers Market
Blackheath Rail Station Carpark, Blackheath, London, Outer London, SE3
Every Sunday 10.00-14.00
Farmers Market with local produce for sale

MARKETS

Shepherd's Bush Market
Between Uxbridge Road and Goldhawk Road, Hammersmith, Outer London, W12 8DG
Tel: 020 8743 5089
Tues, Wed, Fri & Sat 08.30-18.00 Sun 08.30-15.00
Over 200 stalls catering to the local Irish and African-Caribbean communities

Channel Islands

ART GALLERIES/ARTS & CRAFTS

Guernsey Clockmakers Limited

Les Vauxbelets, St Andrews, Guernsey, Channel Islands, GY6 8XY

Tel: 01481 236 360

Website: www.guernsey.net/ mpclocks/

Daily (Mon-Fri) 08.30-17.30 (Sat&Sun) 10.00-16.00

This is the largest clock shop in Guernsey and all the clocks are hand made using traditional methods. Each clock is a work of art and takes a long time to make, making every clock produced an original.

Bruce Russell & Son-Gold & Silversmiths

Le Gron, St Saviours, Guernsey, Channel Islands, GY7 9RN

Tel: 01481 264 321

Website: www.guernseymint.com

Daily 09.00-17.00

Workshop and showroom where traditional gold, silver and platinum jewellery are made. Visitors can visit the workshop and showroom and the 8 acres of winning gardens and nature reserve.

Oatlands Village

Les Gigands, St Sampsons, Guernsey, Channel Islands, GY2 4YT

Tel: 01481 244 282

Daily

The remains of the brick kilns that date back to when brick making was a major Guernsey industry are now the setting for one of Guernsey's most popular tourist attractions. The site now houses shops, cafes and a play area set amongst the restored kilns.

Guernsey Wood Carvers

Les Issues, St Saviours, Guernsey, Channel Islands, GY7 9FS

Tel: 01481 265373

Mon-Fri 08.00-17.00 Sat&Sun 10.00-17.00

Wooden gifts and furniture are produced here from over sixty different types of wood. Visitors can see the different products for sale in the shop or commission their own pieces.

Guernsey Candles Ltd

Les Petites Capelles, St Sampsons, Guernsey, Channel Islands, GY2 4GR
Tel: 01481 249 686
Daily 09.00-17.30
Visitors can see the complicated process of candle making in the workshops and then browse the wide range of varied candles available in the gift shop, there is also a general gift shop and Cat-a-mania an original and unusual shop for all cat lovers.

Jersey Pearl

North End, Five Mile Road, St Ouen, Jersey, Channel Islands
Tel: 01534 862137
Email: info@jerseypearl.co.uk
Website: www.worldpearl.com
Summer Daily 10.00-17.30 Winter Daily 10.00-16.30
Guided tours are available of the largest collection of quality pearls in the Channel Islands, there are also educational displays that explain how pearls and the jewellery are made. Visitors can purchase individual pieces which are crafted in the workshops.

HISTORIC HOUSES

Priaulx Library

Candie Road, St Peter Port, Guernsey, Channel Islands, GY1 1UG
Tel: 01481 721 998
Website: www.gov.gg/priaulx
Mon-Sat 09.30-17.00
This beautiful Victorian building stands in its own stunning grounds and holds important collections of newspapers, documents and photographs. It is also Guernsey's premier centre for family history research and local studies.

HISTORIC SITES

Greve De Lecq Barracks

Greve de Lecq Bay, St Mary, Jersey, Channel Islands
Tel: 01534 483 193
Email: enquiries@nationaltrustjersey.org.je
Website: www.nationaltrustjersey.org.je
May-Sept Tues-Fri 11.00-17.00 Sat 10.00-17.00 Sun 14.00-17.00
This barracks was build between 1810 and 1815 to provide accommodation for the soldiers who guarded the bay from French Invasion, and was in use until 1926. The building retains many original features.

The Elms Pressoir & Boulangerie

La Cheve Rue, St Mary, Jersey, Channel Islands
Tel: 01534 483 193
Email: enquiries@nationaltrustjersey.org.je
Website: www.nationaltrustjersey.org.je
Please contact National Trust For Jersey for opening times

The Headquarters of the National Trust for Jersey are situated in this building which still retains the original rooms for cider pressing and bread making. There is a rare Jersey granite apple crusher and cider press within the Headquarters and the Boulangerie is located in the farmyard.

Morel Farm Pressoir

La Rue de la Fontaine St. Martin, St Lawrence, Jersey, Channel Islands
Tel: 01534 483 193
Email: enquiries@nationaltrustjersey.org.je
Website: www.nationaltrustjersey.org.je
Door is usually left open for visitors during the day time

This is an important farm complex and the Pressoir which is open to the public can be found to the right of the archway entrance. There is a granite apple crusher, cider press and original clay floor within the building.

MUSEUMS

The Guernsey Diamond Museum

Ray & Scott Jewellers Ltd, The Bridge, St Sampsons, Guernsey, Channel Islands, GY2 4QN
Tel: 01481 244 610
Mon-Sat 09.00-17.00

This museum gives a fascinating glimpse into the world of diamonds and lets the visitor follow the journey from the diamonds origin to its final destination when it is set into jewellery.

CHURCHES & CATHEDRALS

The Little Chapel

Les Vauxbelets, Rue de Bouillon, St Andrews, Guernsey, Channel Islands, GY6 8XY
Tel: 01481 237 200
Website: www.thelittlechapel.org
Open daily

This is possibly the smallest chapel in the world and was built by Brother Deodat and started in 1914. The chapel is stunning and decorated with sea shells, pebbles and pieces of broken china.

GARDENS PARKS & WALKS

Guernsey Freesia Centre

Route Carre, St Sampsons, Guernsey, Channel Islands, GY1 3ZF
Tel: 01481 248 185
Daily 09.00-17.00

At the Freesia Centre there are 2 acres of the beautiful flower grown under glass. Visitors can see the flowers being planted, picked, cut and boxed on site, and view the stunning display of the freesias in various stages of bloom.

Candie Gardens

Access from Candie Road, St. Julian's Avenue, or Vauxlaurens lane, St Peter Port, Guernsey, Channel Islands
Open daily until dusk

These gardens were once part of a private estate and have fantastic views to the other Channel Islands. Within the gardens there are the oldest known heated glass houses in the British isles, which date from the late 18th Century.

Strawberry Farm

Les Issues Vinery, St Saviours, Guernsey, Channel Islands
Tel: 01481 264 428
East-October Daily

Visitors can see the different ways of growing strawberries at the farm . There is also a craft centre on site with a pottery, patisserie and fudge shop. The fruit that is grown on site can also be sampled in the tea rooms.

EXHIBITIONS

Kempt Tower Visitors Centre

In the most Northerly Martello Tower, Five Mile Road, St Ouen, Jersey, Channel Islands
May-Sept Daily 14.00-17.00

This Visitors Centre explains the ecology of St Ouen's Bay and tells the history of the Martello Tower where the centre is located. There are also success stories of how the Island's countryside has been managed.

WALES

Wales is a small country perched on the edge of the England with its own fierce identity.

The Welsh have their own language although English is widely spoken and Wales in Welsh is pronounced Cymru. In addition to its own language, Wales has a very distinct nationality and culture that is still very evident today as well as in the country's historical attractions.

More than half of the population of Wales live in the Southern quarter of the country around the area of the Capital City of Cardiff. Cardiff, is Europe's youngest capital city and has only been the capital city of Wales for around 50 years and is fast becoming one of the most fashionable cities in the United Kingdom.

Wales has some spectacular scenery and an abundance of wide open spaces. There are stunning natural features such as Snowdonia National Park and the Brecon Beacons offering fantastic waterfalls, steep passes, lakes and impressive mountain ranges.

The Welsh coastline is also breath taking with towering cliffs, hidden coves and harbours and beautiful deserted sandy beaches. Throughout the country there are an abundance of old fashioned market towns and picturesque villages hidden away in lush valleys and unspoilt countryside.

Wales is a small country approximately 160 miles long by 60 miles wide, which makes it perfect for exploring.

WALES

Cambrian Coast-Wales

ART GALLERIES/ARTS & CRAFTS

The School of Art-Gallery & Museum
University of Wales, School of Art, Brarth Mawr, Aberystwyth, Ceredigion, SY23 1NE
Tel: 01970 622 460
Website: www.aber.ac.uk/art
(Mon-Fri) 10.00-17.00
Home of the Art Department with a public gallery on the ground floor.

Curlew Weavers
Troedyraur, Old Rectory, Rhydlewis, Newcastle Emlyn, Ceredigion, SA44 5RL
Tel: 01239 851 357
Mon-Fri 09.00-17.00 All Year
Producing a wide range of woollen fabrics and products in tweed. There is a large craft shop with demonstrations from the mill and free tours on site.

Aberystwyth Arts Centre
University College of Wales, Penglais, Aberystwyth, Ceredigion, SY23 3DE
Tel: 01970 622 893
Open all year Mon-Sat 10.00-20.00 Sun 12.00-17.30
This arts centre includes four gallery spaces, workshops, craft and design shops, theatre, concert hall, cinema, café and bookshop. This is the main venue for arts in Mid & West Wales. Charge for performances, but free exhibitions and annual festival.

Meirion Mill Woollen Centre
Dinas Mawddwy, Machynlleth, Aberdovey, Powys, SY20 9LS
Tel: 01650 531 311
Mon-Sat 10.00-17.00 Sun 10.30-17.00
Housing outdoor and country clothing as well as woollen and knitwear made on site, this mill has a shop to purchase goods and a coffee shop and picnic area. There is also a scenic walk to King Arthur's battlefield nearby

Corris Craft Centre

Corris, Machynlleth, Aberdovey, Powys, SY20 9RF
Tel: 01654 761 584
Email: information@corriscraftcentre.co.uk
Website: www.corriscraftcentre.co.uk
April-October Mon-Sun 10.00-17.30 November to March please call 01654 761584 to check opening times.
Visitors can watch skilled craft workers produce jewellery, pottery, leather and candles amongst these craft workshops. There is also a restaurant, picnic area, gardens and a children's play area

CASTLES

Aberystwyth Castle

New Promenade, Aberystwyth, Ceredigion
Access at all times
Situated on a rocky headline in the town the ruins of this castle stare blankly out to sea. Built by Edward I in the 13C

Castell-Y-Bere

Llanfihangel-Y-Pennant, Off B4405, Tywyn, Gwynedd
Tel: 029 2050 0200
Email: cadw@wales.gsi.gov.uk
Access at all times Normally daily 10.00-16.00
The remains of a distinctive Welsh native castle built in 1221 by Prince Llywelyn ab Iorwerth to protect the mountain passes

CHURCHES & CATHEDRALS

St Padarn Church

Llanbadarn Fawr, Aberystwyth, Powys, SY23 3QU
Tel: 01970 623 368
Website: www.stpadarns-llanbadarn.org.uk
Open daily
Legend has it that St Padarn and his associate Cadfan sailed from Brittany with 847 monks in the 6C and founded a religious order here.

The Strata Florida Abbey

Pontrhydfendigaid, Tregaron, Ceredigion, SY25 6BT

Tel: 01974 831 261

Website: www.cadw.wales.gov.uk

FREE April-Sept Mon & Tues and Oct-March daily (Charge at all other times) Normal opening hours 10.00-16.00

Strata Florida or " Vale Of Flowers" was founded in 1164. The Princes & Princesses of Wales are buried here in what used to be called the "Westminster Of Wales "

GARDENS PARKS & WALKS

Cenarth Village Waterfalls

7 Miles upstream from Cardigan, Cardigan, Ceredigion

Access at all times

The waterfalls in this little village are close to the main road providing a nice easy walk.

Aberaeron to Llanina Coastal Walk

From Aberaeron to Llanina, Aberaeron, Ceredigion

Access at all times

This walk is approximately 4 miles and has splendid views across Cardigan Bay

Ceredigion Coastal Path

Ynyslas to Cardigan, Borth, Borth, Ceredigion

Access at all times

Along the spectacular Heritage Coast of Cardigan Bay and joins the Pembrokeshire Coast Path National Trail at Cardigan

Aberaeron to Llanerchaeron Cycle Way

Along the Aeron Valley to Llanerchaeron, Llanerchaeron, Ceredigion

Access at all times

The country's first cycle way runs for 3km and takes in beautiful scenery and steep sided valleys

Cregennan Lakes

Near Dolgellau, Arthog, Arthog, Gwynedd

Access at all times

Serene local beauty spot that has a special tranquil beauty.

Cambrian Mountains

Devils Bridge, Aberystwyth, Ceredigion, SY23 3JL

Access at all times

Between 1500 and 2500 in altitude the Cambrian Way long distance trail passes through these Mountains

Borth Sands

Borth, Clarach, Ceredigion, SY24 5LJ

Access at all times

3 miles of unbroken sands and the scenic estuary of the Dyfi River

Mynach Falls

Near the Vale Of Rheidol Railway Terminus, Aberystwyth, Ceredigion

Access at all times

Spectacular 300 foot waterfall with a view of the three bridges one of which is the legendary Devil's Bridge

HISTORIC HOUSES

National Library Of Wales

Penglais, Aberystwyth, Ceredigion, SY23 3BU

Tel: 01970 632 800

Email: holi@llgc.org.uk

Website: www.llgc.org.uk

Mon-Sat 10.00-17.00

Dominating the hill side overlooking Aberystwyth, this library includes exhibitions, a collection of early books, manuscripts and paintings, as well as being research facility

HISTORIC SITES

Gors y Gedol Burial Chamber

Signposted just off main road behind the school in Dyffryn Ardudwy, Near Barmouth, Barmouth, Gwynedd, LL44 2DG

Access at all times

Two supported capstone lie amongst a bed of small boulders, the base stone is though to have been originally 100 feet long.

Llanbedr Standing Stones

3 miles N of Dyffryn Ardudwy, Near Barmouth, Barmouth, Gwynedd
Access at all times
At the Northern end of the village in a field South of the petrol station stand two standing stones.

MUSEUMS

Lampeter Museum

Town Library, Market Street, Lampeter, Ceredigion
Mon-Fri 10.30 -16.30 Also when the library is open.
Situated within the Town Library is a civic museum and old photographs of the town

A Nation's Heritage

National Library Of Wales, Aberystwyth, Ceredigion, SY23 3BU
Tel: 01970 632 800
Email: holi@llgc.org.uk
Website: www.llgc.org.uk
Mon-Fri 09.30-18.00 Sat 09.30-17.00
The Library's permanent exhibition with some of Wales' most precious collections

Y Tabernacl

Wales Museum Of Modern Art, Machynlleth, Powys, SY20 8AJ
Tel: 01654 703 355
Website: www.momawales.org.uk
(Mon-Sat) 10.00-16.00
Program of temporary exhibitions located in an old converted chapel.

RNLI Lifeboat Museum

Pen-y-Cei, Barmouth, Gwynedd, LL42 1HB
Tel: 01341 280 940
Easter-End September (Daily) 10.30-16.30
Workaday exhibitions and displays of lifesaving paraphernalia and artefacts.

Ceredigion Museum

Terrace Road, Aberystwyth, Ceredigion, SY23 2AQ
Tel: 01970 633 088
Email: museum@ceredigion.gov.uk
Mon-Sat 10.00-17.00
This museum is housed in a restored Edwardian theatre and shows the history of Ceredigion from stoneage to modern times

The Camera Obscura

Constitution Hill, Aberystwyth, Ceredigion, SY23 2DN
Tel: 01970 617 642
Daily 10.00-17.00 (Until 18.00 during July & August)
The huge 14 inch lens takes a view of more than 1000 square miles of land and sea in a 360 degree sweep around Aberystwyth

Rheidol Power Station

Cwm Rheidol Reservoir, Cwm Rheidol, Aberystwyth, Ceredigion
Tel: 01970 880 667
Guided tours of the power station Apr-Oct 11.00-15.30 Power Station open daily
April-October 10.30-16.15
An information centre with a 45 minute guided tour of the Power Station.

NATURE AND WILDLIFE

Pendinas and Tanybwlch

Walking distance from Aberystwyth Town Centre, Aberystwyth, Ceredigion
Tel: 01545 570 881
Access at all times
A reserve which combines the largest Iron Age Hill Fort in Ceredigion with a shingle ridge beach where Red Kites and polecat can be seen

Penglais Nature Park

Penglais, Aberystwyth, Ceredigion
Tel: 01545 572 142
Website: www.ceredigion.gov.uk
Open all year
Covering 27 acres of woodland and an old disused quarry

Borth Bog

Cors Fochno, Aberystwyth, Ceredigion

Open all year

These dunes have open access and are used by both locals and tourists, the grazing saltmarshes are encouraged for wintering wildfowl

Dyfi National Nature Reserve

Ynyslas, Borth, Ceredigion

Tel: 01970 871 640

Visitors Centre open daily 09.30-17.00 Reserve access at all times (Reserve Carpark has a £1 charge between Easter and September)

Explore the sand dunes and the local wildlife. Guided walks most weekends and a shop at the visitors centre

South East Wales

ART GALLERIES/ARTS & CRAFTS

Ceri Richards Gallery
Taliesin Arts Centre, University of Wales, Singleton Park, Swansea, Swansea County, SA2 8PZ
Tel: 01792 295526
Website: www.taliesinartscentre.co.uk
Mon-Fri 10.00-18.00 Sat 12.00-15.00 & 15.30-18.00
This gallery situated within the Taliesin Arts Centre hosts a variety of regular touring exhibitions.

Glynn Vivian Art Gallery
Alexandra Road, Swansea, Swansea County, SA1 5DZ
Tel: 01792 516 900
Email: glynn.vivian.gallery@swansea.gov.uk
Website: www.swansea.gov.uk/glynnvivian
Tue-Sun 10.00-17.00
An Edwardian Gallery with an inspiring collection of Welsh art ranging from the works of Old Masters to The 20th Century

Model House Craft and Design Centre
Bull Ring, Llantrisant, Mid Glamorgan, CF72 8EB
Tel: 01443 237 758
Website: www.craftgallerywales.com
(Tue-Sun) 10.00-17.00
A variety of different exhibitions, workshops and conventions. House in a Victorian converted building.

Turner House Art Gallery
Plymouth Road, Penarth, Cardiff, Glamorgan, CF64 3DM
Tel: 029 2070 8870
Email: turnerhouse@ffotogallery.org
Website: www.ffotogallery.org
Open Wed -Sun 11.00-17.00
Turner House Gallery was built in 1888 and given to the National Museums & Galleries in 1921. It is now an established local venue for temporary art exhibitions.

Mission Gallery

Gloucester Place, Maritime Quarter, Swansea, Swansea County, SA1 1TY
Tel: 01792 652 016
Email: missiongallery@btconnect.com
11.00-17.00 Daily
Exhibits and sells works of art of Swansea's magnificent coastal scenery

Albany Gallery

74b Albany Road, Cardiff, Glamorganshire, CF24 3RS
Tel: 029 2048 7158
Email: info@albanygallery.com
Website: www.albanygallery.com
Mon-Sat 10.00-17.00 Sun 11.00-16.00
Wales' premier gallery for contemporary art established in 1965

Cilgwyn Candles

Trefelin, Cilgwyn, Newport, Pembrokeshire, SA42 0QN
Tel: 01239 820 470
Email: cilgwyncandles@macunlimited.net
Website: www.pembrokeshirecandles.co.uk
East-Oct Daily 11.00-17.00 Nov & Dec Daily 12.00-16.00
This small workshop produces hand dipped candles and offers a retail outlet for
their products, there is also Britain's smallest museum with displays on the
history and traditions of candle making

G39-Gallery

Wyndham Arcade, Mill Lane, Cardiff, Glamorganshire, CF10 1FH
Tel: 029 2025 5541
Email: post@g39.org
Website: www.g39.org
Wed-Sat 11.00-17.30
Offers various exhibitions and changing contemporary displays

Bay Art

54 b/c Bute Street, Cardiff Bay, Cardiff, Glamorganshire, CF10 5AF
Tel: 029 2065 0016
Email: bayart@tiscali.co.uk
Website: www.bayart.org.uk
Tues-Sat 11.00-17.00 during exhibitions
This gallery provides exhibitions of contemporary art and is a welcome addition
to the exciting Cardiff art scene

Open Art Gallery

123 Bute Street, Cardiff Bay, Cardiff, Glamorgan
Tel: 029 2048 8772
Mon-Fri 12.00-17.00
Established in 1991 by Cardiff Bay Development Corporation the art work has been commissioned for the Bay's Public Area. There is a great sense of local identity and of the transforming environment.

CASTLES

Castlehill

Monmouth, Opposite Shire Hall, Monmouth, Monmouthshire
Access at all times
Castle hill can be climbed to see the ruins of a castle built in 1068 and rebuilt in stone in the 12C. It was almost completely destroyed during the Civil War, the most noticeable part that remains is the Great Tower.

Pennard Castle

3 miles from Three Cliffs Bay, Gower, Swansea, Swansea County
Access at all times
This ruined castle is best reached from the car park at Southgate.Perched on Pennard Pill, Overlooking Three Cliffs and Oxwich Bay. Dates from the 14C

Ogmore Castle

1 mile N along the coast from Southerdown, Southerdown, Near Bridgend, Bridgend County
Access at all times
Castle dates from the Norman Conquest in around 1100 and is set in stunning surroundings.

Coity Castle

1 mile NE of Bridgend, Bridgend, Bridgend County
Tel: 029 2082 6185
May-Dec Mon-Sun 10.00-16.00
Substantial remains of a once imposing Norman fortification.Raised by The De Londres family

Skenfrith Castle

6 miles NW of Monmouth, Skenfrith, Monmouthshire
Tel: 029 2082 6185
Open Dawn-Dusk
Castle built in the 13C set in a picturesque riverside location.

Grosmont Castle

Grosmont Village, 5 miles from Skenfrith, Abergavenny, Grosmont, Monmouthshire
Tel: 029 2082 6185
Access at all times
The entrance to the castle is over a wooden bridge that spans a dry moat. The ruin include the remains of a former large great hall and is situated on a small hill above the village

Newport Castle

Newport, Newport County
Access at all times
Established in the 14C, the remaining buildings belong to the late 14 and early 15C. The castle was raised by the Staffords

Churches & Cathedrals

Ewenny Priory

2 miles from the village of Ewenny, on the B4524, Ewenny, Mid Glamorgan
Website: www.ewenny.org.uk
Access at all times
Remains of a Benedictine priory founded in 1141, tucked away down leafy lanes.

Neath Abbey

The Vale of Neath, Off the A465 follow the Skewen Signs, Neath-Port Talbot, Glamorgan
Tel: 029 2082 6185
Access at all times
The ruined ghostly remains of an early 12C abbey. Once described as the fairest abbey in all Wales

St Mary's Church

St Mary's Square, Swansea, Swansea County, SA1 3LP
Tel: 01792 655 489
Email: alun-wyn@ntlworld.com
Website: www.swanseastmary.fsnet.co.uk
Jan, Feb, March & Nov Open Mon, Wed, Thurs & Sat Mornings Rest of the year Weekdays
10.00-15.00 Free Organ Recitals on Tues June-Sept
This is the Mother Church of Swansea and the interior houses a number of
works of arts by Swansea and Internationally renowned artists

EXHIBITIONS

Environment Centre

Old Telephone Exchange, Pier Street, Swansea, Swansea County, SA1 1RY
Tel: 01792 480 200
Email: office@environmentcentre.org.uk
Website: www.environmentcentre.org.uk
Mon-Fri 10.00-16.00
A resource centre for all things green and peaceful with a variety of changing
exhibitions.

Swansea Market

Oxford Street, Swansea, Swansea County
Mon-Sat
One of the largest indoor markets in the UK. Consists of shops and stalls of local
produce, flowers, jewellery and Welsh souvenirs

Royal Male Voice Choir

Treorchy Primary School, Glyncoli Road, Treorchy, Cardiff, Glamorgan
Visitors welcome to rehearsals on Tue & Thurs from 19.30
This town is one of the most famous of mining towns due to the International
status of the Royal Male Voice Choir, which is the oldest choir in Wales.

GARDENS PARKS WALKS

Bishops Wood Nature Reserve

Caswell Bay Road, Caswell, Swansea County, SA3 3DS
Tel: 01792 361 703
Visitors Centre open Weekends April-June Daily June-Sept
Only one of two Nature Reserves in Wales to be awarded the prestigious Green
Flag Award. Part of this Nature Reserve is an ancient woodland which has been
wooded since at least the 17C

Clyne Garden

Blackpill, Between Swansea and the Mumbles, Swansea, Swansea County
Tel: 01792 401 737
Access at all times
This is the 50 acre grounds of the Vivian family's old estate. It contains lovely
walks, rhododendron glades, bog gardens, woods and meadows

Parc Bryn Bach

Merthyr Road, Tredegar, Gwent, NP22 3AY
Tel: 01495 711 816
Email: parcbrynbach@compuserve.com
Website: www.blaenau-gwent.gov.uk
Open all year
400 acres of woodland and lakes offering picnic areas, an adventure playground,
campsite and many watersports

Bedford Park

Cefn Cribwr, Near Kenfig Hill, Bridgend, Glamorganshire
Tel: 01656 725 155
Open all year
This country park has been transformed from a former ironworks

Craig-y-nos Country Park

Brecon Road, Pen-y-cae, Swansea, Swansea County, SA9 1GL
Tel: 01639 730 395
Open all year (Charge for car parking)
Once the private grounds of Craig-y-nos Castle this country park has woodlands
and riverside walks in a wonderful setting

Kenfig National Nature Reserve

Kenfig, Near Porthcawl Junction 37 off the M4, Porthcawl, Mid Glamorgan

Tel: 01656 743 386

Reserve open all year Visitors Centre Weekdays 14.00-16.30 Weekends 10.00-16.30

The dunes have been opened as a nature reserve which offers an abundance of local wildlife, various walks and bird watching.

Aberdulais

The Vale of Neath, Neath-Port Talbot, Glamorgan

Access at all times

Great walks start from Neath Museum up into the surrounding wooded hillside and are brilliantly signposted.

Brynmill Park

Uplands, Swansea, Glamorganshire

Daily dawn-dusk

Victorian Swansea Park with wild fowl lake, rose beds, bowling green and basketball ring

Cwmdonkin Park

Uplands, Swansea, Glamorganshire, SA2 0PP

Tel: 01792 280 210

Daily dawn-dusk

Established in 1871 this park contains an ornate Italian water garden, tennis courts and a bowling green.

The Golden Bays of Gower

Gower, Swansea, Glamorganshire

Access at all times

Stretching for ten miles, this attraction covers a dozen beaches, rocky coves and sandy bays.

Singleton Park

Sketty, Swansea, Glamorganshire, SA2 9DU

Tel: 01792 298 637

Open all year

Houses the City's Botanical Collection within a walled garden and includes a boating lake, herb garden and a bright red Swiss Cottage.

HISTORIC HOUSES/MUSEUMS

Great Castle House

Situated next to the castle, Monmouth, Monmouthshire, NP25 3BS
Tel: 01600 772 175
Email: curator@monmouthcastlemuseum.org.uk
Website: www.monmouthcastlemuseum.org.uk
Museum open April-Oct Daily 14.00-17.00 Nov-March Sat & Sun 14.00-16.00
Built in the 17C this house was constructed using bricks from the castle and now
serves as the headquarters of the Royal Monmouth Royal Engineers. Inside
there is a small museum focusing on the Royal Monmouth Royal Engineers.

HISTORIC HOUSES

The Old Station

Tintern, Chepstow, Monmouthshire, NP16 7NX
Tel: 01291 689 566
Website: www.tintern.org.uk/station.htm
10.30-17.30 East-October Daily
This Victorian Station is now a visitors centre, with picnic sites and walks

Sirhowy Ironworks

Graham's Yard, Dukestown, Tredegar, Gwent, NP22 4QD
Tel: 01495 355 972
Email: frank.olding@blaenau-gwent.gov.uk
Website: www.blaenau-gwent.gov.uk
April-Oct Wed-Sat 09.30-16.30 Sun 14.00-17.00
Visitors can wander round this recently restored and conserved ironworks which
are a rare survivor from the iron industry heyday

Elliot Colliery Winding House

White Rose Way, New Tredegar, Tredegar, Gwent, NP24 6DF
Tel: 01443 822 666
Email: museums@caerphilly.gov.uk
East-Oct Wed, Thurs, Fri 11.00-16.00 Sat & Sun 14.00-17.00
Tells the story of Elliot Colliery and the local coal industry

National Assembly for Wales Visitor and Education Centre

Pierhead Building, Cardiff Bay, Cardiff
Tel: 029 2089 8200
Mon-Fri 10.00-17.00
Visitors can discover how the National Assembly for Wales works and what happens at the National Assembly via interactive exhibitions

HISTORIC SITES

Harold Stones

S of Trellech, On the B4293, Trellech, Monmouthshire
Access at all times
Three fingers of rock dating back 3500 years and standing silently in the middle of a field.

Virtuous Well

Off the lane to Tintern, Near Trellech, Trellech, Monmouthshire
Access at all times
This had long been a place of pilgrimage due to the well's reputed healing qualities

Agincourt Square

Monmouth, Monmouthshire
Access at all times
Within the square are a number of interesting sites, including an 18C statue of King Henry V who was born in Monmouth. In front of Shire Hall is a statue of Charles Stewart Rolls, the first man to fly a double flight over the English Channel in 1911

Cat Hole Rock Cave

1 mile N of Parkmill, Follow the footpath from Parkmill Heritage Centre, Gower, Swansea County
Access at all times
A dark cave where flint tools that date back over 12 000 years were discovered.

Paviland Cave

Between the villages of Horton & Port Eynon, South Coast Gower Peninsular, Gower, Swansea County

Permission must be obtained to access the cave as it is on private land. Please telephone the National Trust Warden on 01792 390 636

In 1823 a skeleton of a stone age hunter that dates back at least 19 000 years was found.

King Arthur's Stone

1 mile E of the village of Reynoldston, Reynoldston, Swansea County

Access at all times

Follow the path from the car park to King Arthur's Stone. This is a massive isolated burial chamber capstone that dates from at least 4000BC and weighs over 25 tonnes.

Tinkinswood Long Cairns

N on the A4226 from Barry, Vale of Glamorgan, Barry, Glamorganshire

Access at all times

Capstoned burial chamber around 4500 years old. The legend says that anyone who sleeps under the 50 tonne monolith with either die, go mad or become a poet

Dylan Thomas Statue

Dylan Thomas Square, Maritime Quarter, Swansea, Swansea County

Access at all times

A life size bronze statue of the poet Dylan Thomas as a child can be found outside the Dylan Thomas theatre

Pontypridd's Bridge

Pontypridd, Mid Glamorgan

Access at all times

This arched bridge that dates from 1775 was once the largest single span stone bridge in Wales.

Mynydd Y Gelli

2 mile climb from Llwynypia, Llwynpia, Glamorgan

Access at all times

Remains of an Iron Age hut and Bronze Age stone circle and burial chamber

Newport Transporter Bridge

Off the A4042, Newport, Pembrokeshire
Tel: 01633 250 322
Email: transporterbridge@newport.co.uk
Viewed at all times-Visitors Centre open April-Sept 10.00-17.00 (Wed-Sat) 13.00-17.00
(Sun) Oct-March 10.00-17.00 (Sat) 13.00-17.00 (Sun)
This bridge carries vehicles and pedestrians across the river Usk. The visitors
centre has exhibitions about the history of the bridge

MUSEUMS

Swansea Museum

Museum Square, Victoria Road, Maritime Quarter, Swansea, Swansea County, SA1 1SN
Tel: 01792 653 763
(Tue-Sun) 10.00-17.00
Wales' oldest public museum, including exhibitions of a wizened Egyptian
mummy and local pottery and discoveries.

Big Pit National Mining Museum Of Wales

Blaenafon, Torfaen, Blaenafon, Glamorgan, NP4 9XP
Tel: 01495 790 311
Website: www.nmgw.ac.uk
Daily 09.30-17.00 Underground tours take place between 10.00-15.30. Dec and January
please call for Winter opening hours
A real coal mine and one of Britain's leading mining museums. Where visitors
can go 300 feet underground to see for themselves what it was like to work as a
miner

Neath Museum

Gwyn Hall, Orchard Street, Neath, Neath-Port Talbot, Neath-Port Talbot, Glamorgan, SA11
1DU
Tel: 01639 645 741
Tue-Sat 10.00-16.00
Museum telling the history of Neath over the past 6000 years.

Cardiff Bay Visitors Centre

Harbour Drive, Cardiff, Glamorgan, CF10 4PA

Tel: 02920 463 833

Email: enquiries@cardifftic.co.uk

Mon-Fri 09.00-17.00 Sat-Sun 10.30-17.00

Video presentations, large scale models and panoramic views of the bay are all on offer at Cardiff Bay Visitors Centre. There is also a shop where visitors can purchase mementoes, books and branded clothing.

Dylan Thomas Exhibition Centre

The National Literature Centre Of Wales, Somerset Place, Swansea, Swansea County, SA1 1RR

Tel: 01792 463 980

Email: dylanthomas.lit@swansea.gov.uk

Tues-Sun 10.30-16.30

Dylan Thomas is Swansea's most famous literary son. This exhibition includes manuscripts, gallery, bookshop and bar.

Museum Of Welsh Life

St Fagans, Cardiff, Glamorgan, CF5 6XB

Tel: 029 20 57 3500

Website: www.nmgw.ac.uk

Open daily 10.00-17.00

Displays of a welsh grocer's shop, miner's cottage and school have been recreated within this charming museum

The National Museum & Gallery

Cathays Park, Cardiff, Glamorgan, CF1 3NP

Tel: 029 20 39 7951

Website: www.nmgw.ac.uk

Tues-Sun 10.00-17.00

This is the premier museum of Wales. Housing priceless collections and exhibitions including Monet's " Blue Lady "

Roman Legionary Museum

High Street, Caerleon, Gwent, NP6 1AE

Tel: 01633 423 134

Mon-Sat 10.00-17.00 Sun 14.00-17.00

This museum follows the life of a soldier from his equipment, armour and even to his death.

The Nelson Museum And Local History Centre

Priory Street, Monmouth, Monmouthshire, NP5 3XA
Tel: 01600 713 519
Email: nelsonmuseum@monmouthshire.gov.uk
Mon-Sat 10.00-13.00 & 14.00-17.00 Sun 14.00-17.00
A museum dedicated to Admiral Horatio Nelson commemorating his life and death

Pontypridd Museum

Bridge Street, Pontypridd, Glamorganshire, CF37 4PE
Tel: 01443 490 748
Email: enquiries@pontypriddmuseum.org.uk
Website: www.pontypriddmuseum.org.uk
Mon-Sat 10.00-17.00
This museum and gallery displays the history of Pontypridd and is housed in a restored Welsh Baptist Chapel

Chepstow Museum

Gwy House, Bridge Street, Chepstow, Monmouthshire, NP26 5EZ
Tel: 01291 625 981
Mon-Sat 11.00-17.00 Sun 14.00-17.00
A museum which tells the history of this ancient town and its industries through photographs and displays

Cynon Valley Museum & Gallery

Depot Road, Gadlys, Aberdare, Glamorganshire, CF44 8DL
Tel: 01685 886 729
Email: cvm@rhondda-cynon-taff.gov.uk
09.00-16.30 Mon-Sat
A museum of social history and a contemporary art gallery housed in a 19C ironworks

Newport Museum And Art Gallery

John Frost Square, Newport, Pembrokeshire, NP20 1PA
Tel: 01633 815 880
Email: museum@newport.gov.uk
Mon-Thurs 09.30-17.00 Fri 09.30-16.30 Sat 09.30-16.00
This museum is of local social and industrial history with the art gallery offering 19th and 20C art

Abergavenny Museum

The Castle, Castle Street, Abergavenny, Monmouthshire, NP7 5EE
Tel: 01873 854 282
Email: abergavennymuseum@monmouthshire.gov.uk
March-Oct Mon-Sat 11.00-13.00 & 14.00-17.00 Sun 14.00-17.00 Nov-Feb Mon-Sat
11.00-13.00 & 14.00-16.00 Closed Sundays
Situated within the grounds of a Norman Castle, this museum tells the story of
the Market Town of Abergavenny

FESTIVALS

Cardiff Summer Festival

Various Venues throughout the city, Cardiff, Glamorganshire
Website: www.cardiff-festival.com
Annually during the last two weeks of July and the first week of August
Europe's biggest free festival made up of the Welsh Proms, The Celtic Food and
Drink Festival and numerous events of art, theatre and comedy

Snowdonia And The Llyn-Wales

ART GALLERIES/ARTS & CRAFTS

Trefriw Woollen Mill
Trefriw, 5 miles N of Betws-y-Coed on the B5106, Trefriw, Conwy County, LL27 0NQ
Tel: 01492 640 462
Email: info@t-w-m.co.uk
Website: www.t-w-m.co.uk
Shop & Turbine House All Year (Mon-Sat) 09.30-17.30 Sun 11.00-17.00 Winter 10.00-17.00,
Weaving All Year (Mon-Fri) 10.00-13.00 & 14.00-17.00, Top Floor of Mill East-Oct (Mon-Fri)
10.00-13.00 & 14.00-17.00, Weavers Garden Jun-Sept (Mon-Sat) 09.30-17.30 Sun
11.00-17.00
See the weaving and hydro-electric turbines in our mill where we manufacture
traditional Welsh bedspreads and tweeds from the raw wool

Brynkir Woollen Factory
Golan, Garndolbenmaen, Golan, Gwynedd, LL51 9YU
Tel: 01766 530 236
Mon-Fri 09.00-16.30
Traditional working woollen mill which is over 150 years old

Llwyngwril Gallery of Welsh Art
The Church Room, A493 between Dolgellau and Tywyn, Llwyngwril, Gwynedd, LL37 2JB
Tel: 01341 25005
Email: enquiries@llwyngwril-gallery.co.uk
Website: www.llwyngwril-gallery.co.uk
March-Nov Daily 10.00-17.00
This gallery only sells works created in Wales from walking sticks, jewellery,
pottery and ceramics to painted glass and furniture

Rob Piercy Galley
10 Snowdon Street, Porthmadog, Gwynedd, LL49 9BT
Tel: 01766 513 833
Email: gallery@robpiercy.com
Website: www.robpiercy.com
All year Mon-Sat 10.00-17.00
Home to four exhibiting spaces most of the gallery is dedicated to the work of
Rob Piercy, but there is also another collection of other notable artists

Gwynedd Museum & Art Gallery

Ffordd Gwynedd, Bangor, Gwynedd, LL57 1DT
Tel: 01248 353 368
Email: gwyneddmuseum@gwynedd.gov.uk
Tues-Fri 12.30-16.30 Sat 10.30-16.30
The Museum details the history of North Wales whilst the Art Gallery has changing exhibitions throughout the year

CASTLES

Dolbadarn Castle

Llanberis, 7 miles E of Caernafon of the A4086, Llanberis, Gwynedd
Tel: 029 2082 6185
Access at all times
Perched on a rock between Llyn Peris and Llyn Padarn, the castle has one dramatic tower and other scattered 13C remains

CHURCHES & CATHEDRALS

Gwydyr Uchaf Chapel

Gwydyr, Llanwrst, 1 miles SW of Llanwrst of the B5106, Llanwrst, Conway County, LL26 0PN
Tel: 01490 412 025
Access at all reasonable times
Built in 1673 with a plain exterior and a Baroque interior.

Cymer Abbey

Llanelltud, Near Dolgellau, Dolgellau, Gwynedd
Tel: 029 2082 6185
Access at all reasonable times
The remains of a small abbey founded in 1198. Most notable of the ruins are the three remaining arched windows

St Hywyn Church

Aberdaron, Llyn Peninsular, Aberdaron, Gwynedd
Tel: 01758 760229
Email: office@st-hywyn.org.uk
Website: www.st-hywyn.org.uk
Summer 10.00-18.00 Winter 10.00-16.00
This 19C church with Norman door was built on the site of a 5C church

GARDENS PARKS & WALKS

Parc Padarn Country Park

Llanberis, Gwynedd, LL55 4TY
Tel: 01286 870 892
Email: pardarncountrypark@gwynedd.gov.uk
Access at all times
A countryside park based around the Lake of Llyn Padarn, with unrestricted access, lakeside walks and oak woods.

Black Rock Sands

SW from Porthmadog, Along coastal road to Morfa Bychan, Porthmadog, Gwynedd
Access at all times
Best beach in the area with 2 miles of golden sands and fantastic views

Glasfryn Parc

Yffor, Pwllheli, Gwynedd, LL53 6RD
Tel: 01766 810 202
Email: jwe@glasfryn.co.uk
Website: www.glasfryn.co.uk
Daily 10.00-18.00 Admission to the park is free but there are separate charges for the activities on offer
Located in an area of outstanding natural beauty and surrounded by mountains and sandy beaches. The park is also home to Wales premier activity and adventure centre.

HISTORIC SITES

Capel Garmon Chambered Tomb

On the A5 from Betws-Y-Coed towards Llangollen, Capel Garmon, Gwynedd
Access at all times
A reconstructed but very atmospheric multi chambered communal burial site built between 2500-1900BC.

Bryn Cader Faner

Near the village of Talsarnau, Near Porthmadog, Talsarnau, Gwynedd
Access at all times
15 stones survive of this Cairn Circle, standing up to six feet tall

Waterloo Bridge

Over the Rover Conwy, Betws-y-Coed, Conwy County

Access at all times

Built in 1815 the bridge is complete with emblems of the four countries of the then newly formed Uk. English Rose, Scottish Thistle, Irish Shamrock and Welsh Leek

MUSEUMS

Welsh Slate Museum

Padam Country Park, Llanberis, Gwynedd, LL55 4TY

Tel: 01286 870 630

Email: slate@nmgw.ac.uk

Website: www.nmgw.ac.uk/wsm

East-Oct Daily 10.00-17.00 Nov-Easter Sun-Fri 10.00-16.00 Last admission 1 hour before closing

An insight into the history of slate quarrying in North Wales

EXHIBITIONS

Electric Mountain Visitors Centre

On the Outskirts of Llanberis, 9 miles from Caernarfon, Llanberis, Gwynedd, LL55 4UR

Tel: 01286 870 636

Email: info@electricmountain.co.uk

Website: www.electricmountain.co.uk

Feb, March, Nov & Dec Wed-Sun 10.30-16.30 April, May, Sept & Oct Mon-Sun 10.30-16.30 June, July & Aug Mon-Sun 09.30-16.30

A split level complex containing a range of interactive displays and exhibitions on hydro-electricity. The Visitors Centre is Free but there is a charge to take the tour of the Dinorwig Power Station

NATURE AND WILDLIFE

Mawddach Valley

Penmaenpool, Gwynedd

Tel: 01341 422 071

Email: mawddach@rspb.org.uk

Reserve open at all times. Information Centre open May-Aug 10.00-17.00

Two reserves offering walks, and the chance to see ravens and buzzards

North Coast And Anglesey-Wales

ART GALLERIES/ARTS & CRAFTS

Gwynedd Museum & Art Gallery
Ffordd Gwynedd, Bangor, Gwynedd, LL57 1DT
Tel: 01248 353368
Email: gwyneddmuseum@gwnedd.gov.uk
Website: www.gwynedd.gov.uk/museums
(Tue-Fri) 12.30-16.30, (Sat) 10.30-16.30
This museum has a wide variety of collections that allow the visitor to learn about how previous generations led their lives

Oriel Mostyn
2 Vaughan Street, Llandudno, Conwy, LL30 1AB
Tel: 01429 879 201
Email: post@mostyn.org
Website: www.mostyn.org
(Mon-Sat) 10.00-17.00
A Premier contemporary Art Gallery.Lady August Mostyn originally founded the museum as a spot to house her personal art collection.

CASTLES

Ewloe Castle
1 Mile NW of Hawarden, NW of Ewloe on the A55, Ewloe, Flintshire
Access at all times
The ruins of an English strong hold that fell into Welsh hands in 1146. The ruins are reached through a wooded glen.

Flint Castle
Flint, Flint, Flintshire
Access at all times
The remains of a castle built in the 13C by King Edward I can be reached via a 2 minute walk over the footbridge from the station

Churches & Cathedrals

St Giles Church

College House, 1 Temple Row, Wrexham, Denbighshire, LL13 8LY
Tel: 01978 355 808
Email: wrexhamparish@aol.com
Daily 11.00-15.00
Contains a Gothic tower with a steeple dating from 1520. The tower has five
distinct levels stepping 4 hexagonal pinnacles.Known as one of the seven
wonders of Wales

St Asaph Cathedral

High Street, Denbigh, Denbighshire, LL17 0AX
Tel: 01745 583 429
Email: stasaphcathedral@btopenworld.com
Website: www.stasaphcathedral.org.uk
Open daily 08.00-18.00
This is the country's smallest cathedral,and one of the oldest in Wales. It dates
from the 15C and houses William Morgan's first Welsh translation of the bible.

Basingwerk Abbey

Greenfield Valley Heritage Park, S of A458, Holywell, Flintshire
Tel: 029 2082 6185
Access at all times to Abbey. Visitor's Centre Daily 10.00-17.00 Between April and October
In 1188 the Archbishop Balwin and Giraldus Cambrensis spent the night in this
abbey during their grand tour. There is also a visitor's centre on site

Bangor Cathedral

Glanrafon, Bangor, Gwynedd, LL57 1LH
Tel: 01248 353 983
Email: martin@bangorcathedral.freeserve.co.uk
Open 11.00-17.00
This Cathedral boasts the longest continual use of any Cathedral in the British
Isles.

Penmon Priory

7 miles from Beaumaris, Off the B5109, Penmon, Anglesey
Access at all reasonable times
The Welsh name of the priory is Ynys Seiriol after a 6C saint who became
known as The White Saint. The 12C church and 13C cloisters are still standing
and the lime washed interior has a Norman Font.

St Cadwaladr Church

Llangadwaladr, Near Aberffraw, Llangadwaladr, Anglesey

Open Sunday Mornings, at all other times key can be obtained from the rectory.

13C church built encompassing a Latin memorial plaque dating from 625AD in the interior wall.

Church of St Cybi

Newry Street, On the A5, Holyhead, Anglesey, LL65 1HP

Tel: 01407 763 001

Website: www.stcybi.co.uk

Jun-Sep (Mon-Sat) 11.00-15.00

13C church that has undergone much restoration including new stained glass by Edward Burne-Jones and William Morris. The chapel house next door housed the town's first free school.

EXHIBITIONS

Bersham Heritage Centre

Bersham, Wrexham, Denbighshire, LL14 4HT

Tel: 01978 261 529

Email: bershamheritage@wrexham.gov.uk

April-Sept Mon-Fri 10.00-16.30,Sat-Sun 12.00-16.30 Oct-March Mon-Fri 10.00-15.30 Sat & Sun 12.00-15.30

Collections of archaeology, archives, industry, science, technology and social history

GARDENS PARKS & WALKS

Church Bay And Mynydd y Garn Walk

Starts in the village of Swtan, Swtan, Anglesey

Access at all times

This six mile walk covers the North West coast of Anglesey and offers some of the best views of the area. The footpath starts and ends at the car park in Swtan

Loggerheads Country Park

Loggerheads, Alyn Valley, Mold, Flintshire, CH5 5LH
Tel: 01352 810 614
Email: vanessa.cooke@denbighshire.gov.uk
Open all year
Offers great nature walks and country trails with great views of the Clwydian Range.

Llandudno Pier

Llandudno, Conwy
Access at all times
The pier juts out of Llandudno bay and gives great views back along to the limestone cliffs.

Great Orme Country Park

Llandudno, Llandudno, Conwy, LL30
Tel: 01492 874 151
Access at all times
An ancient mountain almost completely surrounded by the sea. The summit can be reached from the car park.

Holyhead Mountain Walk

2 miles W of Holyhead town centre, Holyhead, Anglesey
Access at all times
Starting from the car park just outside Holyhead town centre, this walk is approx 4.5 miles in length and offers a superb coastal walk with modest to rough terrain

Treborth Botanical Gardens

University of Wales, Bangor, Bangor, Gwynedd, LL57 2RQ
Tel: 01248 353 398
Email: n.brown@bangor.ac.uk
Open during daylight hours
Acres of lush lawns, exotic trees, wild grass areas and ancient woodland

Breakwater Country Park

Holyhead, Holyhead, Anglesey
Tel: 01407 760 530
(Daily) 09.00-Dusk.
The park has been constructed on the site of an old brick works and a few remaining kilns can still be seen. There are great walks along the cliff tops to the foghorn station on the North Stack.

Admiral Nelson Statute
Near the Britannia Bridge, Overlooking the Menai Strait, Anglesey, Anglesey
Access at all times
This statue stands on the shoreline and was erected in 1873 as a navigational aid

Maen Huail
Outside Barclays Bank, Ruthin, Ruthin, Denbighshire
Access at all times
This marks the spot where King Arthur and Huail fought for the same woman.
King Arthur was stabbed by Huail in the thigh.They promised never to mention
the fight, but Huail could not resist taunting Arthur who consequently had Huail
beheaded on this stone

Maen Achwyfaen
4 miles W from Holywell, Holywell, Anglesey
Access at all times
The stone of lamentation and Britain's oldest Celtic Cross.

Menia Suspension Bridge
Connects Angelsey to the mainland, Anglesey, Anglesey
Access at all times
The world's first large iron suspension bridge which lies 100 ft above the water.

Bryn Celli Ddu
1.5 miles S of Llanfair PG, Llanfairpwllgyngyllgogerychwryndrobwllllandysiliogogogoch,
Anglesey
Access at all times
4000 year old religious site with a well proportioned henge and stone circle,
inside one of the chambers is an impressive smooth monolith

MUSEUMS

Wrexham County Borough Museum
County Buildings, Regent Street, Wrexham, Denbighshire, LL11 1RB
Tel: 01978 317 970
Email: museum@wrexham.gov.uk
(Mon-Fri) 10.00-17.00, (Sat) 10.30-15.00
A wide variety of 19C town artefacts. Plus the remains the Bronze Age " Brymbo Man" that was unearthed from a local burial cist.

Mold Museum
Earl Road, 10 miles N of Wrexham, Mold, Flintshire, CH7 1AP
Tel: 01352 754 791
Mon-Tues Thurs-Fri 09.30-19.00 Wed 09.30-17.00 Sat 09.30-12.30
Small but effective museum with memorabilia of the Welsh Writer Daniel Owen.

NATURE AND WILDLIFE

Valley Wetlands
Caergeilliog, Anglesey
Tel: 01407 764 973
Access at all times
One of the best places in Wales to see wildfowl all year round

Point Of Air
Dee Estuary, Near Prestatyn, Prestatyn, Flintshire
Tel: 01352 780 527
Access at all times
At its best in Winter when thousands on wading birds feed on the mud flats

South West Wales

ART GALLERIES/ARTS & CRAFTS

Oriel Myrddin

Old Art College, Church Lane, Carmarthen, Carmarthenshire, SA31 1LH
Tel: 01267 222 775
(Mon-Sat) 10.30-16.45
Victorian School Of Art including a craft centre, art gallery, and the work of local artists.

Jim Harries Woodturners

Siop Fach, Mathry, Haverfordwest, Pembrokeshire, SA62 5HB
Tel: 01348 831 379
Shop 09.30-17.30 Mon-Fri Sat 10.00-16.00 Sun 11.00-16.00 Workshop Mon-Fri 10.30-12.30
& 14.00-16.00 Closed in Winter
A workshop where visitors can watch local craftsfolk at work and buy products in the shop.

Llangloffan Farm Cheese Centre

Castle Morris, 2 miles E of Mathry, Haverfordwest, Pembrokeshire, SA62 5ET
Tel: 01348 891 241
Email: leondowney@welshcheese.co.uk
Website: www.welshcheese.co.uk
May-Sep (Mon-Sat) 10.00-12.30 April-Oct (Mon,Wed, Thur,Sat) 10.00-12.30 (Last admission at 11.45)
Demonstrations of home made cheese making processes.

Melin Tregwynt Woollen Mill

Castle Morris, 2 miles E of Mathry, Haverfordwest, Pembrokeshire, SA62 5UX
Tel: 01348 891 225
Email: info@melintregwynt.co.uk
Website: www.melintregwynt.co.uk
Weaving Demonstrations Mon-Fri 09.00-16.30 Shop open Mon-Fri 09.30-17.00 Sat
10.00-17.00 Sun 11.00-16.30
Visitors can watch the wool being spun and processed in this working woollen mill

Gwili Pottery

Pont-ar-Sais, Carmarthen, Carmarthenshire, SA32 7DU
Tel: 01267 253 449
Website: www.gwili.co.uk
Mon-Sat 09.00-17.00 Sun 11.00-15.00
Hand made and decorated earthen ware, are made and can be purchased at
this pottery

Avondale Glass

Carmarthen Road, Kilgetty, Kilgetty, Pembrokeshire, SA6 0YA
Tel: 01834 813 345
Email: info@avondaleglass.f9.co.uk
Website: www.avondaleglass.co.uk
Craft Shop Open End of April-Oct Mon-Fri 09.00-16.30 Sat 09.00-13.00 Glass Making End
of April-October Mon, Tues, Thurs & Fri 09.00-14.00 Wed 09.00-13.00
Producing original pieces including paperweights and animal figures made
entirely by hand

Trapp Arts & Crafts Centre

Llwyndewi, Trapp, Llandeilo, Carmarthenshire, SA19 6TT
Tel: 01269 850 362
March-Dec Thurs-Sun 11.00-17.00
This centre features an art gallery, art exhibitions, craft shop and
demonstrations, workshops and courses as well as a coffee shop.

Solva Woollen Mill

Middlemill, Solva, Haverfordwest, Pembrokeshire, SA62 6XD
Tel: 01437 721 112
Email: enquiries@solvawoollenmill.co.uk
Website: www.solvawoollenmill.co.uk
Mon-Fri 09.30-17.30 July-End Sept Also Sat 09.30-17.30 Sun 14.00-17.30
Gives visitors the chance to see tweeds, rugs and carpets being made on site.
There is also a shop where products can be purchased.

Narberth Pottery

2 Market Street, Narberth, Pembrokeshire, SA67 7AX
Tel: 01834 860 732
Email: simon@simonrich-narberthpottery.co.uk
Website: www.simonrich-narberthpottery.co.uk
Mon-Sat 10.00-17.30 Closed Mondays during Jan, Feb & March
Simon Rich has been perfecting zinc crystalline glazes for the last 25 years and
his range of pottery can be seen at this gallery

The Pembroke Glass Blowing Studio

Blue Gates Yard, The Parade, Commons Road, Pembroke, Pembrokeshire, SA71 4EA
Tel: 01646 682 482
East-End Oct Mon-Fri 09.30-16.30 Glassblowing Mon-Fri 10.00-12.30 & 13.00-15.30
Come and watch this ancient craft as hot glass is worked, shaped and blown into
a range of glasswear

Oriel Emrys Gallery

15 High Street, Haverfordwest, Pembrokeshire, SA61 2BW
Tel: 01437 779 646
Email: enquiries@emrysart.co.uk
Website: www.emrysart.co.uk
Mon-Sat 09.30-17.00
This gallery has a changing exhibition programme which are mostly one person
shows

Cwm Deri Vineyard

Martletwy, Pembrokeshire, SA67 8AP
Tel: 01834 891 274
Email: enquiries@cwm-deri.co.uk
Website: www.cwm-deri.co.uk
March-Oct Mon-Sat 11.00-17.00 Sun 12.00-17.00
Visitors are welcome to wander freely around the vineyard and see the grapes
on the vines and being picked, the finished wine is on sale in the shop. For a
small fee visitors can sample the wine.

CASTLES

Llansteffan Castle

On the B4312, 8 miles SW of Carmarthen, Llansteffan, Carmarthenshire
Tel: 01267 241 756
Access at all times
Impressive ruins of a castle that loom above the village of Llansteffan.

Llawhaden Castle

Llawhaden, Narberth, Narberth, Pembrokeshire
Tel: 029 2082 6185
Access at all times
This was once the residence of the Bishop of St David's

Nevern Castle

Nevern, 1 mile from Newport, Newport, Pembrokeshire

Access at all times

The overgrown ruins of a 13C castle standing above the churchyard, built by Lord Robert Fitzmartin

Haverfordwest Castle

Castle Street, Haverfordwest, Haverfordwest, Pembrokeshire, SA61 2EF

Tel: 01437 763 707

Open all year round-Castle is free to visit but museum costs £1 and is open East-October Mon-Sat 10.00-16.00

Only the remains of this 12C castle are still visible, but within the remains still stands the old Police Station and Prison which house the Country's archives.

CHURCHES & CATHEDRALS

St Ishmael Chapel and village

Ferryside, Carmarthenshire

Access at all times

Originally built to service a medieval village and was destroyed in a storm 300 years ago. A further storm in 1896 revealed the remains of houses around the site. St Ishmael is known as the lost village near the present day village of Ferryside

Church of St Brynach

On the B4582, Nevern, Pembrokeshire

Exterior View at all times

Founded in the 6C it's Norman Tower is still intact. In the churchyard (the second tree on the right) is The Bleeding Yew whose bark oozes brownish red sap. Legend says that the tree will bleed until a Welsh Lord is reinstated in the village castle.

St Non's Chapel & Holy Well

2 miles W of St David's Cathedral, Near St David's, St David's, Pembrokeshire

Access at all times

Holy Well and ancient ruined chapel from the 6C constructed inside a prehistoric stone circle and dedicated to the mother of St David.

St Dogmael's Abbey

St Dogmael's, Near Cardigan, Cardigan, Pembrokeshire, SA43 3DY
Tel: 01239 820 427
Access at all times
Built by Benedictine Monks in the 12C, only the remains of this Abbey survive.

St Govan's Chapel

Near Bosherston, Bosherston, Pembrokeshire
Access at all times
Built into the cliff at St Govan's is this tiny hermit's cell. It is reputed that the counting the number of steps to and from the cell will always result in a different total number.

EXHIBITIONS

West Wales Eco Centre

Lower St Mary's Street, Newport, Pembrokeshire, SA42 0TS
Tel: 01239 820 235
Email: westwales@ecocentre.org.uk
Website: www.ecocentre.org.uk
April-October (Mon-Fri) 09.00-17.00
A venue for exhibitions and advice and resources on sustainable living.

FESTIVALS

Tenby Arts Festival

Throughout Tenby, Tenby, Pembrokeshire
Tel: 01834 843 898
Email: tenbyartsfest@tenby.org
Website: www.tenbyartsfest.co.uk
September each year-please contact for exact dates
A week long festival to celebrate the arts. Visitors can watch numerous free displays and demonstrations such as sand sculpture and kite flying competitions and many more activities.

GARDENS PARKS & WALKS

Welsh Wildlife Centre

Cilgerran, Cardigan, Pembrokeshire, SA43 2TB

Tel: 01239 621 212

Admission free after 18.00 (Carparking charges of between £3 and £5 apply at other times)

Giving visitors the opportunity to explore seven different natural habitats within the centre.

Bosherston Lily Ponds

Bosherston, Near Stackpole, Bosherston, Pembrokeshire, SA61 1PY

Tel: 01646 661 359

Open all year

Wander the footpath which surrounds these three flooded limestone valleys, now covered with lilies.

Parc Howard

Llanelli, 1 mile from the centre, Off the A476 Fenlinfoel Road, Llanelli, Carmarthenshire, SA15 2LJ

Tel: 01554 772 029

Museum Open April-Sept Daily 11.00-13.00 & 14.00-18.00 Oct-March Daily 11.00-13.00&14.00-16.00

The park which centres around a Victorian House contains pleasant grounds and superb views down to the sea. Inside Parc Howard Mansion is a superb collection of Llanelli pottery and local paintings

Cefin Sidan Sands

Pembrey, Carmarthenshire

Access at all times

A beautiful beach that stretches for 7 miles and curves around the end of the Burrows. Where Bonaparte's wife's niece drowned after being ship wrecked.

Saundersfoot to Tenby Walk

Starts at Saundersfoot Harbour, Saundersfoot, Pembrokeshire

Access at all times

Starting from the harbour at Saundersfoot this 4.5 mile walk is an attractive coastal path

Brechfa Forest

Near Abergorlech, Abergorlech, Carmarthenshire
Tel: 01550 720 394
Email: llanymddyfrifd@forestry.gsi.gov.uk
Access at all times
The starting point for many fabulous walks the forest guarantees peace and solitude.

Pembrokeshire Coastal Path

Tenby, Pembrokeshire
Email: webmaster@pembrokeshirecoast.org.uk
Website: www.pembrokeshirecoast.org.uk
Access at all times
This is a major stopping off point with miles and miles of unrivalled cliff scenery.

Landsker Borderlands Trail

Eastern Cleddau, Pembrokeshire
Access at all times
This walk runs the entire length of the Eastern Cleddau. A circular walk from Whitland of 60 miles, winds through the Pembrokeshire/Carmarthenshire Borderland

Tenby North and South Beaches

Esplanade, Tenby, Pembrokeshire, SA70 7DU
Tel: 01834 842 402
Access at all times
North and South Beaches are one of Wales' most popular tourist resorts, offering clear blue waters and ideal for families

Pembrey Country Park

Pembrey, Llanelli, Carmarthenshire, SA16 0EJ
Tel: 01554 833 916
Access at all times
More than 200 hectares of parkland and beach as well as a nature reserve with pitch and putt and a dry ski slope

Llyn Llech Owain Country Park

Gors Las, Llanelli, Carmarthenshire, SA14 7NF
Tel: 01269 832 229
April-Sep Mon-Sun 10.00-17.00 Oct-March Mon-Sun 10.00-16.00
This park consists of woodland with a central lake. There is also a visitors centre, adventure playground and picnic areas

Freshwater West

On the A4319 from Pembroke, Pembroke, Pembrokeshire
Access at all times
This beach is home to the Welsh National Surfing Championships and a favourite
for surfers all year. There are long sandy beaches that remain uncomercialised.

HISTORIC HOUSES

Penrhos Cottage

3 miles from Maenclochog, Maenclochog, Pembrokeshire, SA66 7XT
Tel: 01437 731 457
Email: Mark.Thomas@Pembrokeshire.gov.uk
Viewed by appointment through Scolton Manor Museum
A traditional thatched cottage which has remained unchanged since the 19C.
Built as a ty un nos (house built in one night) and last occupied in 1967, the last
thatched cottage of its kind in Pembrokeshire.

HISTORIC SITES

Merlin's Hill

1 mile E of Abergwili, Abergwilli, Carmarthenshire
Access at all times
The A40 passes the slopes of Merlin's Hill, where legend has it the famous
wizard Merlin lies sleeping under the slopes imprisoned in a cave and waiting for
the call to return and help his fellow countrymen.

Paxton's Folly

Llanarthne, On the B4300, Llanarthne, Carmarthenshire
Access at all times
A Castellated tower that gives fabulous views over the rural countryside below.

Carreg Samson

Near Long House Farm, Abercastle, Trefin, Pembrokeshire
Access at all times
A 4500 year old burial chamber with a sixteen foot high capstone.

Mynachlogddu Village Historic Sites

Mynachlogddu, Pembrokeshire

Access at all times

Many tracks connect a number of ancient sites including; Beddarthur-an eerie stone circle rumoured to be the burial place of many Great Kings., Foeldrygarn-Very impressive Iron Age ramparts and hill circles and Carn Menyn a stone quarry

Devil's Quoit

Near Broomhill Burrows, Castlemartin, Pembrokeshire

Access at all times

The B4319 meets the B4320 at the Devil's Quoit a Neolithic burial chamber which is topped by an impressive capstone.

Celtic Cross

Carew, Carew, Pembrokeshire

Access at all times

Memorial to Maredydd, the ruler of Deheubarth who died in 1035. The cross is remarkably intact and is covered in fine welsh tracery.

Stack Rocks and The Green Bridge Of Wales

Castlemartin, Near Pembroke, Pembroke, Pembrokeshire, SA71 5EB

Tel: 01646 622 388

Access at all times (Please call to check times)

A natural rock arch and rock pillars, make up the Stack Rocks on the SW coast of Pembrokeshire

MUSEUMS

Kidwelly Industrial Museum

Priory Street, Kidwelly, Carmarthenshire, SA17 4LW

Tel: 01554 891 078

Email: cdelaney@carmarthenshire.gov.uk

Easter, May Day Weekend, June-Aug Weekdays 10.00-17.00 Weekends 14.00-17.00

The museum features exhibitions and displays of old tin works.Unique opportunity to see how tinplate was made by hand.

Carmarthen County Museum

Bishop's Palace, Abergwilli, Carmarthenshire, SA31 2JG
Tel: 01267 231 691
Email: cdelaney@carmarthenshire.gov.uk
(Mon-Sat) 10.00-16.30
Various exhibitions including local pottery, archaeological finds, crime and policing, geology, and education.

Speed Museum

Pendine, Carmarthenshire, SA33 4NY
Tel: 01994 453 488
Email: cdelaney@carmarthenshire.gov.uk
April-Oct 10.00-13.00 & 13.30-17.00 Please phone to confirm the museum is open on the day of your visit
Exhibitions and displays on speed in the days gone by and a collection of motorcycles that were used in record breaking attempts

Nant-Y-Coy Mill

Treffgarne Gorge, On the A40, 7 miles N of Haverfordwest, Haverfordwest, Pembrokeshire, SA62 5LR
Tel: 01437 741 671
Email: info@nantycoy.co.uk
Mon-Sat (East-Oct) Entrance to the mill is Free, small charge for the walk.
14C mill below Great Treffgarne Rocks, with nature trail, small museum and craft shop

NATURE AND WILDLIFE

Pengelli Forest

On minor road from Velindre to Eglwyswrw, Felindre Farchog, Pembrokeshire, SA41 3UJ
Access at all times
This forest comprises of oak and ash woodland with alder and ash. There is a wide selection of birds nesting in this forest including Kestrel, Sparrowhawk, Buzzard and the harder to spot Tawny Owls and Woodpeckers

Central Wales

ART GALLERIES/ARTS & CRAFTS

Oriel Davies Gallery
The Park, Newtown, Powys, SY16 2NZ
Tel: 01686 623 633
Email: enquiries@orieldavies.org
Website: www.orieldavies.org
(Mon-Sat) 10.00-17.00
The gallery holds several different exhibitions over the course of a year,
displaying the work of contemporary Welsh, British and international artists.

Country Works Gallery
Broad Street, Montgomery, Powys, SY15 6PH
Tel: 01686 668 866
Email: countryworks@btconnect.com
Tues-Sat 10.00-17.30 Sun 14.00-17.30 Mondays 10.00-17.30 (Summer and Christmas)
Jan-March Wed-Sat 10.00-17.30
Specialises in showing the work of contemporary British Artists

Meirion Mill Woollen Centre
Dinas Mawddwy, Machynlleth, Gwynedd, SY20 9LS
Tel: 01650 531 311
Email: vs@meirionmill.co.uk
Feb-Dec Mon-Sat 10.00-17.00 Sun 10.30-17.00
Visitors can view and purchase pottery and crafts from this mill which has
stunning views of the mountains and River Dyfi

CASTLES

Dolforwyn Castle
Abermule, Montgomery, Powys
Tel: 029 2082 6185
Access at all times
The remains of a castle that was built in 1273 and captured by the English in
1277, were recently revealed by extensive archaeological excavations.

Montgomery Castle

Near Pool Road, Montgomery, Powys, SY15 6QY
Access at all times
Built along the English Welsh Border the building of this was castle started in
1223 by Henry III

Bronllys Castle

South East off the A438/A479 Junction at Bronllys Village, 9 miles NE of Brecon, Bronllys,
Powys, LD3
Tel: 029 2082 6185
Access at all times
A 12C Keep which towers 80 feet above the motte overlooking the river Llynfi

CHURCHES & CATHEDRALS

Brecon Cathedral & Heritage Centre

Cathedral Close, Brecon, Brecon, Powys, LD3 9DP
Tel: 01874 625 222
Email: hazelbar@aol.com
Cathedral is open daily from 8.30 to 18.00, the Heritage Centre and Shop 10.30-16.00
Monday to Saturday and 12.30- 15.30 Sunday
For over 900 years the Church of St John the Evangelist has stood on this site
and was elevated to cathedral status in 1923. Cathedral Heritage Centre with
exhibitions on the history of the Cathedral, shop and restaurant on site

GARDENS PARKS WALKS

Gregynog Hall

University Of Wales, 5 miles N of Newtown, Newtown, Powys
Grounds open all year round
Extensive woodland with many walks, the grounds contain a hedge of golden
yew and a 19C fountain.

Brecon Beacons National Park

Southern Powys and Northern Monmouthshire, 520 square miles of National Park covering the two counties from West to East., Powys
Website: www.breconbeacons.org
Access at all times
This Park contains the Black Mountain, the most challenging and exhilarating walk in South Wales and the Forest Fawr,a vast expanse of hilly landscape between the Black Mountain and The Central Beacons.There are also a large number of fantastic waterfalls

Newtown to Welshpool Walk

Start at Halfpenny Bridge in Newtown, Newtown, Powys
Access at all times
This is one of the easier sections of the Severn Way, and keeps close to the Montgomery Canal Towpath. The walk is approx 12.5 miles in length

Nant yr Arian Visitors Centre

On the A44, 2 miles W of Ponterwyd, Ponterwyd, Ceredigion, SY23 3AA
Tel: 01970 890 694
Summer 10.00-17.00 Winter 11.00-dusk Charge for Parking
This centre offers mountain bike trails and lakeside walks

Pen y Fan

Brecon Beacons National Park, Start from The Storey Arms Centre, Brecon, Powys, LD3 9NA
Tel: 01874 623598
Email: storeyarms@cardiff.gov.uk
Access at all times
This is the highest summit in the Beacons and the third highest summit in Wales

Elan Valley Visitors Centre

Elan Valley, Rhayader, Powys, LD6 5HP
Tel: 01597 810 898
Email: info@elanvalley.org.uk
Website: www.elanvalley.org.uk
Seven days a week from March-October 10.00-17.30 Entrance to Visitors Centre FREE but there is a £1 parking charge that covers the whole estate
Visitors centre situated on the Elan Estate which covers approx 70 square miles. The Centre details the area around the Elan Valley through exhibitions and audio visual shows.

HISTORIC SITES

Ffynon Drewllyd
Dol y Coed, 20 miles NW of Brecon, Llanwrtyd Wells, Powys
A spring named the Stinking Well wells up inside a domed shaped extension in the field behind a spa building and which has the highest sulphur content of any natural source in Britain

Eliseg's Pillar
400 yards N of Llangollen, On the A542, Llangollen, Powys
Access at all times
An eight feet tall pillar erected to a Prince Of Powys in the 9C. The pillar was originally 25 feet tall.

Maen Llia Standing Stone
Brecknock, Powys
Access at all times
An impressive standing stone at nearly 4 meters high, probably marking an ancient trackway

Duke Of Wellington Statue
Brecon Town Square, Brecon, Powys
Access at all times
A bronze statue of The Duke Of Wellington in military dress on a stone pedestal in front of the Wellington Hotel

Beacon Ring
On Long Mountain, Near Welshpool, Welshpool, Powys
Access at all times
Pre Roman Iron Age Hill Fort with views across the Severn Valley. Near to Offa's Dyke footpath

Bryntail Lead Mine Buildings
Llanidloes, Powys
Access at all times
19C Buildings associated with the extraction and processing of lead ore

Dyfi Furnace

3km NW of Dolgelliau, Machynlleth, Powys

Access at all times

A restored 18C charcoal fired furnace used for smelting iron ore

Brecon Gaer Roman Fort

On a farm near Aberyscir, A minor road off the A40 NW of Brecon, Aberyscir, Powys

Access at all times

Remains of an early fort with corner turrets still preserved. Finds from this site can be viewed at to Brecknock Museum in Brecon

MUSEUMS

Robert Owen Museum

Ground Floor of Town Council Building, The Cross, Broad Street, Newtown, Powys, SY16 2BB

Tel: 01686 626 345

Email: johnd.robert-owen@midwales.com

Website: www.robert-owen.midwales.com

(Mon-Fri) 09.30-12.00, 14.00-15.30. (Sat) 09.30-11.30

Converted house where the early socialist Robert Owen was born. The house now details his life.

W H Smith Museum

24 High Street, Newtown, Montgomeryshire, SY16 2NP

Tel: 01686 626 280

Mon-Sat 09.00-17.30

With displays and memorabilia of the history of W H Smith who pioneered new ways to distribute newspapers from the paper round to horse drawn carts, bicycles and station news stands.

NATURE AND WILDLIFE

Lake Vyrnwy
Near Llanwddyn, Llanwddyn, Powys
Tel: 01691 870 278
Email: vyrnwy@rspb.org.uk
Reserve-open at all times; visitor centre-1 April to 31 Oct, daily 10.30 am to 17.30 pm, 1 Nov to 24 Dec 10.30 am to 16.30 pm, 1 January to 31 March, weekends only 10.30 am to 16.30pm.
Offers nature trails and bird watching hides for both bird watchers and families.

Carngafallt
The Cwm, Llanwrthwl, Llandrindod Wells, Powys, LD1 6NU
Tel: 01597 811 169
Access at all times
You can see Red Kites on a visit to this reserve.

EXHIBITIONS

Rheidol Hydro Electric Scheme Visitors Centre
Cwmrheidol, Aberystwyth, Ceredigion, SY23 3NF
Tel: 01970 880 667
Easter weekend and May -Sept Visitors Centre open 10.30-16.15 Guided tours available from 11.00-15.30
Visitors can take a guided tour of the power station or walk one of the centres nature trails, or drive round the scenic reservoirs

FESTIVALS

Llandrindod Wells Victorian Festival
Old Town Hall, Temple Street, Llandrindod Wells, Powys, LD1 5DL
Tel: 01597 823 441
Email: info@victorianfestival.co.uk
Website: www.victorianfestival.co.uk
August-please telephone for exact dates each year
Over 300 events with a Victorian Flavour including walks, talks, exhibitions and musicals

NORTHERN IRELAND

Northern Ireland is part of the UK, unlike Southern Ireland and is made up of six counties.

The Capital of Northern Ireland is the City of Belfast. Belfast is the second largest city in Ireland and has some impressive and important 19th and 20th Century architecture. The city once famous for its ship building (the most famous of which was the Titanic) is now an all year round bustling and modern tourist destination with a wide variety of attractions.

Away from the Capital City, the counties of Northern Ireland offer the visitor a wide range of attractions and things to see. There are natural features such as the spectacular Giants Causeway, dramatic mountain ranges and large and impressive Loughs (lakes). Northern Ireland also has impressive and beautiful countryside, romantic ruined castles and a wide range of historical buildings and sites.

Throughout Northern Ireland there many museums and places of local historical interest that feature industry and trades such as linen making, farming, crystal factories, porcelain manufacture and of course distilleries.

NORTHERN IRELAND

City Of Belfast-N.I.

ART GALLERIES/ARTS & CRAFTS

Fenderesky Gallery

The Crescent Arts Centre, 2-4 University Road, Belfast, County Antrim, BT7 1NH
Tel: 028 902 35245
Email: michelle.cac@btconnect.com
Website: www.crescentarts.org
Tues-Sat 11.30-17.00
This gallery features various displays and exhibits focused on contemporary art.

Bell Gallery

13 Adelaide Park, Belfast, County Antrim, BT9 6FX
Tel: 028 906 62998
Email: bellgallery@btinternet.com
Website: www.bellgallery.com
Open Mon-Thurs 09.00-17.00 Fri 09.00-14.00
This gallery specialises in works by Irish artists and also has an exhibition of
Irish silver and antiques included in its Summer and Autumn programme.

Cavehill Gallery

18 Old Cavehill Road, Belfast, County Antrim, BT15 5GT
Tel: 028 907 76784
Email: art@cavehillgallery.com
Tues-Sat 13.00-17.30 Closed Mon & Sun Please phone in advance to check there is an
exhibition showing
This gallery hosts 5 exhibitions a year each lasting between 2 and 3 weeks. The
exhibitions are mainly paintings based but include some sculpture. There is an
emphasis on Northern Irish artists. Please telephone for exact dates and times
of exhibitions

Ormeau Baths Gallery

18a Ormeau Avenue, Belfast, County Antrim, BT2 8HS
Tel: 028 903 21402
Email: admin@obgonline.net
Website: www.obgonline.net
Tues-Sat 10.00-18.00
This gallery was established in 1995 and is now the leading contemporary arts
gallery in Northern Ireland. Exhibitions change roughly every six weeks.

Aunt Sandra's Candy factory

60 Castlereagh Road, Belfast, County Antrim, BT5 5FP
Tel: 028 907 32868
Email: enquiries@irishcandyfactory.com
Website: www.irishcandyfactory.com
Mon-Fri 09.30-17.00, Sat 10.00-16.30
Visitors can watch candy being handmade from traditional recipes some of
which are over 100 years old. Candy made on site includes honeycomb, fudge
and novelty lollies.

Gormleys Fine Art

670 Raven Hill Road, Belfast, County Antrim, BT6 0BZ
Tel: 028 902 08942
Email: oliver@gormleys.ie
Website: www.gormleys.ie
Mon-Sat 11.00-17.30 Sun 14.00-17.00
Regular exhibitions displaying works of both local and established artists

Crown Liquor Saloon

46 Great Victoria Street, Opposite Europa Hotel, Belfast, County Antrim, BT2 7BA
Tel: 028 9027 9901
Website: www.nationaltrust.org.uk
Open Mon-Sat 11.30am-23.00 Sunday 12.30-22.00
This is Northern Ireland's best known public houses its ornately extravagant
Victorian exterior and fabulous interior decoration makes it one of the National
Trusts greatest treasures. The interior is lit by gas lamps.

St George's Market

Corner of May Street & Oxford Street, Opposite the Hilton Hotel, Belfast, County Antrim,
BT1 1NN
Market Day Tues & Fri Mornings Farm and Speciality Market Saturday Mornings
Over 100 years old and now restored this colourful covered market covers
everything from fresh produce to second hand bargains as well as festive events

CASTLES

Belfast Castle & Visitors Centre

Antrim Road, North Belfast, Belfast, County Antrim, BT15 5GR
Tel: 028 907 76925
Email: bcr@belfastcastle.co.uk
Website: www.belfastcastle.co.uk
Mon-Sat 09.00-22.00 Sun 09.00-18.00
The castle was presented to the city in 1934. It sits on the top of "cave hill" which has long been the seat of Ulster rulers. Trails lead off from the castle to five caves thought to be ancient mines. Visitors centre has 4 different exhibition rooms.

CHURCHES & CATHEDRALS

Belfast Cathedral

Donegall Street, Belfast, County Antrim, BT1 2HB
Tel: 028 903 28332
Email: assist@belfastcathedral.org
Website: www.belfastcathedral.org
Mon-Sat 10.00-16.00, Sun before and after service
Belfast's Cathedral stands as a Hiberno-Romanesque monument, open under partial completion in 1890 and finished almost a century later. Interesting features include the baptistry, angel head font and mosaics.

Sinclair Seamens Church

Corporation Square, Belfast, County Antrim
Tel: 028 907 15997
Open Wed 14.00-17.00 and during Sunday Services 11.30 and 19.00
This church dates from 1857 and has been refurbished using a maritime theme by the congregation in tribute to the seafaring traditions of the City. Notable features include the stained glass, the bell from HMS Hood and lifeboat shaped collection boxes

Clonard Monastery

Clonard Gardens, Falls Road, Belfast, County Antrim
Tel: 028 904 45950
Mon-Sat 06.00-21.00 Sun 06.00-15.00
This monastery is home to the Redemptorists who were founded in Italy in 1732. The monastery was built in 1897 and is Early French Gothic in style.

St Malachy's Church

24 Alfred Street, Belfast, County Antrim, BT2 8EN
Tel: 028 903 21713
Open daily outwith mass times

A Tudor-Gothic castle of a church with octagular painted pink turrets and stone castellations. The unusual interior ceiling has been described as an upside down fancy iced cake.

GARDENS PARKS & WALKS

Botanic Gardens

Stranmillis Road, Queens University Area, Belfast, County Antrim, BT9 5AB
Tel: 028 903 24902
Gardens open daily to dusk. Greenhouses open Mon-Fri 10.00-17.00 Sat-Sun 14.00-17.00 (until 16.00 in winter).

Inside the landscaped gardens are two 19C greenhouses. The Tropical Ravine House and the Palm House, there is also a beautiful rose garden.

Lagan Valley Regional Park

Belvoir Park Forest, Belfast, County Antrim, BT8 4TQ
Tel: 028 904 91922
Email: Postmaster@laganvalley.co.uk
Website: www.laganvalley.co.uk
Open dawn-dusk

13 miles of a mixture of public parks, picnic areas, wetlands, canal tow paths, woodlands and wildlife sanctuaries, as well as a pre-historic monument. Include everything from way marked trails to an arboretums, Japanese gardens, and riverside areas

Cavehill Country Park

Antrim Road, North of City Centre, Belfast, County Antrim, BT5 5GR
Tel: 028 907 76925
Email: parksinfo@belfastcity.gov.uk
Website: www.belfastcity.gov.uk
Open daily 09.00-18.00

Early stone aged settlers lived in the caves in this park which is how the area got its name. The park contains a mixture of features that provide geological, archaeological and botanical interest. There are also marked walks and an adventure playground.

Minnowburn Beeches

On the B205, 3.5 miles S of Belfast at Shaw's Bridge, Belfast, County Antrim
Open dawn-dusk
Owned by the National Trust this area provided woodlands and walks in the Langan Valley which lead to both the Giants Ring and Edenderry Village.

Sir Thomas and Lady Dixon Park

Upper Malone Road, Belfast, County Antrim, BT9 5PD
Tel: 028 903 20202
Email: parksinfo@belfastcity.gov.uk
Website: www.rosemerald.co.uk
Open dawn-dusk
One of the World's best rose gardens with over 25 000 rose, a spectacular sight in summer. Different themed gardens and over 100 different Camellia trails, a Japanese garden and traditional Rhododendrons.

Grovelands

Stockman's Lane, 3 miles S of Belfast Centre, Belfast, County Antrim, BT9 7JE
Tel: 028 903 20202
Email: parksinfo@belfastcity.gov.uk
Website: www.belfastcity.gov.uk
Open dawn-dusk
Sunken gardens and small ornamental gardens enclosed within impressive Art Deco entrance gates.

Stormont Public Park

Upper Newtownards Road, Belfast, County Antrim
Daily until 19.30
This public park includes the Glen Walk, The Prince of Wales Avenue and a children's playground. The park surrounds the Irish Parliament Buildings.

Redburn Country Park

Old Holywood Road, Holywood, Belfast, County Antrim, BT16 1YP
Tel: 028 9181 1491
Open at all times
Woodland walks within this park provide the visitor with great views of Belfast City and Lough, and over the South Antrim hill. During spring the park is ablaze with bluebells which makes a beautiful sight.

HISTORIC HOUSES

Linen Hall Library

17 Donegall Square North, Belfast, County Antrim, BT1 5GB
Tel: 028 903 21707
Email: info@linenhall.com
Website: www.linenhall.com
Mon- Fri 09.30-17.30 & Sat 09.30-16.00
This is one of the oldest subscription libraries in the UK. Specialising in Irish
Politics and Culture. The building is accessible to all members of the public.

Malone House

Barnett Demesne, Belfast, County Antrim, BT9 5PB
Tel: 028 906 81246
Email: mhreception@malonehouse.co.uk
Website: www.malonehouse.co.uk
Open Mon-Sat 10.00-16.00
An elegant Georgian mansion that gives spectacular views over the beautiful
Lagan valley Regional Park. Built in the 1820s the last resident was a wealthy
Belfast grain merchant, William Barnett. He presented the house to the City Of
Belfast in 1946

Belfast Central Library

Royal Avenue, Belfast, County Antrim, BT1 1EA
Tel: 028 9050 9150
Mon & Thurs 09.30-20.00 Tues, Wed & Fri 09.30-17.30 Sat 09.30-13.00
This imposing Classical building was built in the 1890s using red sandstone from
Scotland. The interior of the building is equally impressive including the splendid
domed reference section

Dundonald Old Mill

231 Belfast Road, Quarry Corner, Dundonald, Belfast, County Antrim, BT16 1UE
Tel: 028 904 80117
Open daily
This 300 year old restored sandstone mill boasts Ireland's biggest water wheel
still in working order and at an impressive 35 feet. The mill itself houses a gift
shop, exotic plants centre and a coffee shop & restaurant

Public Record Office

66 Balmoral Avenue, Belfast, County Antrim, BT9 6NY
Tel: 028 902 51318
Email: proni@doeni.gov.uk
Website: www.proni.gov.uk
Mon, Tues, Wed & Fri 09.00-16.45, Thurs 10.00 -20.45
This building is used by historians, students and genealogy enthusiasts who come to use the public search room. There are also historical exhibits that use the vast documentary resources of the Public Record Offices

Belfast City Hall

Donegall Square, Belfast, County Antrim, BT1 5GS
Tel: 028 903 20202
Jun-Sep (Mon-Fri) 11.00, 14.00 & 15.00 (Sat) 14.30 Oct-May (Mon-Fri) 11.00, 14.30 Sat 14.30 (1 hour guided tours)
Designed in 1906 the 173 ft green copper dome can be seen from any point in the city. Grand marble staircase, 3 elaborate reception rooms and portraits of the City's Lord Mayors. Outside is Queen Victoria's Statue, and commemorative Titanic sculpture

Queens University Belfast

University Of Belfast, University Road, Belfast, County Antrim, BT7 1NN
Tel: 028 909 75252
Email: visitors.centre@qub.ac.uk
Website: www.qub.ac.uk
Visitors Centre Open-Mon-Fri 10.00-16.00, Sat 10.00-16.00 May-September Only
Original buildings of Queens College designed by Charles Lanyon consisted of the Main Building and the peaceful quadrangle behind.Today the University has expanded to include all the houses on University Square.Visitors Centre sells University memorabilia

HISTORIC SITES

Albert Memorial Clock

Queen's Square, Belfast, County Antrim, BT1 3FG
Access at all times
Erected in 1865 to commemorate Prince Albert this is one of Belfast's best known landmarks and features a statue of Prince Albert

Giant's Ring

Ballylesson, Off the B32, 5 miles from Belfast City Centre, Belfast, County Antrim, BT7 1HP

Tel: 028 9024 6609

Open dawn-dusk

This prehistoric enclosure is over 600 ft in diameter with an earthen bank 20 ft wide and 12 ft high. In the centre of the enclosure is a dolmen.During the 18C this prehistoric site, of which there is still little known was used as a site for horseracing

Milltown Cemetery

Falls Road, Belfast, County Antrim, BT12 6EQ

Tel: 028 906 13972

Daily 09.00- Dusk

A famous Belfast landmark which has at its centre a green area to mark the site of the unmarked pauper's grave for victims of Typhoid and Cholera

MUSEUMS

Ulster Museum

In the Botanic Gardens, Off Stranmillis Road, Belfast, County Antrim, BT9 5AB

Tel: 028 903 83000

Website: www.ulstermuseum.org.uk

(Mon-Fri) 10.00-17.00, (Sat) 13.00-17.00, (Sun) 14.00-17.00

Irish and Modern Art, local history, antiquities, The Mummy Of Takabuti and the treasure salvaged from the Spanish Armada ship "Girone"

RUC Museum

Brooklyn, 65 Knock Road, On the A504, 3 miles E of Belfast City Centre, Belfast, County Antrim, BT5 6LE

Tel: 028 906 50222

Email: museum@psni.police.uk

Website: www.ruc.police.uk

Mon-Fri 09.30-12.20 & 13.30-16.30 Prior appointment for visits preferred

This museum houses uniforms, photographs and equipment relating to the Irish Constabulary and dates from its formation in 1822.

Belfast Lough

Belfast Harbour Estate, On the shores of Belfast Lough, Belfast, County Antrim

Tel: 028 9147 9009

Viewpoints open at all times, observation room open Tues-Sun 09.00-17.00

Important feeding area for wading birds and wildfowl. Oyster Catchers and Redshanks can be seen from the viewing points

County Fermanagh-N.I.

ART GALLERIES/ARTS & CRAFTS

The Buttermarket

Boston Quay, Down Street, Enniskillen, County Fermanagh, BT74 7DU
Tel: 028 663 23837
Email: bq@ireland.com
Website: www.thebuttermarket.com
Mon-Sat 10.30-17.30
This market houses various craft workshops and allows visitors to watch the
production, purchase and commission unique pieces by some of Fermanagh's
finest craft people.

Belleek Pottery Visitors Centre

On the A46 from Enniskillen, Belleek, County Fermanagh, BT93 3FY
Email: visitorscentre@belleek.ie
Website: www.belleek.ie
Mon-Fri 09.00-17.50 Visitors Centre Free Charge For Tours
A world famous pottery opened in 1989. Visitors can watch the craftsmen shape
and design the porcelain

CASTLES

Castle Balfour

Main Street, Lisnaskea, County Fermanagh, BT92 0JE
Tel: 028 9023 5000
Access at all times
Built around 1618 by Sir James Balfour, a Scottish Planter this castle was in
continuous occupation until the early 19C.

Monea Castle

7 miles NW of Enniskillen, On the B81, Enniskillen, County Fermanagh
Tel: 028 6632 3110
Access at all times
Imposing plantation castle built by Malcolm Hamilton around 1618. The castle
was abandoned after a fire in 1750.

Tully Castle

On the A46 Enniskillen to Belleek Road, Sign post for castle on right hand side approx 12 miles, Derrygonnelly, County Fermanagh

July & August Wed-Sun 10.00-18.00

Built in 1613 by Sir John Hume and burnt in 1641 by the Maguires. Visitors can find a visitors centre and formal gardens

GARDENS PARKS & WALKS

Marble Arch Forest

Florencecourt, Entrance is off the main Florencecourt to Blacklion Road, Florencecourt, County Fermanagh

Tel: 028 6632 3110

Open end of March to September.

Situated close to the famous Marble Arch caves this forest offers walks along the Claddagh Glen, nature trails and a waterfall.

Castle Archdale Country Park

Rossmore, Irvinestown, County Fermanagh, BT94 1PP

Tel: 028 686 21588

Email: brondi@doeni.gov.uk

09.00-Dusk

This country park offers woodland and loughshore walks. The marina gives access to White Island.

Forthill Park

Forthill, Enniskillen, County Fermanagh

Tel: 028 6632 3533

Park access at all times

A beautiful town park on a steep hill. Within the park is the Cole Monument built in 1857 with 108 steps to the top. (There is a charge to climb the monument but the park itself is free.)

Ely Lodge Forest

Entrance just across the road to Carrickreagh viewpoint, Enniskillen, County Fermanagh, BT74 4EJ

Tel: 028 6634 3032

Website: www.forestserviceni.gov.uk

Access at all times

This forest offers lake shore trails and rambles, picnic area and a jetty.

Lough Macnean Sculpture Trail

Around the shores of Upper and Lower Lough Macnean, Lough Macnean, County Fermanagh

Tel: 028 6632 3110

Access at all times

Along the boundaries for Fermanagh, Cavan and Leitrim on a 40 mile circular trail are unique sculptures carried out by renowned Irish artists

Sliabh Beagh

Rosslea, County Fermanagh

Tel: 028 6775 1918

Email: info@sliabhbeagh.org

Access at all times

The Sliabh Beagh Way is a 25 miles walk starting at St Patrick's Chair and Well in County Tyrone and finishing at Donagh in South East Fermanagh

HISTORIC SITES

Galloon Cross

Galloon Graveyard, Galloon, County Fermanagh

Access at all times

There are two crosses in this graveyard, one at each end. One is quite badly weathered but the other has identifiable Biblical scenes showing Adam and Eve

Drumskinny Stone Circle

North of Irvinestown, A few hundred yards from the Kesh-Castlederg Road, Irvinestown, County Fermanagh

Access at all times

Dating from the New Stone Age 2250BC this stone circle is one of five in the immediate locality. This stone circle consists of 39 stones and a small cairn and is believed to have been used for religious practices and astronomical observations.

Killadeas Churchyard

7 miles N of Enniskillen, Killadeas, County Fermanagh

Access at all times

Stone carvings dating from the 7 & 8C can be found in this old graveyard. The most unusual is that of the Bishop's Stone, one side is a strolling church man with Crozier and Bell and on the other side a grotesque moon face.

Ederney Covered Wishing Well

100 meters outside Ederney Village, On the Main Road to Omagh, Ederney, County Fermanagh

Access at all times

This unusual well is one of a kind in this area and can only be accessed by going through a kissing gate.

The Clock Tower

Main Street, Irvinestown, County Fermanagh, BT94 1GL

Tel: 028 822 47831

Exterior View

This tower that stands at the head of Main Street is the only surviving part of the Old Parish Church. This monument is Irvinestown's best known landmark. The graveyard of the old church can still be seen and the earliest grave dates from 1694

Montiaghroe Standing Stones

1 mile S of Montiaghroe, Montiaghroe, County Fermanagh

Access at all times

Three standing stones and a small cairn on one side, this standing stone is very similar to the Drumskinny Stone Circle

NATURE AND WILDLIFE

Lower Lough Erne Islands

Near Belleek, Belleek, County Fermanagh

Tel: 028 6634 1456

Access at all times-the hides are not owned by the RSPB but there is public access

A mix of forest and islands, this is a breeding reserve for Snipe, Redshanks, Curlews and Sandwich Terns

Londonderry-N.I.

ART GALLERIES/ARTS & CRAFTS

Orchard Gallery
Orchard Street, Derry, Londonderry, BT48 6EG
Tel: 028 712 69675
Tues-Sat 10.00-18.00
Establishing itself as one of Ireland's most innovative art galleries. Houses exhibitions of the work of local and international artists

Glenaden Shirts
Trench Road, Derry, Londonderry, BT47 2US
Tel: 028 7134 4353
Email: info@glenaden.com
Website: www.glenaden.com
Mon-Thurs 08.15-17.00 Fri 08.15-15.00
This unique exhibition lets the visitor learn the history of shirt manufacturing in the city

The Craft Village
Shipquay Street, Derry, Londonderry
Tel: 028 712 60324
Mon-Sat 09.00-17.30
Take a step back in time at this craft village which combines craft shops, balconied apartments, a restaurant and coffee shop

The Laneside Gallery
5 Stable Lane, Coleraine, Londonderry
Tel: 028 703 53600
Email: info@lanesidegallery.com
Website: www.lanesidegallery.com
Tues-Sat 12.00-17.30
As well as accommodating original paintings by leading and emerging artists, Laneside Gallery also offers a selection of prints, original drawings and sculptures

Flowerfield Arts Centre

185 Coleraine Road, Portstewart, Londonderry, BT55 7HU
Tel: 028 708 31400
Email: info@flowerfield.org
Website: www.flowerfield.org
Mon-Fri 10.00-17.00, Sat 12.00-16.00 Admission to the gallery free, charge for some events.
A venue for arts and crafts, exhibitions, events and lectures. There is also two
galleries and a children's play area.

Gallery 33

33 St Paul's Road, Articlave, Coleraine, Londonderry, BT51 4UP
Tel: 028 708 49933
Website: www.irishgallery33.com
Tues-Sun 12.30-17.30
Our artistic style is a blend of modern art and imaginative ideas along with
traditional

CASTLES

Mountsandel Fort

Mountsandel Road, Coleraine, Londonderry
Access at all times
This large oval mound, dominates the bank of the Bann River, beside the site of
Ireland's oldest house that was inhabited 9000 years ago.

Downhill Castle

42 Mussenden Road, Castlerock, Londonderry, BT51 4RP
Tel: 028 708 48728
Email: downhill@nationaltrust.org.uk
Access to grounds all year
Near Mussenden Temple is the 18C ruined palace of the Temple's eccentric
builder the Earl Bishop Of Derry

CHURCHES & CATHEDRALS

Banagher Old Church

2 miles SW of Dungiven, Off the B74, Dungiven, Londonderry
Access at all times
Impressive ruins, the knave was built around 1100 and the chancel added
around 1200 with a tomb in the shape of an Early Irish Church.

Bovevagh Church

7 Connell Street, Limavady, Londonderry
Access at all times
Established in the late Middle Ages by Colm Cille in 557. There is a mortuary house built to house the remains of a Saint, now in a ruined state with a slab stone roof.

St Eugene's Cathedral

Fransic Street, Derry, Londonderry, BT48
Summer 0900-2100; Winter 0900-2030
Completed in 1903 in Gothic Revival style this is one of the City's most magnificent structures.

Saint Patrick's Church

Church Street, Coleraine, Londonderry, BT52 1AR
Tel: 028 7034 4213
Email: admin@stpats.co.uk
Website: www.stpats.co.uk
Tues-Sat 11.00-15.00
The present church dates from 1613 and contains many fine memorials. The church is on the original site of an early Christian Chirch founded by St Patrick in the 5C

St Augustine's Church

Off Bishop's Street, Palace Lane, Derry, Londonderry
Email: st.augustine@btinternet.com
Website: www.btinternet.com/ st.augustine
Open daily
The present building was erected in 1872 on the site of an ancient Augustian Abbey

Dungiven Priory

Dungiven, Londonderry, BT47
Tel: 028 777 60307
Access at all times
This is an Augustinian Priory with a 15C tomb of Cooey-na-Gall an O'Cahan chief who died in 1385.

HISTORIC HOUSES

Guildhall

Shipquay Gate, Guildhall Square, Derry, Londonderry, BT48 6DQ
Tel: 028 713 77335
(Mon-Fri) 09.00-17.00 Free tours available during the Summer
First built in 1887 the building was destroyed by fire in 1908 and devastated by bombs in 1972. The restored building contains replicas of the original stained glass windows and an enormous organ with over 3000 pipes. The hall is haunted by San Mackay

HISTORIC SITES

The Walls Of Derry

Derry, Londonderry
Access at all times
These famous walls have withstood many sieges, the most celebrated lasting 105 days. There are fine views from the top of the walls which encircle the old city in a circuit of one mile.

Auglish Stone Circles

3 miles SSW of Dungiven, Dungiven, Londonderry
Tel: 028 777 60307
Access at all times
Consisting of five circles and five alignments at a very well preserved site

William Ferguson Massey Statue

Outside the Limavady Library, Limavady, Londonderry
Access at all times
A statue to William Ferguson Massey who was Prime Minister of New Zealand from 1912-1925, and who was born in Limavady

MUSEUMS

Harbour Museum

Harbour Square, Derry, Londonderry, BT48 6AF
Tel: 028 7137 7331
Email: museums@derrycity.gov.uk
(Mon-Fri) 10.00-16.30
The museum displays painting and artefacts relating to the harbour history of Derry

Workhouse Museum

23 Glendermott Road, Waterside, Derry, Londonderry, BT47 6BG
Tel: 028 713 18328
Email: museums@derrycity.gov.uk
Mon-Thurs and Sat 10.00-16.30
History of the workhouse, Irish famine and the City's role in World War II.

Amelia Earhart Centre

Ballyarnet Country Park, Derry, Londonderry
Tel: 028 713 54040
Mon-Thurs 10.00-16.00 Fri 10.00-13.00
A cottage exhibition dedicated to Amelia Earhart, the first woman to fly across the Atlantic solo, and who landed here in the field in 1932.

NATURE & WILDLIFE

Lough Foyle

Near Londonderry, Derry, Londonderry
Tel: 028 9049 1574
Access at all times
Large number of waterfowl, geese and swans with excellent views over the mud flats

County Down-N.I.

ART GALLERIES/ARTS & CRAFTS

Breezemount Angora Goat Farm
49 High Bangor Road, Donaghadee, County Down, BT21 0PB
Tel: 028 9188 8125
Email: breezemount.farm@btinternet.com
Website: www.breezemountfarm.com
Jan-Dec 09.00-17.00 Weekdays also open weekends but please contact before visiting to conform opening hours as this is a working farm
This open farm produces Mohair from its herd of Angora Goats. The Mohair is then made into scarves, knitwear, socks and a range of other products. 'Olde world' style craft shop with own products and those from local artists.

CASTLES

Bangor Castle
Castle Park, Bangor, Bangor, County Down, BT20 4BN
Tel: 028 912 70371
Exterior View only of castle
This Elizabethan Jacobean revival style castle was built in 1852 for the Hon. Robert Edward Ward. . The gardens surrounding the castle have won many awards for their displays of flowers.The castle now serves as the Town Hall

Clough Castle
Clough, At Junction A24 and A25, Clough, County Down
Tel: 028 9751 0721
Website: www.ntni.org
Access at all times
Anglo-Norman motte and bailey earthwork castle with added stone tower. Great views of the surrounding area from the top of the mound

Strangford Castle
Strangford, County Down
Tel: 028 902 35000
Access at all times
Built to control ships entering Strangford Lough this castle is a 16C Tower House.

Mound Of Down

English Street, Downpatrick, County Down
Tel: 028 902 35000
Access at all times
This large man made earthwork with steep banks and outer ditch was the site of
a much earlier fortification on which the Normans built a later castle. Today only
the mound remains.

CHURCHES & CATHEDRALS

Downpatrick Cathedral

English Street, Downpatrick, County Down
Tel: 028 446 14922
Website: www.downcathedral.org
Mon-Sat 09.30-16.30 Sun 14.00-17.00
A 12C Cathedral on the historic hill of Down. Next to the Cathedral is where
Saint Patrick is believed to be buried.

Movilla Abbey

Millisle Road, 1 mile E of Newtownards, Newtownards, County Down
Access at all times
Refounded as an Augustinian Abbey in the 12C. The structure of this abbey
includes one stone from the pre-Norman monastery, ruins from the 13C church
and additions from the 15C.

Derry Churches

Off Cloghy Road, 1.5 miles NE of Portaferry, Portaferry, County Down
Access at all times
These churches are associated with Saint Cumain and are pre-Norman in date.
Features include a small cross and carved stones.

Nendrum Abbey and Monastic Site

Mahee Island in Strangford Lough, Strangford, Mahee Island, County Down
Tel: 028 905 43037
Access at all times
Created by Saint Mochaoi all that now remains is a Round Tower stump and the
foundations of other buildings. There is also a sundial and cross slabs dating
from the 12C that are still visible.

Raholp Church

4 miles SW of Strangford, On the A25, Strangford, County Down, BT30
Access at all times
This small church is associated with Saint Lassach who traditionally gave Saint Patrick the last sacrament. The church dates from early 10 or 11C with a west door and narrow east window.

The Church Of The Narrows

Centre of Kilkeel, Kilkeel, County Down
Access at any reasonable time
The 14C ruined church pales in insignificance to the nearby graveyard. Where William Hare, murderer of 16 people in Edinburgh and of the infamous Burke and Hare. Hare ended up in the workhouse in Kilkeel after turning King's evidence for his freedom

GARDENS PARKS & WALKS

Cairnwood

Ballysallagh, County Down
Tel: 028 9064 7256
Access at all times
Offering a mixture of marked paths for rambling and orienteering, this is a haven for mature conifers and young trees.

Stricklands Glen

Bangor West, Approached by narrow Glen Road off Bryansburn Roundabout, Bangor, County Down
Access at all times
A wooded glen which follows the Bryans Burn, a stream which runs from Connor Park into Smelt Mill Bay. Enchanting walks take you along tree lined roads, stunning waterfalls and ponds.

Kilbroney Park

Rostrevor, off the A2, Rostrevor, County Down, BT34 3DQ
Tel: 028 417 38134
Open dawn to dusk
Features of this park include a stunning 2 mile forest drive with panoramic views over Carlingford Loch, riverside walks and arboretum.

Redburn Country Park

Old Holywood Road, Jackson's Road, Holywood, County Down, BT16 1YP

Tel: 028 918 11491

Access at all times

Wooded walks with views of Belfast City, Lough and South Antrim Hills.
Spectacular displays of bluebells in Spring.

Scrabo Country Park

Scrabo Road, Newtownards, County Down, BT23 4SJ

Tel: 028 918 11491

Park open at all times Tower open 10.30-18.00 from 30th March-25th September (Closed on
Fridays)

The park has wooded walks and stunning views and also includes Scrabo Tower
a memorial to the third Marquis of Londonderry

Tyrella Beach

Killough Road, Follow signs off the A20 and A21, Downpatrick, County Down

Access at all times

Waymarked walks, beach centre, information displays and a shop all feature on
this award winning beach.

HISTORIC HOUSES

North Down Visitor's And Heritage Centre

Town Hall, Castle Park Avenue, Bangor, County Down, BT20 4BT

Tel: 028 912 71200

Email: ian.wilson@northdown.gov.uk

Website: www.northdown.gov.uk

Daily except Mondays 10.30-16.30, Sundays 14.00-16.30 (Open until 17.30 July & August)

An Elizabethan Revival style house that belongs to the Hamilton family who were
once the owners of all the land around Bangor. The estate also includes 2 parks
in the 129 acres of grounds. Castle Park and Ward Park.

Hilden Brewery Visitors Centre

Hilden House, Hilden, Lisburn, Hilden, County Down, BT27 4TY

Tel: 028 9266 3863

Email: hilden.brewery@ukgateway.net

Visitors Centre open all year Tues-Sat 10.00-17.00 Exhibitions Free Charge for Brewery
Tours

A working brewery with visitors centre in a historic setting at Hilden House

Bangor Tower House And Tourist Information Centre

34 Quay Street, Bangor, County Down, BT20 5ED
Tel: 028 912 70069
Summer 10.00-19.00 Winter 10.00-17.00
Built in 1637 this Tower and adjoining Tower House were the original Customs House on Bangor's sea front. In 1979 it was added to the "list of buildings of special interest".

Cockle Row

The Harbour, Groomsport, County Down, BT19 6JR
Tel: 028 9145 8882
Daily June July & August
300 year old fishermen's cottages with 1910 furnishings. Within the building there is a heritage centre, tourist information, shop and craft demonstrations

HISTORIC SITES

St Patrick's Shrine

On the summit of Slieve Patrick, Near Downpatrick, Downpatrick, County Down
Access at all times
A granite stature of the saint with bronze panels depicting his life. 360 degrees views of the Lough and mountains.

St Patrick's Grave

Cathedral Hill, Down Cathedral, Downpatrick, County Down
Access at all times
Reputedly the grave of Saint Patrick buried in 461 AD and also of Saint Brigid and Saint Colmeille, who foretold the joint burial of the Irish Trinity. A place of pilgrimage on the 17th March St Patrick's Day

Millin Bay Cairn

Portaferry, County Down
Access at all times
A Neolithic burial ground excavated in 1953, and which was found to be the tomb of 15 people dating back over 4000 years

Scrabo Tower

Scrabo Country Park, Killynether Wood, Newtownards, County Down
Tel: 028 918 11491
10.30-18.00 from 30th March-25th September (Closed on Fridays)
Built in 1857 as a memorial to the third Marquis of Londonderry. There are 122 steps which take you to the viewing level which gives breathtaking views across Strangford Lough and beyond to Scotland.

St Cooeys Wells

South of Portaferry, Towards Ballyquintin Point, Portaferry, County Down
Access at all times
Just south of Portaferry are a collection of 7C holy wells founded by Saint Cowey, a drinking well, a wishing well and an eye well. Pilgrims still journey to these wells which are reputed to have healing powers.

The Market Cross

East end of High Street, Newtownards, County Down
Access at all times
Built in 1636 and destroyed by Commonwealth Troups in 1653 the present building was finished in 1666. Legend says the cross used to flow with wine at the birth of a Royal baby.

The Maypole

Junction of High Street and Shore Street, Holywood, County Down, BT1 2AR
Tel: 028 902 70069
Access at all times
Dating pre 1700 this is Ireland's only remaining Maypole. It is said to be constructed from a broken mast from a Dutch ship which went aground on the nearby shore line.

Struell Wells

Off B1, Just E of Downpatrick, Downpatrick, County Down
Access at all times
Healing wells nestled in a rocky valley that are strongly associated with Saint Patrick

Finnis Souterrain

Off the Carrigagh Road, 2.5 miles S of Finnis, Dromara, County Down
Access at all times
An underground stone lined tunnel dating from the 9C possibly used as a place of refuge, for storing food or as a safe for valuables. Although common in Ireland there are few that visitors can actually go inside and this one has solar powered lighting.

MUSEUMS

Down County Museum

The Mall, English Street, Downpatrick, County Down, BT30 6AH
Tel: 028 446 15218
Email: museum@downdc.gov.uk
Website: www.downcountymuseum.com
Monday to Friday from 10.00 to 17.00, Saturdays and Sundays from 13.00 to 17.00
Restored 18C jail housing a museum which tells the story of Saint Patrick. There is a restored cell block with life size figures of jailers and prisoners.

Newry Museum

Arts Centre,, Bank Parade, Newry, County Down, BT35 6HP
Tel: 028 3026 6232
Mon-Fri 10.30-16.30
History of the Gap Of The North, robes of the order of Saint Patrick. There is a restored 18C room with period furniture and Nelson's table from HMS Victory. This Museum will relocate to Bagenal's Castle in late 2006

Portaferry Visitors Centre

The Stables, Castle Street, Portaferry, County Down, BT22 1NZ
Tel: 028 427 29882
Email: tourism@ards-council.gov.uk
Website: www.portaferry.freeserve.co.uk
East-Sept Mon-Fri 10.00-17.00 Sun 14.00-18.00
Restored stable that houses exhibitions on the history, heritage and environment of Portaferry and Strangford Lough. Also audio visual display on the town houses of County Down.

Scarva Visitors Centre
Main Street, Scarva, County Down
Tel: 028 388 32163
April-Sept Tues-Sun 09.00-17.00
History of Irish Canals. The building of the Newry canal and the history of Scarva which developed as a direst result of the canal.

NATURE & WILDLIFE

Ballywhiskin Open Farm
216 Ballywalter Road, Millisle, County Down, BT22 2LY
Tel: 028 918 62262
March-October 10.00-13.00 & 14.00-18.00
This open farm allows visitors to view and touch animals in their natural environment. Animals include sheep, rabbits, duck and pea fowl.

Quoile Countryside Centre
Off the A245 North of Downpatrick, 5 Quay Road, Downpatrick, County Down, BT30 7JB
Tel: 028 446 15520
April-Sept daily 11.00-17.00 Oct-March Weekends only 13.00-17.00
Rare breads of cattle, sheep, pigs and ponies. Ornamental pheasants, pet corner and pony rides also on site.

County Armagh-N.I.

ART GALLERIES/ARTS & CRAFTS

Ballydougan Pottery
Bloomvale House, 171 Plantation Road, Craigavon, County Armagh, BT63 5NN
Tel: 028 383 42201
Email: info@ballydouganpottery.co.uk
Website: www.balldouganpottery.co.uk
Mon-Sat 09.00-17.00
Visitors can watch the pottery being hand thrown, decorated and designed all within this historic thatched house. It is also the winner of the British Airways Northern Ireland Tourist Board Award

Shambles Market
Cathedral Road, Armagh, County Armagh, BT61 7QX
Tel: 028 375 28192
Market on Tues & Fridays 09.00-17.00 , car boot sale every second weekend 09.00-12.00
This market was built in 1827 as a grain market. The market originally housed the city's butchers who did their own slaughtering on the premises. The enclosed area was used for the sale of pork, hay, straw and hides.

CASTLES

Grey Point Fort
Within Crawfordsburn Country Park, Helen's Bay, Helen's Bay, County Armagh
Tel: 028 918 53621
Open April-Sep Mon, Wed-Sun 14.00-17.00 Oct-March Sun 14.00-17.00
This fort was built to defend the Lough during the Two World Wars. There are still gun emplacements, quarters and stores.

Kirkistown Castle
Between Cloghy Bay and Kearney, On the Eastern Side Of the Ards Peninsula, Kearney, County Armagh
External View Only
Built by the Savage family, who were Anglo-Norman landlords of the peninsular , in 1622 this impressive Tower House is well worth a view, even though the house is on private ground and not accessible to the public.

St Patrick's Roman Catholic Cathedral

Cathedral Road, Armagh, County Armagh, BT61 9DL

Tel: 028 375 22802

Website: www.armagharchdiocese.org

Open Daily dawn-dusk

This imposing cathedral was started in 1840 but the magnificent interior was not completed until the early 20C

Church Of Ireland Cathedral Of St Patrick

Abbey Street, Armagh, Armagh, County Armagh, BT61 7DY

Tel: 028 375 23142

Email: armroblib@aol.com

Website: www.stpatricks-cathedral.org

(daily) Apr-Oct 10.00-17.00, Nov -March 10.00-16.00 Tours Jun-Aug Mon-Sat 11.30-14.30

19C restoration of a 13C structure that enlarged upon the 5C original building. The Cathedral is the final resting place of the Irish King Brian Boru. There is also an Iron Age sculpture of a King with a false arm.

Armagh Friary

Access at the entrance to Palace Stables Heritage Centre, Armagh, Armagh, County Armagh, BT61

Tel: 028 375 29629

Access at all times

Ruins of the longest Friary in Ireland (163 feet). Founded by Founded by Arch Bishop Patrick O'Scanail in 1263

Creggan Churchyard and Visitors Centre

Grounds of Creggan Parish Church, Glassdrumman Road, Crossmaglen, County Armagh

Tel: 0429 371921

Email: creggan@armagh.anglican.org

Website: www.creggan.armagh.anglican.org

Access to the churchyard at all times Guided tours given by the Visitors Centre June-Sept 15.00-17.30

Within this serene church yard are tablet memorials to a number of 18C poets including Art McCooney (1738-73) and the bandit port Seamus Mor MacMurphy (1720-1750)

Killevy Churches
Forkhill, 3.5 miles SW of Newry on the B113, Newry, County Armagh
Tel: 028 375 21800
Access at all times
These two churches date from medieval times, the west church from the 11C and the east church from the 15C and the site also includes O'hanlon cemetery. The site was previously the location of a nunnery that was founded by St Monnena in the 5C.

GARDENS PARKS & WALKS

Tannaghmore Garden Farm
Silverwood, Craigavon, County Armagh
Tel: 028 383 43244
Daily 10.00-1 hour before dusk
Rose gardens surround this Georgian farmhouse. The farm has many rare breeds of animals that were found on Ulster farms 100 years ago. The farm is next to Craigavon Lakes which is a great location for walks.

Ballymoyer Forest
Off Whitecross to Newtownhamilton road, Newtownhamilton, County Armagh
Access at all times
Ballymoyer is a wooded glen surrounded by the dramatic scenery of the Fews Mountains. Douglas Firs dominate the skyline

Slieve Gullion Forest Park
Forkhill Road, 5 miles from Newry, Newry, County Armagh
Access at all times
There is a route that leads to the top of Slieve Gullion Mountain where a passage grave, cairn and volcanic lake can be found.

Peatlands Park
Derryhubbert Road, Dungannon, 10 miles N of Armagh, Dungannon, County Armagh
Tel: 028 388 51102
Park (Daily) East-Sep 09.00-21.00, Oct-east 09.00-17.00 Visitors Centre. Jun-Sep (Daily) 14.00-17.00
Nature reserves and an interpretative displays on the natural and human history of the peat bogs. Turf cutting demonstrations and a small railway that used to carry turf. (£1)

Maghery Country Park

8 miles E of Dungannon, Exit 12 from M1, Maghery, County Armagh, BT66 6NJ
Tel: 028 383 22205
Open daily 09.00-17.00
Bird watching, fishing and nature trails are all attractions of this Country
Park.Spectacular views of Lough Neagh

Carnagh Forest Nature Reserve

Castleblayney Road, Keady, County Armagh, BT60 3QP
Tel: 028 3755 1277
Access at all times
Consisting of three small lakes and home to a variety of birds and wildfowl

HISTORIC HOUSES

Armagh Public Library-Robinson Library

43 Abbey Street, Armagh, County Armagh, BT61 7DY
Tel: 028 375 23142
Email: armroblib@aol.com
Website: www.armaghrobinsonlibrary.org
Open Mon-Fri 10.00-16.00 Closed 13.00-14.00
Built in 1771 and named after its founder Richard Robinson was the first public
library outside Dublin. Inside the library is a superb collection of antiquities
including, ancient manuscripts, a facsimile of the Book Of Armagh

Moneypenny's Lock

Horseshoe Lane, Brackagh, Portadown, County Armagh
Tel: 028 3832 2205
Open weekends 14.00-17.00 Easter-September
A 2 mile walk along the tow path from Shillingtons Key Carpark leads you to a
restored lock-keepers house, bothy and stables.

HISTORIC SITES

Emain Macha-Navan Fort
Signposted off A28, 2 miles W of Armagh, Armagh, County Armagh, BT61 4LD
Tel: 028 9054 6552
Access at all times
Ancient seat of the Kings and earliest capital of Ulster. There is an impressive earthworks, settlement sites and sacred places which reflect over 7500 years of activity.

Ballykeel Dolmen
Western foot of Slieve Gullion, SW of Village of Camlough, Camlough, County Armagh
Tel: 028 9023 5000
Access at all times
A graceful dolmen with an immense capstone sits at the side of the B134 to Forkhill.

Ballymacdermot Cairn
Near Bernish Viewpoint, SW of Newry, Newry, County Armagh, BT61
Access at all times
On the way to this viewpoint take the time to sop off at this ancient site. The Cairn is a tomb that dated back more than 500 years.

Kilnasaggart Pillar
On the slopes of Slieve Gullion, 1.25 miles S of Jonesborough, Jonesborough, County Armagh
Access at all times
This 8C pillar which has cross inscribed circles also has an inscription in Irish.

MUSEUMS

Armagh County Museum
The Mall East, Armagh, County Armagh, BT61 9BE
Tel: 028 3752 3070
Email: acm.um@nics.gov.uk
Website: www.armaghcountymuseum.org.uk
Mon-Fri 10.00-17.00 Saturday 10.00-13.00 & 14.00-17.00
The museum houses an assortment of 18C artefacts including wedding dresses, pictures, stuffed birds, jewellery and militia uniforms.

Cardinal O' Fiaich Memorial Library

15 Moy Road, Armagh, County Armagh, BT61 7LY

Tel: 028 375 22981

Email: eolas@ofiaich.ie

Website: www.ofiaich.ie

Mon-Fri 09.30- 13.00 & 14.00 -17.00 Access to all but please make an appointment to view the archive or other special collections

A library and archive which concentrate on the Irish Language and Literature as well as History. Houses the Cardinal's papers and books.

Royal Irish Fusiliers Museum

Sovereigns House, The Mall, Armagh, County Armagh, BT61 9DL

Tel: 028 3752 2911

Email: amanda@rirfus-museum.freeserve.co.uk

Website: www.rirfus-museum.freeserve.co.uk

Mon-Fri 10.00-12.30 & 13.30-16.00

Housed in an 18C house which was the former residence of the Mayor of Armagh, the history of the Royal Irish Fusiliers is told through a series of displays and exhibitions

NATURE & WILDLIFE

Lough Neagh Discovery Centre

Oxford Island, Lurgan, Craigavon, County Armagh, Bt66 6NJ

Tel: 028 3832 2205

Email: oxford.island@craigavon.gov.uk

Website: www.oxfordisland.com

October-March Wed-Sun 10.00-17.00 Closed Mon & Tues Summer April -Sept Daily 10.00-19.00

This centre houses exhibitions and displays all about the culture, wildlife and history of Lough Neagh. Footpaths, woodland walks, bird watching hides, picnic area and craft shop all on site

County Antrim-N.I.

Art Galleries/Arts & Crafts

Coloured Rain Art Gallery
886 Antrim Road, Templepatrick, County Antrim, BT39 0AH
Tel: 028 944 39494
Email: art@colouredrain.com
Website: www.colouredrain.com
Mon-Fri 10.30-16.30 Sat 10.30-17.00
A contemporary showcase offering a wide range of artists including major and important pieces

Clotworthy Arts Centre
Antrim Castle Gardens, Randalstown Road, Antrim, County Antrim
Tel: 028 944 28000
Email: clotworthyarts@antrim.gov.uk
Mon-Fri 09.30-21.30 Sat 10.00-17.00 July & August Sun 14.00-17.00
Once a coach house and stables for Antrim Castle, this Arts Centre now provides performance spaces, galleries, exhibitions and workshops

Irish Linen Centre and Lisburn Museum
Market Square, Lisburn, County Antrim, BT28 1AG
Tel: 028 926 63377
Email: irishlinencentre@lisburn.gov.uk
Website: www.lisburn.gov.uk
Mon-Sat 09.30-17.00
This exhibition recreates the great linen industry of Ulster through weaving workshops with hand looms, audio visuals, local history exhibits and a linen and craft shop.

Churches & Cathedrals

Ballymoney Parish Church
Top of Church Street, Opposite St Patrick's Church Of Ireland, Ballymoney, County Antrim
Access at all times
The ruins of the ancient Parish Church and the Old Church Graveyard is one of Ballymoney's most beautiful and historic places.

Bonamargy Friary

On the A2, 0.5 miles E of Ballycastle, Ballycastle, County Antrim

Tel: 028 2076 2225

Access at all times

These are the remains of a Franciscan Friary founded circa 1500. The E range of the cloisters, gatehouse and church are virtually complete except for the roof, which was originally thatched

Layde Old Church

1 mile N of Cushendall, Via a footpath on coast road to Torr Head, Cushendall, County Antrim

Access at all times

This Franciscan Friary was a Parish Church from 1306 to the end of the 18C. It is also the chief burial place of the MacDonnells after Bonamargy.

St Nicholas Church

Market Place, Carrickfergus, County Antrim

Website: www.saintnicholas.org.uk

Open mornings

This building was founded in the 12C by the Anglo-Norman John de Courcy. Over the centuries there have been many changes and additions to the building but it has managed to retain its ecclesiastical beauty and historical ambience

GARDENS PARKS & WALKS

West Light Seabird Viewpoint

West Lighthouse, Rathlin Island, 4 miles from the harbour, Ferry from Ballycastle, Ballycastle, County Antrim, BT54 6RT

Tel: 028 2076 3948

Free access to Kebble Nature Reserve. Access to view point only with supervision of the RSPB Warden during April-August. To avoid disappointment please contact the warden before your visit

Spectacular views of puffins, razorbills, guillemots, kittiwakes and fulmars.

Portrush Countryside Centre

8 Bath Road,, Next to Fossil Ammonites Nature Reserve at Landsdown Crescent, Portrush, County Antrim, BT56 8AP

Tel: 028 7082 3600

March to May Saturday to Tues from 10.00 -16.00 June to September daily 10.00-18.00

This Countryside Centre's attractions include rock pool animals in a touch tank, exhibitions and video presentations. Once the bath-house (with hot and cold salt-water bathing) for the patrons of the famous Northern Counties Hotel.

White Park Bay Nature Trail

On the A2, 0.5 miles W of Ballintoy, Ballintoy, County Antrim

Free access at all times Car park charge May-Aug weekends and holidays

One mile trail showing vegetation types that have been developed on sand and chalk. There are also geological features displayed.

Antrim Castle Gardens

Randalstown Road, Antrim, County Antrim, BT41 4LH

Tel: 028 944 28000

Website: www.antrim.gov.uk

Mon-Fri 09.30-21.30 (or dusk if earlier) Sat 10.00-17.00 Sun 14.00-17.00

These restored 17C Anglo Dutch water gardens have a parterre, ponds and woodland and riverside walks.

Tardree Forest

W of Main Doagh to Ballymena Road, 4 miles to the north of Parkgate village. Access from Duncan's car park, Antrim, County Antrim

Tel: 028 9049 1264

Access at all times

This is a mixed conifer forest with marked footpaths and picnic areas. There are stunning views over County Antrim and Lough Neagh. There is also a nature reserve with a rhyolite quarry.

Portmore Lough Nature Reserve

George's Island Road, Gawleys Gate, Aghalee, County Antrim

Tel: 028 9265 2406

Access at all times

In winter large flocks of Geese visit the Lough as well as swans, ducks and other wildlife. During the Summer months the area is full of dragonflies, butterflies and wild flowers. There are also nature trails and a hide.

Randalstown Forest

Entrance off Staffordstown Road, 1 mile W of Randalstown, Randalstown, County Antrim

Tel: 028 9049 1264

Open 10.00-sunset

This mixed conifer forest also contains a visitors centre, deer park, a national nature reserve and a wild fowl refuge. To see the whole site on foot will take approximately 2.5 hours.

HISTORIC SITES

Giant's Causeway
Causeway Head, Bushmills, County Antrim, BT57 8SU
Tel: 028 207 31855
Email: giantscauseway@nationaltrust.org.uk
Stones and coastal paths accessible all year Visitors Centre daily 10.00-17.00
This is Ireland's first World Heritage Site. Over 40 000 stone columns eerily interlock to form amazing natural patterns and features. Just east of the causeway at Port-na-Spaniagh is the wreck of the Spanish Armarda Treasure Ship

Big Lamp Carrickfergus
High Street, Carrickfergus, County Antrim
Email: touristinfo@carrickfergus.org
Access at all times
This new " Big Lamp" was unveiled in March 1990 to replace the original gas lamp and water fountain that dated from 1881. The Big lamp has been used as a meeting point for locals in the town centre for over a century.

The Holestone Marriage Stone
Holestone Road, Parkgate, Parkgate, County Antrim
Tel: 028 944 28331
The stone is on private farmland so please contact the landowner to gain permission
Bronze Age Hole Stone, 1.5 meters high with a 10cm hole gut into it. Since the early 18C couples seeking eternal love and devotion have travelled to the stone and held hands through the hole through its centre, pledging to love one another forever

Ossian's Grave
Off the A2, 3 miles S of Cushendall, Cushendall, County Antrim
Access at all times
On the slopes of Tievebulliagh Mountain is a megalithic tomb that is said to be the grave of Ossian, the son of the legendary Finn McCool.

Ballylumford Dolmen
91 Ballylumford Road, Island Magee, Larne, County Antrim
Tel: 028 902 35000
Can be viewed at all times
This stone tomb literally sits in someone's front garden and possibly dates from 4000 years ago. There are four upright stones, with a heavy capstone and a second fallen stone.

Cranfield Point Church & Holy Well

Cranfield Road, Cranfield, County Antrim

Open dawn-dusk

Here are the ruins of a church and St Olcans Holy Well which are still a place of pilgrimage. St Olcan is said to be buried at the church in soil brought from Rome.

The Town Walls and North Gate

Carrickfergus, County Antrim

Email: touristinfo@carrickfergus.org

Access at all times

The town walls of Carrickfergus are the earliest and largest urban defence structure in Ulster. Built in 1608-1618 the remains of the walls can be seen at several points around the town. The North gate was partially rebuilt in 1849 and refurbished in 1911

Springfarm Rath

Off Stiles Way, In the Meadow Housing Development, Antrim, County Antrim

Tel: 028 944 28331

Access at all times

A rath was usually built to house a farming family and their livestock and dates from around 700-900AD,. This rath now stands as a local landmark with mature trees and a variety of plants and wildlife covering this ancient site.

Antrim Round Tower

Off Steeple Road, Antrim, County Antrim

Tel: 028 944 28331

Access at all times

These are the remains of a Celtic monastic settlement. The tower is roughly 1000 years old and stands a staggering 93 feet tall.

MUSEUMS

Ballycastle Museum

59 Castle Street, Ballycastle, County Antrim, BT54 6AS

Tel: 028 207 62942

Mon-Sat July-Aug 12.00-18.00

Situated in the town's 18C court house this museum tells the story of the folk and social history of the Glens. Exhibits include the Glemtaisie banner of the First Feis na nGleann (1904)

Ballymena Museum

3 Wellington Court,, Ballymena, County Antrim, BT43 6EG
Tel: 028 2564 2166
Email: ballymena.museum@ballymena.gov.uk
Mon-Fri 10.00-17.00 Sat 10.00-13.00
This museum tells history of the town of Ballymena and the surrounding Borough. There is a permanent exhibition as well as a programme of changing temporary exhibits

Morrow's Shop Museum

13-15 Bridge Street, Ballymena, County Antrim, BT42 1A
Email: william.blair@ballymena.gov.uk
Mon-Fri 10.00-13.00 & 14.00-17.00 sat 10.00-13.00
Collection of displays based on the history of Ballymena, housed in a former drapers shop with original fittings.

Larne Museum

Carnegie Arts Centre, 2 Victoria Road, Larne, County Antrim, BT40 1RN
Tel: 028 282 79482
Email: larnetourism@btconnect.com
April-Oct Tues-Fri 14.00-17.00
Exhibits include a country kitchen from the turn of the century, an old time smithy and a collection of agricultural implements.

County Tyrone-N.I.

ART GALLERIES/ARTS & CRAFTS

Tattykeeran Gallery and Crafts
25 Drumeen Road, Beragh, County Tyrone
Tel: 028 807 58763
Mon-Sat 10.00-17.30
Most products are exclusively sourced from all over Ireland as well as some items hand crafted on the premises. Items include hand made jewellery, ceramics, paintings and prints and leather goods.

Spires Art
2 Brookmount Road, Omagh, County Tyrone, BT78 5HZ
Tel: 028 822 46613
Email: info@mail.spiresart.com
Website: www.spiresart.com
Mon-Fri 09.00-17.30 Sat 10.30-17.30
Spires Art Gallery offers paintings, photography and rare prints as well as tailor made art, which uses the very latest techniques and equipment to produce paintings and digitally created images on canvas, card or paper

CASTLES

Harry Avery's Castle
0.5 miles SW of Newtonstewart, in a field off the Rakelly Road, Newtonstewart, County Tyrone
Access at all times
Majestic ruins of a Gaelic stronghold. The twin towers of the keep date from the 14C.

Castle Caulfield
Castlecaulfield, 3 miles W of Dungannon, Dungannon, County Tyrone
Access at all times
Ruins of a mansion built in 1619 with murder holes, the Caulfield Arms and a plaque to the poet Charles Wolfe

Tullaghoge Fort

2.5 miles SE of Cookstown, Off the B162, Cookstown, County Tyrone

Access at all times

This is where the Great Hugh O'Neill was crowned in 1593. It was the headquarters of the Chief Justices of Ireland who performed the coronations of the O'Neills from the 12-17C. The fort also gives great views over the old kingdom of Tyrone

Benburb Castle

In Benburb Valley Park, Main Street, Benburb, County Tyrone

Tel: 028 375 48241

Castle grounds open at all times

Positioned high above the Black Water River is this magnificent 17C castle.

Castlederg Castle

Signposted from Castlederg Main Street, Castlederg, County Tyrone

Tel: 028 9054 3034

Access at all times

Located on the River Derg these ruins consist of a rectangular brawn with square flankers at each corner

GARDENS PARKS & WALKS

Benburb Valley Park

Main Street, Benburb, Benburb, County Tyrone

Tel: 028 375 49752

Daily 10.00-dusk

The park includes walks along the Black Water River. The ruins of the 1615 Benburg Castle and limestone gorge are surrounded by Ash, Beech and Conifer trees. There is also a conservatory with Jasmine and Vines.

Parkanaur Forest Park

4 miles W of Dungannon, Ballygawley, County Tyrone

Tel: 028 877 67432

Open daily 10.00-dusk

A nature trail runs through Oak and Beech trees, passing a Victorian garden, wishing well and an old archway. The park is full of daffodils and rhododendrons and home to a herd of white fallow deer.

Favour Royal Forest Walk
Between Augher and Aughnacloy, On the A28, Augher, County Tyrone
Access at all times
The walk includes a visit to a gigantic Druid's stone with nearby well accredited
with healing powers

Binevenagh Forest
5 miles N of Limavady off the A2, Binevenagh, County Tyrone
Tel: 028 2955 6003
Email: customer.forestservice@dardni.gov.uk
Website: www.forestserviceni.gov.uk
Access at all times
Known for its impressive cliffs and the Finn MacCool Finger Stone

Davagh Forest
10 miles NW of Cookstown, Cookstown, County Tyrone
Tel: 028 2955 6003
Email: customer.forestservice@dardni.gov.uk
Website: www.forestserviceni.gov.uk
Access at all times
Davagh Forest has a series of trails suitable for everyone

The Memorial Garden
In the grounds at County Hall, Drumragh Avenue, Omagh, County Tyrone, BT78 1DP
Tel: 028 8224 7831
Access at all times
Following the bomb atrocity in Omagh on the 15 August 1998 this memorial
garden was constructed

HISTORIC HOUSES

Omagh Court House
High Street, Omagh, County Tyrone, BT78 1DU
Tel: 028 822 42056
Exterior View
The Court House which was built in 1820 has retained much of its original
character and Classical architecture and has a resident friendly ghost.

The Wilson Ancestral Home

2 miles SE of Strabane, On the B536 to Plumbridge, Dergalt, County Tyrone
Tel: 028 7138 2204

July & August Tues-Sun 14.00-17.00 or by arrangement

Visitors can learn how the fate of the 28th Presidency of the USA was to lie in the hands of local man James Wilson

HISTORIC SITES

Knockmany Passage Grave

Knockmany Hill, 2 miles NW of Augher, Augher, County Tyrone

Access at all times

This pre-historic tomb contains stones carved with zig zags, circles and spirals which have been protected by a modern cairn.

Loughmacrory Wedge Tomb

Loughmacrory, 2 miles from An Creggan, Omagh, County Tyrone

Access at all times

A burial chamber believed to be 4000 years old which has a front chamber and doorway. It has double walls and a roof and is known as the Wedge Tomb because of its unusual shape.

Beaghmore Stone Circles

Beaghmore, Between Cookstown and Gortin, 8.5 miles NW of Cookstown, Cookstown, County Tyrone

Access at all times

Mysterious complex of seven Bronze Age stone circles and alignments.

Ardboe Cross

Ardboe, Off the B73, east of Cookstown, Cookstown, County Tyrone

Access at all times

Richly carved 10C High Cross with old testament scenes on the East side and New testament on the West

Creggandevesky Tomb

Lough Mallon, West of Pomeroy, Omagh, County Tyrone

Access at all times

This is the site of a Megalithic court grave.

Donaghmore Cross

Donaghmore, Donaghmore, County Tyrone

Access at all times

This High Cross stands in the main village street near the O'Neill memorial pillar.

Aghascrebagh Standing Stone

1 mile NE of Sheskinshule, Sheskinshule, County Tyrone

Access at all times

The stone is 1.2 meters high and seven letters of the inscription can still be read. It is one of the most impressive standing stones in County Tyrone

Moy Iron Gates and Screen

In the village of Moy, Moy, County Tyrone

Access at all times

Cast Iron gates and screen from the 19C which provided a grand entrance to what was then Roxburgh castle

SOUTHERN IRELAND

Southern Ireland (Republic of Ireland-Eire) is not part of the United Kingdom but is an independent Country, although it is physically attached to Northern Ireland. The currency of Southern Ireland is the Euro not the British Sterling as used in the UK.

The Capital City of Southern Ireland is Dublin which is one of the top European tourist destinations. Dublin is renowned for its friendly atmosphere, fantastic pubs with live Irish music, Guinness and Irish Whisky and beautiful buildings and parks. Dublin is a lively and exciting place to visit or stay.

Southern Ireland is made up of 26 Counties and its long history gives this region an abundance of archaeological and historical attractions many dating back thousands of years.

SOUTHERN IRELAND

Dublin City-Southern Ireland

ART GALLERIES/ARTS & CRAFTS

Hugh Lane Gallery
Charlemont House, 22 Parnell Square North, Dublin, County Dublin
Tel: 01 874 1903
Email: info@hughlane.ie
Website: www.hughlane.ie
(Tue-Thurs) 09.30-18.00, (Fri-Sat) 09.30-17.00 (Sun) 11.00-17.00 Admission to the
Permanent Collection is Free
The gallery was founded in 1908 by wealthy Sir Hugh Lane. The Lane Bequest
pictures which form the main exhibition in the gallery contain some important
paintings including Manet's Eva Gonzales, Pissarro's Printemps, Berthe
Morisot's Joor D'Ete and Renoir

National Gallery Of Ireland
Merrion Square West, Dublin, County Dublin
Tel: 01 661 5133
Email: info@ngi.ie
Website: www.nationalgallery.ie
Mon-Sat 09.30-17.30 Thurs 09.30-20.30 Sun 12.00-17.30
Houses the National Collection of Irish Art and European Master Paintings

Irish Museum Of Modern Art
Royal Hospital, Military Road, Kilmainham, Dublin, County Dublin
Tel: 01 612 9900
Email: info@modernart.ie
Website: www.modernart.ie
(Tue-Sat) 10.00-17.30, (Sun) 12.00-17.00 Free Guided Tours Tuesday to Sunday
12.00-17.30
The gallery contains a regularly changing collection of works that combine items
from European Collections with Irish Collections

Solomon Gallery

Powerscourt Townhouse Centre, South William Street, Dublin, County Dublin
Tel: 01679 4237
Email: info@solomongallery.com
Website: www.solomongallery.com
Mon-Sat 10.00-17.30
One of Ireland's leading contemporary art galleries which hosts 12 to 13 exhibitions a year

Temple Bar Gallery And Studios

5-9 Temple Bar, Dublin, County Dublin
Tel: 01671 0073
Email: info@templebargallery.com
Website: www.templebargallery.com
Tues-Sat 11.00-18.00 Thurs 11.00-19.00
One of the largest galleries/studio complexes in Europe. With more than 30 Irish artists on display

The Douglas Hyde Gallery

Trinity College, Nassau Street, Dublin, County Dublin
Tel: 01608 1116
Email: dhgallery@tcd.ie
Mon-Fri 11.00-18.00 Thurs 11.00-19.00 Sat 11.00-16.45
Focusing on Contemporary Irish Art, but also houses exhibitions from London, Paris and New York

Gallery Of Photography

Meeting House Square, Temple Bar, Dublin, County Dublin
Tel: 01671 4654
Email: gallery@irish-photography.com
Website: www.irish-photography.com
Tues-Sat 11.00-18.00 Sun 13.00-18.00
Dublin's only photographic gallery with exhibitions of International and Irish Contemporary photographs

CHURCHES & CATHEDRALS

Saint Ann's Church

18 Dawson Street, South of the river Liffey, Near St. Stephen's Green, Dublin, County Dublin
Tel: 01 676 7727
Email: stannschurch@eircom.net
(Mon-Fri) 10.00-16.00
The church was built in 1720, but now has a 1868 façade. The best view of the church is from Grafton Street and the church is famous for its lunch time recitals

Saint Stephen's Church

Upper Mount Street, Near Meridon Square, Dublin, County Dublin
Tel: 01 478 0638
Exterior View
This church was built in 1824 in the Greek Revival style, hence it's cupola. The building has now been converted into business units. The church is nicknamed the Peppercanister church due to it's unusual architecture.

Saint Werburgh's Church

Werburgh Street, South of Christchurch Cathedral, Beside Dublin Castle, Dublin, County Dublin
Tel: 01 872 4154
Sunday services 11.00
The church has a long history of fine deign and interesting interior. However it is now only used for Sunday Mass, but visitors can obtain the key and see inside the building when it is not in use.

St Mary's Pro Cathedral

83 Marlborough Street, Dublin, County Dublin
Tel: 01874 5441
Email: procath@dublindiocese.ie
Website: www.procathedral.ie
Mon-Fri 07.30-18.45 Sat 07.30-19.15 Sun 09.00-13.45 & 17.30-19.45
St Mary's is Dublin's Catholic Cathedral. The facade is based on the Temple Of Theseus in Athens

Whitefriar Street Carmelite Church

Aungier Street, Dublin, County Dublin
Tel: 01475 8821
Email: whitefriars@eircom.net
Mon, Wed, Thurs, Fri 07.45-18.00 Tues 07.45-21.15 Sat 07.45-19.30 Sun 07.45-19.30
Built in 1827 on the site of a 16C Priory, this Catholic Church contains the remains of St. Valentine

GARDENS PARKS & WALKS

National Botanic Gardens

Glasnevin, On Botanic Road, North of the city centre, Dublin, County Dublin
Tel: 01 837 4388
Email: botanicsv@duchas.ie
Summer (Mon-Sat) 09.00-18.00, (Sun) 11.00-18.00 Winter (Mon-Sat) 10.00-16.30 (Sun) 11.00-16.30
This relaxing Botanic garden includes a "Yew Walk" that contains trees that date from the 18C, a palm house and a number of attractive glass houses that date from between 1843 and 1869.

St Stephen's Green

Top of Grafton Street, Dublin, County Dublin
Tel: 01 475 7816
Open daylight hours normally Mon-Sat 08.00-dusk Sundays 10.00-dusk
A 22 acre park landscaped with a fountain and a lake, trees and flower beds and a band stand that was built in 1887

The Grand Canal

Dublin, County Dublin
Access at all time
The Grand Canal joins the River Liffey at Ringsend where 1796 locks still stand. In the North West corner of the Dock is Misery Hill where criminals used to be publicly executed. Further upstream there is the Waterways Visitor's Centre

Phoenix Park

Parkgate Street, Dublin, County Dublin
Tel: 01677 0095
Email: phoenixparkvisitorscentre@ealga.ie
Main gates never close. Side gates open 07.00-23.00
One of the largest parks in Europe covering 1760 acres. Including nature trails, ornamental gardens, forested areas and polo fields

Garden Of Remembrance

Parnell Square East, Dublin, County Dublin

Jan, Feb, Nov & Dec Daily 11.00-16.00 March, April, Oct Daily 11.00-19.00 May-Sept Daily 09.30-20.00

Dedicated to the men and women who died in the pursuit of Irish Freedom

Iveagh Gardens

Clonmel Street, Dublin, County Dublin

Mon-Sat Dec & Jan 08.00-16.00 Sun 10.00-18.00 Feb & Nov Mon-Sat 08.00-17.00 Sun 10.00-17.00 March-Oct Mon-Sat 08.00-18.00 Sun 10.00-18.00

Designed in 1863 and one of the finest of Dublin's parks and gardens

Blessington Street Basin

Blessington Street, Dublin, County Dublin

Tel: 01661 2369

Access at all times during daylight hours

A quiet haven with local wildlife which was fully refurbished in 1994 and is known as Dublin's Secret Garden

St Anne's Park & Rose Gardens

Raheny and Clontarf, Dublin, County Dublin

Tel: 01605 7700

Daily 10.00-17.00

St Anne's Estate was the former home of the Guinness family and is now the largest enclosed Dublin City Park covering 270 acres

St Audoen's Park

High Street, Dublin, County Dublin

Access at all times

A small park which uses part of the Old City Wall and City Gates which date from the 12C as part of its boundary

War Memorial Gardens

Islandbridge, Dublin, County Dublin

Tel: 01647 2498

Mon-Fri 08.00-18.00 Sat & Sun 10.00-18.00

Dedicated to the 49,400 Irish soldiers who died in the 1914-1918 War.

HISTORIC SITES

Arbour Hill Cemetery

Stoneybatter, West of the old Jameson Distillery, Dublin, County Dublin
Tel: 01 605 7700
(Mon-sat) 09.00-16.30, (Sun) 09.30-12.00
This small cemetery contains the graves of all 14 of the leaders of the 1916 Easter Rising, all of whom were executed. In the graveyard beside their graves is a cenotaph inscribed upon which is the Easter Proclamation.

Prospect Cemetery (Glasnevin)

Finglas Road, North West of the city centre, Dublin, County Dublin
Tel: 01 830 1133
Email: cemetery@indigo.ie
Website: www.glasnevin-cemetery.ie
Cemetery open daily 08.00-16.00 Free Guided Tours commence from the main gate of the Cemetery at 14.30 every Wed & Fri and last approx 2 hours
This cemetery is the largest in Ireland and is the final resting place of many famous Irish men. Make sure you check out the SE end of the cemetery where there are two watchtowers which were used to keep a look out for body snatchers.

Merrion Square

Dublin, County Dublin
Access at all time
One of Dublin's largest and grandest Georgian Squares. Many of the houses have plaques detailing the rich and famous who once lived in them

Ireland Famine Imigrants Statues

Near The Customs House, Dublin, County Dublin
Access at all time
The statues are in memory of the Native Irish who were forced to emigrate to the United States during the 1840s famine years

Oscar Wilde Statue

Merrion Square Park, Dublin, County Dublin
Access at all time
A colourful statue of the Victorian playwright Oscar Wilde

Molly Malone Statue

Grafton Street, Dublin, County Dublin
Access at all time
A statue of Molly Malone immortalised in the famous Irish song " Cockles and Mussels" The statue shows Molly with her cart selling her cockles and mussels

James Joyce Statue

North Earl Street, Dublin, County Dublin
Access at all time
This statue depicts James Joyce, who was considered to be the greatest writer of the 20C

Ha'penny Bridge

The City Centre, Dublin, County Dublin
Access at all times
Erected in 1816 this bridge is one of the earliest cast-iron structures of its kind and the oldest pedestrian crossing over the River Liffey

HISTORIC HOUSES

General Post Office

O'Connell Street, Dublin, County Dublin
Tel: 01 705 7000
Mon-Sat 08.00-20.00 Sun 10.30-18.20
The GPO became a symbol of the 1916 Easter Rising. Inside the building is a sculpture of the legendary Irish Warrior Cuchulainn

Leinster House

Kildare Street, Dublin, County Dublin
Tel: 01 618 3000
Email: info@orieachtas.ie
Website: www.orieachtas.ie
Exterior view at all times-interior visits can be made with prior arrangement please contact for details
Originally built for the Duke of Leinster in 1745 and was obtained by the Government for Parliamentary use in 1922.

Four Courts

Inns Quay, Overlooks the River Liffey, Dublin, County Dublin
Tel: 01 872 5555
Mon-Fri 11.00-13.00 and 14.00-16.00 (Public is admitted only when the court is in session please phone to check before visiting)
Home of the Irish Law Courts since 1796. Designed by James Gandon. Public is admitted only when the court is in session

President's House

The Phoenix Park, Dublin, County Dublin
Tel: 01677 0095
Email: phoenixparkvisitorscentre@ealga.ie
Website: www.irlgov.ie/aras
Free Admission Tickets to the President's House are issued at the Phoenix Park Visitors Centre on the day. Open Saturdays Only
Guided tours are available every Saturday Summer 10.00-17.00 Winter 10.30-16.00 of the residence of the President Of Ireland including the main State Reception Rooms and Exhibition Centre

MUSEUMS

Chester Beatty Library and Gallery Of Oriental Art

Dublin Castle Grounds, Reached from Ship Street, Dublin, County Dublin
Tel: 01 407 0750
Email: info@cbl.ie
Website: www.cbl.ie
(Tue-Fri) 10.00-17.00, (Sat) 14.00-17.00, (Tours On Wed & Sat 14.30)
This building houses the collection of Sir Alfred Chester Beatty who was a mining engineer, (1875-1968) His collection comprises over 20 000 manuscripts, paintings, rare books, clay tablets, costumes and other objects.

Natural History Museum

Merrion Square West, Beside the National Gallery, Dublin, County Dublin
Tel: 01 677 7444
Website: www.museum.ie/naturalhistory/
(Tue-Sat) 10.00-17.00, (Sun) 14.00-17.00
The first floor of the building contains skeletons and stuffed animals that covers all of Ireland's Fauna and includes three skeletons of the Irish Giant Deer which became extinct around 10 000 years ago.

Dublin Civic Museum

58 South William Street, Dublin, County Dublin
Tel: 01 679 4260
(Tue-Sat) 10.00-18.00, (Sun) 11.00-14.00
The building contains a variety of changing exhibitions and displays that are dedicated to the history of the city from Viking times to the 21 Century. The building itself has some stunning architectural features.

National Museum Of Decorative Arts and History

Collins Barracks, Benburb Street, Dublin, County Dublin
Tel: 01677 7444
Email: marketing@museum.ie
Tues-Sat 10.00-17.00 Sun 14.00-17.00
This museum charts Ireland's social, political and military progress through the ages

Pearse Museum

St Enda's Park, Grange Road, Rathfarnham, Dublin, County Dublin
Tel: 01493 4208
All Year Daily 10.00-14.00 Afternoon Opening Nov-Jan Daily 14.00-16.00 Feb-April & Sept-Oct Daily 14.00-17.00 May-August Daily 14.00-17.30
This museum includes exhibitions, displays on flora and fauna and a Nature Study room

Heraldic Museum

2 Kildare Street, Dublin, County Dublin
Tel: 01603 0311
Email: herald@nli.ie
Website: www.nli.ie
Mon-Wed 10.00-20.30 Thurs-Fri 10.00-16.30 Sat 10.00-12.30
With displays of paintings, porcelain, shields, stamps and coins, and including the office of the Chief Herald of Ireland

Irish Jewish Museum

3/4 Walworth Road, Portobello, South Circular Road, Dublin, County Dublin
Tel: 01490 1857
Sun, Tues, Thurs May-Sept 11.00-15.30 Sundays Only Oct-April 10.30-14.30
Housed in a former Synagogue this museum displays memorabilia including Irish Jewellery and a collection on Jewish Life

National Museum of Ireland-Archaeology and History

Kildare Street, Dublin, County Dublin
Tel: 01677 7444
Tues-Sat 10.00-17.00 Sun 14.00-17.00
Built in the 1880s this museum displays Irish Silver and Glasswear and The War
Of Independence Exhibition

NATURE & WILDLIFE

North Bull Island

North Bull Wall, North City, Dublin, County Dublin
Tel: 01833 1859
Visitors Centre Daily 10.00-16.30
This 300 hectare island is now a Nature Reserve and Bird Sanctuary of
International importance.

South West-Southern Ireland

ART GALLERIES/ARTS & CRAFTS

Crawford Municipal Art Galley

Emmet Place, Cork, County Cork
Tel: 021 427 3377
Email: crawfordinfo@eircom.net
Website: www.crawfordartgallery.com
(Mon-Sat) 10.00-17.00
This building built in 1724 as a customs house and converted into a school of art
in 1884. It now houses an excellent permanent collection which includes works
by Jack Yeats and Sean Keating as well as works of the British Newlyn and St
Ives Schools

Triskel Arts Centre

Tobin Street, Old City, Cork, County Cork
Tel: 021 427 2022
Email: info@triskelart.com
Website: www.triskelart.com
(Mon-Sat) 10.00-17.30
This small arts centre houses two galleries with rotating exhibits. In addition is
also organises a variety of cultural events including music, film, literature, theatre
and visual arts.

West Cork Arts Centre

The Sutherland Centre, North Street, Skibbereen, County Cork
Tel: 021 822 090
Email: westcorkarts@eircom.net
(Mon-Sat) 10.00-18.00 Winter closing times 17.00
This art centre shows changing exhibits of Irish art and a permanent collection of
Cork crafts

Cork Vision Centre

At St Peters, North Main Street, Cork, County Cork
Tel: 021 427 9925
Email: visioncentre@eircom.net
Website: www.corkvisioncentre.com
Tues-Sat 10.00-17.00
Offers visitors the opportunity to explore Cork's past, present and future through
exhibitions and events

Edman Collection-Factory & Visitors Centre

Kilnamartyra, Macroom, County Cork
Tel: 01264 0222
Email: info@edmancollection.com
Website: www.edmancollection.com
Mon-Fri 09.00-17.00 All year May-August Mon-Fri 09.00-18.00 Sat 10.00-16.00 Sun 12.00-16.00
This collection includes Lord Of The Ring figures, Irish Military figurines and chess sets. Visitors can watch the manufacturing and painting process

CASTLES

Parkavonear Castle

Aghadoe, Killarney, County Kerry
Access at all times
The remains of a 13C Round Castle which consist of circular walls to the height of the second level. There would have been further levels but these have now gone.

James Fort

Cross Duggan Bridge, turn left, Kinsale, Kinsale, County Cork
Access at all times
The fort which is now heavily grass covered has a wealth of secret passageways and panoramic views over Kinsale.

Carrigafoyle Castle

2 miles N of Ballylongford, Ballylongford, County Kerry
Open all year
The castle is protected by the Carrig island and has a vaulted tower, it was once a stronghold of the O'Connors of Kerry and is now uninhabited.

CHURCHES & CATHEDRALS

Lislaughtin Abbey

1 miles N of Ballylongford, Ballylongford, County Kerry
Access at all times
The ruins of a Franciscan monastery built in 1477. The ruins have three finely carved sedilia and a good east window.

Aghadoe Church

Aghadoe, Killarney, County Kerry
Access at all times
The ruined remains of a 12C church built on the site of a 7C monastery. A Romanesque doorway has survived in excellent condition.

Colman's Cathedral

Cobh, Cobh, County Cork
(Daily) 07.00-20.00
The gothic spire of the cathedral dominates the surrounding landscape and was completed in 1915. The cathedral has the largest carillon or harmonised bell system in Ireland which consists of 47 bells weighing over 7700 pounds.

Saint Mary's Cathedral

Cathedral Place, Off Port Road, Killarney, County Kerry
Tel: 021 443 1014
Daily 10.30-18.00
The cathedral has three huge altars and can seat 1400 people inside its rough limestone structure.

Muckross Friary

Muckross Estate, Killarney, County Kerry
Tel: 01643 1440
June-Sept Daily 10.00-17.00
Founded in the 15C and in a remarkable state of preservation, this friary has the only Franciscan Tower in Ireland

GARDENS PARKS & WALKS

Fota Arboretum

Fota Island, Carigtwohill, County Cork
Tel: 021 481 2728
Email: fotaarboretum@eircom.net
April-Oct Mon-Sat 10.00-18.00 Sun 11.00-18.00 Nov-March Mon-Fri 10.00-17.00 Sun 11.00-17.00
The arboretum has a wide range of exotic plants and trees that are both diverse in their collections as well as rare.

Doneraile Forest Park

Doneraile, Near Mallow, Doneraile, County Cork

Tel: 021 425 5100

Free on weekdays

An 18C landscaped park with a special attraction of a herd of deer

Keyser Hill

South Main Street, Proby's Quay, Cork, County Cork

Access at all times

Great views of Cork from top of Keyser Hill. At the top of the hill is an Elizabethan Fort, a star shaped ivy covered building. The fort houses the Garda station. For the best views of the surrounding area climb the stairs inside the main gate of the fort

Killarney National Park

On the N71 Kenmare Road, Killarney, County Kerry

Tel: 01643 1440

Email: killarneynationalpark@ealga.ie

Access at all times

This National Park famous for its natural habitats, Red Deer and mountain scenery is over 24000 acres.

Rossbeigh Beach

Glenbeigh, Glenbeigh, County Kerry

Access at all times

Four miles of golden sands with views of the surrounding mountains of Kerry. Ideal for picnicking and walking, this beach is popular but rarely crowded.

Ladies View

Kenmare Road, On the N71, Killarney, County Kerry

Access at all times

This viewpoint gives a spectacular panorama of the lakes of Killarney. The name comes from the fact that it was a favourite spot for Queen Victoria's ladies in waiting when she visited the area in 1861.

HISTORIC SITES

Drombeg Stone Circle

On R591, 16kms W of Clonakilty, Glandore, County Cork

Access at all times

This group of 17 stones dates from around 100BC and is one of the most impressive of West Cork's stone circles. Nearby is a cooking area in which hot stones can bring 318.5 litres if water to the boil in 18 minutes and keep it hot for roughly three hours

The Round Tower of Rattoo

Just beyond the village of Ballyduff, 3 miles S of Ballybunion, Ballyduff, County Kerry

Exterior View

One of the most perfect extants with a restored cap.

MUSEUMS

Cork Public Museum

Fitzgerald Park, Off Western Road, Mardyke, County Cork

Tel: 021 427 0679

Email: museum@corkcity.ie

Mon-Fri 11.00-13.00 & 14.15-17.00 (June -August open till 18.00) Sun 15.00-17.00

The ground floor of the museum details Cork's fight for independence whilst the first floor of the building is dedicated to archaeological displays and finds

NATURE & WILDLIFE

The Donkey Sanctuary

Knockardbane, Liscarroll, County Cork

Tel: 01224 8398

Email: donkey@indigo.ie

Website: www.thedonkeysanctuary.ie

Mon-Fri 09.00-16.30 Sat & Sun 10.00-17.00

Rescuing over 2000 donkeys from all parts of Ireland has been the purpose of this sanctuary. There is an information centre, walks and picnic areas

Western-Southern Ireland

ART GALLERIES/ARTS & CRAFTS

Croagh Patrick Visitors Centre

Murrisk, 5 miles from Westport, Murrisk, County Mayo

Tel: 098 64115

Email: info@croagh-patrick.com

Website: www.croagh-patrick.com

April-May 10.00-18.00 June-August 10.00-19.00 Sept & Oct 11.00-17.00 Nov-March (limited opening times please call)

Croagh Patrick is Ireland's Holy Mountain. At the base is Croagh Patrick Visitors Centre, craft shop and tea room

Limerick City Gallery Of Art

Carnegie Building, Pery Square, Limerick, County Limerick

Tel: 061 310 633

Email: lcgartzz@iol.ie

Mon-Fri 10.00-18.00 Thurs 10.00-19.00 Sat 10.00-13.00

Founded in 1948 and houses 18, 19 and 20C collections by Irish Artists

Angela Woulfe Gallery

16 Pery Square, Limerick, County Limerick

Tel: 061 310 164

Email: angelawoulfe@eircom.net

Website: www.angelawoulfegallery.com

Mon-Fri 11.00-17.00 Sat 11.00-14.00

Original oil paintings by Angela Woulfe and guest artists. The gallery hosts an annual Christmas exhibition.

Chris Doswell's Gallery

Nicholas Street, Limerick, County Limerick

Tel: 061 318 292

Email: info@doswellprints.com

Website: www.doswellprints.com

Mon-Fri 09.00-17.30 Sat 10.30-14.30

This gallery offers regular exhibitions as well as original prints from leading Irish print makers.

CASTLES

Newtown Castle
Burren College Of Art, Ballyvaughan, County Clare
May-Sept Mon-Fri 10.00-16.00
This 16C Towerhouse has been beautifully restored and has some unique architectural features. Free for non guided visits

Carrigogunnel Castle
Near Clarina, 5 miles W of Limerick, Limerick, County Limerick
Access at all times
Known as the rock of the O'Connells, the castle was built between the 14 & 16C and is now in ruins with a collection of isolated towers.

Shanid Castle
South of Shanagolden, On the Ardagh Road, Shanagolden, County Limerick
Access at all times
The ruins of a 13C castle that was a former Desmond fortress

CHURCHES & CATHEDRALS

Killinaboy Ruined Church
Killinaboy, County Clare
Access at all times
This 16C church has two interesting features, a Sheela-Na-Gig above the doorway and a double barred cross on the church gable

Augustinian Friary
Church Street, Adare, County Limerick
Tel: 061 396 227
Please phone for opening times
The Friary was built around 1315 by John the 1st Earl Of Kildare and now is Adare's Church Of Ireland Parish Church

Cictercian Abbey of Knockmoy
Abbeyknockmoy, County Galway
Access at all times
A Cistercian Abbey founded in 1189 by King Cathal Crowdearg O'Connor the last of the O'Connor Kings to be buried in its sanctuary

Moyne Abbey

1.5 miles from Killala Town, Ballina, County Mayo
Access at all times
The church consists of a rectangular nave and chancel there is also a chapel, well preserved cloisters and a variety of buildings surrounding it

Church Of Iomar Graveyard

Killimer, Killimer, County Galway
Access at all times
Ellen Hanley is buried in this graveyard, her beauty lead to a tragic end at the hands of her secretly married husband, who drowned her in the Shannon in a fit of jealousy in 1819 when she was only sixteen.

Tuam Catholic Cathedral

To the east of Market Square, Tuam, County Galway
Open all year
This is one of the finest examples of early Gothic Revival architecture with an impressive spire and windows.

Strade Abbey

Strade, County Mayo
Access at all times
The remains of Strade Abbey that was originally founded for Franciscans but transferred to the Dominicans in 1252. Much of the present building is 15C, and there is a sculptured tomb on the north wall of the Chancel.

GARDENS PARKS & WALKS

Knockpatrick

The hill between Foyes and Shanagolden, Shanagolden, County Limerick
Access at all times
The hill between Foyes & Shanagolden gives great views of the Estuary. The hill is named after a ruined church that was said to have been built by St Patrick.

The Cliffs of Moher

The Burren, County Clare
Access at all times
One of the most impressive stretches of the coast in the West of Ireland. The best views can be seen from O'Brien's Folly which leads off left from the main road.

Moore Bay

Kilkee, 13km NW of Kilrush, Killkee, County Clare
Access at all times
This bay is protected from the full fury of the Atlantic by a reef known as
Duggerna Rocks, the sandy beach resort offers good bathing opportunities.

Spanish Point

In the centre of Mal Bay, Miltown Malbay, Just N of Quilty, Miltown Malbay, County Clare
Access at all times
The point is famous for the fact that numerous bodies were washed ashore here
from the Armada and buried at the point.

Benwee Head

following the road to Portacloy, Portacloy, County Mayo
Access at all times
This is a fabulous cliff with views towards Archill and the Donegal Coast.

Lissoughter Hill

Immediately North of Recess, Recess, County Galway
Access at all times
A walk on the slops of this hill/mountain gives great views of the Maumturk
Mountains, the most obvious summit of which being Letterbreekaum, and the
Twelve Bens.

Dromore Wood

Off the Ennis/Galway Road, Ruan, Ennis, County Clare
Wood open daylight hours
1000 acres of diverse habitat including river, lakes, woodland, flooded meadows
and reed beds. Within the wood there is also the 17C O'Brien's Castle 2 ring
forts a church and a lime kiln

HISTORIC SITES

The Sword of Galway and the great Mace

Galway City Council, City Hall, College Road, Galway, County Galway
Tel: 0191 536 400
Email: enquiries@galwaycity.ie
Located in the reception area of Galway City Hall-City Hall open Mon-Fri 09.00-16.00
Dating from 1610 and 1710 respectively the Sword and Mace were acquired by
William Randolph Hearts in 1938 and generously returned to Galway in 1960 by
the Hearst Foundation.

Cahercommaun

N of Killinaboy, Killinaboy, County Clare

Access at all times

This rock fort has been excavated to reveal the interior chambers.

The Tait Clock

Baker Place, Limerick, County Limerick

Access at all times

Erected in 1867 to the then Mayor of Limerick, Sir Peter Tait. The clock is a Gothic octagonal tower clock with four faces

Doonamo Point

Belmullet, Between Bangor and Ballina, Belmullet, County Mayo

Access at all times

A fine promontory Iron Age fort with a wall 5.5m high which encloses three clochans and a ring fort.

The Seven Monuments

Loughrea, Loughrea, County Galway

Access at all times

This megalithic stone circle comprises of a circle of seven stones set into a low circular bank near the remains of a square chamber tomb

Turoe Stone

4 miles North of Loughrea, West of the village of Bullaum, Loughrea, County Galway

Access at all times

This stone is interesting for it's richly ornamented carvings that cover its surface.

Dolmen Of The Four Maols

Ballina, Ballina, County Mayo

Access at all times

A Neolithic dolmen that dates back to 3000BC. Legend says that it marks the grave of four foster-brothers who murdered their master , the Bishop of Kilmoremoy and were hanged by the Bishop's brother.

MUSEUMS

Limerick Museum
Castle Lane, Nicholas Street, Limerick, County Limerick
Tel: 061 417 826
Email: lwalsh@limerickcorp.ie
Website: www.limerickcity.ie
Tues-Sat 10.00-13.00 & 14.15-17.00
A collection of almost 50 000 objects from the city's earliest times to present day

National Museum Of Ireland Country Life
Turlough Park, Castlebar, Castlebar, County Mayo
Tel: 094 903 1773
Email: tpark@museum.ie
Website: www.museum.ie
Tues-Sat 10.00-17.00 Sun 14.00-17.00 Closed Mondays
Experience the Irish Country Life between 1850 and 1950

EXHIBITIONS

Scattery Island Centre
Merchants Quay, Kilrush, County Clare
Tel: 01905 2139
Email: scatteryisland@ealga.ie
June-Sept Daily 10.00-18.00
This exhibition situated on the mainland tells the history of the monastery, monuments and wildlife on the island.

Eastern-Southern Ireland

ART GALLERIES/ARTS & CRAFTS

Tinahely Courthouse Centre
Couthouse Arts Centre, Tinahely, County Wicklow
Email: tinahely@iol.ie
Website: www.tinahely-courthouse.ie
Tues-Fri 10.00-17.00 Sun (Summer) 14.00-18.00 (Winter) 12.00-16.00
A premier venue for fine art exhibitions, the gallery hosts ten exhibitions a year each lasting for four weeks.

CASTLES

Black Castle
Wicklow, Just outside the town on the seaward side, Wicklow, County Wicklow
Access at all times
The sparse ruins of this fortification were originally built in 1169 by the Fitzgeralds after the Anglo Saxon invasion. It was almost entirely demolished by the O'Byrnes and the O'Tooles in 1301.

CHURCHES & CATHEDRALS

Fore Abbey
Near the village of Fore, 3 miles E of Castlepollard, Fore, County Westmeath
Access at all times
Founded originally in 630AD by St Fechin and now home to the remains of a 13C Benedictine Priory

Monasterboice
On the road from Drogheda, On the main N1 Dubin to Belfast Road, Or by following the Drogheda to Collon Road, Drogheda, County Louth
Access at all times during daylight hours
This impressive monastic site contains two 10C high crosses and a round tower which is 110 feet tall, both of which are reputed to be the finest examples of their kind in Ireland. The site also houses two 13C churches.

Hill Of Slane

Slane, 10 miles from Tara, Slane, County Meath

Access at all times

This is where St Patrick lit his Paschal fire in 433AD to announce the arrival of Christianity. Near the top of the hill are the ruined remains of Friary Church which was built in 1512.

GARDENS PARKS & WALKS

Lough Ennel

3 miles South of Mullingar, Mullingar, County Westmeath

Access at all times

This is a major bird sanctuary favoured by trout fishermen. The Lough is 3250 acres in area, 4.5 miles long by 2.5 miles wide

Carlingford Lough

Near Carlingford, Cooley Peninsular, Carlingford, County Louth

Access at all times

This particular spot on the Lough which faces the Mountains of Mourne has some of the best scenery in the area, and is a delightful spot to take in the view.

Glendalough

Near Roundwood, Glendalough, County Wicklow

Within Wicklow Mountains National Park-Park Open May-August Daily 10.00-18.00 April & Sept Weekends 10.00-18.00

This is one of the most important and best preserved monastic sites in Ireland. The site also includes many numerous walks that start from Glendalough and venture off into the nearby mountains.

Bray Head

Bray, Wicklow Coast, Bray, County Wicklow

Access at all times

A piece of rock pushing into the sea. A huge cross was erected here in 1950 to remind you that you are now in Catholic Europe. There are also many secluded coves in the area where you can swim.

Hill Of Uisneach

On the road to Kilbeggan, Kilbeggan, County Westmeath

Access at all times

The summit of this hill was an ancient assembly point. The hill gives some stunning views of the surrounding area.

Clara Bog

Clara, County Offaly
Access at all times
This is one of the largest and well preserved raised bogs in Ireland. It is the perfect habitat for a wide variety of plant and moss species which flourish in the area.

The Cavan Way

From Dowra to Blacklion, Dowra, County Cavan
Access at all times
A 17 mile walk that gives some fabulous views over Lough MacNean, The Fermanagh Islands and the Sligo and Lentrim Mountains. Along the walk is the Shannon Pit the source of Ireland's mightiest river.

Wicklow Mountains National Park

Centered around Glendalough, Glendalough, County Wicklow
Tel: 0404 45338
Access at all times
This National Park includes Glendalough Wood Nature Reserves and Glenealo Valley.

Kilmacurragh Arboretum

9km from Rathdrum Village, Rathdrum, County Wicklow
Tel: 01837 7896
Summer Mon-Sat 09.00-18.00 Sun 11.00-18.00 Winter Mon-Sat 09.00-16.30 Sun 11.00-16.30
Containing a magnificent collection of exotic trees and shrubs, but famous for its conifers planted in the 19C by Thomas Acton

Heywood Gardens

Ballinakill, County Laois
Tel: 01562 1450
Email: heywoodgardens@duchas.ie
Open daylight hours
Offers gardens, lakes and woodlands.

HISTORIC HOUSES

Dwyer McAllister Cottage
Derrynamuck, Knockanacarrigan, County Wicklow
Tel: 0404 45325
Mid June-Mid Sept Daily 14.00-18.00
A 200 year old thatched cottage with plenty of history.

HISTORIC SITES

Twyford Cross
west from Mullingar, Towards Athlone on the R390, Mullingar, County Westmeath
Access at all times
The cross stands on a lonely hillside roughly 4 miles before Athlone. The cross dates back to the 10C and was erected on the hillside after it was found sunk in a bog.

Magdalene Tower
Millmount Hill, Drogheda, County Louth
Exterior View Only
This belfry tower was originally part of a Dominican friary that was founded in 1224. The tower rises above a Gothic arch where the transept and nave would have met. Inside a spiral staircase ascends through two floors

Battle Of The Boyne Site
Oldbridge Estate, Oldbridge, County Meath
Tel: 01988 4343
Website: www.battleoftheboyne.ie
1 May-30 Sept 10.00-18.00
This is the site of the famous battle between King William III and his father in law King James II.

MUSEUMS

The People's Museum
Catholic Club, Main Street, Portarlington, County Laois
(Sun) 11.30-13.00 & 15.00-17.30
The museum houses a variety of exhibits ranging from 4000 year old axe heads to 20C artefacts.

Ballitore Library and Quaker Museum

Mary Leadbeater House, Ballitore, Athy, County Kildare
Tel: 01862 3344
Email: ballitorelib@kildarecoco.ie
June-Sept Wed-Sat 12.00-17.00 Sun 14.00-18.00 Oct-May Tues-Sat 12.00-17.00
Within this library is a museum of memorabilia of local nature and items of
Quaker interest.

South East-Southern Ireland

ART GALLERIES/ARTS & CRAFTS

The Old Market House Arts Centre
Lower Main Street, Dungarvan, County Waterford
Tel: 058 489 44
Email: artscentre@waterfordcoco.ie
Tues-Sat 10.00-17.00
Housed in a 17C buttermarket this centre has exhibition space for local, national and international artists. The area in front of the market is reputed to have been used for public executions.

Smithwicks Brewery
In the Abbey yard, Parliament Street, Kilkenny, County Kilkenny
Tel: 05 621936
Free audio visual presentation and ale tasting July-Aug (Monday-Friday) 15.00
This is the oldest brewery in Ireland which was started in 1710. Which offers an audio visual presentation of the brewery which includes free ale tasting.

Kiltrea Bridge Pottery
3.5 miles from Enniscorthy, Just off the Kiltealy, Enniscorthy, County Wexford
Tel: 054 35107
Email: kiltreapottery@eircom.net
Website: www.kiltreapottery.com
Daily 10.00-13.00 14.00-17.30
This is one of the few Irish potteries that still uses native clays. All products are individually thrown on the potter's wheel and visitors can watch the potters at work from the viewing gallery.

Garter Lane Arts Centre
O'Connell Street, Waterford, County Waterford
Tel: 051 855038
Email: info@garterlane.iol.ie
Website: www.garterlanewaterford.com
Gallery Open Daily 10.00-18.00
One of Ireland's largest art centres exhibiting works by contemporary and local artists

Waterford Pottery and The Dyehouse Gallery

Dyehouse Lane, Waterford, County Waterford
Tel: 051 844 770
Email: info@dyehouse-gallery.com
Website: www.dyehouse-gallery.com
Dyehouse Gallery Open Mon-Sat 11.00-18.00
Liz McCay is both the resident potter and the gallery director of this combined
venue. The Gallery hosts seven or eight exhibitions per year

CASTLES

Ferns Castle

At the NW end of the village of Ferns, Gorey, Gorey, County Wexford
Access at all times
The remains of a castle that date back to 1220, and are thought to stand on the
site of Dermot MacMurrough's old fortress. A complete tower, ruined walls and
part of the moat still survive, and the views from the top of the tower are fantastic

CHURCHES & CATHEDRALS

Saint Iberius Church

South of The Bull Ring, On Main Street, Wexford, County Wexford
Tel: 053 430 13
May-Sept Daily 10.00-17.00 Oct-April Tues-Sat 10.00-15.00 Free Guided tours available
The church was built in 1760 on the site of several previous churches. The 18C
interior boasts altar rails from a Dublin church and a set of 18C monuments in
the Gallery.

Saint Mary's Church

Church Lane, New Ross, New Ross, County Wexford
Exterior View Only, to view the interior the church key is available from the caretaker
The ruined remains of a church founded by Isabella of Leinster and her husband
in the 13C. She died around 1220 and was buried in England but inside the
church is a large stone slab that is her memorial.

Hore Abbey

Down the cow path from the Rock Of Cashel, Cashel, Cashel, County Tipperary
Access at all times
This conglomeration of ruined arches and walls was built by Cistercian monks

Tintern Abbey

Saltmills, 16 miles S of New Ross, Saltmills, County Wexford

Mid June-Late Sept 09.30-18.30

Visitors are free to wander around the ruins of this 13C Abbey, but there is a charge for guided tours

St Laserian's Cathedral

Old Leighlin, Carlow, Old Leighlin, County Carlow

Tel: 0503 21411

Mid June-End August Mon-Fri 10.00-18.00

This present 13C cathedral replaces a 7C monastery which once accommodated 1500 monks

Mount Melleray Abbey

On the Glenshelare River Walk, 5 miles N of Cappoquin, Cappoquin, County Waterford

Tel: 058 544 04

Access at all times-Visitors are asked to respect the fact that this is still a working monastery

3 miles along the river walk you will come across a Cistercian Monastery that welcomes visitors in search of solitude.

Black Abbey

Abbey Street, Kilkenny, County Kilkenny

Tel: 056 772 1279

April-Sept Mon-Sat 07.30-19.00 Sun 09.00-19.00 Oct-March Mon-Sat 07.30-17.30

Founded in 1225 and restored in 1866 the elements that remain from the original abbey include a sculpture of the Holy Trinity and a statue of St Dominic

GARDENS PARKS & WALKS

Kilkenny Castle Rose Gardens

The Parade, Kilkenny, County Kilkenny

Tel: 056 772 1450

Summer 09.00-20.30 Winter 09.00-15.00

A 52 acre landscaped park that adjoins the nearby castle. Unfortunately the castle has an entrance fee but you can enjoy the relaxing grounds for free.

Ardmore Cliff Walk

Ardmore, County Waterford

Access at all times Free map and guide pamphlets for the walk are available at the Tourist Information Centre.

This 3 mile cliff walk has some great views of the ocean and encompasses most of Ardmore's historic sites, including the cathedral, St Declan's Stone, St Declan's Well and St Declan's Way.

Stradbally Cove

Stradbally, County Waterford

Access at all times

This beautiful beach has a spectacular location as a result of its lush oak and ash covered slopes.

Glenshelane River Walk

0.5 miles E out of the village take the right fork by the statue of the Virgin Mary., Cappoquin, Cappoquin, County Waterford

Access at all times

The walk flows through a deep valley lined with pine trees. 3 miles along the walk is Mount Melleray a Cistercian Monastery that welcomes visitors in search of solitude.

The Raven Nature Reserve

R741 North from Wexford, 1 mile from Curracloe, Wexford, County Wexford

Access at all times

This Nature Reserve contains a long walk through the forest that brings you out on dunes where there are Greenland white fronted geese and various waders.

Wexford Wildfowl Reserve

North Slob, North 3.5km from Wexford, Wexford, County Wexford

Tel: 035 23129

Email: cwilson@duchas.ie

Apr-Sep (Daily) 09.00-18.00, Oct-March 10.00-17.00

Throughout the year there is a wide selection of wildlife including, mallards, pochards, godwits, mutes, berwick swans, redshank, terns, coots and oystercatchers. There is also a visitors centre, and observation tower and an assortment of hides.

Curracloe Beach

15km NE of Wexford, Off the Dublin Road, Curracloe, County Wexford

Access at all times

The location of the Omaha Beach sequence from the film " Saving Private Ryan " A magnificent beach stretching over 11 Km and flanked by extensive dunes that provide shelter.

HISTORIC HOUSES

Waterford City Hall

The Mall, Waterford, County Waterford

Tel: 051 73501

Mon-Fri 09.00-13.00 & 14.00-17.00

A late 18C building with a display dedicated to Thomas Francis Meagher

HISTORIC SITES

Brownshill Dolmen

Rathvilly Road, 3 miles from Carlow on the R726, Carlow, County Carlow

Tel: 01647 3000

Access at all times

This capstone is believed to be the largest in Europe and most likely marks the burial place of a local King of long ago

Waterford Medieval Town Walls and Tower

Waterford, County Waterford

Access at all times

Waterford boasts the largest collection of medieval towers and town walls in Ireland

The Metalman

Westown, County Waterford

Access at all times

This painted figure on the headland in Westown is a tribute to the 360 people who died when the "Seahorse" was wrecked off the coast of Tramore in 1816

MUSEUMS

Dungarvan Museum

Old Town Hall, St. Augustine Street, Dungarvan, County Waterford
Tel: 058 459 60
Email: website@dungarvanmuseum.org
Website: www.dungarvanmuseum.org
Winter Mon-Fri 10.00-13.00 & 14.00-16.30 Summer Mon-Sat10.00-13.00 & 14.00-17.00
This museum shows the history of Dungarvan and West Waterford through displays of individual items and collections of local interest

Tipperary S.R. County Museum

Borstal Gate, Emmet Street, Clonmel, County Tipperary
Tel: 052 25399
Email: museum@southtippcoco.ie
(Tue-Sat) 10.00-13.00 & 14.00-17.00
The museum contains travelling art exhibitions, local history displays and a 1000lb skull belonging to the long extinct Irish Elk.

EXHIBITIONS

Cashel Heritage Centre

Town Hall, Cashel, County Tipperary
Tel: 062 625 11
Email: cashelhc@iol.ie
March-Oct Daily 09.30-17.30 Nov-Feb Mon-Fri 09.30-17.30
Providing exhibitions on the rich heritage of Cashel

North West-Southern Ireland

ART GALLERIES/ARTS & CRAFTS

Sligo Art Gallery
Yeats Memorial Building, Hyde Bridge, Sligo, County Sligo
Tel: 071 458 47
Email: sagal@iol.ie
Website: www.sligoartgallery.com
Mon-Sat 10.00-17.30
The gallery hosts up to twenty exhibitions and events each year, please contact before visiting to see what exhibitions are available at the time

Model Arts and Niland Gallery
The Mall, Sligo, County Sligo
Tel: 071 914 1405
Email: info@modelart.ie
Website: www.modelart.ie
Tues-Sat 10.00-17.30 Sun 11.00-16.00 Closed Mondays
A premier arts centre in Ireland with collections of Paul Henry and Louis Le Broquy

Taylor's Art Gallery and Picture Framing
Castlebaldwin, Castlebaldwin, County Sligo
Tel: 0719 165 138
Mon-Sat 09.00-18.00
Five large exhibition rooms with exhibits from local, national and international artists

Leitrim Crystal
Market Yard Centre, Carrick on Shannon, County Leitrim
Tel: 0719 622 255
Mon-Sat 09.00-18.00
Visitors are welcome to view this crystal being designed , cut and engraved

Carrickmacross Lace Gallery
Market Square, Carrickmacross, Carrickmacross, County Monaghan
Tel: 0429 662 506
Open between 30th May and 1st September
An Irish craft dating back to 1816 when a piece of applique lace was brought back from Italy, this locally hand made lace is on display and for sale in the gallery

Donegal Parian China
Portnason Industrial Estate, Ballyshannon, County Donegal
Tel: 072 518 26
Email: sales@donegalchina.ie
Website: www.donegalchina.ie
Visitors Centre Open Mon-Fri 09.00-17.30 Summer open daily
Produces hand crafted delicate wafer like china. Visitors can take a guided tour, watch an audio visual presentation and visit the showrooms to view the final products

CASTLES

Roscommon Castle
Immediately North of the town of Roscommon, Roscommon, County Rosscommon
Access at all times
The dramatic and imposing ruins of a castle that was erected in 1280 by Sir Robert de Ufford

CHURCHES & CATHEDRALS

Donegal Old Franciscan Monastery
The Quay, Donegal, County Donegal
Access at all times
Founded in 1474 by the first Red Hugh O'Donnell and his wife, the impressive ruined remains of this church and cloister are where the " Annals Of The Four Masters " were compiled

GARDENS PARKS & WALKS

Letterkenny Town Park
High Road, Just off the Hospital Roundabout, Letterkenny, County Donegal
Tel: 074 919 4222
Access at all times
This park houses a Garden Of Remembrance, a herb garden and orchards, numerous walks and a play area for children

Glenveagh National Park & Visitors Centre
Churchill, 15 miles NW of Letterkenny, Churchill, County Donegal
Tel: 01743 7090
March-Early Nov Daily 10.00-18.30 No charge for National Park, Visitors Centre or Gardens, but a charge for the Castle
This National Park contains 16,540 hectares of mountains, lakes, woods and even a herd of Red Deer. There is also one of the finest gardens in Ireland which surrounds a Scottish style castle, and a visitors centre

Lough Muckno Leisure Park
Castleblaney, County Monaghan
Access at all times
This scenic 364 hectare lake and forest park has walks, picnic areas and many amenities. In the grounds of the park is Hope Castle

Donegal Bay Walk
From Ballyshannon to Rossnowlagh, Ballyshannon, County Donegal
Access at all times
An 8 mile walk which includes views of Kilbarron Castle and two beaches, which is rich in wildlife.

The Leitrim Way
48 km walk from Drumshanbo to Manorhamilton, Drumshanbo, County Leitrim
Access at all times
This walk covers some 48Km from Drumshanbo to Manorhamilton. It follows the East shore of Lough Allen up to its highest point of Doo Lough

HISTORIC SITES

Knockdoe Battlefield
On the N63, South West from Roscommon towards Galway, Lackagh, County Rosscommon
Access at all times
This is the battlefield of Knockdoe where in 1504 Gerald Fitzgerald the great Earl Of Kildare defeated his son in law Ulick de Burgh in battle.

Drumcliffe High Cross
Drumcliffe, County Sligo
Access at all times
Magnificent 10C High Cross which stands at almost 4 meters in height and features carved scenes of Adam and Eve and David and Goliath as well as many other Biblical characters

Coolkill Burial Ground and Standing Stone

Portaleen Pier, Glengad, Inishowen, County Donegal

Access at all times

Situated on a small low headland just above Portaleen Pier, this burial site was used for infants and there are small stones marking the graves. The standing stone has a small cross carved into its West side, and there are unrestricted views of the sea.

Yeats Grave

In Drumcliffe Churchyard, Drumcliffe, County Sligo

Access at all times

A simple headstone marks the final resting place of the world famous poet W B Yates who died in France in 1939 and was buried here in 1948.

Queen Maeve's Mound

On Knockarea Hill, 4 miles W of Sligo, Sligo, County Sligo

Access at all times

Even though this gigantic cairn pre dates Maeve who was a queen of Connaught in the first century AD, legend has it that she was buried here in full battle dress, with her spear in her hand ready to face her enemies even in death.

Beltany Stone Circle

Letterkenny, On a hill top at Beltany, Letterkenny, County Donegal

Access at all times

This fine stone circle stands on a hill top at Beltany. It is reputed to be older than stone henge and 64 of the original 80 stones remain.

W B Yates Statue

Infront of Ulster Bank, Sligo, County Sligo

Access at all times

A bronze statue of the famous poet W B Yates, which has been engraved with lines of his own poetry

Creevykeel Full Court Tomb

North of Creevykeel Crossroads, On the Sligo to Bundoran Road, Drumcliffe, County Sligo

Access at all times

A short passage leads into a large oval court approximately 15 meters long. There are three single chambered tombs and the remains of a much later kiln.

MUSEUMS

Monaghan County Museum
1-2 Hill Street, Monaghan, County Monaghan
Tel: 047 829 28
Email: comuseum@monaghancoco.ie
Mon-Fri 11.00-17.00 Sat 12.00-17.00
This museum tells the story of the County of Monaghan using records, displays and objects of the County's Heritage

Donegal County Museum
High Road, Letterkenny, Letterkenny, County Donegal
Tel: 0749 124613
Email: museum@donegalcoco.ie
Open all year, (Mon-Fri) 10.00-16.30 (Sat) 13.00-16.30. Closed daily 12.30-13.00
The museum has various exhibits including archaeology, historical and folklore sections

ACCOMMODATION

SCOTLAND

The Highlands

Self Catering Accommodation

Loch Ness Cottages
Contact: Scott Sutherland
Loch Ness Cottages, Loch Ness-side, Inverness, IV3 8LA
Tel: 01456 459 469
Email: relax@lochnesscottages.com
Website: www.lochnesscottages.com
Loch Ness Cottages is a family run development of traditional luxury highland cottages. Each cottage is set within its own private garden and all cottages command panoramic views across beautiful and mysterious Loch Ness. A luxurious retreat awaits!!

Self Catering Cottages On Corrour

Corrour Trust, Corrour, By Fort William, Inverness Shire, PH30 4AA
Tel: 01397 732 000
Fax: 01397 732 203
Email: mainoffice@corrour.co.uk
Website: www.corrour.co.uk
Corrour, at the heart of a Highland Estate, is one of the few places left in Britain where you can get away from it all and live in comfort. The cottages are twelve miles along a private road and are situated in the most beautiful lochside setting surrounded by spectacular mountain scenery, including 8 Munros. Visit Corrour and experience the wilderness.

Oak Dale

Ardaneaskan, Lochcarron, Stathcarron, Ross-shire, IV54 8YL
Tel/Fax: 01520 722281
Email: mackay@oakdale2.freeserve.co.uk
Website: www.ardaneaskan.com
We offer 2 self catering cottages and a caravan. Fasgadh Cottage which comprises of sitting/dining room, kitchen, bathroom, one double bedroom and two twin bedrooms Rental from £200 - £350 / week. Clachan Cottage which comprises of living/dining room, kitchen, bathroom, one twin bedroom and one single/twin - Rental from £175 - £230 per/week.. Both cottages have electric heating and are fully equipped except for linen although duvets and pillows are provided. Our caravan comprises of one double bedroom, one bunk bedroom and two single beds/day seats in lounge - Rental from £110 - £125/week.

Self Catering Accommodation Highlands

Greenaway Holiday Home nr Aviemore

Skye of Curr, Nr Aviemore, The Highlands
Tel: 01497 831 063
Email: greenaway@aviemore-holiday-home.co.uk
Website: www.aviemore-holiday-home.co.uk

Greenaway is a spacious four bedroomed, self catering detached house which comfortably sleeps eight people, it is set in a quiet location within seven miles of the popular, all year round resort of Aviemore. The house id set in an elevated position with panoramic views of the Cairngorm Mountains and is set in about an acre garden –perfect for dogs and children. It's the perfect location, whether you want a relaxing break, or enjoy walking, climbing, skiing, fishing, golf, sailing, canoeing or bird watching. Please visit our website for very competitive rates from £280 all inclusive per week.

Forglen Cottage

Contact: Mrs Sue Kulle
8 Croft, Poolewe, Ross-shire
Tel: 0208443 0967
Mobile: 07977206109
Email: forglencottage@hotmail.co.uk
Website: www.forglencottage.co.uk

A beautiful cosy cottage in the most beautiful part of Scotland sits alone in its own grounds surrounded by spectacular scenery and wildlife only 5 minutes walk to the village shops, pub and restaurant. Also within easy reach to most fine beaches and lochs. Explore and enjoy the beautiful mountains or just relax in front of the cozy open fire. Forglen is suitable for anyone who wants peace and tranquility and a taste of rural life but within easy reach of ones needs. The cottage is we4ll equipped, linen, towels, bedding and pillows are all supplied and electricity and hot water and heating are included in the cost per week, no extras. £250-£550 per week and sleeps up to 8 people.

North Haven Cottage, Kirtomy, Sutherland

Contact: Margaret Emmott, 3 Durdar Cottage, Durdar, Carlisle, Cumbria, CA2 4TY
Tel: 01228 532808
Mobile: 07751410134
Email: magsemmott@btopenworld.com
Website: www.northhavencottage.co.uk

'North Haven' was sympathetically renovated in 2003 and has retained its rustic charm. It is cosy and comfortable with a large multi fuel stove in the spacious lounge. The gallery bedroom, with a double bed, is accessed by an ornate Victorian spiral staircase (if stairs are a problem this may need to be considered) and the room has large Velux windows, which give fantastic views. In the lounge there is a sofa bed with additional folding beds available if required. The kitchen is well equipped and again spacious. It has a fridge, cooker, microwave and washing machine. It also contains a large dining table which will seat 6 people comfortably. All bed linen & towels are provided and electricity is included. Rates from £210 - £280 per week.

Self Catering Accommodation Highlands

Strone Farm, Fort William
Contact: Mrs E. Cameron, Strone Farm, Banavie, Fort William, PH33 7PB
Tel/Fax: +44[0]1397 712 773
Email: info@stronefarm.co.uk
Website: www.stronefarm.co.uk

Standing just a stone's throw from the famous Caledonian Canal, in the shadow of Ben Nevis, Strone Farm offers unbeatable value self catering accommodation all year round in a spacious wing of the farmhouse. The accommodation consists of a self-contained apartment, made up of: 3 en-suite bedrooms (2 double, 1 twin), Large lounge with window overlooking Ben Nevis and the Caledonian Canal. Fully equipped kitchen. Dining room. The apartment will comfortably accommodate six adults and prices include all heating and electricity costs. Available to rent by the week prices range from £150-£650 depending on the time of year.

Bed & Breakfast Accommodation Highlands

Birch Cottage
7 Station Road, Garve, Ross-shire, IV23 2PS
Email: raywalt4@aol.com

Set amidst spectacular mountain scenery, Birch Cottage is ideally situated for walking, fishing and touring. With the capital of the Highlands –Inverness– and its' airport only 30 miles drive away. There are many Munros within easy driving distance, and the beautiful East and West coasts make for great days out. We have created a welcoming and comfortable retreat. All rooms are en-suite, and furnished and decorated to a high standard, with central heating, hairdryer, TV, DVD and tea/coffee making facilities. What makes Birch Cottage really special however is the quality of the food –it is truly outstanding. The breakfast menu is extensive offering both continental and full Scottish. Dinner is a daily changing menu, and served in the intimate, candle-lit dining room which overlooks the cottage garden. Ray personally sources all food locally, selecting the best for quality and freshness. Whilst unlicensed, guests should feel free to bring their own wine with no corkage charged. Prices are per person per night. Bed and Breakfast 2 Sharing £22.00, Single Occupancy £27.00. 3 course dinner £15.00

Islands

Bed & Breakfast Accommodation

Old Mission House
Upper Garafad, Staffin, Isle Of Skye IV51 9JX
Tel: 01470 562 490
Email: nick@oldmissionhouseskye.com
Website: www.oldmissionhouseskye.com

Comfortable Bed and Breakfast at the Northern end of the mystical Isle Of Skye. Within easy reach of the world famous Quiraing range and Staffin Bay, this is the ideal stopping place for your travels round the island. The house is situated 16 miles North or Portree and the same distance south of Uig Ferry Terminal, and is beside the famous candle workshop Skyelight Candles.

Green Gables House
Harrapool, Broadford, Isle Of Skye, IV49 9AQ
Tel: 01471 820211
Fax: 01471 820212
Email: info@greengableshouse.co.uk
Website: www.greengableshouse.co.uk

Comfortable and affordable bed and breakfast accommodation in private house with stunning views over Broadford Bay. No smoking throughout. Adults only –no children under 14 years of age. Sorry no pets. Single, double and twin rooms available (some on ground floor) all with double glazing and central heating. Full Scottish breakfast included in the price or continental buffet if preferred. Guest lounge with TV, DVD and Video. Special offers available. Groups of up to 10 people welcome. Car parking, city link and local bus stops outside. Full fire certificate.

Grampians

Self Catering Accommodation

Croft Of Muicken, Braemar
Contact: Stewart
11 Russell Place, Edinburgh, EH5 3HQ
Tel: Day Time 0131 247 1021
Evening 0131 552 3866
Email: ehstewart@btconnect.com

Accommodation comprises of a large sitting room with wood burning stove. A kitchen with a separate dining area; 2 double bedrooms, one bunk room with sizable bunks; bath and shower; porch; fenced garden. Panoramic views up Glen Cluny and across to the mountains. Approximately one mile from the center of the village. Nice riverside walk. Rent £450 per week –this includes electricity, linen and logs.

Ardvaine
Contact: Mairi Steele
Carbost, Iale of Skye
Tel: 01224 823154
Email: mairi-steele@beeb.net

Welcome to this comfortable house in a quiet Highland village, with views over Loch Harport and the Cuillin Hills. The bungalow sleeps three in two bedrooms, and a cottage annex immediately behind has a bathroom and two further bedrooms, so up to five guests can have space and privacy, with one double and three single rooms. Enjoy the open fire in the sitting room, or the convenience of electric heating. There is a large garden and ample parking space. The village has a pub, a shop and Talisker Distillery, which is open to visitors. The climbing centre of Glenbrittle is nearby and Dunvegan Castle a pleasant drive away. Explore the lovely island, or just sit in the garden and relax.

Bunk House Accommodation-Grampians

Loch Park Swan Bunkhouse (Bunkhouse)
Loch Park Adventure Centre, Drummuir Castle Estate, Drummuir, Keith, Banffshire, AB55 5JX
Tel: 01542 810 334
Fax: 01542 810 323
Email: manager@lockpark.co.uk
Website: www.lochpark.co.uk

Situated between the 2 major malt whisky capitals of the world, Dufftown and Keith, in the picturesque Strathisla Valley and central to the delights of the North East Of Scotland. Our newly renovated former Village Shop has a combination of centrally heated rooms from en-suite to 6 bedded family rooms with large kitchen diner and quiet sitting area will give you ample space to relax after your hectic day. It is and ideal location for walking, sightseeing or that introduction to adventure that Lock Park is renowned for. Cost: £12.50 pp per night including linen (min 4 people or £50.00)

Edinburgh & The Lothians

Hostel Accommodation

Budget Backpackers

37-39 Cowgate, Old Town, Edinburgh
Tel: 00 44 (0) 131 226 6351
Email: info@budgetbackpackers.com
Website: www.budgetbackpackers.com

Wow, Wow, Wow! Are the only words to describe Edinburgh's newest 4 star Hostel. Located a stones throw away from the castle, in the heart of Edinburgh's historic old town and next to the city's vibrant nightlife. This means your bed in only 2 minutes away from your last drink. You will love our rooms designed for your maximum comfort. Modern with loads of character, private bed lights and lockers for every bed and cleaned every day. Our staff are friendly and will tell you all the best places to go and more importantly where not to go! We have 6 Ultra modern kitchens (Yes 6), 36 Ultra Modern Rooms (Yes 36). Stunning chill out room with 42 inch plasma screen. Free City Tour for every guest and only 5 mins from bus.

Caravan Park

Drummohr Caravan Park

Levenhall, Musselburgh, East Lothian, EH21 8JS
Tel: 0131 665 6867
Fax: 0131 653 6859
Email: bookings@drummohr.org
Website: www.drummohr.org

The Drummohr Park itself was originally the walled garden of a monastery. At Drummohr we have 12 fully equipped, superior lodges in a combination of 2 or 3 bedrooms suitable to sleep from 2-6 people. We also have 3 bedroomed lodges fitted to a slightly higher standard, again suitable to sleep 2-6 people. Also available on site are a small shop and excellent touring caravan/tent facilities. Situated only 7 miles from the heart of Scotland's' capital, Edinburgh, and only a short drive from East Fortune Museum Of Flight, final home of the supersonic Concorde.

Central Scotland

Self Catering Accommodation

Loch Tay Lodges
Contact: A & J Duncan Millar, Remony, Aberfeldy, Perthshire, PH15 2HR
Email: remony@btinternet.com
Website: www.lochtaylodges.co.uk

Six self catering lodges sleeping up to 4, up to 6 and one sleeping up to 8, set in a modernized listed stone built building, which was formerly accommodation for estate workers on the famous Taymouth Castle Estate, home of the Earls of Breadalbane. Open all year so you can enjoy all the delights of the seasons in the highland heart of Scotland. Fish or sail on the loch.

Bunk House Accommodation

Cairnwell Mountain Sports
Gulabin Lodge, Spittal Of Glenshee, By Blairgowrie, Perthshire, PH10 7QE
Tel/Fax: 01250 885 255
Mobile: 07799847014
Email: admin@cairnwellmountainsports.co.uk
Website: www.cairnwellmountainsports.co.uk

Located at the Spittal of Glenshee, under the watchful eye of the Ben Gulabin, 2643 ft, Cairnwell Mountain Sports is run out of Gulabin Lodge by Darren and Tereza Morgan and their ever growing clan. From the Ski hire and school in the winter months to Multi activities in the summer season, Cairnwell Mountain Sports has it all.. Gulabin Lodge offers very comfortable reasonably priced bunkhouse accommodation, for individuals, families or organised groups. From the home from home feel of the comfy sitting room, which is available all day, where you can relax in front of a real log fire after a hard day on the hills, to the dining room and a fully equipped kitchen for those who choose the self catering package. In total the lodge can sleep up to 35. There are 2, 4, 5, 6, and 7 person rooms, all equipped with wash hand basins. Bed only accommodation from £12 per person. Bed and full cooked breakfast from £17 pp. Family room (5 persons) from £45 per night. The entire Lodge can also be booked by arrangement.

Hostel Accommodation-Central

Comrie Croft Hostel and Bike Hire
Comrie Road, By Crieff, Perthshire, PH7 4JZ
Tel: 01764 670 140
Email: info@comriecroft.com
Website: www.comriecroft.com

At Comrie Croft you can get away from it all and be only an hour from Glasgow or Edinburgh. The accommodation is in a beautiful old farmstead set in the rugged glens of the Southern Highlands. Converted to offer luxury hostel self-catering to suit all pockets, we offer superb facilities (including en-suite rooms), a relaxed atmosphere and the ultimate peaceful location. The surrounding mountains and valleys offer loads of things to see and do including mountain biking or rafting, distilleries, exploring abandoned castles, standing stones, waterfalls, Loch Lomond National Park at Loch Earn and fishing on our own loch.

Hostels 4 Groups
Nethy Station, Nethy Bridge, PH25 3DS
Tel/Fax: 01479 821 370
Email: info@hostels4groups.co.uk
Website: www.hostels4groups.co.uk

Our hostels in the heart of the Cairngorms National Park are all ideally situated for all activities available in this All-Season area of Strathspey during winter or summer. So many activities are available –they can't be listed here– but anything to do with mountains, water, biking or on foot –try us– maybe we can provide it. The groups who could benefit from our accommodation are varied. Families wanting to get together on budget can take over a whole building –one even has a bar. Educational establishments, the Forces, student trips. . . you name it –we've probably had it!

Ayrshire, Strathclyde, Lanarkshire

Bed & Breakfast Accommodation

Carlton Seamill Bed & Breakfast
Contact: H & A Rennie
53 Ardrossan Road, Seamill, West Kilbride, Ayrshire, KA23 9NE
Email: carlton@westkilbride.net
Website: www.carlton-seamill.co.uk

For guests who love traditional Victorian architecture and panoramic Scottish scenery, Carlton Seamill has much to offer. An impressive, stone built, Scottish Victorian house, dated 1883, Carlton occupies an ideal location at Seamill on the Ayrshire Coast. It enjoys a commanding view over Seamill shore and beach, to the world famous Firth of Clyde and the beautiful mountainous Isle of Arran. The Rennie family have cherished Carlton carefully for over 50 years. With most of its original period features still intact, it is a fine example of a Scottish Victorian family home. Guests frequently remark on the house's relaxing "get away from it all " atmosphere and on the craftsmanship, style and graciousness that characterize the Victorian era. Carlton's handsome historically-detailed rooms afford magnificent views, over the Rose Garden and the Croquet Lawn, towards the peaks of Arran.

Bunk House Accommodation

Aldersyde Bunkhouse
Lamlash, Isle Of Arran, KA27 8LS
Tel: 01770 600 959
Email: jpricelamlash@hotmail.com

Bunkhouse excellently situated on the beautiful island of Arran. Close to numerous amenities including transport and entertainment. Outdoor activities well catered for on Arran. Rates: £10 per night or £200 per night to book the entire bunkhouse.

Argyll

Holiday Park Accommodation

Port Ban Holiday Park
Kilberry, Tarbert, Argyll, PA29 6YD
Email: portban@aol.com
Website: www.portban.com

Port Ban Holiday Park is a small family run caravan and camping site situated on the beautiful unspoilt coastline of the knapdale peninsula in Argyll. We are in the far west of Scotland, 15 miles down a single track road and look out over the sea to the Isles of Jura and Islay. We have plenty of activities available on site (large playground, football nets, tennis court, putting green etc.) and there is an abundance of wildlife and rare plants to be found. Caravans are well equipped and very generously spaced.

ENGLAND

North West England

Self Catering Accommodation

High Swinside Holiday Cottages
High Swinside Farm, High Lorton, Nr. Cockermouth, Cumbria, CA13 9UA
Tel: 01900 85206
Email: bookings@highswinside.demon.co.uk
Website: www.highswinside.demon.co.uk

High Swinside comprises three comfortable, well equipped, family run, self-catering cottages, each with wonderful views and modern facilities. The cottage sleeps 2,5 and 8 respectively. Fires in the two larger ones. We are situated above Lorton Vale which leads to Crummock and Buttermere, and we enjoy 180 degree panoramic views, from Melbreak in the South to Dumfries and Galloway to the North. Birds, (including Ospreys), squirrels, peace and tranquility are here for you. Walk or bike from your door. Lakes, golf, mountaineering, walking, biking are all here. We are child friendly but regretfully do not accept pets.

Guest House Accommodation

THREAPLAND MOSS COUNTRY GUEST HOUSE & HOLIDAY COTTAGE
Bothel, Nr Bassenthwaite Lake, Cumbria
Tel: 01697 322 275
Email: hattersleythreaplandmoss@yahoo.co.uk
Website: www.threaplandmoss.co.uk

Threapland Moss is idyllically situated on the edge of the national park, near Keswick, Cockermouth and Bassenthwaite Lake and offers Bed and Breakfast or Self Catering accommodation. Set in woodland with views of the fells, it offers peace and tranquility and an ideal base for enjoying all that the Lake District has to offer. As members of Horse Holidays in Cumbria we can provide accommodation to both horse and rider.

North East England

Self Catering Accommodation

Gate House
Contact: Mrs K Haigh
Bridge End, Allendale, Hexham, Northumberland, NE47 9NF
Tel: 01524 720626
Email: bookings@gatehouse-allendale.org.uk
Website: www.gatehouse-allendale.org.uk

A single storey stone-built old toll house on the edge of Allendale. This attractive village lies 11 miles SW of Hexham, in the North Pennines Area of Outstanding natural Beauty. The cottage has one bedroom with twin beds, good size living room with open fire, piano, bed-settee. Ideal for a couple, but families have stayed here quite happily and come again for more! There is a small modern kitchen, and a shower room with WC, wash basin and shower. Easy access to Hadrian's Wall, Durham, MetroCentre; local golf, pony trekking, craft centres etc. £131-£210 p.w.

Bed & Breakfast Accommodation

The Chirnells
Thropton, Morpeth, Northumberland, NE65 7JE
Tel: 01669621507
Email: thechirnells@aol.com
Website: www.thechirnellsfarmhousekitchen.com

The Chirnells is a Georgian farmhouse which stands in its own grounds, with spectacular views of the Coquet Valley. 2.5 miles from the picturesque town of Rothbubury, within easy driving distance of the coast, Alnwick Castle and Gardens, Cragside, Wallington Hall, Roman Wall, Kielder Water, 7 Castles, 30 mins from Newcastle, 45 mins from the Scottish Border and much more. We have 3 en-suite bedrooms with central heating, television, tea/coffee making facilities, hair dryers. Breakfast is a full English and served at 8.30 It will set you up for a days exploring. The Chirnells is open from April until October.

Yorkshire

Hotel Accommodation

Golden Lion Hotel
Contact: Mrs Anne Wood
Market Place, Leyburn, North Yorkshire
Tel: 01969 622161
Fax: 01969 623836
Email: annegoldenlion@aol.com
Website: www.thegoldenlion.co.uk

The Golden Lion Hotel is a busy family run market place hotel in the heart of the Yorkshire Dales. Open seven days, closed Christmas and Boxing Day. Children and pet friendly. Wide selection of traditional hand pulled Real Ales and Fine Wines. Good food freshly prepared to order. 15 letting rooms available with all facilities.

Bed & Breakfast Accommodation

Laskill Grange Holidays
Contact: Mrs S. Smith
Laskill Grange, Nr Hawnby, Helmsley, York, YO62 5NB
Tel: 01439 798268
Email: suesmith@laskillfarm.fsnet.co.uk
Website: www.laskillgrange.co.uk

Laskill Grange has earned its reputation from attention to detail, friendly and personal service and value for money. Our lovely bed and breakfast accommodation caters for people who are looking for comfort and luxury in superb surroundings. We also have 7 luxury self catering cottages which we offer to people seeking complete comfort in tranquil surroundings. We were featured on BBC1 holiday programme. Please visit our website for more information.

Self Catering Accommodation-Yorkshire

Pinecroft and Timberlodge
Pinecroft, Ingleton, North Yorkshire, LA6 3DP
Tel/Fax: 01524 241 462
Email: mail@pine-croft.co.uk
Website: www.pine-croft.co.uk

Pinecroft and Timberlodge is a small site of Scandinavian Pine log cabins at Ingleton on the Southern edge of the Yorkshire Dales National Park. The Pinecroft cabins, located in an area of outstanding natural beauty, are suitable for use all year by couples or families and the Timberlodge is a large log cabin fully equipped for self catering groups from schools, clubs, outdoor activity organizers, team trainers or larger families.

Merricote Cottages

Contact: Andrew Williamson

Malton Cottages, Stockton on the Forest, York

Tel: 01904 400256

Email: merricote@hotmail.com

Website: www.merricote-holiday-cottages.co.uk

Our cottages offer a holiday experience and standard of self catering accommodation second to none. Once a traditional working farm, Merricote has been converted to provide 7 superb cottages, each one different in size and character with a 4 bedroomed bungalow. In each cottage, meticulous attention to details has been given, the décor and choice of rich, soft furnishings add to the quality of your holiday experience. The historic city of York is only 3 miles away and the Yorkshire moors and Coastline within an hours drive makes Merricote Cottages a good place for exploring this beautiful part of Yorkshire. Children and dogs welcome.

Country/Coast Holiday Cottage Near Whitby

Grosmont Cottage, Ruswarp, Whitby, North Yorkshire

Tel: - 01274 546884

Email: paul.rushworth@hotmail.co.uk

Fully equipped two bedroom single storey stone cottage with newly fitted kitchen and dining area, sleeps up to 4+cot. Located in a quite rural location surrounded by beautiful countryside yet only 2 miles from the charming seaside resort of Whitby. The cottage comes with ample parking, outdoor sitting and play areas, views of Eskdale and Whitby Abbey. With full gas central heating and new double glazing the cottage is ideal for short breaks out of season, minimum 3 nights. Close to coastal attractions and the stunning scenery of Captain Cook Country and the North York Moors National Park. Local attractions include mini-golf and boating at Ruswarp, the North York Moors Steam Railway and Heartbeat Country. PLEASE E-MAIL OR PHONE PAUL RUSHWORTH FOR DETAILS AND MENTION FD2.

Central England

Bed & Breakfast Accommodation

Moseley Farm Bed & Breakfast
Moseley Road, Hallow, Worcester, WR2 6NL
Tel: 01905 641 343
Fax: 01905 641 416
Email: moseleyfarmbandb@aol.com
Website: www.moseleyfarmbandb.co.uk

Spacious 17th Century former farmhouse with views over the Worcestershire countryside. Set in a rural location just 4 miles from Worcester City Centre, Moseley Farm Bed and Breakfast aims to provide comfortable accommodation. Weekdays we offer room only, whilst at weekends we offer a Full English Breakfast (including free range eggs from our own chickens). Both en-suite rooms and twin rooms with private bathroom available. Cooking facilities available by prior arrangement. Dogs by prior arrangement. Secure off-road parking for several vehicles, including transit vans and trailers. Open all year round.

Tachbrook Mallory House
Contact: Jennifer
Oakley Wood Road, Bishops Tachbrook, Leamington Spa, Warwickshire, CV33 9QE
Email: tmhouse@btinternet.com
Website: www.tachbrookmalloryhouse.co.uk

Tachbrook Mallory House is a beautiful 16th Century manor house, with all the original features, set in a lovely rural location within a very large and attractive grounds. Located centrally and within minutes of Warwick Castle, Leamington Spa, Warwick town centre, the Motorway Network and the famous Cotswolds. We are also within easy reach of Stratford Upon Avon, NEC, NAC. We offer spacious luxury accommodation in a very peaceful location and a warm and friendly welcome.

Caro's Bed & Breakfast
1 Higher Netley, Dorrington, Nr. Shrewsbury SY5 7JY
Tel: 01743 718790
Mobile: 07739 285263
Email: info@carosbandb.co.uk
Website: www.carosbandb.co.uk

Stay at Caro's and enjoy: AA Red Diamond accreditation, Easy off road parking, Real log fire, Fabulous views, No-smoking environment, Prices from just £55. Each bedroom has: Colour television , Tea & coffee making facilities, En suite bathroom, Full central heating. Available on request: Ironing facilities, Cot. *We regret pets are not allowed.* We look forward to seeing you soon!

Self Catering Accommodation-Central England

Cotswold Property Lettings
4 Keil Close, High Street, Broadway, Worcs, WR12 7DP
Tel: 01386 858 147
Fax: 01386 854 930
Email: gill@cotswoldholiday.com
Website: www.cotswoldholiday.com

High Quality Cotswold cottages throughout the north Cotswold villages ranging from a cosy cottage for 2 to a large 3 bedroomed property suitable for the larger party or family group. Short breaks available at most of our properties as well as weekly holidays. Full colour brochure available.

Ashwater House
Contact: Mrs Holly Mapletoft
19 Willow Drive, Louth, Lincs, LN11 0AH
Tel: 0845 126 0442
Email: enquiries@ashwaterhouse.co.uk
Website: www.ashwaterhouse.co.uk

Self catering pine log cabins and cottages in the Georgian market town of Louth, on the edge of the Lincolnshire Wolds. Quality accommodation set in over 2 acres of grounds with a half acre coarse fishing lake, play area for children, complimentary use of an off site private health and leisure club, within walking distance of the town but bordered by fields. Ranging from Ashpot Cottage, our 5 bedroomed cottage sleeping 8, with exposed beams, inglenook fireplace and enclosed gardens to Teal Cabin a cosy 1 bed log cabin on the bank of the lake. Guestbook Quotation: " What luck, a little piece of heaven. Have so enjoyed this peaceful corner, the beautiful view with wildlife around".

Manor Holding
Contact: Nigel & Penny Dobson-Smyth
32 Church Street, Hagley, Stourbridge, West Midlands, DY9 0NA
Tel: 01562 883 609
Mobile: 07970 260 010
Email: nds@landscapeconsultancy.freeserve.co.uk

Romantic deer frequent the wild flower meadows and ancient orchards of Manor Holding, in the tranquil Forest of Wyre. Restored with earth daub, lime plaster and green oak, the cottage is warm and sunny. Pale terracotta and oak floors add to the charm of crooked timber frame, leaning walls and low ceilings, complete with inglenook and old stone bread oven. It has a sheltered south facing garden and ample parking. 4 miles cycle ride along the network of forest paths, through a national nature reserve, lies Bewdley's Georgian port. Steam trains from here connect to Birmingham and London via Kidderminster.

Self Catering Accommodation-Central England

Langstone Court Farmhouse

Contact: Mrs Sonia Davies, Langstone Court Farmhouse, Langstone, Llangarron, Ross-on-Wye, HR9 6NR

Email: sonialangstone@aol.com

Website: www.langstonecourtfarmhouse.co.uk

Self-catering holiday accommodation within a fourteenth century farmhouse. Langstone is warm, welcoming and family friendly, great for reunions. Situated only 6 miles from the old market towns of Ross-on-Wye and Monmouth. Ideal touring centre for the Cathedral cities of Hereford and Worcester, Wye Valley, Forest of Dean and Wales. Golf, fishing, pony trekking and cycling can all be found locally along with lovely Forestry Commission walks or hire a canoe taking you along the River Wye to Symonds Yat. There is a first class choice of restaurants and public houses nearby or catering in house undertaken by local caterers.

Raven House Farm

Contact: Paul Rowlands

High Street, Tibshelf, Derbyshire, DE55 5NY

Tel: 07004246543

Email: paul@07004aholiday.com

Website: www.07004aholiday.com

Raven House Farm is over 400 years old; its size and old world charm makes it the ideal weekend getaway. Its thick walls isolate you from the outside world and the muffled silence creates an inner calm, well at least until the rest of your party arrives, then it transforms into a spacious party environment. We regularly have family Celebrations, Birthdays and Anniversaries. Or maybe you just want a quiet gentle weekend sightseeing, walking or shopping at the numerous factory shops in the area. Then back for the evening to a roaring fire and a bottle of wine or two.

Campden Cottages

Folly Cottage, Paxford, Chipping Campden, Glos, GL55 6XG

Tel: +44 (0)1386 593315

Email: info@campdencottages.co.uk

Website: www.campdencottages.co.uk

Campden Cottages is a small, locally based agency with a wide range of character holiday cottages in the beautiful Chipping Campden/Broadway area of the North Cotswolds –a designated Area of Outstanding Natural Beauty. All cottages are privately owned, individually situated and are very well equipped and maintained. Prices include all fuel ,linen and towels and welcome tea tray with home made cake and fresh flowers. Brochure available. Ideally situated for visiting Stratford-upon-Avon, Warwick castle, Blenheim Palace, Cheltenham, Oxford. Many gardens to visit nearby including Hidcote Garden (National Trust), Kiftsgate, Sezincote, Batsford Arboretum.

London

Hotel Accommodation

Crystal Hotels, London
Central Reservations
Tel: +44 (0) 7259 2888
Fax: +44 (0) 7259 2999
Email: cro@crystalhotels.co.uk
Website: www.crystalhotels.co.uk
Crystal Hotels welcome their guests with a range of accommodation in the three star markets. All six hotels have ideal locations within easy access for both the businessman and the tourist to the major areas of the Capital City. They stand out as preferred suppliers of commercial and Leisure accommodation in each of their locations offering good value with no frills. Our other prices are generous to the guest and we have no hidden extras. Our friendly staff speak a wide range of languages, and will be happy to help you make the most of your stay in London with us.
AMBASSADORS HOTEL, Kensington-Rooms from £50
BRUNEL HOTEL, Bayswater-Rooms from £50
DUKE OF LEINSTER, Bayswater-Rooms from £69
EDWARD HOTEL, Paddington-Rooms from £52
KENSINGTON COURT, Earls Court-Rooms from £55
REEM HOTEL, Bayswater-Rooms from £45

Self Catering Accommodation

London Flats And Houses
Email: stella@londonflatsandhouses.com
or stella@rentalondonapartment.com
Website: www.londonflatsandhouses.com
At London Flats And Houses I will do my very best to help you find the apartment in London that you require for your vacation. I will give you as much help and time as you need to find your perfect home from home. Just take a look through the apartments on my website and choose those you like and I can check the dates available for you. I can also recommend many others that are not on the website. **Most apartments are 7 nights minimum but occasionally they will do 4 or 5 nights if they have a slot available. The prices vary from £695 a week for a two bedroom at Notting Hill to over £2000 a week for very luxurious 3 bedrooms in Kensington, Mayfair and other areas.**

Bed & Breakfast Accommodation-London

Bluebelle Mansion B&B-Guest House

Contact: Ms Yvette Peacock, 17 Chertsey Road, Lower Feltham, Middlesex, TW13 4RA

Tel: 0208 707 9822 or 07956 940346

Email: bluebelle17@hotmail.com

Website: http://www.where2stay-com/html/bluebellemansion.html

Bluebelle Mansion is a family run relaxed Guest House. Our B&B is very clean, comfortable and quiet with the personal touch you would expect of a small privately owned business. Heathrow is just 5 mins away by car. Whether you are staying for one night or two weeks, everything possible will be done to make your stay as comfortable as possible with taxis, car hire or bus journeys arranged and booked as and when you require. We are a non-smoking establishment. Bluebelle Mansion is a Luxury large clean house. We offer a home from home feel that's relaxed, friendly and welcoming. We have a lot of repeat business from our visitors since our opening over the 4 years that we have been in business.

London To The Severn

Guest House Accommodation

Nanford Guest House
137 Iffley Road, Oxford, OX4 1EJ
Tel: 01865 244 743
Fax: 01865 249 596
Email: b.cronin@btinternet.com
Website: www.nanfordguesthouse.com
Budget Guest House located 5 minutes on foot from the University of Oxford. Wide range and number of rooms at budget prices. All rooms have private shower and toilet, colour TV and tea set. Single @ £30 per night, Double £40 per night. Twin single £40 per night, Family £60 per night, Triple £60 per night, Quadruple £80 per night and Family room for 5 £100 per night. All prices include a full English breakfast. Private off street parking available. Large groups welcome. Earliest check in time is 2 pm. We require 24 hours notice to cancel.

Bed & Breakfast Accommodation

Highfield Farm
Tempsford Road, Sandy, Bedfordshire, SG19 2AQ
Tel: + 44 (0) 1767 682332
E-mail: margaret@highfield-farm.co.uk
Website: www.highfield-farm.co.uk
Awarded the highest grade of Five Diamonds plus a Gold Award. B&B available in Highfield or in our barn conversion "Sunnyside" Full breakfast served in the large, airy dining-room in Sunnyside, which overlooks the open fields. We also offer 4 super self catering cottages. Equipped to a very high standard with a bathroom per bedroom, linen and heating included, fully fitted kitchens, and washing and drying machines on site . B&B rates: Double or twin £70, Single occupancy of double or twin £55-60, Family rooms from £80 inclusive of breakfast and VAT. Self catering from £250 - £600 per week.

East Anglia

Guest House Accommodation

The Old Rectory Hopton
Contact: Sarah or Bobby Llewellyn
The Old Rectory, High Street, Hopton, Suffolk
Tel: 44 (0) 1953688135
Email: Llewellyn.hopton@btinternet.com
Website: www.theoldrectoryhopton.com

A retreat in which everyone can relax and be assured of their own space in beautiful surroundings, this lovely Grade II listed timber framed building dates from the 16th Century. Behind its symmetrical Georgian façade, lie high quality furniture and furnishings which are in keeping with the times when the occupants of rectories were the younger sons of the landed gentry. Outside, in the mainly walled garden, stands a magnificent copper beech tree with the carvings of the names of evacuees during the war. Peace and tranquility prevail, whether it's outside on the terrace in the Summer, inside in the Winter with log fires or in beautifully decorated en-suite bedrooms which enjoy spectacular views of the garden with its old English roses, mature shrubs and trees.

Self Catering Accommodation

Apartments Plus In Cambridge
86b Barton Road, Cambridge, CB3 9LH
Tel: 07748 347096
Email: apartments_plus@hotmail.com
Website: http://apartments-plus.4t.com

Apartments-Plus welcomes you to stay in Cambridge. Whether you are on business or pleasure, with your family or taking some time off to visit by yourself. The apartments are *fully* furnished and *serviced, well presented, welcoming spaces,* each with its *own garden* and its *own car parking* facility. The apartments sleep from 1-5 people and have 2 bedrooms (1 master bedroom with kingsize bed and second bedroom either single or twin * 1 apartment has an additional sofa bed in the living room). Bathroom with shower and toilet Kitchen-diner (fully stocked) Storage spaces. The apartments are of a quality and standard to meet the needs of: The individual independent visitor , The group visitor , The family visitor , Visiting students , Visiting academics , Visitors on business. £30 - £45 pppn based on 2 adults sharing Kids are FREE.

Hampshire, Dorset & Wiltshire

Bed & Breakfast Accommodation

Harmshay Farmhouse B & B

Contact: Tina Hutchings, Harmshay Farm, Marshwood, Bridport, Dorset, DT6 5QJ
Email: tinahut@hotmail.co.uk
Website: www.harmshayfarm.co.uk

Our B&B is a 16th Century Thatched Farmhouse set in one hundred acres of own land. It overlooks the beautiful Marshwood Vale and the Hill Forts of Lamberts Castle and Coneys Castle. There are many footpaths and lovely walks and a country pub which serves good food and is a short walk or a two minute drive away. The bedrooms are 1 en-suite with double(king) bed, 1 double(king) with single in room, 1 twin room and bathroom with shower close to both rooms. Rooms have exposed beams and brickwork and double rooms are large with sofas, colour televisions and tea making facilities.

Pebble Villa Bed & Breakfast

Contact: Martin Hill, Pebble Villa, Preston, Weymouth, Dorset, DT3 6JT
Tel: 01305 837469
Email: stay@pebblevilla.co.uk
Website: www.weymouthbedandbreakfast.net

Pebble Villa is a rather special Weymouth Bed and Breakfast. We have just one letting room where you will be treated as house guests, rather than visitors. Our non-smoking villa is situated about ten minutes walk from the beach and the South-West Coast Path. We are just over 2 miles from the centre of Weymouth. We have one double bedroom with a full en-suite bathroom. There is a TV/video, tea/coffee facilities, hair-dryer, radio/alarm and iron. The bedroom overlooks the peaceful Mediterranean style garden. On fine warm days breakfast is served on the sea-view terrace.

Wisteria House

14 Mays Lane, Stubbington, Fareham, Hampshire
Tel: 01329 511 940
Email: info@wisteria-house.co.uk
Website: www.wisteria-house.co.uk

Wisteria House is a comfortable and tastefully decorated home in Stubbington, near Fareham in Hampshire offering Bed and Breakfast accommodation. All bedrooms have en-suite bathrooms and are located on the ground floor. Bedrooms also have remote control colour television with video, teletext and Freeview, radio alarm, coffee and tea making facilities, hairdryers and full central heating. Off road parking is available. Wisteria House is conveniently located on the edge of Stubbington Village just a 3 minute flat walk to all local amenities and approximately 1 mile to the beach and coast at Lee-on-the-Solent, where you can enjoy panoramic views of the Isle of Wight. It is also ideally placed for access to the M27 and within easy reach of Portsmouth, Southhampton and Winchester. Wisteria House has been awarded 4 Diamonds and a Silver Award by the English Tourist Council which recognises the service and comfort provided.

Self Catering Accommodation Hampshire, Dorset & Wiltshire

Marston Holiday Flats (S/C)

16 Burlington Road, Swanage, Dorset, BH19 1LS
Tel/Fax: 01929 422 221
Email: marstonflats@btinternet.com
Website: www.swanageholidayflats.co.uk

Marston is a large Edwardian Purbeck stone property standing on the cliff top, in the north of Swanage, with lovely views across to the Isle of Wight and Ballard Down. It is ideally located for family holidays with the sandy beach only a two minute walk away and no roads to cross. The three flats have all been recently refurbished and comfortably accommodate up to six people. Children are very much welcome but unfortunately we do not take pets. The flats have newly fitted kitchens, a separate lounge, two bedrooms and newly renovated bathrooms. Cots and high chairs are also available on request. Marston is open all year round and caters for short breaks in the low season, long weekends and longer family holidays. Prices range from £200 per week, or £60 per night (for a minimum of two nights). Please contact Jackie by phone, fax or email for availability and further information.

Surrey, Kent & Sussex

Bed & Breakfast Accommodation

The Silverdale
21 Sutton Park Road, Seaford, East Sussex
Email: silverdale@mistral.co.uk
Website: www.silverdale.mistral.co.uk

We are a town centre establishment with prices of a B&B and facilities of a hotel. Seaford is an Edwardian seaside town which has managed to avoid the commercialization of many other seaside towns despite being next to the lovely Seven Sisters. We were awarded AA Pet Friendly Guest Establishment of the Year 2005 so really welcome visiting dogs. In addition to this we were runner up in 2006 to the Considerate Hotel of the Year for our waste and recycling practices. We have double four poster and canopied rooms, family rooms and two suites. All our rooms have their own en suite facilities.

Woodacre Bed & Breakfast
Arundel Road, Fontwell, Arundel, West Sussex, BN18 0QP
Tel: 01243 814301
Fax: 01243 814344
Email: wacrebb@aol.com
Website: www.woodacre.co.uk

Woodacre offers Bed and Breakfast in a traditional family house set in beautiful grounds. We can accommodate up to 10 guests in 4 rooms. On the ground floor there is a Double En-Suite room with private entrance and parking and there is also a Family Room (sleeps 4 in one double bed and 2 singles) with doors opening onto the garden. 2 Twin Rooms (not en-suite) on the 1st floor. Woodacre is easy to find from A27 and conveniently situated for touring the South of England. Everyone is made welcome including children and pets. Credit cards accepted.

Guest House Accommodation Surrey, Kent & Sussex

Manor Guest House
100 Broadwater Road, Worthing, West Sussex, BN14 8AN
Tel: 01903 236028
Email: stay@manorworthing.com
Website: www.manorworthing.com

Hotel facilities and service and Guest House prices. We offer newly refurbished single and double standard rooms and a brand new four poster en-suite. A further twin en-suite and a family room that sleeps 4 are also available. We welcome children aged 8 plus and your well behaved pets. "The Manor Restaurant' is open 7 days a week to non-residents for breakfast, lunch, dinner, Sunday roasts and for small, personal wakes and other functions. We are fully licensed and offer themed food evenings for special occasions. Close to local business parks, Worthing town centre and bowling greens.

The West Country

Bed & Breakfast Accommodation

The Paddock
Contact: Sue Russell
Edmonton, Wadebridge, North Cornwall
Email: srus14@aol.com
Website: www.paddock-bedandbreakfast.co.uk

The Paddock is a small guest house with a great reputation for being Home from Home. We are ideally situated for you to explore this beautiful county and we can personally recommend many places for you to see. The Paddock is a smallholding and houses many friendly pets, we are dog and horse friendly so bring em along too. All of our rooms are en-suite and rates include full breakfast. Rates one night 25 pounds, two nights or more 20 pounds. We don't charge a single supplement unless the single room is already booked. Look forward to meeting you.

Manor Farm Bed & Breakfast
Contact: Mrs. Fiona Fridd
Old Frome Road, East Horrington, WELLS, Somerset, BA5 3DP
Tel: 01749 679832
Mobile: 07774 733702
Email: info@somersetbed.co.uk
Website: www.somersetbed.co.uk

Manor Farm is a huge and stunning 15th century home offering luxury yet relaxing B&B all year round. Open fires, flagstone floors, beans galore, accommodation is spacious and light and offers excellent facilities. Residents' Drawing Room, Games Room, walled garden. Private wing available for romantic getaways. Wonderful breakfasts served anytime to suit guests. Situated in a charming village just 2 miles from central Wells. 1 mile character pub/restaurant. Easy access to many local attractions to suit all ages –Bath, Cheddar, Glastonbury, Longleat, Wookey Hole caves, Wells Cathedral, and a good stopover for guests en route to Devon/Cornwall.

Hunters Moon
Contact: John & Diane Ware, Bridestowe, Okehampton, Devon, EX20 4EN
Tel: 01837 861193
Email: enq@huntersmoon-devon.co.uk
Website: www.huntersmoon-devon.co.uk

Bed & Breakfast accommodation in a 17th Century stone and cob cottage with oak beams and inglenook fireplaces but with modern day comforts. A full Devon breakfast is included and a three course, set menu, evening meal is offered as an optional extra. All food is homecooked using local produce where possible and our own fresh eggs and homemade preserves. An ideal base for touring, walking or cycling located on the edge of Dartmoor on both the Two Castles Trail and the National Cycle Network and the Granite Way. Stunning views and scenery.

Bed & Breakfast Accommodation-West Country

Ivydene Bed & Breakfast

19 Southbourne Road, St Austell, Cornwall
Tel: 01726 61759
Email: info@ivydenebedandbreakfast.co.uk
Website: www.ivydenebedandbreakfast.co.uk

A very friendly family run Bed and Breakfast in St Austell, Cornwall. We like to make our guests comfortable and relaxed and encourage them to come and go as they please, so they can make the most of St Austell, and Cornwall's many attractions. Ivydene is close to many attractions including The Eden project, Heligan Gardens, Charlestown (the setting for Poldark), Mevagissey and much more. There is 1 double room with an ensuite shower room, and 1 twin room with an ensuite bathroom. Rates are from £25 per person per night. Children are very welcome, and there is ample off street parking. The rooms have tea/coffee making facilities and televisions. There is also a television in the guest lounge. Ivydene is a non smoking house.

Guest House Accommodation-West Country

Rivendell Guest House

Contact: Angela & Barrie Walker
7 Porthminster Terrace, St Ives, Cornwall
Tel: 01736 794923
Email: rivendellstives@aol.com
Website: www.rivendell-stives.co.uk

Rivendell is a family run Guest House with an excellent reputation for friendly hospitality. A perfect location for your holiday. Close to all amenities, all rooms have en-suite facilities except the single room. It is highly recommended with beautifully appointed rooms, some with sea views. Evening meals are optional and are prepared using local fresh produce. Barrie is a qualified chef.

Molesworth Manor

Little Petherick, nr. Padstow, North Cornwall
Tel: 01841 540292
Email: molesworthmanor@aol.com
Website: www.molesworthmanor.co.uk

Molesworth Manor is a licensed guesthouse in a former rectory dating from the early 17th Century. Situated in an attractive garden, 2 miles from the pretty fishing port of Padstow, and provides comfortable relaxed accommodation with a warm and friendly atmosphere. Awarded four diamonds by the English Tourism Council. All the rooms are centrally heated and enjoy splendid views of open countryside. Guests may relax in the drawing room, the library or the T.V. morning room all of which have open fires in the colder weather. Accommodation is on a bed and breakfast basis, with breakfast consisting of a variety of fruits, fruit juices, cereals, yoghurts, hams, cheeses and toasts.

Self Catering Accommodation-West Country

Rosecraddoc Lodge Holiday Bungalows
St Cleer, Liskeard, Cornwall, PL14 5BU
Freephone: 0800 458 3886
Email: andy@contact.go-plus.net
Website: www.gotocornwall.info
'Get away from it all'. Come and have a peaceful, relaxing break in one of our bungalows at Rosecraddoc Lodge, Liskeard. Formerly part of the Rosecraddoc Manor Estate, this is now a well maintained, purpose built holiday retreat. Pub/Restaurant on site but NOT holiday camp style. No noisy nightclubs or 'red coats'. Great base for visiting many of Cornwall's top attractions including the Eden Project (30 minutes). Many <u>free</u> attractions within easy reach. Liskeard 2 miles, Looe 9 miles, Plymouth 20 miles. Well equipped bungalows, sleep 4-5. Everything you need. Please visit our website for more information.

Two Coastal Apartments South Cornwall
Morweth Court, Downderry, Cornwall
Tel: - 01274 546884
Email: paul.rushworth@hotmail.co.uk
Modern fully equipped 2 bedroom, ground and first floor apartments, sleep 2 to 4. Situated in the lovely coastal village of Downderry, South East Cornwall. The apartments have a balcony and a large decking area to soak up the sun with sea and countryside views. Private parking area provided and only 5 minutes walk to the beach and Inn on the Shore. You will find many local holiday attractions in this area for both adults and young children including the world famous Eden Project. Visit the quaint fishing villages of Kingsand, Cawsand and Polperro together with the larger centres of Looe and Plymouth and the beautiful Tamar estuary. Local facilities include a Cafe and beach shop, Spar/Post Office, Hotel and Restaurant. PLEASE E-MAIL OR PHONE PAUL RUSHWORTH FOR DETAILS AND MENTION F2D.

Brean Sands Holiday Flats
Contact: V Beale, 53 Hillview, South Road, Brean, Somerset, TA8 2RD
Tel: 01278 751979/751741
Email: valbeale@breansands.fsbusiness.co.uk
Website: www.somersetaccommodation.co.uk
Privately owned holiday flats with parking space and access to beach. Close to all Holiday Facilities. Open all Year, fully equipped shower room with separate WC, TV, Weekend and Mid week breaks off-season. Pets welcome by arrangement. Four sharing. 10 minutes from the M5. Good beach and sea fishing. Near Golf Course.

Self Catering Accommodation-West Country

Towan Beach Chalet
Contact: John Reddick and Helena Ragg-Kirby
Nr. Portscatho, St Anthony Head, Roseland, South Cornwall.
Tel: ++(0) 113 274 6474
Email: reddragg@waitrose.com
Website: www.hoadworks.com/towan.htm

Secluded, beautifully appointed and super-comfortable chalet set amongst grass and trees with spectacular views over rolling countryside, and just 400m from a never-crowded sandy beach, while 50m in the other direction –through our own woodland– lie a picture-book tidal creek and its winding estuary. With full length veranda and fall-asleep sofas, woodburning stove and triple-aspect picture windows, two bathrooms and well-equipped kitchen, it is a perfect summer and winter retreat –complemented by a brilliant 7-days local store and superb country inns. Such delights as the Eden Project, the Lost Gardens of Heligan and the Tate at St Ives, are all within easy reach. £195-640 pw.

Solis
Contact: Paul Rowlands
Coast Road, Berrow, Somerset, TA8 2QS
Tel: 0700 424 6543
Email: paul@07004aholiday.com
Website: www.07004aholiday.com

A very large 1920's house sleeping 16 people, close to the beach and overlooking Berrow dunes and a links golf course. A few miles from the M5 it is accessible from most of the UK in only a few hours. Recently refurbished it is the ideal place to hold family Celebrations, Birthdays and Anniversaries or stay with family and friends for a quiet break. Solis is an ideal gateway for exploring the South West being on the doorstep of the world famous Somerset Levels with Glastonbury, Wells and Taunton within 30 minutes drive.

Burrell's Beach Properties
Contact: Peter, Denise, Samantha Burrell
8 Beach Rd, Perranporth, Cornwall, TR6 0DQ
Tel: 01872 573628
Email: info@burrellsholidays.co.uk
Website: www.burrellsholidays.co.uk

All of our properties are situated 150m or less level walk from Perranporths beautiful 3 mile beach and the local town and amenities and have private parking. They vary from 1 bed apartments through 2 bed apartments, bungalows and a cottage to a 4 bedroom detached house situated right on the beachfront. We are a family run business and own our properties ourselves, so we can be confident of the accommodation standard and that they all provide an ideal location from which to explore all the regions attractions, the quaint villages, dramatic coastlines, the Eden Project, Rick Steins Seafood restaurant and plenty more...

WALES

Self Catering Accommodation

Granary Cottages

Ystradgynwyn, Torpantau, Merthyr Tydfil, CF48 2UT
Tel: 01685 383358
Email: sian@selfcateringcottageinwales.co.uk
Website: www.selfcateringcottagesinwales.co.uk

Two delightful cottages and The Stable Loft (all WTB 4 Star) in the heart of the Brecon Beacons, close to the Taff Trail, Pen Y Fan and the Beacons Way and 15 minutes from Merthyr Tydfil and 25 minutes from Brecon. Sympathetically converted with many traditional features (open fires, exposed beams, stonework). The cottages sleep up to 5 with fitted kitchen, seating and eating areas. The Stable Loft sleeps 2 in oodles of space ideal base for walking, cycling and exploring the South Wales Valleys.

Lleyn-Farm-Holidays

Contact: Jane Owen, Towyn, Llanengan, Abersoch, Gwynedd, LL53 7LS
Tel: 01758 712302 or 01758 712570
Email: annie@towynfarm.co.uk
Website: www.lleyn-farm-holidays.co.uk

Superb self-catering and bed and breakfast accommodation on the Lleyn Peninsula, North Wales. Pwllheli, Abersoch, Nefyn, Portmeirion and Snowdonia are all within easy reach. Lleyn was voted the 4th best holiday area in Britain in 2003, and is designated an Area of Outstanding Natural Beauty. With 50 miles of heritage coast, and a wealth of sandy beaches and rocky headlands. The narrow country lanes provide an abundance of flora and fauna while prehistoric cairns, castles churches and Snowdon are all within a 30 mile radius. Lleyn is a place where you can unwind and enjoy a peaceful tranquil stay or where you can have an active energetic holiday, coupled with a warm Welsh welcome. Select self catering, B&B or camping holidays at various prices-the choice is yours.

The Hay Barn & The Bull Pen

Tor-Y-Mynydd Farm, Devauden, Chepstow, Monmouthshire, NP16 6NU
Email: brian.tor-y-mynydd@virgin.net

Converted from a stone Barn high on a hillside stunning views over the Vale of Usk to the mountains. Peace and Relaxation. THE HAY BARN ; sleeps 6. Ground floor King sized double bed with en-suite shower room W/C Basin. 1st Floor Large sitting room with Dining area, fully fitted kitchen Seating for 6/7 on leather sofas and chairs. T.V. Video, CD Radio. 1 Large Double en-suite Bathroom, 1 Twin en-suite bathroom. THE BULL PEN Sleeps 4. G/F Flagstone floors & whitewashed walls. Sitting Room fantastic views, Dining Area, & Fully fitted Kitchenette T.V. 1st Floor Twin en-suite bathroom. Both Cottages have Full C/H Towels, Linen, Heating and Electricity included. Pets welcome. No smoking Please.

Self Catering Accommodation-Wales

4 Norton Avenue
Contact: Mrs M. Stone, Rotherslade, 341 Rochester Road, Chalk, Gravesend, Kent
Mumbles, Swansea, SA3 5TP
Tel: +44 (0) 1474 365775
Email: kmstone@hotmail.co.uk

Semi-detached house, which accommodates 7 people, situated 2 minutes from the promenade at Mumbles. The promenade extends for some 5 miles around Swansea Bay. The accommodation comprises of, lounge dining room with seating for 7, well equipped 'Shaker style' kitchen, cloakroom with toilet and wash-hand basin. The main bedroom has a sea view and double bed. The second bedroom contains 3 single beds, and the third bedroom contains two full size bunk beds. The family-sized bathroom has a wash basin, a full size bath and electric shower. There is a separate WC.A travel cot and high chair can be provided at an additional cost. There is a secluded rear garden with patio and garden furniture. Regretfully pets are not allowed. This is a non-smoking establishment.

Guest House Accommodation Wales

Bryn-y-Ddafad Country Guest House
Contact: June & Glyn Jenkins
Welsh Saint Donats, Cowbridge, Vale Of Glamorgan, CF71 7ST
Tel: +44 (0) 1446 774451
Email: junejenkins@bydd.co.uk
Website: www.bydd.co.uk

Experience the peace and tranquility of our spacious 4 Star Guest House and lovely garden lying in the heart of beautiful countryside. We offer guests on holiday or business comfort, good food and a warm friendly relaxed atmosphere. En-suite rooms, guest lounges. Self contained ground floor apartment also available on a self catering basis. Outdoor enthusiasts will find fine golf courses, fishing and forestry walks nearby. The elegant town of Cowbridge lies three miles away with many fine shops and restaurants whilst Cardiff and the Heritage Coast are within easy reach. An ideal touring base. Strictly non-smoking, sorry no pets.

Bunk House Accommodation Wales

Hardingsdown Bunkhouse
Contact: Allison Tyrrell, Lower Hardingsdown Farm, Llangennith, Gower, Swansea, SA3 1HT
Tel: 01792 386222
Email: info@bunkhousegower.co.uk
Website: www.bunkhousegower.co.uk

Hardingsdown Bunkhouse is a renovated stone barn situated on an organic working farm on the Gower Peninsula approximately 15 miles from Swansea. A perfect location for all that the area has to offer –safe sandy beaches, walking, biking, surfing etc. Open 12 months of the year the bunkhouse provides comfortable, fully equipped self catering accommodation for groups or families sleeping up to 12/14 people on a weekend, midweek or weekly basis. Accommodation consists of 4 bedrooms sleeping 5,2,2,3 plus 2 comfy chair beds in the living room. There is a garden and patio that catches the afternoon and evening sun –perfect for barbeques. There is ample parking and a separate drying room and lock-up for safe storage of bikes, surfboards etc.

Hostel Accommodation Wales

Cardiff Backpacker Caerdydd

98 Neville Street, Riverside, Cardiff, CF11 6LS
Tel: 02920345577
Fax: 02920230404
Email: info@cardiffbackpacker.com
Website: www.cardiffbackpacker.com

Cardiff Backpacker Hostel is within a stone's throw from the centre of Europe's youngest and fastest growing capital. Cardiff is a vibrant compact city with a large student and multicultural population. Enjoy a warm welcome in the Welsh capital whilst relaxing and socialising with fellow travelers from around the world. All our friendly staff are experienced travelers; multilingual in Welsh, English and other languages; and highly knowledgeable about sights and activities throughout Wales. Accommodation is a combination of twin/double rooms and dorm beds. Facilities include reception, information desk, telephone and internet access, guest bar with pool table and big screen TV, lounge with DVD library, roof garden with BBQ, launderette and car parking. Foreign passport holders only. Prices from £17.70 pppn.

NORTHERN IRELAND

Bed & Breakfast Accommodation

Avarest Town House
64 Mark Street, Portrush, Co. Antrim, BT56 8BU
Tel: 02870823121
Email: relax@avarest.com
Website: www.avarest.com
Avarest is a beautiful Victorian town house located in the centre of Portrush, Ireland's N° 1
holiday resort. Indulge yourself with our breathtaking views of harbour west bay and Downhill
before casting your eyes further along to the Donegal Hills. All rooms excellently appointed to
include small fridges, hairdryers and ironing facilities. Internet Access also available (small fee).
Only 15 minutes from the world famous Giants Causeway and the Old Bushmills Distillery.

SOUTHERN IRELAND

Bed & Breakfast Accommodation

Northwood House B & B
Muckross View, Killarney, Co. Kerry, Ireland
Email: info@northwoodhouse.com
Website: www.northwoodhouse.com
        www.aanson.com

Enhance your visit to Killarney by staying at one of our newly built homes. You can have Bed and Breakfast at Northwood House, our family run B&B which enjoys panoramic views over Killarney National Park, Lakes and Mountains. Set in a quiet peaceful location yet only 5/7 minutes walk from Killarney town centre and National park entrance. Or you can enjoy a weeks self catering at one of our 4/5 star self catering homes. To view all accommodation please visit our websites.

Forest Park House
Contact: Helen & Eileen Kelly, Rockingham, Boyle,County Roscommon
Tel: +353 (71)9662227
Email: forestparkhse@hotmail.com
Website: www.bed-and-breakfast-boyle.com

Forest Park House is a purpose built, wheelchair friendly guesthouse nestling among the trees at the entrance to the beautiful **Lough Key Forest Park**. We are just minutes from Boyle and we are on the N4 route between Dublin and Sligo. All bedrooms are modern, spacious, ensuite with power showers and tastefully decorated with cable TV in each room. Wheelchair access is available and all rooms have been finished with wooden floors and other natural materials. There is a large private car park at the rear. Our dining room modern, spacious and overlooks the guest patio and landscaped gardens. We have a drying room and bait fridges for fishermen. We offer an extensive breakfast menu to cater for all dietary needs.

Whitestrand B&B
Crega, Malin Head, Co. Donegal
Tel: 074 93 70335
Mobile: 0868229163
Email: whitestrand@eircom.net
Website: http://homepage.eircom.net/~whitestrand

On arrival at Whitestrand you will receive a warm welcome, home baking with tea or coffee. It has beautiful views of the surrounding mountains and countryside. Nearby there is the fishing port and some really beautiful unspoilt beaches. It is within easy traveling distance of the golf course, famine village, diving, horse riding and two ferries. One ferry goes from Greencastle to Magilligan in Northern Ireland and the other ferry from Buncrana to Rathmullan which is in the Fanad Penninsula. The Seaview Tavern and Restaurant plus other bars are close by.

Bed & Breakfast Accommodation-Southern Ireland

Old Mill House
Dingle Town, Avondale Street, Dingle, Co. Kerry
Tel: 353 66 91 52349
Fax: 353 91 51120
Email: verhoul@iol.ie
Website: www.old-mill-house.com

Family run B&B, offering, en-suite with TV and hairdryer, some with sea views, superking beds, and Jacuzzi baths. Breakfast menu, pancakes, Irish and Vegetarian. Located near the main drag, less than 1 minute walk to all 52 pubs and restaurants. Ideal place to stay to visit the Dingle Peninsula and the Ring of Kerry. Off street parking, Family, twin, single and double rooms available.

Guest House Accommodation-Southern Ireland

Rusheen Bay House
Contact: Anne Buckley
8 Cashelmara, Salthill, Galway, Ireland
Tel: 00 353 91 520729
Email: rusheen@indigo.ie
Website: www.rusheenbayhouse.com

Rusheen Bay House is situated in Salthill, Galaway, overlooking Galway Bay. It is a charming and intimate guesthouse where the comfort of our visitors is our priority. With this in mind we furnished our guesthouse to the highest standard to ensure your stay with us is an enjoyable experience. We look forward to welcoming you in the near future and trust you will enjoy your stay with us. Enjoy a substantial breakfast in the Dining Room or the adjoining conservatory. A selection of fresh fruits, juices, cheeses, yoghurts, etc. are available along with the famous traditional Irish Breakfast, served between 8am and 10am. Special dietary requirement are catered for, please inform your host on arrival. Free Wireless Internet Broadband Available at Rusheen Bay House.

Self Catering Accommodation-Southern Ireland

Latchfords Self Catering Accommodation
Contact: Jody Gettins
99 Lower Baggot Street, Dublin 2, Ireland
Tel: 00353-1-6760784
Fax: 00353-1-6622764
Email: info@latchfords.ie
Website: www.latchfords.ie

Latchfords of Baggot Street id located in the heart of Georgian Dublin. The accommodation offers a variety of self catering serviced apartments from studio to two bedroom units all with en-suite facilities, TV, telephone, etc. Independent access allows complete freedom of lifestyle and movement to guests. Ideal for long or short stays, business or family. Within walking distance of a wide selection of Theatres, Museums and Art Galleries.

No. 1 Redwood Park
Contact: RoseMarie Dempsey
Clonakilty, West Cork
Tel: 023-48011
Email: dempseyrm@eircom.net
Large detached house in upmarket park, in quiet area of town. 5 minutes walk to town centre. House has 4 bedrooms, bathroom, 2 living rooms, downstairs WC, kitchen/dining and utility. Private Parking. Sleeps 8/9. Has all mod cons. Electricity and heating included. Clonakilty is the beach centre of West Cork on the Southern tip of Ireland. There are many activities available locally such as sea/freshwater fishing, windsurfing, swimming, golf, pitch and putt, ring fort, model railway village, museums, cinemas, standing stones, award winning restaurants and pubs, tidy towns winner, farmers market etc. Please ring/email for brochures.

Self Catering Accommodation-Southern Ireland

Drim House
Crega, Malin Head, Co. Donegal
Tel: 074 93 70335
Mobile: 0868229163
Email: whitestrand@eircom.net
Website: http://homepage.eircom.net/~whitestrand
A five bedroom house with two bedrooms downstairs and three bedrooms upstairs, two of which are en-suite. There is also a kitchen, dining room, laundry room, sitting room, main bathroom with bath and separate shower. Drim house has spectacular views.
Nearby there is the fishing port and some really beautiful unspoilt beaches. It is within easy traveling distance of the golf course, famine village, diving, horse riding and two ferries. One ferry goes from Greencastle to Magilligan in Northern Ireland and the other ferry from Buncrana to Rathmullan which is in the Fanad Penninsula. The Seaview Tavern and Restaurant plus other bars are close by.

Hostel Accommodation Southern Ireland

The Four Courts Hostel
15 -17 Merchant's Quay, Dublin 8
Tel: + 353 1 6725 839
Fax: + 353 1 6725 962
Email: info@fourcourtshostel.com
Website: www.fourcourtshostel.com
The world famous Four Courts Hostel was voted N° 1 Hostel Worldwide by customers in 2003, best hostel in Ireland 2003 and 2nd best hostel in the world 2003. Highly recommended by all major guidebooks, we offer a range of high quality accommodation for backpackers, students and budget travelers. Large selection of en suite facilities with keycard security in 3 beautifully restored Georgian buildings. 24 hour access/reception, free continental breakfast, free internet access, excellent security, laundry facilities, games room, Bureau de Change, car parking on request, lift and tour desk with car hire. City centre with easy access to all the major sites of interest. Children under 14 require private accommodation rooms are sold by the bed so if private occupancy required ,all beds in the room will need to be reserved. We will do everything possible to ensure you enjoy your time in Dublin.

INDEX